PHOTO FEATURES

Photo features offer visual coverage of major sights or unusual attractions. Where relevant, there is a map showing the location and essential information on opening times, entrance charges, transport and contact details.

The Essentials

Address: www.centre pompidou.fr
Tel: 01 44 78 12 33
Opening Hrs: Wed–Mon 11am–9pm
Entrance Fee: charge
Transport: Rambut

SHOPPING AND RESTAURANT LISTINGS

Shopping listings provide details of the best shops in each area. Restaurant listings give the establishment's contact details, opening times and price category, followed by a useful review. Bars and cafés are also covered here. The coloured dot and grid reference refers to the atlas section at the back of the book.

Le Grand Véfour
17 rue de Beaujolais, 1st
Tel: 01 42 96 56 27
Open: L & D Mon–Fri.
€€€€ 34 [p336, B1]
Hiding under the arches of the Palais Royal is one of the most beautiful restaurants in Paris. Le

TRAVEL TIPS

aged 4–11,
4 travel free but are n
aranteed a seat.
Paris has six mainline railway stations, with lines radiating across France and Europe. Each connects with several Métro or RER lines, and all have left-luggage facilities (consignes) and coin-operated lockers (consignes automatiques).The SNCF's Train à Grande Vitesse (TGV) high-speed trains offer comfortable services

Travel Tips provide all the practical knowledge you'll need before and during your trip: how to get there, getting around, where to stay and what to do. The A–Z section is a handy summary of practical information, arranged alphabetically.

Contents

Introduction

The Best of Paris 6
A City for All Seasons 17
Parisiens, Parisiennes 19

History

Decisive Dates 24
The Making of Paris 29

Features

Architecture 45
Paris on a Plate 51

Insights

MINI FEATURES

The Outsiders.............................. 41
Café Life 101
The Métro.................................. 176
Paris Schooling 226

PHOTO FEATURES

Chic Shopping............................. 58
The Market Scene....................... 60
Paris after Dark 62
Paris at the Movies 64
Notre-Dame de Paris 88
Centre Pompidou...................... 116
The Louvre 140

The Arc de Triomphe 160
Cabaret Life 180
Jardin du Luxembourg 218
The Eiffel Tower......................... 248
Musée d'Orsay.......................... 250
La Défense................................ 266
Versailles 286

Places

Orientation 71
◼ Ile de la Cité and Ile St-Louis .. 75
◼ The Marais 91
◼ Beaubourg and Les Halles .. 105
◼ The Louvre and Quartier
   des Tuileries 121
◼ Grands Boulevards
   and Champs-Elysées 145
  Montmartre.......................... 163
◼ Bastille and East Paris......... 183
◼ The Latin Quarter and
   St-Germain-des-Prés........... 197
◼ Montparnasse
   and Beyond 220
◼ The Eiffel Tower and
   Les Invalides 231
◼ Paris Parks 257
◼ Disneyland Paris 268
◼ Trips out of Town 277

SQUARE D'ANVERS

Maps

Paris **72**
Cité, Marais, Beaubourg
  and Les Halles **76**
Louvre and Grands
  Boulevards **118**
Montmartre **164**
Bastille and the East **185**
Latin Quarter, St-Germain
  des-Prés and
  Montparnasse **198**
Eiffel Tower and Les
  Invalides **232**
Paris Parks **259**
Trips Out of Town **279**
Street Atlas **331**

Inside front cover: Paris.
Inside back cover: Paris metro.

Travel Tips

TRANSPORT
Getting There **292**
Getting around **294**

ACCOMMODATION
Booking and Prices **298**
Holiday Flats **298**
Bed & Breakfast **298**
Hostels **298**
Ile de la Cité, Ile St-Louis and the
  Marais **299**
Beaubourg, Les Halles, Louvre and
  Tuileries **300**
Grands Boulevards and Champs-
  Elysées **301**
Montmartre, Bastille and
  East Paris **303**
Latin Quarter and St-Germain-des-
  Prés **304**
Montparnasse, the Eiffel Tower and
  Invalides **306**

ACTIVITIES
The Arts **307**
Nightlife **308**
Cinema **310**
For Children **311**
Sports **312**
Courses **313**
Sightseeing Tours **313**

A – Z
Addresses **314**
Admission charges **314**
Budgeting for Your Trip **314**
Business Visitors **314**
Children **315**
Climate **315**
Complaints **315**
Crime and Safety **316**

Customs Regulations **316**
Disabled Travellers **317**
Electricity **318**
Etiquette **318**
Gay Travellers **318**
Health & Medical Care **318**
Internet **319**
Maps **320**
Media **320**
Money **321**
Opening Hours **321**
Postal Services **322**
Religious Services **322**
Student Travellers **322**
Study in France **322**
Telephones **323**
Time Zone **323**
Tour Operators **323**
Tourist Offices **324**
Useful Addresses **324**
Visas and Passports **324**
Weights & Measures **324**

LANGUAGE
General **325**
Useful Words & Phrases **325**

FURTHER READING
History **330**
Art and Architecture **330**
Expat Memoirs **330**
Fiction **330**
Food **330**
Other Insight Guides **330**

THE BEST OF PARIS: TOP ATTRACTIONS

At a glance, everything you can't afford to miss in Paris, from the emblematic Eiffel Tower and Arc de Triomphe to the world-class museums and cutting-edge architecture of what is a thoroughly modern city.

▷ A palace fit for a king: the **Château de Versailles** is an awe-inspiring confection of gilt, paintings, mirrors, lavish fabrics, stunning architecture and landscaped gardens. As extensive restoration work progresses it is becoming more gorgeous. See page 286

△ The **Arc de Triomphe** honours Napoleon's armies, and is the focus of national celebrations in France. The view from the top is breathtaking. See page 160

◁ As well as an art museum, the **Jardin du Luxembourg** boasts an apiary, an orangery, a bandstand, a boating pond, tables for chess, tennis courts and a lovely civilised atmosphere. See page 218

▷ The glass-and-steel pyramid is an inspired addition to the venerable architecture of the **Louvre**, the best museum in the world. See page 140

◁ Once a railway station, the **Musée d'Orsay** is now one of the world's finest museums of Impressionist art. See page 250

◁ **St-Germain-des-Prés** still evokes memories of its 1950s heyday of intellectual prowess and easy-going chic – though these days fashion has largely replaced philosophy. See page 213

▽ One of the three wonderful rose windows of **Notre-Dame** cathedral, the best-known sacred building in Europe. See page 88

▷ The **Eiffel Tower** was built for the centenary of the Revolution, and the city authorities originally planned to take it down after a few years. The tower is the city's number one visitor attraction, and a global icon. See page 248

▽ The **Centre Pompidou** is an international icon of inside-out high-tech and is as much of an attraction as its contents, which include the Musée National d'Art Moderne. See page 116

8

THE BEST OF PARIS: EDITOR'S CHOICE

Unique attractions, festivals and events, top cafés and shops, family outings and money-saving tips personally selected by our editor.

ONLY IN PARIS

The view from the top of the **Eiffel Tower** one hour before sunset, and the tower's shimmering costume of light after dark. See page 248
The view of the city, as night falls, from the steps in front of **Sacré-Cœur**. See page 167
The lift ride to the top of the **Grande Arche de la Défense**, and the view across the Bois de Boulogne. See page 266
The *Mona Lisa*'s enigmatic smile at the **Louvre**. See page 125
The Impressionists at the **Musée d'Orsay**. See page 250
Rodin's beautiful sculpture garden. See page 241
Picasso's legacy to the French state. See

page 98
The 19th-century shopping arcades around the **Palais Royal**. See page 135
The elegant mansions of the **Marais** and its glorious centrepiece, the Place des Vosges. See page 94
The offbeat boutiques and hip cafés of **Bastille**. See page 184
The quiet backstreets, arty shops and bars of **Montmartre**. See page 171
Napoleon's tomb in **Hôtel des Invalides**. See page 239
The famous graves of **Père-Lachaise** cemetery. See page 188
Subterranean passages, packed with skulls and bones in the

catacombs. See page 223
Enjoy a coffee and a croissant in a literary café and browse through the boutiques of **St-Germain-des-Prés**. See page 213
Mint tea in the **Paris Mosque**. See page 207
Evening picnic with wine, on the **Pont des Arts**. See page 215
Late-night contemporary art at the **Palais de Tokyo**. See page 235
Open-air swimming fol-

lowed by drinks on the terrace at the floating pool on the **Seine**. See page 224
The stunning **Cinémathèque Française**. See page 193
The two MK2 cinemas on opposite banks of the **Canal St-Martin**, linked by a nifty little ferry. See page 225
A 21st-century take on public transport: the driverless trains on **Métro line 14**. See page 191

BEST MUSEUMS AND MONUMENTS

Centre Pompidou Masterpieces of modern and contemporary art in an icon of high-tech architecture. See page 116
Les Invalides Testament to the imperial ambitions of Louis XIV and Napoleon. See page 241
Musée Carnavalet A fascinating insight into the history of Paris. See page 97
Musée Guimet Buddhist sculptures from Angkor and other treasures from the Orient. See page 236
Musée du Quai Branly Tribal art housed in one of the city's most dynamic buildings. See page 237
Musée du Louvre The *Mona Lisa*, *Venus de Milo*, the new Depart-

ment of Islamic Art and much, much more – all in palatial surroundings. See page 140
Musée de l'Orangerie A refurbished Monet showcase. See page 130
Musée d'Orsay A treasure trove of Impressionist masterpieces. See page 250
Musée Zadkine An intimate glimpse of the artistic past of Montparnasse. See page 221
Notre-Dame and Sainte-Chapelle Two of the finest Gothic churches in the world. See pages 75, 88 and 81
Palais Garnier Opulence at the opera in the grand staircase and magnificent foyer. See page 147

BEST SHOPPING

Printemps The department store that tops them all: six floors of fashion. See page 149
The Marais Funky boutiques and designer stores on and off Rue des Francs-Bourgeois. See page 100
Colette Pioneering concept store that picks the best of what's stylish and innovative. See page 137
Galerie Vivienne The best preserved of the capital's 19th-century shopping galleries, elegant precursors of the

department store. See page 136
Diptyque Gorgeous candles and perfumes. See page 215
Le Bon Marché The oldest, and still the most chic department store in Paris. See page 244
Rue de Rivoli From souvenir shops to high-street fashions, they're all here. See page 131
Marché aux Puces de St-Ouen Wander among the bric-a-brac stalls of this huge flea market. See page 59

TOP LEFT: the breathtaking view over Paris from the Eiffel Tower. **LEFT:** Art Nouveau Métro Station.
TOP: the opulent foyer of the Opéra Garnier.
RIGHT: Printemps is a long-established fashion mecca.

PARIS FOR FAMILIES

Aquarium Tropical Catch up with the crocs and tropical fish at the Palais de la Porte Dorée. See page 263
Bois de Boulogne The Parisian's favourite Sunday afternoon playground, with woods, gardens, lakes and cycling tracks, an amusement park for children and even a folk museum. See page 257
Canal St-Martin With its nine locks, the tranquil canal makes for an attractive boat trip, starting from Bastille. See page 186
Disneyland Paris The most popular tourist attraction in Europe. See page 268
Grande Galerie de l'Evolution Revamped natural history museum with a truly impressive collection of stuffed animals. See page 209
Jardin du Luxembourg Puppet shows, tennis courts, model boats, playgrounds, chess tables and honey bees in the quintessential Parisian park. See page 218

Jardin des Tuileries The well-manicured garden adjacent to the Louvre is the perfect pleasure park: avenues of trees, statues, pony rides, toy boats, cafés and children's trampolines, as well as a giant Ferris wheel at Christmas and Easter. See page 128
Musée Grévin A fun waxworks museum, full of cheerfully incompatible figures from Marie-Antoinette to Spiderman. See page 146
Notre-Dame Kids love climbing steps: ascend the towers of Notre-Dame for a bird's-eye view of the gargoyles. See page 79
Parc des Buttes-Chaumont Ice-skating, a boating lake, a fake mountain and waterfall, puppet shows and donkey rides. See page 261
Parc de la Villette Science museum, music and dance conservatory, a giant IMAX screen and children's museum, all set in futuristic gardens. See page 259

GOURMET PARIS

Berthillon ice-cream on the Ile St-Louis. See page 86
Chez René Timeless bistro atmosphere and the perfect *coq au vin*. See page 216
Drouant A revamped classic that puts a new spin on the hors d'oeuvre concept. See page 159
Fauchon and Hédiard Famous delicatessens brimming with visually stunning and mouthwatering delicacies. See page 150
Guy Savoy Light and sophisticated dishes: a gastronomic treat. See page 159
La Coupole For an oyster feast and classic brasserie experience. See page 228

Ladurée This elegant *salon de thé* is a Paris institution, famous for its melt-in-the-mouth macaroons. See page 159
Le Comptoir Yves Camdeborde's no-choice set meal is the talk of the town – but you'll need to book for it months ahead. See page 216
L'Ourcine Run by one of a new generation of young chefs revisiting bistro cuisine. See page 217
Marché d'Aligre Sells some of the best and cheapest produce in Paris. See page 191
Marché Biologique Organic food and veg at the Sunday morning market on Boulevard Raspail. See page 212

ABOVE: tempting macaroons at Ladurée.
BELOW: enjoy some family fun at the Mad Hatter's Tea Cups ride in Disneyland Paris.

BEST EVENTS & FESTIVALS

Feb–Mar: *Salon de l'Agriculture.* A festival of regional food.
Apr–early June: *Foire du Trône.* A huge funfair comes to town.
June–July: Open-air jazz in the Parc de Vincennes.
21 June: *Fête de la Musique.* Free street concerts and dancing.
Late-June: Gay Pride.
July: Bastille Day. Street party on the night of 13

July at Place de la Bastille. On 14 July, a military parade and fireworks.
July–Aug: *Paris Plage.* The seaside comes to the Seine.
Sept: *Festival d'Automne.* Modern theatre and dance.
Oct: *La Nuit Blanche.* Museums, monuments, cinemas open all night.
Dec-Jan: Ice-skating at the Eiffel Tower.

BEST CAFES

Bistrot Beaubourg Terraced designer café by the Centre Pompidou with a chic clientele. See page 115
Café Charbon A coal shop turned café that's a neighbourhood fixture. See page 195
Café de Flore The Left Bank literary café still retains something of the charm of its intellectual heyday. See page 217
Café de la Ville Trendy hangout on the Grands Boulevards. See page 159
Café du Marché Classic neighbourhood café with a good menu of market-inspired food. See page 247
Café Marly The Louvre's classiest café, with a superb terrace looking onto the Pyramid. See page 139
Chez Prune A cornerstone of the trendy Canal St-Martin area. See page 194
Le Procope The oldest café in Paris, established In 1686. See page 217
Le Sancerre One of the best cafés in Montmartre, drawing an eclectic, young, arty crowd. See page 179

ABOVE: make sure to be bikini-ready for Paris-Plage
RIGHT: the foodie and the trendy gather at Chez Prune.

MONEY-SAVING TIPS

Paris Museum Pass (sold at museums, tourist offices, FNAC and airports) gives you priority entrance at the Louvre and enables you to skip the queues while saving money. See www.parismuseumpass.com for details.
Tickets to Ride A *carnet* of 10 tickets (available from bus or Métro stations) gives reduced fares on public transport. The Paris Visite card is valid for one, two, three or five consecutive days on the Métro, bus and railway.

Le Kiosque Théâtre (15 place de la Madeleine, Montparnasse Square and Ternes Square) sell half-price theatre tickets from 12.30pm for performances that day.
The sales Traditionally the sales *(soldes)* are held in July and early January but many shops offer mid-season reductions.
Free museums Entry to the permanent collections of the municipal Paris museums is free, including the Musée

Carnavalet, Musée d'Art Moderne, Musée Cognacq-Jay, Musée Zadkine, Musée de la Vie Romantique, the Petit Palais, Maison de Victor Hugo and Maison de Balzac. Most Réunion des Musées Nationaux (RMN) museums are free on the first Sunday of the month. See http://en.parisinfo.com/affordable-paris for free or inexpensive activities including free music concerts, free museums, free sports activities and free meals.

A CITY FOR ALL SEASONS

France's chic capital has as much substance as style and offers plenty to entertain visitors whatever the month. Scratch the surface and uncover a liveable city where old meets new and the finer things in life make up for an often-painful past.

"I love Paris in the springtime," wrote American composer and lyricist Cole Porter, who then went on to say that he also loved it in the fall, the summer and the winter. The capital of France is a seductive destination at any time of year, whether strolling along the banks of the Seine in muggy August, when most of the city has shut up shop, or ice-skating on the first floor of the Eiffel Tower in the chilly depths of December.

Wherever you head in Paris you are surrounded by its (often turbulent) history, usually in places you least expect to find it: the reconstructed Roman amphitheatre off Rue Monge in the Latin Quarter; the 14th-century city walls, underground, in the Carrousel du Louvre; the church of St-Roch on Rue St-Honoré, whose facade is dotted with the scars of 18th-century Revolutionary shoot-outs.

Paris has long been known as the place to go for a good time: from the 19th-century Montmartre cabarets famously painted by Henri de Toulouse-Lautrec to the surfeit of stylish cocktail bars in 2012. Then there is the galaxy of

Michelin-starred restaurants, not to mention a few of the world's best sports events like the French Open tennis tournament and the final leg of the Tour de France cycle race. Look hard enough and you'll find something to suit all tastes and budgets.

This might be one of the world's greatest cities but Paris manages to retain the feel of a large town; it is very easy to get around on foot. Each district has its own unique character – from the smart shops and cafés in St-Germain to the ethnic markets and restaurants of Belleville – and it is often said that the French capital is merely a collection of villages.

In recent years, thanks to (now ex) President Sarkozy's reforms including the *Grand Paris* project, which aims to improve transport links with the suburbs and build 1.5 million new homes by 2030, Paris has been reluctantly dragged into the 21st century. The successful *cohabitation* between ancient and modern is exactly what makes Paris attractive to so many visitors.

PRECEDING PAGES: dim lighting is *de rigueur* in any Parisian café; the Pont des Arts aptly attracts musicians, street performers and romantics alike. **LEFT:** the most iconic and photographed monument in Paris. **ABOVE, FROM LEFT:** métro sign; artwork in Montmartre.

PARISIENS, PARISIENNES

Everyone knows something about Paris, even without ever having visited. But the legends and stereotypes have more truth to them than you might think, and there are many exceptions that confound the rules.

Paris is divided by the Seine into two halves, with the Ile de la Cité and Ile St-Louis in the centre. According to an old saying, the Left Bank was where you did your thinking – the Sorbonne University has been located there since the Middle Ages – and the Right Bank was the place to spend money. Over time, the city was organised into *arrondissements* (districts), running outwards in a clockwise spiral from the Ile de France (1st *arrondissement*) to the northeast (20th *arrondissement*), all contained within the *Périphérique* (ringroad).

Within the various *arrondissements* there are recognised *quartiers*, or neighbourhoods, often worlds apart though linked by a short Métro ride. Each has its own shops, markets, cafés and local eccentricities. Parisians develop lifetime attachments to their *quartier*. Although supermarket chains are ubiquitous, residents still support local merchants and shop in specialist shops and local markets.

The east-west divide

The most important unofficial division in Paris is between the traditionally working-class east end and the mostly bourgeois west. In general, the further east you go, the further left you'll find its inhabitants on the political spectrum. Rents are exorbitant in the western *arrondissements*, but there's a substantial reservoir of affordable real estate in the east. City planners have been struggling for decades to improve the balance, hence the massive urban renewal

projects at Bercy and the "new" Left Bank in the southeast.

The east-west dichotomy is rooted in recent history. When Baron Haussmann began to demolish the city's medieval slums in 1860, the middle classes tended to relocate to the west, whereas the working class moved east. The following decade was one of the most turbulent in the history of Paris and ended in the terrible events of the Commune (see page 36).

Immigrants live on both sides of the Seine, east and west, from Chinatown in the 13th to the predominantly African Goutte d'Or in the 18th. However, the most diverse community of all is probably in the 19th *arrondissement*; in

LEFT: exuding that *je ne sais quoi…*
RIGHT: Parisians have a real love affair with dogs.

Parisians topped a national survey on the most-hated people in France, above traditional targets such as civil servants, Corsicans and policemen; although many of the city's inhabitants were born and raised elsewhere.

Belleville is also on the map, and for gay or lesbian hotspots, head straight for the Marais.

Outside the *Périphérique*

Paris proper has few ghettos to speak of. For the most part, they're beyond the *Périphérique* where many of the poor are housed in the *cités* (housing estates) of the *banlieue* (suburbs). Until recently, Paris seems to have turned a blind eye to the problems of its poorer suburbs, and most Parisians were rarely confronted with ghetto life unless they wanted to be.

The *cités* in the French suburbs were built in response to the housing shortage after World War II. Row upon row of ugly, grey rectangular high-rises were built to house French workers. Immigrants, encouraged to come to France during the economic boom of the 1960s, moved in later. With the oil crisis and recession of the 1970s, there was less and less employment. Crime and drug use soared (see page 41).

Culture and multiculture

Paris considers itself to be the capital of everything French. Despite an official effort to promote regional development, there's still a

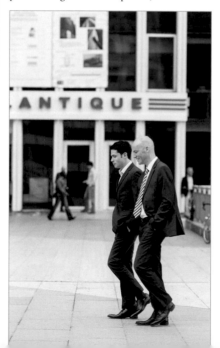

some schools half of the children speak Arabic as a first language, and there are nearly seventy other ethnic groups. Although the iconic *rive gauche* (Left Bank) still pulls millions of tourists south of the Seine in search of the literary vibe, there have been huge changes in the social geography of Paris since the days of Sartre and de Beauvoir. The Left Bank's Latin Quarter is one of the city's most expensive neighbourhoods, more notable for designer boutiques than it is for literary activity and bohemian lifestyles.

So, where do you go in Paris if you're young and adventurous? From the 1980s up until recently, the simple answer was Bastille. The labyrinth of cobbled backstreets around Place de la Bastille still has a great bar scene, trendy art galleries and cabaret theatre. However, nearby Rue Oberkampf and Rue Ménilmontant are now much cooler, particularly for clubbing.

lot of one-way traffic to Paris for the best and the brightest provincials in almost every field of human endeavour. The tendency of the capital has long been to look down on the provinces. In return, many French people who live outside Paris are disdainful of its inhabitants: "*Parigot, tête de veau*" (which means "the Parisian is pig-headed" – or, literally, calf-headed).

But, as France moves gradually away from its rigidly centralised history, attitudes about the provinces are changing. The Paris press is full of stories about stressed-out Parisians who escape to a better life in the countryside. Regional development programmes are pumping a great deal of capital into cities like Bordeaux and Toulouse. And the new high-speed trains, that zap south in a flash, are worshipped not so much by provincials, but by Parisians who, much as they love their city, can't get out of it fast enough.

Aside from the provinces, the largest contributors to the Parisian cultural and racial *pot au feu* are the former colonies of West and North Africa. Other, earlier waves of immigration

> "If you are lucky enough to have lived in Paris as a young man, then wherever you go for the rest of your life, it stays with you, for Paris is a moveable feast." Ernest Hemingway, A Moveable Feast

have brought an influx of Chinese, Vietnamese, Poles, Russians, Bosnians, Serbs, Armenians, Turks and Greeks. France has the largest Muslim population in Europe and its largest Jewish minority outside of Russia. If Paris on the whole displays genuine tolerance of other races and religions, "immigration" is still used as a code word – particularly by right-wing extremists – to express their fear of foreigners. Legislation has been passed in recent years to beef up the country's security, expand the police force and make it harder for foreigners to move to the country.

The people who live here

Incredibly, Paris is more densely populated than Tokyo, London and New York, and Parisians' high stress levels can partly be put down to the fact that they live literally on top of one

FROM LEFT: browsing the Marché aux Fleurs; suits heading out for lunch; a balmy summer evening along the Canal St-Martin.

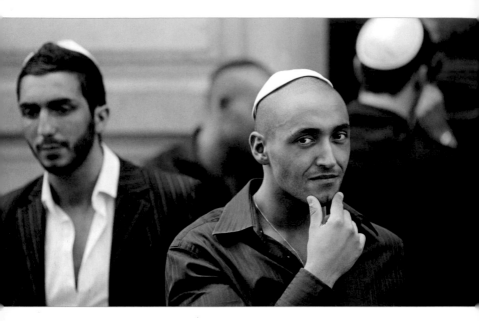

another, squeezed into small apartments, packed into the city's 100 sq km (40 sq miles). There's intense competition for desirable living space. Moreover, high rents mean that many Parisians have neither the time nor the money to appreciate their city, being trapped in a routine they call *Métro-boulot-dodo* (commuting, working, sleeping). Nonetheless, for anyone fortunate enough to live in the city centre, the rewards far outweigh the demands. Human in scale, clean, safe, cosmopolitan and lively, Paris deserves its reputation as one of the best cities in which to enjoy the good life.

Parisians, as a whole, are such a diverse collection of races and cultures that it's virtually impossible to stereotype them. Still, there are ties that bind. Parisians are proud and often impatient, always complaining about their social services, yet often defending them, too. In general they are class-conscious and fashion-savvy, largely traditional when it comes to food and etiquette, refreshingly open-minded about art, politics and lifestyle. They're the most orderly people on the planet, and the most chaotic. They're forever in a hurry – and always late.

Appearances matter in a city where people-watching is a popular pastime. Almost everyone pays attention to *le look* (pronounced "louk"): an English word used to describe not only your wardrobe but also your "style". And if you change your style you are *relooké(e)*.

A French sociologist once claimed that in his country there were not three social classes but 63. One entrenched classification is BCBG (*bon chic, bon genre*): the French equivalent of the British Sloane ranger or the American preppie. The rich suburbs of the 16th and 17th *arron-dissements*, Neuilly, Auteuil and Passy (known

PARI-ROLLER

Every Friday night at 10pm hundreds of roller skaters meet at Place Raoul Dautry in Montparnasse to head off on a three-hour, 30km (19-mile) tour around Paris; the route varies each week. Originally launched as an ad hoc gathering in 1993, Pari-Roller, a not-for-profit organisation, has now become part of the city's fabric thanks to a successful working partnership with the police, which ensures a safe and fun evening out for all; motorbikes lead the way and mobile officers mingle with participants. While Pari-Roller is for experienced skaters, there is a meeting more suited to beginners at 2.30pm on Sundays in Place de la Bastille. For further information see www.pari-roller.com.

collectively as NAP), are their stamping grounds. If you are BCBG, your clothes are well cut, but not daring or flashy. Another taxonomic is *bobo (bourgeois bohème)*. These are the sort of bohemians who can afford the high rents of St-Germain-des-Prés or the Marais. They're just as bourgeois as the BCBG crowd, only they play up their informality with more youthful clothes.

Breaking the rules

Paris is riddled with rules and regulations, but Parisians have a special talent for breaking them. Things like building codes, labour laws or pollution will probably not come to the visitor's immediate attention. What will hit home, however, are things like clouds of cigarette smoke wafting through public spaces marked "smoking forbidden". In theory, you can be fined for allowing your dog to leave its mess, yet dog dirt is by no means rare on Paris pavements.

La politesse

This is not to suggest the city is one big free-for-all. Parisian anarchy does not extend to etiquette, and their reputation for rudeness is largely undeserved. Good manners are considered essential to everyday life. Indeed, *la politesse* can often become outright chivalry. Visitors would be well advised to follow the same rules of courtesy. Whether you're buying a baguette or a Hermès scarf, starting any transaction with a "*Bonjour Madame/Monsieur*," and finishing with "*Merci, au revoir*" will make the

world of difference to the service you receive. If you forget, you may be reminded with an unspoken reprimand.

Taking to the streets

Somewhere in Paris, someone is on strike almost every day of the year. The expression for going on strike – *faire la grève* – refers to the still current practice of besieging Paris's Town Hall (located on what was once called Place de Grève) or marching from Nation and blocking streets all the way to Bastille. The strikes can involve many groups – transport workers, teachers, air traffic controllers, hospital staff, illegal immigrants, etc. These "social actions" might involve picketing school teachers, farmers dumping tomatoes on the Champs-Elysées or lorry drivers blockading roads. Perhaps going on strike is compensation for the decline of the trade unions and the weakening of political parties. But it can also seem rather more banal – a national sport in which Parisians are top of the league.

The protest march is part of the great Paris tradition of "the people" rising up. Parisians from all walks of life are willing to participate in street demonstrations for causes that matter to them. Several hundred thousand people packed the streets in 2003 to protest against the war in Iraq. In fact, there were so many marches and strikes that year, there was even a major protest march against strikes.

FROM LEFT: attending synagogue in the Marais; Parisian waiter; *Santé!*

DECISIVE DATES

The Gallo-Roman era

c.300 BC
A Celtic tribe, the Parisii, settle on the Ile de la Cité.

58–52 BC
Julius Caesar conquers Gaul; Lutetia is founded.

c.AD 250
Gaul converts to Christianity.

451
St Geneviève's troops fend off Attila the Hun.

The Dark Ages
486
Frankish king Clovis expels the last Romans. In 496, he is baptised at Reims; in 508, he makes Paris his capital.

751
The Carolingian dynasty: Emperor Charlemagne rules from 768 to 814.

845–80
Paris sacked by the Vikings.

885
Count Eudes is king of the Western Franks in 888.

The Middle Ages
Paris develops into a city of learning and political power. It spreads north of the river.

987
The Capetian dynasty starts.

1108–54
Paris becomes an important trading centre.

1163
Notre-Dame is started.

1190–1223
The Louvre fortress is built.

1246–8
Sainte-Chapelle is built.

1253
Sorbonne University created.

1340
Beginning of the Hundred Years War.

1358
Jacquerie uprising.

1364
Charles V moves his court to the Louvre.

1380
The Bastille prison is built.

1420
English rule until 1436, despite Joan of Arc's military campaign of 1429.

The Renaissance
Wars with Italy expose the French to new ideas of art, wealth and luxury.

1469
First French printworks.

1516
François I brings Leonardo da Vinci to France; rebuilding of the Louvre starts in 1528.

1572
St Bartholomew's Day Massacre of Protestants.

1589
Henri III is assassinated.

1593
Henri IV becomes a Catholic.

1598
The Edict of Nantes ends the Wars of Religion.

1609
The Place Royale (now Place des Vosges) and Pont Neuf are built.

1610
Henri IV is assassinated.

"Le Grand Siècle"

Louis XIV spurs an age of extravagance by moving to Versailles and launching an opulent building programme.

1629
The Palais Royal is built.

1631
Launch of the first Paris newspaper, *La Gazette*.

1635
Académie Française set up.

1648–53
The Fronde rebellion.

1672–1705
The Grands Boulevards are built.

1677
Hôtel des Invalides finished.

1680
Comédie Française founded.

1682
Court moves to Versailles.

1686
The first café, Le Procope, opens in Paris.

Age of Enlightenment

The arts flourish, science develops and philosophers spread new ideas.

1715
Louis XIV dies and Philippe

d'Orléans becomes regent.

1751
First volume of Diderot's *Encyclopédie* published.

1755
Place Louis XIV (now Place de la Concorde) is started.

1758
Panthéon is started.

The First Empire

The French Revolution leads to a republic then an empire under Napoleon Bonaparte.

1789
Bastille stormed; Louis XVI leaves Versailles for Paris.

1791
Louis is caught fleeing Paris.

1792
The Republic is declared; the royal family is imprisoned.

1793
Louis and Marie-Antoinette are guillotined.

1794
The ensuing Terror claims more than 60,000 lives. The Directoire takes over.

1799
Napoleon seizes power and is crowned emperor in 1804.

1806
Arc de Triomphe started.

1814
Napoleon is defeated; the Russians occupy Paris.

1815
Napoleon briefly regains power before his downfall at the Battle of Waterloo; the Bourbon monarchy is restored with Louis XVIII.

The Restoration

Two more revolutions shake Paris, unseating the monarchy once and for all.

1830
Charles X is overthrown and Louis-Philippe d'Orléans becomes "the Citizen King".

1837
First French passenger railway service.

1848
Louis-Philippe is deposed. Louis-Napoleon Bonaparte is elected president of the Second Republic.

The Second Empire

Under Louis-Napoleon, Paris becomes the most efficient, modern city in Europe.

1852
Louis-Napoleon crowns himself Emperor Napoleon III; the Second Empire begins.

1852–70
Baron Georges Haussmann redesigns the city.

1852
Le Bon Marché, the first department store, opens.

1855
Paris's first World Fair.

1862
Hugo's Les Misérables published.

1863
Manet's Le Déjeuner sur l'herbe causes a scandal.

1867
Second World Fair.

1870
Franco-Prussian War.

The Belle Epoque

New inventions and a great artistic élan.

1871
Defeated France signs an armistice with Prussia. During the Paris Commune, 25,000 people are killed.

1875
The Third Republic begins.

1887
Louis Pasteur founds the Institut Pasteur.

1889
Gustave Eiffel completes his tower for the World Fair. The Moulin Rouge opens.

1894–1906
Dreyfus scandal.

1894
President Sadi Carnot assassinated.

1895
Lumière brothers screen the world's first public film.

The Age of Anxiety

Social tensions multiply, and France is shaken by two world wars.

1900
The first Métro line opens. Pont Alexandre III, the Grand and Petit Palais are finished.

1914–18
World War I. Paris is saved from German attack by the Battle of the Marne.

1919
Versailles Peace Conference.

1924
André Breton publishes his Surrealist Manifesto.

1934
The Depression gives rise to riots and a series of strikes.

1936
Popular Front leader Léon Blum elected prime minister.

1939
World War II begins; France sides with Britain against Nazi Germany.

1940
Germany invades France.

1941–2
Paris Jews are deported.

1944
Paris liberated by the Allies. General de Gaulle in power

until 1946, when the Fourth Republic is proclaimed.

1949
Simone de Beauvoir publishes *The Second Sex*.

1958
The Algerian crisis topples the Fourth Republic.

The Fifth Republic
De Gaulle returns as president of the Fifth Republic.

1958
Work begins on La Défense.

1962
End of the Algerian War.

1968
Strikes and student riots force de Gaulle to call an election. He wins.

1969
Georges Pompidou becomes president.

1972
The Tour Montparnasse is completed.

FROM LEFT: the Paris uprising of 27, 28 and 29 July, known as the Trois Glorieuses ("Three Glorious Days"), saw Charles X replaced as king by Louis-Philippe; chemist and microbiologist Louis Pasteur; crowds gather on the Champs-Elysées to cheer General de Gaulle two days after Paris's liberation from Nazi occupation on 24 August 1944; Autolib' is an electric car sharing service launched in 2011.

1973
The Boulevard Périphérique (ringroad) is opened.

1977
Centre Georges-Pompidou opens. Jacques Chirac elected mayor of Paris.

1981
Socialist François Mitterrand elected president. First TGV (high-speed) railway service.

1986
Chirac becomes prime minister in an unprecedented "cohabitation". The Musée d'Orsay and Cité des Sciences at La Villette open.

1988
Louvre Pyramid completed.

1989
Bicentenary celebrations of the Revolution. Inauguration of the Grande Arche de la Défense and Opéra Bastille.

1995
Chirac elected president.

1997
Socialist Lionel Jospin becomes prime minister in a second "cohabitation".

1998
France wins the football World Cup. The Bibliothèque Nationale de France is relocated to Tolbiac.

2000
Presidential term shortened from seven to five years.

2001
Bertrand Delanoë elected mayor of Paris.

2002
The euro replaces the franc. Chirac is re-elected.

2003
Chirac opposes the war in Iraq and his popularity soars, then plummets with a reform of the French state pensions and benefit systems.

2005
French voters say *Non* to the European Constitution. Chirac's standing in the opinion polls is at an all-time low. Riots flare up in the *banlieues* (suburbs).

2006
New tram service in the south of the city.

2007
Right-wing Nicolas Sarkozy is elected president.

2009
65th D-Day anniversary in Normandy. "Grand Paris" proposals unveiled.

2011
Autolib' electric car scheme launched.

2012
Socialist François Hollande is elected president.

THE MAKING OF PARIS

The Parisii tribe discovered it, the Romans usurped it, the Franks invaded it and Napoleon ruled it. The city's refined culture and revolutionary politics changed the world.

Paris has been a site of human habitation since the Stone Age, and its history spans well over two millennia. A giddy whirl of invasions, uprisings, murders, building, demolishing, writing, painting, invention, song and dance; a past that's eternally present, reliably thrilling. And lucky too. Unlike many European cities, Paris almost entirely escaped wartime destruction in the 20th century: the buildings that were world-famous at the outbreak of war in 1939 are still standing.

The roots of the city

Paris has grown outwards, in fairly uniform rings from an island in the Seine, the Ile de la Cité. The foundations for the city as we know it today are deemed to have been laid down

> The author of a visitor's guide wrote,
> "One would be wrong if, seeing the vast number of books devoted to Paris, one imagined there was nothing more to be said." That was in 1765.

in around 300 BC by the Celtic tribe of the Parisii, who set up a trading settlement on the island. It was perfect for the transport of goods, from east to west by the river and from north to south along major overland routes that had converged there for centuries: the Seine was much wider then than today, and crossing it at the island was easier than elsewhere.

In 53 BC, some Gallic tribes failed to appear in Ambiani (Amiens) at the annual council convened by the Romans, who were in the process of colonising Gaul. Julius Caesar, Roman commander in Gaul, sensed rebellion and transferred the council to the Parisii settlement. The Romans realised the advantage of the position, and developed the site for themselves, naming it Lutetia. A town grew up with all the hallmarks of Roman civilisation, and it spread to the Left Bank. Buildings were also scattered on the Right Bank, including a hilltop temple to Mercury where, in around

LEFT: fourteenth-century peasants sowing in the shadow of the Louvre. **RIGHT:** Roman stonework at the Thermes de Cluny.

AD 250, Christian missionary St Denis, the first bishop of Paris, was beheaded; according to legend, he picked up his severed head and walked 6,000 steps before being buried on the spot where the St-Denis Basilica now stands. The hill subsequently acquired the name Mons Martyrum (Martyr's Mound), now Montmartre.

Lutetia soon fell victim to sackings by barbarians. In 358, Emperor Constantine sent his son-in-law, Julian, to Gaul to deal with them. Julian promptly fell in love with Lutetia and some say that it was he who renamed it Paris.

Geneviève, patron saint of Paris

Just under a century later, in around 451, the armies of Attila the Hun circled for the kill. The Parisians prepared to flee, but were assured by the pious 19-year-old Geneviève that the Huns would not harm the city, provided they stayed with her and prayed. The marauders passed southwest of the town and ran straight into the swords of a hastily raised army of legionaries. Geneviève later became the patron saint of Paris.

She was still alive when Clovis I, king of the Salian Franks and founder of the Merovingian dynasty, invaded much of Gaul, seeing off the Romans and sweeping into Paris. He promptly made it his capital and reconverted it to Christianity. Later a basilica was built where

he and St Geneviève were buried. The church was demolished; on its site now stands the Panthéon, the last resting place for France's great and good.

The Merovingian law of succession was simple: the empire was divided among the previous ruler's offspring. As a result, for the next 250 years, instead of serving as an administrative centre, Paris became a battleground for the murderous family bickering of Clovis's descendants.

CURRENT AFFAIRS

The Parisii tribe set up camp on the Ile de la Cité in around 300 BC but they were not the first people here: there's evidence of human habitation in these parts dating back to the Stone Age. In 1991, when archaeologists were working at Bercy in the 12th arrondissement, a mile or so from the site of the Parisii settlement, they unearthed several Neolithic dugout canoes, or pirogues, dating from 4500 BC – among the world's oldest known records of the use of canoes by hunter-gatherers. A nearby street was named Rue des Pirogues de Bercy in their honour and three of the craft are now exhibited in the Musée Carnavalet.

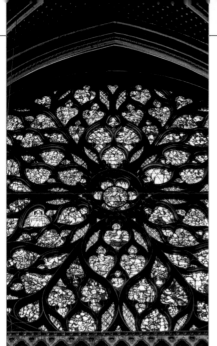

Vikings ran amok. Finally, the power struggle saw Hugh Capet, son of Hugh the Great, a descendant of Eudes, become king of all France in 987. This marked the beginning of a new, long-lasting dynasty – the Capetians.

Paris prospered under the Capetians: new fountains were built to provide fresh drinking water, and armed *sergents de ville* walked a beat. With new churches and a cosmopolitan population, Paris soon became an intellectual hotspot. At the start of the 12th century, monks, scholars, philosophers, poets and musicians came to the city to learn, exchange ideas and teach.

Economic power rested in the hands of merchants and craftsmen, organised into guilds. The most powerful was the water merchants' guild, which included all river workers and gave its coat of arms to Paris. Philippe-Auguste (1180–1223) built Les Halles for the guilds and improved the docks. The guilds took care of levying taxes, town-crying and other municipal duties. In 1200, Philippe-Auguste founded the University of Paris.

The first revolution

By the mid-14th century the Capetians had been replaced by the Valois dynasty, and the devastating Hundred Years War with England began. In 1356, the English captured King Jean ("the Good") at Poitiers. Parisians, tired of incompetent leadership, rebelled; their leader was Etienne

Into the Middle Ages

The Carolingians, who ruled from 751, moved the political centre away from Paris, which was left in the charge of a count and his municipal guard. Charlemagne died in 814, leaving his son Louis – the first Louis of many – in charge.

The Norman (or Viking) invasions of the mid-9th century brought Paris back into the limelight. After several sackings of the city, in 885 Eudes, count of Paris, had fortifications built around the Ile de la Cité. The first siege of Paris lasted a year and almost bore fruit: the Carolingian army came to the rescue. But King Charles ("the Fat"), instead of attacking the siege-weary aggressors, let them sail up the Seine to pillage Burgundy. In defiance of the king, Eudes took the crown and Carolingian unity dissolved. A period of instability followed, as the French crown was passed from one dynasty to the next. The Saracens appeared in the south, Hungarians in the east, and the

FROM LEFT: St Geneviève as a shepherdess with the Butte Montmartre in the background; detail from a tapestry depicting the baptism of Clovis (c.1525); Sainte-Chapelle stained glass; Charlemagne, founder of the Carolingian dynasty.

Most historians view the coronation of Hugh Capet (c.940–96), Count of Paris, as the beginning of modern France. The city flourished under his rule.

Marcel, a wealthy cloth maker and guild chairman. He also provided troop reinforcements to impoverished townspeople and peasants under Jacques Bonhomme, who chose the moment to start a revolt known as the *Jacquerie*.

For support, Marcel unwisely chose the king of Navarre, Charles ("the Bad"), an ally of the English. When the Parisians learned of the alliance, they turned on Marcel, who was killed in July 1358. Three days later, Jean's son entered the capital. The new regent, the future Charles V (1364–80), hammered out a truce with the English. But Parisians were seething. In 1382, during the reign of Charles VI (1380–1422), a group called the Maillotins rebelled against high taxes and were brutally repressed. Then, in 1407, they were enmeshed in the struggle for power between the Burgundian Jean ("the Fearless") and his cousin Louis d'Orléans. Jean had Louis murdered and, in 1409, took control of Paris.

The advance of the English

While Louis's Armagnac son, Charles, raised a new army, Paris celebrated. Into the fray stepped butcher Caboche, demanding reforms. All hell broke loose as Jean's authority slipped into Caboche's hands. Profiting from the reign of terror, Charles's army re-entered the city. With France torn apart by civil war, the English resumed hostilities and, siding with the Burgundians, beat the Armagnacs at the Battle of Agincourt in 1415.

Four years later, Jean "the Fearless" was murdered, whereupon Henry V of England married Catherine, daughter of the mad King Charles, and occupied Paris in December 1420. The dauphin, the legitimate French heir, had some support in the capital, but could not keep out the English. Joan of Arc, a 17-year-old girl from Lorraine, came to his rescue in 1429 by defeating the English at Orléans; a year later, Charles VII was crowned at Reims. However, Paris remained English until 1436, when

FROM LEFT: Henri III, son of Catherine de Médicis; siege of Paris by Charles VI during the Hundred Years War; Henri IV welcomed by Parisians on 22 March 1594 after converting to Catholicism.

Charles recaptured his capital and drove the English back to Calais.

By the early 16th century, Louis XII (1498–1515) was embroiled in the Italian Wars. His successor, François I (1515–47), began the struggle against the Habsburgs but was captured at Pavia in 1525. The Parisians paid his ransom and he moved into the Louvre. In his wake came Italian architects, painters, sculptors and

> In 1516, François I enticed Leonardo da Vinci to France. He lived in a manor house called Clos Lucé near the king's residence in Amboise and died there in 1519 at the age of 67.

masons, whose task was to reshape the city's lugubrious Gothic face. With the rebirth of the capital gathering pace, French culture also returned to life.

The advent of the printing press underpinned the Renaissance; however, it also helped spread the new gospel of Protestantism through Catholic France. Paris, dominated by the conservative Sorbonne theologists, pushed for measures against the Protestants, known as Huguenots, often burning religious agitators. Henri II's sons and heirs, François II (1559–60), Charles IX (1560–74) and Henri III (1574–89),

were not able to control France's religious factions; nor were they helped by the intrigues of the Queen Mother, Catherine de Médicis. The country was plunged into a religious war.

War between the Henris

King Henri III's concessions to the Protestants infuriated the Catholics, led by Henri de Guise and his Holy League. In 1584, the Protestant Henri de Navarre, a Bourbon, became heir to the throne, but had to fight de Guise for the right to accede to power. To this end, in 1589, Henri III had de Guise killed. Paris threw up its barricades, and the Holy League's Council of Sixteen took power and deposed Henri III, who joined forces with Navarre. His army, however, sided with the Catholics. That summer, Henri III was murdered and Henri de Navarre became Henri IV.

Civil war dragged on for another five years. In 1593, Philip II of Spain, who had entered the war on the Catholic side, pressed to usurp the French throne. Henri IV chose that moment to convert to Catholicism, whereupon Paris welcomed him, and overnight the war-weary nation fell in line.

Henri IV patched up France spiritually and economically; in 1598, his Edict of Nantes set up guidelines for cohabitation between the religious groups. In 1610, Henri IV was murdered, and the young Louis XIII took to the throne.

The Bourbons

In spite of the massive debts incurred by their foreign wars, the Bourbons lavished huge sums on Paris, while keeping it on a short political leash. Two marshy islets east of the Ile de la Cité were amalgamated to become the residential Ile St-Louis. New bridges crossed the Seine. Avenues cut through the dingy labyrinth. Architects built new houses, parks, palaces and schools and restored the old ones. Cardinal Richelieu, who largely

THE EDICT OF NANTES

The Edict of Nantes, signed by Henri IV on 30 April 1598, enshrined religious tolerance in French law, and was a significant step on the road to the secularism of the French state that holds today. The Edict's immediate purpose was to end the long-running French Wars of Religion by giving rights to French Protestants, also known as Huguenots, in what was a predominantly Catholic state. Once the Edict became law, all subjects of the French crown, with the exception of Muslims and Jews, were granted freedom of worship, the right to work in any sphere, including for the state, and the right to bring grievances directly to the king.

governed on behalf of the young Louis XIII (1610–43), founded the Académie Française. Under the Sun King, Louis XIV (1643–1715), the spending spree reached its zenith. His minister, Colbert, sanitised entire sections of the city and set up manufacturing plants. Louis XIV also had hospices constructed for the poor, and Les Invalides was built to house war veterans.

The influx of money and the proximity of the court attracted crowds to the capital. Theatres rang with the dramas of Racine and Corneille, and audiences roared at the comedies of Molière.

But trouble loomed. In 1648, Paris revolted, demanding greater political representation. The 12 provincial parliaments joined a body lobbying for change, as did a conspiracy of nobles under Prince Condé. This alliance, known as the Fronde, eventually collapsed, but Louis XIV later had his lavish palace built outside the city in Versailles, away from the Parisian mob.

The early 18th century was a time of great inequality in Paris. French high society enjoyed

FROM LEFT: the storming of the Bastille, 1789; Boulevard Haussmann at the turn of the 20th century.

greater comforts and luxuries than ever before, and the court of the Sun King was a fertile breeding ground for debauchery and political intrigue. But the poor still had a raw deal. They were to make their displeasure felt with shattering consequences as the century drew to a close.

The revolutionary years

By the latter part of the 18th century, France's international renown rested increasingly on the writings of its intellectuals such as Voltaire, Rousseau and Diderot. But the poverty worsened; a bad harvest in 1788 caused the price of bread to soar and the people to become restless.

By 1789, France's debts had reached a critical level. King Louis XVI had to summon the Estates General, a legislative body of three estates: the Clergy, the Nobility and the rest of the populace, the Third Estate, to vote for reforms. Craftily, the king allowed only one vote per estate, so the huge Third Estate could be outvoted two to one by the smaller Clergy and Nobility. Eventually forced out, the Third Estate created a National Assembly to oppose the king. On 14 July, Parisians stormed the Bastille prison for weapons, proclaimed a Commune and formed a National Guard under liberal aristocrat and soldier Lafayette. The explosion of 1789 swept the past away. The

First Republic was proclaimed and, in January 1793, Louis was guillotined in public, followed in October by Queen Marie-Antoinette. Paris was the epicentre of the French Revolution and its radical leaders Mirabeau, Danton and the fanatical Robespierre, egged on by Marat, whose murder in July 1793 threw the Reign of Terror into top gear. Anyone suspected of stepping out of line got the chop; in July 1794, it was Robespierre's turn. The young brigadier-general Napoleon Bonaparte finally ended the Revolution, after quashing a royalist uprising in 1795. Four years later he was First Consul. In 1804 he crowned himself emperor of a totalitarian and military state.

The Napoleonic Empire

A masterful administrator, Napoleon drew up plans for a Bank of France, reformed the judiciary and local government, improved secondary education, instituted the Légion d'Honneur and restored the Church. He greatly strengthened France's power in Europe, and its trade links with the rest of the world.

Though he ruled supreme at home, he could not have things all his way on the battlefield for ever. His glorious empire ended with Paris occupied after the Battle of Waterloo in 1815. Bourbon Louis XVIII headed a constitutional monarchy, focusing on law and order and laissez-faire economics. In cultural circles,

Romanticism was in the air; one of the movement's bearers was Victor Hugo (1802–85). Inspired by the anti-establishment spirit of 1789, the Romantics railed against creaky academia and bourgeois respectability. The revolutionary spirit also remained in the Republican forces, who reached for the Parisian mob whenever despotism reared its head. In July 1830, Charles X revoked some electoral laws, sparking three days of rioting; he had to abdicate. His cousin, Louis-Philippe, Duke of Orléans, held power until 1848, when another revolution brought about his abdication in turn; the monarchy was finished.

The Second Empire

The first president of the Second Republic was Napoleon's nephew, Charles-Louis-Napoleon Bonaparte. The family traits didn't take long to show: he crowned himself Emperor Napoleon III in 1852, and arrested over 20,000 opponents to make his life easier.

The Commune

In 1870, Napoleon III went to war with Prussia. Two months later, he had been humiliatingly beaten, the Second Empire had become the Third Republic, and the Prussians were besieging Paris. In Bordeaux, the government of Adolphe Thiers waited for an uprising, which never materialised.

In January 1871, Thiers agreed to a ceasefire; the National Assembly ratified a peace treaty a month later. The Prussians marched through Paris, avoiding the eastern districts full of the starving and vengeful National Guard, which felt betrayed by the French government. Sensing trouble, Thiers moved his government to Versailles. In March, a Commune was proclaimed at the Hôtel de Ville after the bourgeoisie boycotted a municipal election. Civil war erupted and the Hôtel de Ville was burned. While the Communards hoisted red flags and argued over strategies, Thiers was busy raising a new army. The govern-

> *In Paris, Napoleon's architects and engineers improved the sewers and initiated a building boom. Paris wouldn't be the city it is today had it not been for Napoleon.*

ment forces succeeded where the Prussians had failed, and some 25,000 Communards were killed in the last weeks of May.

With the working class brutally tamed, Paris became host for the squabbles and plots of the Third Republic. The Republicans split into pro- and anti-clerical factions. In the 1890s, the left gathered around socialist Jean Jaurès. On the right were diehard monarchists and nationalists with a strong vein of anti-Semitism, as revealed by the Dreyfus Affair in the 1890s. This bitterly divisive scandal revolved around a Jewish army captain, Alfred Dreyfus, imprisoned on trumped-up spying charges. But amid the political acrimony, Paris hailed impressive new facilities: the first Métro lines were dug, the Eiffel Tower was built for the 1889 World Fair, and the first films were shown. Between 1880 and 1940, Paris was home to more artists than any other city.

World War I put a dampener on the high spirits, and in September 1914 the German artillery came within earshot. The city's military governor, Galliéni, rushed reinforcements (including the Paris taxi service) to the counter-offensive on the Marne; his rapid response ensured that the city was spared.

Normal life began to return after the armistice in 1918. From the east came Russian émigrés and from the west came American writers and composers. In the 1930s, Paris became a temporary haven to the refugees of fascism in Europe.

FROM LEFT: the French army crosses the river Isère on improvised gateways under enemy fire, 1917; Adolf Hitler visits occupied Paris in 1940.

Between the wars

With 1 million dead, millions of others crippled and the agricultural north destroyed by shelling, France's part in the victory over Germany in 1914 was bittersweet. Conservative Republicans and left-wing coalitions, including the Communist Party (founded in 1920), tried to come to grips with the economic and social after-effects of the Great War. The extreme right, meanwhile, made some important gains.

AN ERA OF GRANDEUR

The Second Empire was a grandiose era. New railway lines were built, and Paris hosted the World Fair in 1855 and 1867. Basking in financial ease, the city abandoned itself to masked balls, Offenbach operettas and salon conversation. Its prefect, Baron Haussmann, gave Paris a new face, demolishing most of the medieval city and rebuilding vast areas. Water mains and sewers were installed; parks were created and bridges built. Elegant boulevards and squares appeared, notably Avenue de l'Opéra and Place de l'Etoile, where all roads lead to the Arc de Triomphe; these served an aesthetic purpose, but also facilitated swift troop deployment and were hard to barricade.

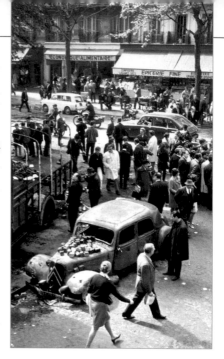

Fascist-type groups had appeared in France in the late 19th century. In the 1920s and 30s they proliferated, fuelled by general discontent and fear of Bolshevism, and inspired by Mussolini and Hitler. They focused their efforts on Paris, parading and campaigning against the internationalists, the socialists and, above all, the Jews. On 6 February 1934, a coalition of fascist factions attempted a *coup d'état* in Paris. It failed, but the left was finally goaded into concerted action. In 1936, a front of radicals, socialists and communists, headed by the socialist Léon Blum, won the election. The so-called Front Populaire promised to fight fascism and improve the workers' lot, but the initial euphoria was short-lived. The Front disappeared after a series of wildcat strikes.

World War II

When war broke out against Nazi Germany in September 1939, France hunkered down behind its fortifications along its eastern border, the Maginot Line, mobilised its ill-equipped army and waited. In Paris, Louvre curators prepared paintings for transport to safety.

General de Gaulle, born in Lille and a veteran of both world wars, was the first president of the Fifth Republic, still in place today.

On 14 June 1940, the Nazis marched into the City of Light after a lightning push through France from the Ardennes; the Germans had simply skirted the northern end of the Maginot Line. There was no siege, no National Guard, no *levée en masse*. Marshal Philippe Pétain, the 84-year-old hero of Verdun, became the head of a puppet regime in Vichy, in what was (at first) the unoccupied southern half of France.

While many Parisians were quiescent under the Nazi occupiers, and a number actively collaborated, there were those who bravely resisted, joining the Free French Movement led from London by General Charles de Gaulle. Their defiance often cost them their lives. On 6 June 1944, Allied forces landed in Normandy and advanced on Paris. Dietrich von Choltitz, the German commander, received orders to blow up the city, but chose to surrender instead; for this action he was dubbed "the saviour of Paris".

On 24 August 1944, Paris was liberated and, two days later, General de Gaulle paraded down the Champs-Elysées. De Gaulle immediately formed a provisional government, which lasted until 1946. Tourists returned in droves. Bebop and rock 'n' roll arrived from across the Atlantic.

Post-war thought was dominated by the dark ideas of writers such as Jean-Paul Sartre and Albert Camus. In addition, France lost two major colonial wars, the first in Indochina (1946–54) and the second in Algeria (1954–62).

May 1968: the barricades are back

A wave of bombings hit Paris in the early 1960s, when it became clear that President de Gaulle, who had come out of retirement to head the Fifth Republic in 1958, wanted to pull out of the Algerian quagmire. His manner in dealing with internal matters was patriarchal and authoritarian.

The 1968 agitation began uneventfully enough in March, with a sit-in by students to revise the antiquated university system. But instead of initiating a dialogue with the students, the *ancien régime* called in the CRS (the riot police) to restore order.

On the night of 10 May 1968, the police stormed 60 barricades in the Quartier Latin. Unrest spread to the factories and other cities. France was soon paralysed and Paris was left in a state of siege. The state-run media broadcast heavily monitored programming, while Parisians received the news from France's periphery. At the end of the month, de Gaulle announced new elections and warned against impending totalitarianism. The Parisian bourgeoisie awoke, and an hour later, over 500,000 supporters of de Gaulle were flowing down the Champs-Elysées.

The Gaullists won the election, but were not in power for long. Discontent continued, and the President resigned in 1969, leaving his Republic to his ardent disciple Georges Pompidou.

Mitterrand and Chirac

The 1970s were a time of relative stagnation, so when the Independent Republican president Valéry Giscard d'Estaing lost to socialist leader François Mitterrand in 1981, it felt like the dawn of a new era. However, the contrary Parisian character revealed itself again in 1986, during the legislative elections. Voters on the left were dismayed by what

they viewed as Mitterrand's capitulation to business interests, and conservative forces, led by Paris mayor Jacques Chirac, swept in with a right-wing coalition; an unprecedented "cohabitation" was begun.

The 1993 elections maintained the swing to the right and two years later Chirac succeeded François Mitterrand as president. Mitterrand died in January 1996. His *grands projets* made an indelible contribution to the Paris landscape. Besides, by 1997, Chirac's popularity had plummeted, and when he made the disastrous decision to dissolve the National Assembly and call new legislative elections in June, the socialist Lionel Jospin was swept in on a flood of votes as prime minister.

The French presidential elections of 2002 produced a dramatic run-off between Chirac and the xenophobic far-right agitator Jean-Marie Le Pen. Parisians took to the streets in vast numbers to express their opposition to Le Pen. Chirac finally won 82 per cent of the vote, the largest in the country's history. His opposition to the war in Iraq saw his approval ratings soar. But the bubble soon burst with public protests against reforms to the state pension and benefit system.

FROM LEFT: Chirac and Mitterrand, 1995; burned out vehicles testify to the riots in the Latin Quarter, May 1968; Nicolas Sarkozy, president from 2007 to 2012.

Sarkozy comes to power

Perhaps Chirac's longest-lasting contribution will be the law he pushed through in 2000 to shorten the presidential term from seven to five years. His party's candidate to succeed him, Nicolas Sarkozy, won the presidency in 2007 with a clear six point lead over socialist Ségolène Royal.

Unfortunately, Sarkozy's taste for luxury and his marriage to former supermodel Carla Bruni, along with doubling his own salary, increasing the pension age from 60 to 62, his coziness with Germany during the Euro crisis and public faux pas, made him France's most unpopular president ever. In May 2012 he was beaten at the polls by the Socialist François Hollande, surprisingly by just 3.2 per cent. Sarkozy has now retired from political life but will be remembered on the world stage for strengthening France's ties with the UK and US, pledging to reduce his country's CO_2 emissions by 50 per cent and taking a lead role in Allied military action against Libya.

The future is Left

Drenched and then struck by lightning (at least his plane was) on the day of his inauguration, things can only get better for Hollande. This unassuming man, who has never held a ministerial post, is getting on the right side of the French by eschewing the grand ways of his predecessor, travelling by train and living in his own apartment instead of the Elysée Palace. Time will tell if his plans to increase taxes on the wealthy, cut the public deficit by 2017 and increase public spending will keep France afloat during these difficult economic times and take him into a second term.

BERTRAND DELANOË

In 2001 Bertrand Delanoë became the first Socialist mayor of Paris for 130 years, elected by a populace who were disenchanted with the sleaze-ridden administration of his far-right predecessor. By the end of his second administration in 2014, the Tunisian-born mayor will probably be best known for bringing the beach – Paris Plage – to the banks of the Seine each summer since 2002, for introducing the *Vélib'* free bike scheme and for developing subsidised pre-school care for the city's toddlers. But his political ambitions may not end here – in 2008 openly gay Delanoë stood for (and lost) the leadership of his party with a view to becoming a presidential contender.

ABOVE: faced with a downturn in the economy and possible recession, François Hollande has his work cut out.

The Outsiders

Dictionaries translate banlieue as "suburbs", but whereas its English counterpart is relatively unproblematic, the French word is loaded.

Banlieue means "outskirts". Historically, it was the loop of land within a distance of one league ("lieue") from a city's perimeter; nowadays the word applies to any residential area on the edge of a large city or town. Some *banlieues*, like St-Germain-en-Laye, west of Paris, are affluent and picturesque; but out of context, "la banlieue" puts most French people in mind of high-rise estates like La Courneuve, Argenteuil and Aulnay-sous-Bois, sinkholes of burned-out cars, delinquency and boiling-point tempers.

Long-term problems

Such estates have been a running sore for years, and not only on the Paris periphery. Most were built in the 1960s and 70s, cheap housing for a growing workforce – in particular first- and second-generation immigrants from Algeria, Morocco and former French colonies in Africa. The effects of cack-handed urban and social engineering were compounded when industry slumped; and so began a vicious circle, whereby poor social facilities fuel local resentment, and chronic vandalism gives the state the perfect excuse not to invest.

Riots

In October 2005, the subject that many politicians and middle-class voters preferred to ignore made headline news. In the Paris *banlieue* of Clichy-sous-Bois, two teenagers, running from the police, climbed into an electricity substation and died. The resulting riots spread across the country; there were 23 nights of violence, 9,000 cars were torched, and a state of emergency was declared.

RIGHT: hanging out at the entrance of a run-down block on an estate in the northeast suburb of Paris.

An inspiration

Still, not all of France was in denial. It's a measure of how heavy the topic weighs on the national conscience that there's even an established cinematic sub-genre, the "*banlieue* film", of which the best-known is Matthieu Kassovitz's incendiary 1995 hit *La Haine*; reportages such as the Taverniers' *De l'autre côté du périph'* are frequent; and there's the occasional film made "from the inside", like *Wesh Wesh, qu'est-ce qui se passe?* (2001). Indeed, it's one of the ironies of the *banlieues* that their cultural scenes should be so vigorous and influential. In fashion, the "banlieue look" has entered the mainstream.

The future

The *banlieues* remain at the core of France's struggle to define and understand itself. They were in the news again in 2012 when random shootings took place in the suburbs of Paris and Toulouse. In spite of a €43 million renovation programme launched in 2003, the deeply ingrained social problems remain due to the lack of opportunities.

ARCHITECTURE

Paris is probably the loveliest and widest-ranging display of building styles in the world – and, with few exceptions, ancient and modern complement each other flawlessly.

Two thousand years of history and seven centuries of artistic brilliance have made Paris a city rich in architecture. Although invasions, sieges, insurrections and city planners destroyed a number of the capital's early masterpieces, fine examples remain, making modern-day Paris one of the most beautiful, fascinating – and intact – cities anywhere in the world.

Over time, the best architects have preserved this heritage, while looking forward and making room for the new. This explains the amazing juxtaposition of different architectural idioms.

Roman remains

Unsurprisingly, almost nothing remains of the wooden huts occupied by the Parisii. However, thanks to the Romans' development of a most

> Paris is a textbook of architectural history, boasting a full set of French architectural styles, especially from the 12th century and the beginnings of the Gothic era onwards.

durable concrete, their ruins can still be found in the Quartier Latin. Streets such as Rue St-Jacques and Boulevard St-Michel are built on ancient Roman roads.The vestiges of a bath can be seen in the garden at the Musée National du

PRECEDING PAGE: Haussmannian-style apartments.
LEFT: old and new – the Louvre and its glass pyramid.
RIGHT: Second-Empire style architecture on the Champs-Elysées.

Moyen Age–Thermes de Cluny, and the ruins of the arena (Arènes de Lutèce) have also survived.

Unfortunately, nothing is left of the Merovingian and Carolingian eras (6th–9th centuries); the Vikings burned and pillaged Paris on several occasions during this period.

Romanesque and Gothic

The Romanesque era (10th–11th centuries), with its ponderous, gloomy structures, left hardly a trace either. The steeple of St-Germain-des-Prés church is a rare remnant. In the 12th century, Paris turned to the newest rage in religious architecture – Gothic, discerned by pointed arches and the use of ribbed vaults with flying buttresses, which allowed windows to replace walls and stone to soar towards the heavens.

The most famous sacred building in Paris, Notre-Dame cathedral, epitomises the perfection of Gothic style. Its construction began in 1163 on the site of a Romanesque church, which had been built on the foundations of a Carolingian basilica, which in turn had been built on the site of a Roman temple. It took 200 years to finish. The building began to decay in the 17th century, but restoration by 19th-century Gothic revivalist Eugène Viollet-le-Duc (1814–79) only started in 1841. The restoration took nearly 23 years.

Close by stands Sainte-Chapelle, a fragile-looking church in High Gothic style, which differs from Notre-Dame in that the vast stained-glass windows are supported by only a thin framework of stone. It was built by Louis IX in 33 months to shelter the Crown of Thorns.

The Renaissance

War in Italy, in 1495, brought the French into contact with Renaissance grandeur, and the style, characterised by contempt for all Gothic forms and a rediscovery of antiquity, was imported to France. In architecture, the ribbed vault disappeared in favour of flat ceilings with wooden beams. Medieval fortresses gave way to genteel palaces with Greek-style colonnades.

Among Paris's main exponents of the Renaissance were architect Pierre Lescot (1510–78), who's finest work is the west wing of the Louvre, and Jean Goujon (1510–68), who sculpted the reliefs on Lescot's Louvre facade and worked on the Hôtel Carnavalet (1544). Goujon's work can also be seen on Lescot's Fontaine des Innocents, an example of Renaissance sensuality.

The Classical influence

While the Renaissance had succumbed to the Baroque in the rest of Europe at the end of the 16th century, a desire for strength and clarity born of rationalism dominated architecture. French architects were still looking towards sobriety and Classicism; the Classical style is based on symmetry, simplicity of line and great, wide-open perspectives. The Pont Neuf (1606), the first bridge to be built without houses on it, was one of the first examples. During this period, large squares were created, surrounded by uniform buildings and displaying a statue of the king in the middle of the large central garden. The Place des Vosges, commissioned by Henri IV in 1609, was the first and most elegant of the Classical-style royal squares.

> Lighter, more slender and luminous than previous styles, Gothic coincided with the strengthening of the French crown and a religious fervour inflamed by the Crusades.

With the coronation of a triumphant Napoleon and the installation of a new empire at the beginning of the 19th century came the triumphal arches (Arc de Triomphe du Carrousel and Arc de Triomphe) and the triumphal Neoclassical Rue de Rivoli.

The Haussmann effect

Except for a few upper-class neighbourhoods, post-Revolution Paris was a squalid city. Poverty-stricken communities, in filthy, narrow alleyways and miserable, overpopulated shacks were constantly on the brink of revolt. For obvious sanitary reasons, but also to defeat riots, Napoleon III and the prefect Baron Georges Haussmann began a sweeping programme to redraw the city map in the 1850s. Medieval Paris all but disappeared: whole quarters were razed, and wide, tree-lined avenues, harder to barricade than narrow alleys, cut through the maze of backstreets.

The grand style

The Sun King, Louis XIV, left his mark on Paris and its surrounding region, but imposed his personality most forcefully on the palace of Versailles. Begun in 1668, the palace symbolised the absolute power of the monarch and employed the top talents of the time: architects Louis Le Vau and Hardouin-Mansart, painter Charles Le Brun and landscape gardener André Le Nôtre. Other fine examples of the Classical style are the Palais du Luxembourg (1631) and the Hôtel des Invalides (1677).

After Louis's death, building was kept to a minimum until the 1750s, when the neoclassical movement turned to forms lifted directly from antiquity, taking the utmost care to reproduce what recent progress in archaeology had brought to light. Jacques-Ange Gabriel laid out Place de la Concorde and built the Ecole Militaire, and Jacques-Germain Soufflot designed the Panthéon on the site of an older church.

FROM LEFT: the Gothic splendor of Notre-Dame de Paris; gateway to Place des Vosges, the most superb Classical-style royal square in Paris; the Eglise du Dôme in Les Invalides is also a fine example of the Classical style.

THROUGH THE AGES
Here are a few examples of Paris's many architectural styles:
Roman: Arènes de Lutèce (1AD)
Romanesque: Steeple of St-Germain-des-Prés (990–1014)
Gothic: Notre-Dame (1163–1345), Sainte-Chapelle (1245)
Renaissance: Cour Carrée facade of the Louvre (1556)
Classical: Versailles (1668), Les Invalides (1677)
Neoclassical: Panthéon (1790), Arc de Triomphe (1806–36)
Second Empire: Gare du Nord (rebuilt 1861–65), Pont St-Michel (rebuilt 1857), Opéra Garnier (1875)
Modern: Institut du Monde Arabe (1981–87), Louvre Pyramid, Opéra Bastille (both 1989), Bibliothèque Nationale François Mitterrand (1998).

Amazingly, the Eiffel Tower was originally intended to be merely a temporary exhibit, to be dismantled after the 1889 World Fair. It is now the world's most visited paid monument.

Paris still bears the indelible stamp of Haussmann's achievements. After clearing out slums and opening up the area around the Louvre, he concentrated on expanding the system of boulevards through the city centre begun by Louis XIV. A small hill then known as the Butte St-Roch, occupied by windmills, a gallows and a pig market, was intended to be their centre. It is hard to picture that today as you stand on the busy Place de l'Opéra, looking at Garnier's opera house, the Second Empire's most sumptuous construction.

Monsieur Eiffel's tower

The second half of the 19th century was rich in architectural creativity. Wrought iron made its debut with the Grand Palais, the Pont Alexandre III and, of course, the iconic Eiffel Tower. Panned by writers and critics during its construction for the World Fair in 1889, the

tower is now the symbol of Paris. The tower embodied the uneasy relationship between science, industry and art in Paris. When the engineer climbed its 1,665 steps to plant the French flag atop his iron latticework fantasy, crowds of ordinary Parisians who admired his vision cheered; the aesthetes stayed away.

It was an eclectic era. Having burned down during the Commune of 1871, the Hôtel de Ville (City Hall) on the Right Bank was rebuilt in Renaissance style, while Sacré-Cœur cathedral fused neo-Byzantine and Romanesque styles. Numerous churches toed the neo-Gothic line. Reacting against these academic approaches and inspired by Japanese art, the Belgian Hector Guimard established the Art Nouveau movement. The sinuous organic forms and curving lines, natural and Baroque at the same time, were decried by some as "noodle style". Guimard designed several buildings in the 16th *arrondissement*, including the Castel Béranger (14 rue de la Fontaine), and also the city's Métro entrances, many of which, including those at Porte Dauphine and Abbesses, still remain.

The modern age

Both the modern movements of the 1920s and 1930s and Art Deco were born in the 16th *arrondissement*. Mallet-Stevens and Le Corbusier were the main exponents of the Cubic style of architecture, all pure lines and concrete. At the same time, a grandiose, neoclassical form

FROM LEFT: the exquisite grand staircase inside the Musée Jacquemart-André; Iraqi architect Zaha Hadid's Chanel Mobile Art Pavilion won the 2004 Pritzker Prize and has now found a permanent home at the Institut du Monde Arabe; the Grande Arche at La Défense aligns with the Arc de Triomphe along the *Axe historique* which runs through Paris.

of modernism appeared, as epitomised by the Palais de Chaillot.

From the 1960s, Paris underwent a transformation. Facades were cleaned, the Métro was modernised and old parts of the city were demolished. New architectural projects were developed, keeping up with technical advances by building upwards (La Défense and the much-decried Tour Montparnasse), expanding indoor space (Centre Pompidou, Cité de la Villette, Palais Omnisports at Bercy) and experimenting with new materials that capture, reflect and admit light.

In the 1980s, Sino-American architect I.M. Peï designed a new entrance for the Louvre: a "landscape" of pyramids in stainless steel and specially made glass. Lauded for its beauty and efficiency, the central pyramid has undoubtedly earned its place on the city's architectural stage.

Like Peï's pyramid, the bankside Institut du Monde Arabe (designed in 1987 by Jean Nouvel) achieves a kind of harmony by reflecting the neighbouring buildings and the ever-changing Parisian sky.

Into the future

Innovation continues. The imposing 1997 Bibliothèque Nationale François Mitterrand, also known as the TGB (Très Grande Bibliothèque), is at the heart of the 'new' Left Bank, a vast renewal project in the 13th *arrondissement*.

MK2 Bibliothèque, a cinema complex designed by Jean-Michel Wilmotte, opened nearby in 2003.

Two new footbridges have sprung across the river in recent years: the Passerelle de Solférino between the Tuileries and the Musée d'Orsay, in 1999, and the Passerelle Simone de Beauvoir between the TGB and the Parc de Bercy in 2006. In the Parc de Bercy itself, the former American Center, a 1992 Frank Gehry building, became the new home for the iconic Cinémathèque Française in 2006. An even newer building, another Nouvel design, is the Musée du Quai Branly, a museum of art from Asia, Africa, the Americas and Oceania that opened in 2006 in the shadow of the Eiffel Tower.

In 2012 work started on Le Triangle (a glass-and-steel pyramid at the Porte de Versailles) and Le Phare (situated in La Défense, this will become one of the tallest buildings in Paris at 300m/984ft). These are two of several new skyscrapers planned by Mayor Delanoë on the outskirts of Paris after he successfully overturned a law restricting the height of new buildings to 37m/121ft.

To get a complete overview of the history of architecture in Paris, pay a visit to the permanent exhibition in Le Pavillon de l'Arsenal (21 boulevard Morland, 4th), itself a remarkable piece of 19th-century design, with natural light pouring through a superb glass roof.

PARIS ON A PLATE

This is a city that worships food – and recent years have brought plenty of notable new talents and intriguing new addresses to keep the dining scene alive.

The news of the death of French food has been greatly exaggerated. Critics hail Spain, or London, or Sydney, or New York, as the "new France" – whereas Paris, they whine, is stuck in a rut. But that's not an entirely fair evaluation. It's important to remember when you eat in Paris, where the cooking of the whole country converges, that you're sampling a long-established cuisine: a vast, yet coherent repertoire of dishes, ingredients and techniques that have stood the test of time. A new ingredient or dish won't be welcomed into the cuisine until it proves itself worthy.

For the traveller, if not for locals, such conservatism is a boon. You want real French onion soup? You've got it. The menu says *steak au poivre*? That means it's *steak au poivre*: flat, rare, with creamy peppercorn sauce. This is not to say that contemporary and international experiences are not to be found. In recent years, a wave of young chefs has been opening snazzy yet relaxed restaurants serving French food with a fresh, contemporary face, and integrating (ever so cautiously) more exotic flavours like ginger, peanut, coriander, curry and lime. Even stellar chefs like Joël Robuchon and Alain Senderens have taken a more unbuttoned approach to their trade by opening their own bistros.

The international scene, although perhaps not as widespread as elsewhere, is also an integral

French cooking may be slow to evolve, but it's because France is a country that truly knows its food. The French are incredibly protective, disciplined and judicious in this regard.

part of the city's taste experience. Indeed, one thing that makes it exciting to eat in a country other than one's own is discovering the influences that immigrants from other places have brought to it. Paris has a lot of good North African, Vietnamese, Japanese, Lebanese and Afro-island cooking.

LEFT: the fabulous Belle Epoque interior of Le Train Bleu, which serves traditional fare. **RIGHT:** some Parisian bistros have small crêperie stands, like this one in Montmartre.

Street food and cafés

Street vendors are a welcome sight, especially in winter, with chestnuts roasting over beds of coal, waffle irons and crêpe grills ever at the ready. Falafels are sold through the windows on the Rue des Rosiers. Middle Eastern kebabs and savoury turnovers are sold throughout the city. Ice-cream stands abound on the Ile St-Louis.

To fill a picnic basket with traditional French fare, your best bet is a *charcuterie*, where you'll find ready-cooked dishes such as quiches, salads, pâtés, sausages, cheeses and prepared dishes like *poulet basquaise* (chicken with tomatoes and red peppers). Next, go to the bakery for a baguette or ready-made sandwiches.

If you're in a rush in the midst of shopping, traditional cafés will cater quickly while you give your feet a rest. Many will serve no more than simple baguette sandwiches. Others offer omelettes, or the quintessential café favourite, *croque-monsieur* (grilled ham and cheese on toast), or *croque-madame* (the same, but with a fried egg on top). Café salads are often hefty and filling, such as *Paysanne* (with potatoes, bacon and cheese) *Norvégienne* (with smoked salmon), *Landaise* (with duck breast), to name but three.

VEGETARIANS WILL SURVIVE

The vegetarian dishes of French cuisine are few and far between. In traditional restaurants, a solution is to order two meat-free starters instead of a main course. In an upmarket establishment, you can telephone ahead and request a vegetarian meal; this gives the cook time to concoct something just for you. Another option is to explore the city's ethnic restaurants, which serve meat-free snacks as well as elaborate three-course meals. However in recent years, vegetarian restaurants have been popping up all over Paris from Saveurs Végét'Halles (see page 115) to Tien Hiang (14 rue Bichat, 10th, tel: 01 42 00 08 23), whose menu consists solely of meat-free dishes from South East Asia.

Bistros and brasseries

No restaurants are more popular – or more emblematic of Paris – than the neighbourhood bistros and brasseries. Brasseries (breweries) were introduced to the city in the 19th century,

FROM LEFT: the much-loved baguette; charcuterie and cheese board; cooking with panache at brasserie La Coupole, where Picasso was a regular.

around the time when modern methods of brewing were being perfected. Many brasseries serve Alsatian specialities such as *choucroute* and *steins* of beer; others specialise in shellfish. Outside the latter, you'll spot heaps of clams, mussels and langoustines on beds of ice, and burly men in overalls shucking oysters from dawn until dusk. All brasseries serve a wide range of dishes, including standard bistro fare. They're a jolly experience: spacious, clamorous and festive, usually decorated in Belle Epoque style.

For quieter, more intimate meals, opt for the bistros. These are smaller, more humble nooks, offering similar menus: *hareng pommes à l'huile* (smoked herring marinated in oil with warm potatoes), *œufs en meurette* (poached eggs with red wine sauce), *blanquette de veau* (veal in a white sauce), *coq au vin* (braised chicken in wine), *mousse au chocolat* (chocolate mousse) and *tarte Tatin* (caramelised upside-down apple tart). Some bistros have a regional bent, proudly boasting their provincial specialities. In Auvergnat bistros, think blue cheese, potatoes, walnuts and superb beef; with Southwestern ones it's *foie gras* and duck; Basque flavours include

hot pepper, salt cod and ham; and Provençal bistros guarantee ratatouille, lamb and *bouillabaisse*.

The star experience

For those who want to dress up and spend a bomb on dinner, there are countless prestigious restaurants in the city. A Michelin guide will point you in the direction of establishments that meet these starry standards. Be ready to spend several hours at the table, to eat seven courses, and to have waiters buzzing around you like winged butlers. The food in starred restaurants (whether one star or three) should produce meals you'll remember for a lifetime, but some restaurants, unfortunately, rest on their laurels.

> The name "bistro" supposedly derives from the days of the Allied occupation of Paris in 1814. Russian soldiers were forbidden to drink, so whenever they dived into a bar, they demanded their refreshments urgently – bistrot – to avoid being caught.

Contemporary French cooking

There is no single term for the sprouting of contemporary French restaurants: sleek, trendy, moderately priced, and with good, interesting food. Dinner usually consists simply of an *entrée*, *plat* and *dessert*. Dishes are lighter than in a bistro, less complicated than in starred establishments; the wine list will probably include international bottles; the service is pleasant; and the crowds are *branché* (fashionable).

All in all, they're a good way to get a taste of the future of French food. The only drawback is that they don't feel particularly French.

> Part of the excitement of dining in France is having the option of – if not the appetite for – pig's ears, beef muzzle and blood sausage.

Food for thought

Not all visitors to Paris are as enthusiastic about certain French classics as the locals. Almost everyone knows that *escargots* are snails and *cuisses de grenouille* are frogs' legs, but many a tourist has unwittingly ordered calf's head *(tête de veau)*, expecting simply veal, or *andouillette* in hope of pork sausage only to discover tripe-filled concoctions. But dishes like these sound more frightening than they really are: after all, millions of French people relish their taste.

Fish, of the truly excellent kind, is not especially easy to find in Paris, and where one does find it, it comes at a price. Brasseries usually have a promising array, for example on their *plateaux*

de fruits de mer (shellfish platters). Of course, it's generally in the more expensive restaurants that it will be cooked best. In France, meats tend to be served at one extreme or another: at the one end, raw (for example, *tartare de bœuf* or beef tartare) or *saignant* (rare); and at the other, *confit* (preserved) or cooked tender until falling from the bone. If you order steak, it will come rare unless you specify "*à point*" (medium) or "*bien cuit*" (well done). Don't hesitate to send a dish back if the meat is not cooked to your liking. Fish is trickier. At mid-range restaurants it tends to be overcooked, so if you like it just done, it's important to ask for your fish cooked "*rose à l'arête*" (rare at the bone).

Cheese

Nowhere in the world is there a wealth of cheese to match that of France, where cheese is considered so important that an entire dinner course is devoted to it alone. Between the main course and dessert, out comes the trolley or platter, laden with a delectably smelly array. The most pungent are generally cheeses such as Epoisses, Mont d'Or and Munster. If you prefer mild ones, steer instead towards goat's cheeses, young Comté or Mimolette. Blue cheeses vary greatly in creaminess and strength, but usually aren't too overpowering; Brie and Camembert are well known, mild and deliciously smooth. Try not to be overwhelmed by the number of options. It can take years to become familiar with French cheeses. Just remember two rules: in a cheese tasting, always start with the mildest cheese and work your way around to the strongest; and never steal the "nose" off a piece; always slice cheese in such a way as to preserve its shape, so the last person served won't be left with just the rind.

Drinks

It is usual to be offered an *apéritif* before a meal. A glass of champagne, white wine, or a *kir* (white wine with *cassis* – a blackcurrant liqueur) are most popular, but whisky and port are also common. Of course, you don't have to order an *apéritif*; you can jump straight to the wine list.

In the minds of the French, wine is the *de rigueur* accompaniment not only to French food, but to eating in general. In starred restaurants, a deal of care is generally taken over which wine will go with what, but in most casual places, the rule is drink what you like.

Simple restaurants, in addition to bottles,

sell wine by the glass or by the jug: *un pichet de rouge* (a jug of red) will get you an inexpensive, potentially rough but entirely drinkable red wine. Beer is usually only ordered with sandwiches, Alsatian meals or Asian lunches; cider accompanies Breton and Norman specialities (crêpes or mussels). Several mineral waters are on offer; request *pétillante* for sparkling, *plate* for still, or *en carafe* for tap water.

The French meal

Entrée (Americans, take note) means starter, not main course. *Plat* is the main dish. *Dessert* is, not surprisingly, dessert or pudding. All three are often included in *prix fixe* (fixed-price) menus, although a choice of either *entrée* and *plat* or *plat* and *dessert* is increasingly common.

In unpretentious places, nobody minds if you order two *entrées* instead of a full meal. What is often frowned upon, especially in upmarket restaurants, is passing dishes around the table to share, as chefs take pride in balancing the flavours on each plate. For a widely roaming meal,

FROM LEFT: contemporary cooking at Les Cocottes; andouillette and potatoes; coffee is served after dessert; French cheeses come in all shapes and sizes.

opt for a *menu dégustation* (tasting menu).

Coffee is served after dessert. *Café* means espresso, strong and black. If you like milk, order a *café noisette*. *Café crème* (coffee with milk) is considered a breakfast drink. Finally, if you're avoiding caffeine, ask for a *café décaféiné* (*déca* for short) or *une tisane* (herbal tea).

Last but not least, the *digestifs* (after-dinner drinks), ranging from Cognac to Armagnac to Calvados to other liqueurs. Beware: too many and you'll pay for it in the morning.

Due to the large American expat community, there are several places to get a decent brunch including Breakfast in America (17 rue des Ecoles, 5th and 4 rue Mahler, 4th) while Le Bal Café (6 impasse de la Défense, 18th), where apple crumble is usually on the menu, is a "must visit" for homesick Brits.

FROM LEFT: North African specialities at Zerda Café in the Marais; chocolate and coffee éclairs aligned with precision at La Maison du Chocolat.

OTHER CUISINES

North African restaurants are most certainly the best-represented in the French capital, serving hearty dishes like *couscous* (steamed semolina with spicy meat or stewy vegetable toppings) and *tagine* (braised meat that is often cooked with preserved lemons and dried fruits).

Parisians have well and truly fallen in love with Japanese food, and dozens of restaurants have opened around the city in recent years, ranging from cheap noodle joints to more sophisticated, top Michelin-star establishments like Aida (1 rue Pierre-Leroux, 7th, tel: 01 43 06 14 18), where a menu can set you back €160. If your budget doesn't stretch that far, head to the Porte d'Italie neighbourhood, south of the Latin Quarter, for cheap and cheerful Vietnamese and Chinese eateries.

For Indian fare (not just restaurants, but also eclectic grocers), explore the 10th *arrondissement* around the Gare du Nord; this area is the place to look for Turkish restaurants too.

A good place to try out African food is the Belleville area, northeast of Place de la République, and Lebanese restaurants are dotted all over Paris, as are Thai establishments.

CHIC SHOPPING

From chic boutiques to mouth-watering food shops and from strutting-edge fashions to antique dealers and flea markets: welcome to the best collection of shops in Europe.

Though shopping abroad is an increasingly predictable affair, Paris can still claim to offer something different. It hosts an incredible variety of shops and has, by and large, retained its tradition of small specialist addresses and personal attention. Take a walk through the Passage des Panoramas (Rue Montmartre, 2nd) to see some fine examples.

Despite a tendency for fashion labels to aim for a citywide spread, there are fewer chain stores here than in most European capitals. With the exception of the Forum des Halles and a couple of small shopping centres, Paris remains largely free of the *centres commerciaux* (shopping malls) that disfigure its suburbs. Instead, boutiques ensure that Paris stays vibrant and alive.

The fashion industry is still a tangible presence in Paris; however, French designers no longer dominate the world fashion stage. But between the couture tags and the high-street chains, you can find boutiques with their own take on French style, retailers picking out exciting new talents, and the one-off boutiques of individual designers. And at some atelier-boutiques, in Bastille and Montmartre, you can buy direct.

Other aspects of French design are also worth exploring. Paris has a strong art and craft tradition, from the classic hallmarks of quality such as Lalique glass and Pierre Frey fabrics to contemporary design gurus such as Philippe Starck, and the rising talents Tsé & Tsé Associées and the Bouroullec brothers.

Then there's food, of course. Every *quartier* has its *chocolatiers*, *pâtisseries* and *boulangeries*, ripe-smelling cheese shops and bustling street markets.

ABOVE: Galerie de Valois, near the Palais-Royal, hosts luxury brands like Marc Jacobs, Stella McCartney and Jérôme L'Huillier.

LEFT: Anne Fontaine, the queen of the white shirt.

ABOVE LEFT: St-Germain-des-Prés is a great area for shoes, sensible or not.

ART AND ANTIQUES

As you'd expect from a city that has contributed significantly to the arts over the centuries, Paris has plenty to offer those looking to buy art or antiques. At the top end of the scale, Le Louvre des Antiquaires, housed in a beautiful 19th-century building on rue de Rivoli opposite the famous museum, has 150 galleries and showrooms selling everything from Old Masters to Art Deco dancer sculptures, while over in the Marais, the Village St-Paul has a more affordable, eclectic mix of galleries and designers.

Serious art collectors should head over to St-Germain as most of the major dealers are based on Rue de Seine and Rue des Beaux-Arts. Near here Librairie Taschen (2 rue de Buci) has dozens of books on the visual arts. For those on tighter budgets, a Marché de la Création takes place in Place de la Bastille on Saturday and in front of the Montparnasse tower on Sunday, where around 150 artists and craftspeople sell their wares from 10am to 7pm.

For iconic images of Paris, such as original posters by Toulouse Lautrec and photos by Henri Cartier-Bresson, the place to go is L'Ile aux Images (51-53 rue St-Louis-en-l'Ile, 4th) on Ile St-Louis.

ABOVE: vintage posters for sale in Passage Jouffroy.

BELOW: hip design store merci in the Marais is a one-stop shop for a stylish life.

ABOVE: window shopping at the Dior store on Avenue Montaigne.

ABOVE: under its stunning Art Nouveau glass dome, Galeries Lafayette offers a colossal fashion choice, from hip designer labels and classical womenswear to popular labels. There is an adjoining Lafayette Homme for men.

THE MARKET SCENE

The city's lively, colourful and sense-stunning street markets are a vital part of life for many residents – all are different, which makes shopping endlessly interesting.

Visitors wanting a change from the cool chic of haute couture Paris should seek out a street market: there are more than 100. Foodies will be beguiled by the tantalising smells of the roving street food markets; photographers intrigued by the predominantly North African Marché d'Aligre; and browsers may prefer the *bouquinistes*, open-air booksellers whose stalls line the banks of the Seine. There are markets specialising in flowers, postcards and stamps; funky Left Bank markets selling second-hand designer clothes; rural markets overflowing with fresh farm produce and bargains; or genuine antiques to be had at the city's regular flea markets.

Non-French speakers need not worry too much. Items are usually marked clearly and many stall-holders speak English or are used to dealing with visitors from around the world; don't be afraid to barter when buying antiques or bric-à-brac. It's a good idea to have lots of change available, especially at food markets, as credit cards are not usually accepted. Markets can be a fun place to take children – just be sure to keep a close eye on them – due to the wide variety of produce and objects on offer, many of which are unlikely to be commonly found in other countries and which have a distinctly French or colonial feel.

Most of all, markets are one of the best opportunities for visitors to experience the real buzz of the various quartiers: whether rubbing shoulders with couture-clad grandes dames in the 8th or being serenaded by African drummers in brightly coloured tunics in Belleville.

LEFT: food markets provide a variety of produce not always found in supermarkets.

RIGHT: a brocante stall near the Canal St-Martin.

BELOW: at the Puces de St-Ouen, although a few of the markets remain shabby, much of what is on sale is classy and often quite pricey. Many of the stalls have the allure of shops, and stallholders are knowledgeable enthusiasts. The whole complex is now listed as a historic monument in an attempt to preserve its character.

THE BEST MARKETS

Paris is known for its many flea *(puces)* and food markets. Here are some of the best:

Marché de St-Ouen: in the north of Paris (Métro Porte de Clignancourt). Reputedly the largest flea market in the world, with over 2,500 dealers spread over a dozen markets and arcades. Be ready to bargain. Sat–Mon 9am–6pm.

Marché de Montreuil: tattier and more anarchic than St-Ouen, Montreuil (Métro Porte de Montreuil) sells car parts, tools and unwashed clothes. Sat–Mon 7am–7pm.

Marché de Vanves: smaller than St-Ouen and Montreuil, Vanves (Métro Porte de Vanves) is a relaxed flea market within the Périphérique. Weekends 7am–3pm.

Marché d'Aligre: the oldest flea market in Paris, on the square next to the Rue d'Aligre (Métro Ledru-Rollin) food market. Handful of stalls selling over-priced antiques and junk. Tue–Sun am.

Marché Bastille on boulevard Richard-Lenoir (Thur and Sun am; Métro Bastille) and Avenue Daumesnil (Tue and Fri am; Métro Daumesnil): street markets with a great range of seasonal produce.

Rue Mouffetard: characterful food market street in the Latin Quarter (Métro Censier-Daubenton). Tue–Sat (closed for lunch) and Sun am

Marché St-Quentin: 85 boulevard Magenta, 10th (Métro Gare de l'Est), was built in the 1880s and remains the best-preserved cast-iron covered market. Stalls sell fresh produce and exotic snacks. Tue–Sun am.

ABOVE: food markets say a lot about the way Parisians live. The key to most is that they sell fresh, quality ingredients. Prices are not cheap, but the emphasis is on the best that is in season. There are two main types of food market: the roving street markets that appear a couple of mornings a week, and the historic covered markets.

ABOVE: old postcards for sale at the Puces de St-Ouen.

LEFT: vegetable-shopping at the Marché Saxe-Breteuil, Les Invalides.

ABOVE: blooms for sale at the Marché aux Fleurs on Ile de la Cité.

PARIS AFTER DARK

The city's nightlife offers a multitude of options for drinking and dancing until the small hours, but live music and cabaret have their fans too.

Paris still isn't really a clubbing city, and stringent anti-noise laws mean most music venues can't stage late-night gigs. But there's no shortage of after-dark revelry if you know where to look. There has been an increase in the range and number of venues: upmarket clubs like VIP Room (188bis rue de Rivoli, 1st) and Neo (23 rue du Ponthieu, 8th) attract celebrities and the jet set; in 2005, an old warehouse on the bank of the Canal St-Martin was turned into a giant arts and nightlife complex Point Ephémère; and in 2007, "hangars" underneath the Pont Alexandre III opened as glam club Le Showcase. And other stalwarts, like the live music venues La Flèche d'Or (102bis rue de Bagnolet, 20th) and Le Bus Palladium (6 rue Fontaine, 9th) have been given new leases of life. There's also a lot of jazz, blues, chanson and world gigs, and lively backroom gig spaces to complement the larger, more traditional music venues. The coolest bars are around Ménilmontant and Oberkampf while the Marais is the place to go for gay and lesbian venues. But going out in Paris isn't solely restricted to bars and dance clubs; the city has long been associated with cabaret, from the magnificent costumes of the Bluebell Girls at Le Lido (116 avenue des Champs Elysées, 8th) to the racy gyrations at adults-only Crazy Horse (12 avenue George V, 8th). Keep your ears to the ground and look out for flyers and free listings booklets in bars.

ABOVE: La Flèche d'Or (102bis rue de Bagnolet, 20th) is an enjoyable anarchic music and clubbing venue housed in an old train station.

RIGHT: the bar at Le Milliardaire (68 rue Pierre Charron, 8th), whose red-and-black décor give a nod to the venue's theatrical days.

BELOW: the Ducs des Lombards (42 rue des Lombards, 1st) is one of the main jazz clubs in the capital.

LEFT: located in an upbeat street in a trendy neighbourhood in the heart of St-Michel quarter, the Bistro de la Huchette will have you dancing to salsa beats all night long.

THE COCKTAIL HOTSPOTS

Parisian trendsetters still love Hôtel Costes (239 rue St-Honoré, 1st), which has a sleek bar and plays classic "lounge music". Kong, the super-stylish Asian-Fusion restaurant on the top floor of the LVMH building (1 rue du Pont Neuf, 1st), is a bar at weekends and offers wonderful views across the French capital from its dome home. Tucked away on a Marais backstreet, Candelaria (see page 103) is a Mexican restaurant with a cosy candlelit cocktail lounge where tequila rules, while gin reigns supreme in the G'Bar and Lounge at Le Parc Trocadéro Hotel (55–57 avenue Raymond-Poincaré, 16th). Harry's Bar (5 rue Daunou, 2nd), with its dark-wood pub-like interior, is the oldest cocktail bar in Europe and where the Bloody Mary was invented in 1920. For a more casual and exotic night, try Andy Wahloo (see page 103) to savour Moroccan tapas, funky decor and mint-and-vodka concoctions.

ABOVE: glamorous Le Showcase boasts a great location under the Pont Alexandre III.

LEFT: Le Kitch, in oh-so-trendy Rue Oberkampf, is a cosy, intimate bar, popular with the equally hip locals.

BELOW: another fashionable Oberkampf hangout is Café Charbon, where DJs spin their decks on Friday and Saturday nights.

PARIS AT THE MOVIES

In 1895, the first public film screening was held in Paris – and the city and cinema have been inseparable ever since.

If Paris feels eternally familiar, thank the movies. Indeed, you're in film-set Paris the second you get off the train at the Gare du Nord, filmed by Orson Welles (*F for Fake*), Jean-Pierre Jeunet (*Amélie*) and many others. Next, naturally, you make your way to the Métro – an even more popular film location, used by everyone from Henri-Georges Clouzot to the Coen brothers. Perhaps you come out at the Champs-Elysées – another classic setting; as you walk up, imagine the Wehrmacht's daily parade coming the other way, as recreated to sobering effect in Jean-Pierre Melville's *L'Armée des Ombres*. The oldest bridge in Paris, the Pont Neuf, was the focus of a 1991 film, *Les Amants du Pont Neuf*, starring Juliet Binoche. And it's hard to miss the Eiffel Tower: not only filmed more times than it has rivets (the pioneering Lumière brothers were first – their 1900 portrait of the 11-year-old tower is still extant), it even starred in its own cartoon, *Bonjour Paris*. Hollywood has long been enchanted by the City of Light, from the 1950s films *An American in Paris*, starring Gene Kelly, and *Funny Face*, featuring Audrey Hepburn, to the controversial 1970s Marlon Brando movie *Last Tango in Paris* and Woody Allen's time-travelling 2011 offering, *Midnight in Paris*.

ABOVE: Vincent Cassel as a bad boy from the *banlieue* in Matthieu Kassovitz's ferocious 1995 agitprop drama *La Haine*, which won its director a major prize at the Cannes Festival that year. In its portrayal of the urban underclass, the film is still all too relevant.

BELOW: Woody Allen's 2011 time-travelling comedy *Midnight in Paris*, in which former First Lady Carla Bruni-Sarkozy plays a museum guide.

BELOW: Marlon Brando and director Bernardo Bertolucci on the set of *Last Tango in Paris* in 1972.

Above: Audrey Tautou as the eponymous heroine of Jean-Pierre Jeunet's 2001 smash hit *Amélie (Le Fabuleux Destin d'Amélie Poulain)*. The Métro stop shown is not, in fact, Abbesses – but a disused station used exclusively for filming.

Left: Rufus Sewell and Emily Mortimer in one of the 18 short films that make up *Paris, je t'aime (Paris, I love you)*, each set in a different *arrondissement*.

Below: Christopher Nolan's visually innovative *Inception* (2010) features a memorable 'folding Paris' scene.

Above: Jean Seberg and Jean-Paul Belmondo in probably the most famous Paris film, Jean-Luc Godard's *Breathless (A Bout de Souffle)*.

GOOD OLD NEW WAVE

When people think of Paris movies, they often have in mind a small clutch of films – usually including *Breathless* and *The 400 Blows* – made by a small group of people in a short space of time. These Nouvelle Vague ("new wave") films were made between the late 1950s and mid-1960s, by a loosely affiliated group of directors opposed to what they saw as the stuffiness of cinema of the day; its leading figures were Jean-Luc Godard, François Truffaut, Claude Chabrol, Eric Rohmer and Jacques Rivette – only Godard and Rivette, now in their eighties, are still alive at the time of writing. The films brought international recognition to the actors Jean-Paul Belmondo, Jeanne Moreau and Jean Seberg, the late American actress who starred in *Breathless*. One of the movement's few women directors was Agnès Varda, whose 1962 film *Cléo de 5 à 7* is one of the best of the bunch.

ORIENTATION

A detailed guide to the entire city,
with principal sites clearly cross-referenced
by number to the maps.

Paris is set in a natural basin, cut through the middle by the meandering River Seine and edged with gentle hills. Situated on longitude 2° 20'W and latitude 48° 50'N, the city itself covers an area close to 100 sq km (40 sq miles), spanning 13km (8 miles) from east to west, and 9km (6 miles) north to south. On the
map, 20 *arrondissements* (administrative districts) spiral out like a snail's shell, a pattern reflecting the city's historical development and successive enlargements. The Seine enters Paris close to the Bois de Vincennes in the southeast, and weaves gently past three small islands – Ile St-Louis, Ile de la Cité and, on its way out, Ile des Cygnes. Several hills rise up to the north of the river, including Montmartre, the city's highest point at 130 metres (425ft), Ménilmontant, Belleville and Buttes Chaumont; and to the south, Montsouris, Mont Ste-Geneviève, Buttes aux Cailles and Maison Blanche. Mont Valérien is the highest point on the outskirts at 160 metres (525ft), providing an immense panoramic view of Paris from the west. The lowest, at 25 metres (85ft) above sea level, is at Grenelle.

The city is contained by the *Boulevard Périphérique*, a ring road stretching 35km (22 miles). Built in 1973 to try to reduce traffic jams, the Périph' is invariably congested itself. Forming two concentric rings around Paris, the suburbs *(la banlieue)* are divided up into *départements* or boroughs. The inner ring incorporates Hauts-de-Seine, Val-de-Marne and Seine-St-Denis, and the outer ring consists of Seine-et-Marne, Essonne, Yvelines and Val-d'Oise. These counties, together with Paris and the Greater Paris conurbation around it, constitute the Ile-de-France region and are linked by eight major roads, five RER lines and an extensive rail network branching out from five stations in the capital. The city's calmest transport route is its river, barely ruffled by the daily flow of boat traffic. Barges and pleasure boats on their way to Burgundy use the St-Martin and St-Denis canals, cutting across the northeast of Paris.

PRECEDING PAGES: the awe-inspiring Arc de Triomphe at dusk; the Louvre is a masterpiece of symmetry. **LEFT:** sweeping view over Paris from its most iconic landmark, the Eiffel Tower. **ABOVE:** postcards for sale at a *bouquiniste* with a view over to Paris's oldest bridge, the Pont Neuf; the view from Paris's tallest building, Tour Montparnasse.

CIMETIÈRE DE
MONTMARTRE
St-Pierre
Basilique du
Sacré-Cœur
Moulin
Rouge
St-Jean
Place
de Clichy
Rue des Abbesses
Bd Barbès
Rue de Maubeuge
0   500 m
0   500 yds
N
Boulevard de Clichy
MONTMARTRE
Pl. Pigalle
Boulevard de Rochechouart
Rue Louis-Blanc
l'Aqueduc
St-Martin
Fayette
Rue Notre-Dame-de-Lorette
Rue La Bruyère
Avenue Trudaine
Rue
Rochechouart
de Dunkerque
Boulevard
Rue
Condorcet
de
Maubeuge
de
Magenta
Gare
du Nord
Rue du Faubourg St-Denis
la
du
Faubourg
Quai de Valmy
Quai de Jemmapes
Pl. du
Colonel-
Fabien
Rue d'Amsterdam
Rue de Clichy
Blanche
Rue Rodier
Rue St-Lazare
Rue de Châteaudin
Fayette
Rue de Chabrol
Gare
de l'Est
Rue
du
Canal St-Martin
Rue de la Grange
de Londres
de Provence
la
Rue
d'Hauteville
de
Paradis
Rue du Faubourg St-Denis
Rue du Faubourg St-Martin
Boulevard de Strasbourg
Château d'eau
de
Magenta
Rue du Faubourg-
du-Temple
St-Lazare
Folies
Bergère
Rue Richer
R. des Petites Écuries
Quai
de
Jemmapes
Av. de la
République
levard
Haussmann
de la Chaussée
du
Fg
R. des Petites Écuries
Bd St-Martin
Pl. de la
République
Palais
Garnier
Bd Montmartre
Bd des Italiens
Bd Poissonnière
Bd de Bonne Nouvelle
Rue St-Denis
Boulevard Voltaire
Bd du Temple
Bd des Capucines
Rue du Quatre-Septembre
La Bourse
Rue N.D. des Victoires
Poissonnière
Bd St-Martin
Pl. de la
République
Th. des
Capucines
Richelieu
Rue de Cléry
Turbigo
Bd des F.
du Calvaire
Place
Vendôme
Rue de la Paix
Bibliothèque
Nationale-
Richelieu
Rue Réaumur
Rue Montmartre
Rue Montorgueil
Sébastopol
Musée des Arts
et Métiers
Rue
de
Réaumur
R. de Bretagne
Bd des F.
du Calvaire
de
l'Opéra
R. des Petits Champs
Rue
Rue Étienne-Marcel
Rue
Temple
MARAIS
St-Roch
JARDIN DU
PALAIS
ROYAL
St-Eustache
St-Denis
Martin
Rue Beaubourg
Archives
Rue
Turenne
Rue
de
Rivoli
Honoré
Comédie
Française
Palais
Royal
Bourse de
Commerce
Forum des
Rue Halles
Berger
Rambuteau
Centre
Georges
Pompidou
Musée des
Archives
Nationales
Temple
des Francs-
Musée
National
Picasso
Bd du Temple
JARDIN DES
TUILERIES
JARDIN DU
CARROUSEL
Rue
Rivoli
Boulevard
Rue du Temple
Vieille
Musée
Carnavalet
Bd Beaumarchais
des Tuileries
Seine
Pont
Royal
Quai Fr.-Mitterrand
Musée du
Louvre
Rue
St-Merri
de
Rivoli
Bourgeois
Pl. des
Vosges
usée
Orsay
de
Anatole-France
Pont du
Carrousel
Pont Neuf
Palais
de Justice
Hôtel
de Ville
Hôtel
d'Aumont
Rue St-Antoine
Maison de
Victor Hugo
Place de la
Bastille
GERMAIN-
de
Bac
Lille
Quai de Conti
École
Nationale Supérieure
des Beaux-Arts
Institut
de France
Ste-
Chapelle
Bd du Palais
Rue de la Cité
Île de
la Cité
de
l'Hôtel
de
Ville
Hôtel
de Sens
Île
St-Louis
Bd Henri IV
usée
aillol
Germain
St-Germain-
des-Prés
Rue
Sts-
Pères
de
l'Université
Rue
Mazarine
Rue
Dauphine
Quai
des
Grands
Augustins
R. André-des-Arts
Notre-Dame
St-Julien-
le-Pauvre
Quai de la Tournelle
Quai
des
Deux-Ponts
Bd Morland
Quai Henri IV
Bd de la Bastille
Bourdon
Grenelle
Raspail
Rue
Four
St-Sulpice
R. St-Sulpice
Boulevard
St-Germain
Germain
Institut de
Mode Arabe
Quai
St-
Bernard
Seine
Pont d'Austerlitz
Quai de la Rapée
ERMES
Rue
Bonaparte
Madame
Théâtre National
de l'Odeon
de
Vaugirard
St-
Jacques
des
Écoles
Rue Clovis
Monge
JARDIN
TINO
ROSSI
Palais du
Luxembourg
La
Sorbonne
R. Cujas
R. Soufflot
Rue
Lhomond
Panthéon
Rue
Jussieu
Cuvier
JARDIN
DES
PLANTES
Raspail
Boulevard
d'Assas
Rue Guynemer
JARDIN DU
LUXEMBOURG
Boulevard
St-
Rue Gay-
Lussac
Rue A.-Comte
Musée Zadkine

ILE DE LA CITÉ AND ILE ST-LOUIS

Paris's Gothic heart, where the soaring towers and buttresses of Notre-Dame and the Sainte-Chapelle rise up next to the glowering fortress-prison of the Conciergerie, only a short walk from the 17th-century refinement of the Ile St-Louis.

The Ile de la Cité in the middle of the Seine is the birthplace and topographical centre of Paris, and has been its spiritual and legislative heart for more than 2,000 years. Invading the already established Parisii settlement in 53 BC, the Romans built a prefect's palace, law court and temple to Jupiter on the island. Across the river on the Right Bank, the Hôtel de Ville has been a cauldron of political debate since the Middle Ages (though the current building dates from the 1870s), while just to the north, the area of Les Halles fed the city's stomachs from 1110 until 1969. This is the core of the capital, an area which in many ways embodies the essence of Paris.

NOTRE-DAME ❶

Address: www.cathedraledeparis.com
Tel: 01 42 34 56 10
Opening Hrs: Mon–Fri 8am–6.45pm, Sat–Sun 8am–7.15pm
Entrance Fee: free
Transport: Cité

The Ile de la Cité is dominated by the soaring cathedral, Notre-Dame de Paris, which fills the eastern end of the island. Gazing up at its finely

sculpted facade, it's hard to imagine the building's condition when Victor Hugo (see page 94) wrote his novel *Notre-Dame de Paris* in 1830–1. He and fellow Romantics were appalled by the state of the building, and in 1841 succeeded in triggering a massive restoration programme, headed by Viollet-le-Duc. For 23 years, the meticulous architect repaired Notre-Dame from the foundations to the roof tiles, recreated stained-glass windows by copying extant ones and replaced sculptures destroyed in the

Main Attractions
NOTRE-DAME
PALAIS DE JUSTICE
SAINTE-CHAPELLE
CONCIERGERIE
MÉMORIAL DES MARTYRS DE LA DÉPORTATION
MUSÉE ADAM MICKIEWICZ

Maps and Listings
MAP, PAGE 76
SHOPPING, PAGE 86
RESTAURANTS, PAGE 87
ACCOMMODATION, PAGE 299

LEFT: the Gothic towers of Notre-Dame.
RIGHT: most brasseries and cafés on the island sell Berthillon ice creams.

Cité, Marais, Beaubourg and Les Halles

Revolution, such as the Gallery of Kings, by studying those of other Gothic cathedrals.

He also added a sacristy on the south side, now the Trésor de Notre-Dame (Mon–Fri 9.30am–6pm, Sat until 6.30pm, Sun 1.30–6.30pm; charge), housing the alleged Crown of Thorns, among other relics. For more on Notre-Dame, see page 88.

Royal shrine

The church of "Our Lady" was built on the site of earlier pagan fertility worship by Celts and Romans. In the 6th century, Clovis, the conquering Frankish king, erected a Christian basilica, which was replaced by a Romanesque church. In 1159, the young bishop Maurice de Sully decided that Paris deserved bigger and better. Work on the cathedral began in 1163 and took just under 200 years to complete, following plans by Pierre de Montreuil, also the architect of Sainte-Chapelle.

Even before it was finished, Notre-Dame had become the venue for state ceremonies, funerals and thanksgivings; in 1239 Louis IX deposited

the Crown of Thorns and other relics acquired on Crusade here, while Sainte-Chapelle was being built. Since then Notre-Dame has been witness to a string of historical events: in 1572, the cathedral's strangest wedding took place. The bride, Marguerite de Valois (a Catholic), stood at the altar, while bridegroom Henri de Navarre (a Protestant), called in his vows from the doorstep. Later, in 1589, Henri was crowned in the cathedral, having decided to

ABOVE: the ascent of the towers rewards you with a glorious view of Paris.
BELOW: the Portal of the Last Judgement.

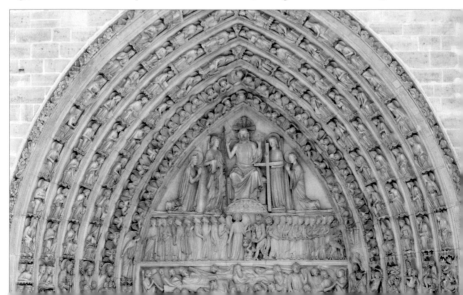

convert to Catholicism. The famous comment attributed to him, "Paris is well worth a Mass" is almost certainly apocryphal.

Come the Revolution, Notre-Dame was ravaged by looters, who melted down and destroyed anything that hinted of royalty, lopping off the heads of the kings of Judah along the top of the main portals. The cathedral was then turned into a "Temple of Reason", and by the end of the Revolution was being used to store wine.

By the time Napoleon decided to be crowned emperor in 1804, the cathedral was in such a shabby state bright tapestries were hung up to cover the crumbling decor. Pope Pius VII attended reluctantly, and when he hesitated at the altar, Napoleon took the crown and to cheers of *"Vive l'empereur!"* placed it on his head himself. Another dramatic event came in August 1944, at the thanksgiving ceremony for the Liberation of Paris, when the leader of the new government, General Charles de Gaulle, was shot at during the Te Deum.

Gothic architecture

Notre-Dame is magnificent from any angle, but its facade is particularly impressive. Viewed from Place du Parvis, the twin towers soar to the heavens with dramatic grace. The three porticoes each have a distinct design: an asymmetry typical of medieval architecture. Originally, the stone figures were finely painted against a gilt background, to illustrate Bible stories for an illiterate populace.

On the left, the Portal of the Virgin depicts the Ark of the Covenant and the coronation of the Virgin. The Portal of the Last Judgement, in the middle, shows the Resurrection, the weighing of souls and their procession to heaven or hell. The Portal of St Anne portrays the Virgin and Maurice de Sully. Above the doorways, the rose window, depicting the Virgin and Child in deep blues and rich reds, is a miracle of engineering. Picture the rickety scaffolding and the armies of stonemasons, who with simple measuring techniques constructed an intricate masterpiece that has lasted for 750 years. The glass, however, has been restored.

Tours de Notre-Dame

Tel: 01 53 10 07 00
Opening Hrs: daily Apr–Sept 10am–6.30pm (June–Aug Sat–Sun until 11pm), Oct–Mar 10am–5.30pm, last admission 45 minutes before closing time

Entrance Fee: charge
Transport: Cité

The ascent of the towers (be prepared to queue) is a religious experience for those who love heights and a taste of hell for claustrophobics and vertigo sufferers. The ascent is long (387 steps) and narrow, but the reward is a breathtaking view over Paris. "Emmanuel", the 13-tonne bell, is rung only on state occasions. Legend has it that the purity of its tone is due to the gold-and-silver jewellery thrown into its heated bronze by the most beautiful women of Paris.

Cathedral interior

Inside, the cathedral is bounded by 37 side chapels. Supported by flying buttresses, the vault of the chancel seems almost weightless, with stained-glass windows distributing rays of coloured light into the solemn shadows. The exquisite 13th-century north and south rose windows are the two star attractions. The spectacular north window still retains most of its 13th-century glass, but the south rose had to be reconstructed completely by Viollet-le-Duc.

ABOVE: Gothic perfection.
BELOW: the superb rose window.

When the north–south Métro line 4 was being built in the first decade of the 20th century, its builders solved the problem of getting past the two channels of the Seine by building colossal iron frameworks, in the shape of flattened tubes, and driving them into the river bed. These tubes are the tunnels the trains have passed through ever since.

ABOVE: the entrance to the Palais de Justice.
BELOW: delicate statuary dot the exterior facades.

The 18th-century carved choir stalls, depicting the life of the Virgin Mary, were commissioned by Louis XIV, fulfilling a vow his father made 60 years earlier that he would devote the east chancel to the Virgin if he were to have an heir. Louis XIII's statue stands behind the high altar, with Guillaume Coustou's *Pietà*.

Hôtel-Dieu ❷

Address: 1 place du Parvis Notre-Dame 4th
Opening Hrs: courtyard daily
Entrance Fee: free
Transport: Cité

Just north of Notre-Dame is the Hôtel-Dieu, the oldest hospital in the city. Founded in 651 by Saint Landry, it was the recipient of generous donations from Louis IX during the 13th century. Many famous doctors have worked here through the ages including Ambroise Paré (1510-1590) who is regarded as the father of prosthetics and forensic pathology. The hospital has remained in the same location despite several fires throughout the ages and the current building, which was constructed by Baron Georges Haussmann in the 1860s, was the scene of intense battles between police and the Germans in 1944.

Civil Court. In the 14th century, the monarchy, in the person of Charles V, moved out, and parliament, with full judiciary rights, moved in. A wander around the hushed building, past fleeting black-robed figures, might recall the tense days of the Revolution when the public prosecutor, Fouquier-Tinville, sent thousands of people to the guillotine. The present legal system is still based closely on the one founded by Napoleon Bonaparte. How the 4,000 people who work here find their way around the 24km (15 miles) of corridors is anyone's guess.

SAINTE-CHAPELLE ❺

Address: www.monuments-nationaux.fr
Tel: 01 53 40 60 80
Opening Hrs: daily Mar–Oct 9.30am–6pm (until 9pm Wed 15 May–15 Sept), Nov–Feb 9am–5pm
Entrance Fee: charge
Transport: Cité

Within the walls of the Palais de Justice, Sainte-Chapelle stands like a skeletal finger pointing heavenwards – an ethereal counterpoint to the stones of the establishment.

Vedettes du Pont Neuf (tel: 01 46 33 98 38; www.vedettesdupont neuf.com) run cruises along the Seine lasting about an hour. Boats leave from the Square du Vert-Galant (Métro: Pont Neuf) every half-hour in the high season.

Crypte archéologique ❸

Address: www.crypte.paris.fr
Tel: 01 55 42 50 10
Opening Hrs: Tue–Sun 10am–6pm
Entrance Fee: charge
Transport: Cité

Underneath the parvis in front of the cathedral, inside the crypt, are excavations of buildings dating back to the Roman city of Lutetia in the 3rd century AD, including parts of a house inhabited by the Gallic Parisii, amid the remains of medieval cellars.

A short walk west of Notre-Dame are the imposing walls of the Palais de Justice and the Conciergerie.

Palais de Justice ❹

Tel: 01 44 32 50 50
Opening Hrs: Mon–Fri 9am–6pm
Entrance Fee: charge
Transport: Cité

At one time, the Palais de Justice was a royal palace, and Louis IX had his bedroom in what is now the First

LEFT: the delicate interior of Sainte-Chapelle, a masterpiece of High Gothic style.
BELOW: admiring tourists.

ABOVE: the flower market on Ile de la Cité is the oldest in Paris (1808).

BELOW: the "veils" of stained-glass in Sainte-Chapelle.

This miracle of High Gothic ingenuity is one of the most gorgeous buildings in Paris. Completed in just 33 months by Pierre de Montreuil and consecrated in 1248, the chapel was built to house the Crown of Thorns, bartered from the Venetians by Louis IX. Seemingly constructed without walls, the chapel's vaulted roof is supported by a thin web of stone, from which descend veils of richly coloured stained glass. A replica Crown of Thorns decorates the top of one of the pinnacles.

Built in two tiers, the lower chapel was designed for the palace staff, and is consequently smaller and gloomier. From the shadows, climb the spiral staircase into the crystalline cavern of the upper chapel. The soaring windows catch the faintest of lights, creating kaleidoscopes of colour that are still vivid, despite being nearly 800 years old. Depicted are 1,134 scenes from the Bible, which begin by the staircase with Genesis and proceed round the church to the 15th-century rose window. Regular concerts of chamber music are held in the chapel.

THE CONCIERGERIE ❻

Address: www.monuments-nationaux.fr
Tel: 01 53 40 60 80
Opening Hrs: daily 9.30am–6pm
Entrance Fee: charge
Transport: Cité

In the northeast wing of the Palais de Justice, the Conciergerie looks like an intimidating castle, its four towers rising menacingly above impenetrable walls. It isn't hard to imagine this fortress as a merciless medieval prison – which it was (although much of the facade is 19th-century). It was originally built as a palace, administered by the Comte des Cierges or royal concierge – hence the name, Conciergerie – but after Charles Martel's revolt in 1358 King Charles V moved his main residence to his new palace of the Louvre.

The Comte was in charge of the king's seals, lodgings and taxes, until the Conciergerie was made a prison in 1391, when his job changed to that of chief gaoler. The Capetian palace came into its own during the Revolution, when it housed nearly 2,600 prisoners awaiting the guillotine, including Marie-Antoinette. Ironically, her prosecutor, Danton, resided in the next cell before his trip to the guillotine, as, in turn, did his nemesis Robespierre. In the merry-go-round of retribution, 1,306 heads rolled in one month at Place de la Nation. To the west is the Cour

des Femmes, a rough courtyard where the women were allowed during the day.

The tower at the back is called Bonbec (the Squealer), for it was here, from the 11th century, that torture victims told all. At the front is the 14th-century clock tower containing the first public clock in Paris, which is still ticking today.

ABOVE: relaxing in the autumn sunshine on the Square du Vert-Galant.
BELOW: the Conciergerie, where Queen Marie-Antoinette spent her last days before her execution.

Notable Inmates

A prison for five centuries, the medieval Conciergerie housed, among others, Captain Montgomery, a Scot, who fatally wounded Henri II during a tournament in 1559, and Ravaillac, assassin of Henri IV in 1610. During the Revolution, its big-name inmates ran from figures of the *ancien régime* such as Marie-Antoinette – whose cell has been carefully reconstructed – and Louis XV's favourite mistress, Madame du Barry, to Charlotte Corday, murderer of the Revolutionary leader Marat, and her defender the poet André Chenier, and finally the revolutionaries themselves, such as Danton, Camille Desmoulins, St-Just and even the architect of the Terror, Robespierre. In September 1792, more than 300 Revolutionary prisoners were killed here.

Escape the shadows of the Revolution on Quai des Orfèvres, on the south bank of the island, where goldsmiths (*orfèvres*) once fashioned Marie-Antoinette's jewellery, but which is now home to the Police Judiciaire (the equivalent of the English cid). Beyond the Square du Vert-Galant and the statue of Henri IV, the river slides past the tip of the island. Pont Neuf, bisected by the island, is the oldest surviving bridge in Paris. It was made of stone, rather than wood, and was the first bridge to be built without houses on it. In 1985, the artist Christo wrapped the whole length of the Pont Neuf in golden fabric. Between 1994 and 2007, the bridge underwent a major restoration project completed in time for its 400th anniversary, as a result of which it is looks particularly resplendent today. No small part of the Pont Neuf's charm, are the 385 grotesque faces below its cornices.

You can return to the east end of the island via the colourful Marché aux Fleurs in Place Louis-Lépine, opposite the Préfecture de Police and the Hôtel-Dieu.

ABOVE: café life on Ile St-Louis.
BELOW: Charles Baudelaire, an Ile St-Louis resident.

Inside, the original kitchens are still intact. They were built to feed up to 3,000 people using four huge fireplaces and have a Gothic canopied ceiling supported by buttresses. The adjacent Salle des Gens d'Armes is a magnificent four-aisled Gothic hall where the royal guards, or men-at-arms, used to live.

The Urban Nomad

One of the 19th-century's most towering literary figures, the poet Charles Baudelaire, lived on the Ile St-Louis, on the ground floor of the Hôtel de Lauzun from October 1843 to September 1845. While here, the young writer took hashish, fell obsessively in love with his mixed-race mistress and wrote several poems that were later to form part of *Les Fleurs du Mal*. Baudelaire enjoyed a nomadic lifestyle and rarely lived at one address for such a long period of time: between his birth in 1821 and death in 1867 he lived at 45 different Paris addresses. The street named after him is in the 12th *arrondissement* – a part of the city he never called home.

In contrast to these forbidding structures, the market is an array of small glasshouses selling flowers and plants underneath classical black street lamps. On Sunday, the stalls become a market for caged birds, and the jabbering of parakeets fills the air.

On the north side of Notre-Dame is the Quartier des Anciens Cloîtres (Ancient Cloister Quarter), home and study area for 12th-century monks and scholars who belonged to the cathedral chapter, including the theologian Pierre Abélard, famous for his love letters to the beautiful Héloïse. The area was once a warren of medieval churches and houses until Haussmann razed them to the ground, moving 25,000 inhabitants to the suburbs, to create the present vista. As you pass along Rue de la Colombe, note the remains of the Gallo-Roman wall in the pavement.

Mémorial des Martyrs de la Déportation ❼

Tel: 01 46 33 87 56

Opening Hrs: Tue–Sun Apr–Sept 10am–noon, 2–7pm, Oct–Mar until 5pm
Entrance Fee: free
Transport: Cité

On the eastern tip of the island lies this bleak but moving monument commemorating the 200,000 French deportees (Jewish, homosexual or resistant) sent to their deaths in Nazi

ABOVE: the streets of Ile St-Louis are surprisingly tranquil.
BELOW: Berthillon boasts some unusual ice cream flavours – all delicious.

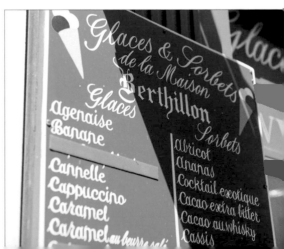

concentration camps. The chambers of this prison-like structure are engraved with quotations and the names of concentration camps.

ILE ST-LOUIS

Away from the tourists and camcorders, across the pedestrian Pont St-Louis, Ile St-Louis is a privileged haven of peace and wealth. The island's elegance recalls the 17thcentury, the era of Louis XIII and Cardinal Richelieu, and its mansions are home to Paris's elite.

Musée Adam Mickiewicz ❽

Address: 6 quai d'Orléans
Tel: 01 55 42 83 88
Opening Hrs: by reservation, Thur 2.15–5.15pm
Entrance Fee: charge
Transport: Pont Marie

Turning right along the south bank, you will come to this small museum. Adam Mickiewicz (1798–1855) was a Polish poet, living in Paris from 1832–40, who devoted his work to helping oppressed Poles. The 17th-century building includes

BELOW: the ever-popular savon de Marseille.

a Polish library and memorabilia of the Polish composer Frédéric Chopin, who often visited and played here.

Continuing eastwards round the island to the north bank, you will pass the private mansion Hôtel Lambert. Built in 1640 by Louis Le Vau, architect to Louis XIV, who built many of the houses on the Ile St-Louis and also worked on Vaux-le-Vicomte and Versailles, it is now owned by the Rothschilds. Further on is another mansion, the Hôtel de Lauzun, where the poets Théophile Gautier and Charles Baudelaire lived in 1843–5 and where Baudelaire wrote part of *Les Fleurs du Mal*.

The building now belongs to the City of Paris, and is reserved for official guests. Behind, the Rue St-Louis-en-l'Ile is full of chic gift shops, bars, restaurants and quaint tearooms. Also on this street is the church of the same name. Built between 1664 and 1765, the **Eglise St-Louis-en-l'Ile** has a classic Baroque interior and hosts popular classical concerts.

SHOPPING

Purchases in well-heeled Ile St-Louis range from unusual-yet-inexpensive knick-knacks to blingy costume baubles.

Gifts

Pylones
57 rue St-Louis-en-l'Ile, 4th.
Tel: 01 46 34 05 02.
www.pylones.com
This shop sells hundreds of quirky items from dog-shaped alarm clocks to smartphone covers of the Eiffel Tower.

Home

La Maison du Savon de Marseille

29 rue des Deux Ponts, 4th.
Tel: 01 43 29 11 82
No need to head to Provence to buy these fine soaps. You'll find 90 different kinds, from rose and cinnamon to spot-calming Alep, here in the centre of Paris.

Jewellery

Sucre Bleu
64 rue St-Louis-en-l'Ile, 4th.
Tel: 01 46 33 55 81
Anne Grima's little boutique sells contemporary jewellery by leading French designers like Les Néréides and Linda Lacroix, who work with Swarovski crystals. There is a gorgeous selection of fans too.

BEST RESTAURANTS, BARS AND CAFÉS

Restaurants

French

Brasserie de l'Ile St-Louis

55 quai de Bourbon, 4th
Tel: 01 43 54 02 59
www.labrasserie-isl.fr
Open: L & D Thur–Tue.
€€ (set menu), €€€ (à la carte)
❶ [p336, C3]

If you eat on the island, you pay for it. Here, at least, the terrace is marvellously placed for people-watching and admiring Notre-Dame's soaring buttresses. The menu is hearty Alsatian fare: terrine with Riesling, pork with apple marmalade and *choucroute*. Wines are reasonable; skip the overpriced coffee and ice cream and head for Berthillon instead.

Café Med

77 rue St-Louis-en-l'Ile, 4th
Tel: 01 43 29 73 17
Open: L & D daily.
€ (set menu) €€ (à la carte)
❷ [p336, D4]

Great value little restaurant with just 12 tables in a high-ceilinged, stone-walled dining room. Light bites include quiches, crêpes and pizza but for the best deal go for the three-course. Decent, inexpensive wines too.

L'Escale

1 rue des Deux Ponts, 4th
Tel: 01 43 54 94 23
Open: non-stop Mon–Sat.
€€ **❸** [p336, C3]

This old-fashioned, pleasantly bustling brasserie-cum-wine bar serves good, heartening

dishes like leek quiches, *chou farci* and *clafoutis*. The wines are well sourced and affordable, and the chips are far better than the average brasserie frites.

L'Ilot Vache

35 rue St-Louis-en-l'Ile, 4th
Tel: 01 46 33 55 16
www.restaurant-ilotvache.com
Open: D daily.
€€€ (set menu) €€€€ (à la carte) **❹** [p336, C3]

Housed in a former butcher's shop, this gourmet address is instantly recognisable by the little cow ornaments in the windows. Steak with Béarnaise sauce followed by white and dark chocolate mousse is unmissable here.

Taverne Henri IV

13 place du Pont-Neuf, 1st
Tel: 01 43 54 27 90
Open: non-stop Mon–Fri, L Sat.
€€ **❺** [p336, B2]

This diminutive spot on

the Ile de la Cité offers straightforward French cuisine and wines. Try the excellent eggs baked with blue cheese and ham, washed down with a glass of white Beaujolais. Prices are reasonable, especially given the location.

Japanese

Isami

4 quai d'Orléans, 4th
Tel: 01 40 46 06 97
Open: L & D Tue–Sat.
€€ (set menu) €€€ (à la carte)
❻ [p336, C3]

There is something marvellous about eating the freshest seafood imaginable and then stepping out onto a full view of the Seine on the Ile St-Louis. The sushi and sashimi are a work of art and the Seine-side dining room is cosy. This small Japanese restaurant has a minimalist menu to match the stripped-back

Price includes dinner and a half-bottle of house wine:

€ = under €25
€€ = €25–40
€€€ = €40–60
€€€€ = more than €60

decor. Prices reflect the quality. Book ahead.

Bars and Cafés

Le Flore en l'Ile

42 quai d'Orléans, 4th.
Tel: 01 43 29 88 27.
Open: Non-stop daily.
❶ [p336, C3]

The views from this café of the river and Notre-Dame are the main draw – that and, in summer, the Berthillon ice cream it serves. If you want something warmer and more substantial, it also does a range of brunch dishes based on eggs and seafood. The *gratin aux poires* is truly delicious.

RIGHT: al fresco lunch option on Place Dauphine.

Notre-Dame de Paris

On the eastern tip of the Ile de la Cité stands the Gothic cathedral of cathedrals, "parish church of the history of France".

Notre-Dame cathedral's fortunate position – at one end of an island, with river to its north and river to its south – has meant it never got hemmed in by urban clutter: visitors are all the better able to appreciate its beauty for the vast open space around it. It has had an eventful history. It stands on the site of a former Gallo-Roman temple to Jupiter, and was damaged by rioting Huguenots in 1548. It was sacked during the Revolution, then turned to new use as a "Temple to Reason" and a warehouse; it remained in poor repair – some city planners even propounded its demolition – until an extensive renovation programme was begun in the mid-19th century, after a campaign led by Victor Hugo. In 1965 the late decorative artist and glassmaker Jacques Le Chevallier was commissioned to design stained-glass windows for high up in the nave. In 1991 another programme of restorations got under way, with a timetable that was expected to run for a decade; the primary job was to clean the western facade. Work is still going on, most recently to renovate the organ, but the results are simply stunning. Amazingly, the architect of this awe-inspiring monument is unknown.

ABOVE: the cathedral is a superb venue for sacred music. As well as free organ concerts held daily at 4.30pm, prestigious vocalists and ensembles perform here at various times in the year.

BELOW: angels flanking the Portal of the Last Judgement.

The Essentials

Address: www.cathedraledeparis.com
Tel: 01 42 34 56 10
Opening Hrs: Mon–Fri 8am–6.45pm, Sat–Sun 8am–7.15pm
Entrance Fee: free
Transport: Cité

Hugo, the Hunchback and History

Notre-Dame's largest bell weighs 13 tonnes and was cast in the 14th century; it was recast in 1631, and is famous for the purity of its F-sharp tone. "The bells", of course, are a distinguishing element in one of the great love stories of literature: the love of the cathedral's hunchbacked bell-ringer, Quasimodo, for the beautiful Esmeralda, in Victor Hugo's 1831 novel *Notre-Dame de Paris*. There have been numerous film adaptations of the story over the years starting with *Esmeralda*, a ten-minute silent short film in 1905; to the contemporary French comedy *Quasimodo d'El Paris* in 1999; Lon Chaney Jr (1923), Charles Laughton (1939) and Anthony Hopkins (1982) have taken the lead role in Hollywood versions; while Disney released an animated adaptation in 1996. Hugo had a special regard for the cathedral, then a tatty place seen by most as a leftover from a barbaric age; he said he was inspired to write the book by a graffito – "*FATE*" – he found in one of the towers.

RIGHT: Notre-Dame's north and south rose windows are both masterpieces of stained glass.

RIGHT: services are in French, but the 11.30am Mass on Sunday is the International Mass with part of the readings and prayers said in English.

BELOW: the south tower is home to Notre-Dame's largest bell, known as the Emmanuel Bell. It is sounded for major holidays like Christmas and Easter, or for more important events, like the death of a pope.

ABOVE: Charles Laughton as Quasimodo (1939).

THE MARAIS

Left behind by history for three centuries but now restored to vibrant life, this charming quarter offers elegant *ancien régime* mansions, trendy bars and boutiques, a whole array of intriguing museums and the city's oldest and most beautiful square.

There's nowhere quite like the Marais, an elegant district that oozes charm and character. There's so much to recommend it: mansions and museums, chic boutiques and kosher grocers, gay bars and cosy cafés, all bundled together in a labyrinth of narrow streets and alleyways. Stretching west to east from Beaubourg to Bastille, straddling the 3rd and 4th *arrondissements*, with the Rue des Francs-Bourgeois pulsing across it like a central artery, the Marais offers a wonderfully compact package of history, local colour and plain fun. Few parts of the Right Bank have so much in so little space.

It's hard to believe that for many centuries the area was a mosquito-infested swamp ("marais" means marsh), cut right through the middle by Rue St-Antoine, the old Roman road. The marshes were drained in Philippe-Auguste's reign, and when Charles V moved his royal court from the Ile de la Cité to the area around the Tuileries in 1358, a royal influx to the Right Bank began.

In 1609, Henri IV had sumptuous accommodation built for his court all around the Place des Vosges, thereby shifting the political and financial focus from the Louvre. As a result, the finest architects and stonemasons in Europe descended on the Marais, building countless grand residences, or *hôtels particuliers*, for the nobility, each more spectacular than the last.

The Place des Vosges itself, initially known as the Place Royale, was the first planned square in Paris, and, with its red brick-and-stone facades tapering into arched walkways, remains as beautiful as ever.

Main Attractions
HÔTEL DE SENS
PLACE DES VOSGES
MAISON DE VICTOR HUGO
JEWISH QUARTER
MUSÉE CARNAVALET
MUSÉE NATIONAL PICASSO
MUSÉE COGNACQ-JAY
MUSÉE DES ARCHIVES NATIONALES

Maps and Listings
MAP, PAGE 76
SHOPPING, PAGE 100
RESTAURANTS, PAGE 102
ACCOMMODATION, PAGE 299

LEFT: one of the elegant archways leading off the 17th-century Place des Vosges.
RIGHT: the archways are lined with restaurants and art galleries.

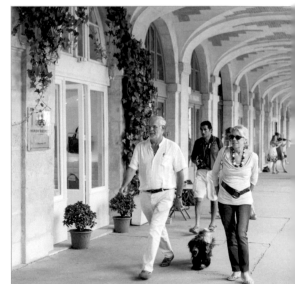

RIGHT: hip design concept store merci (111 boulevard Beaumarchais, 3rd).
BELOW: Rue des Francs-Bourgeois is a busy shopping street.

THE MARAIS'S FALL AND RISE

The pendulum of fashion swung away from the Marais after Louis XIV moved his court to Versailles in the 1680s, and the nobility moved to the Ile St-Louis, then westwards to the Faubourg St-Honoré and the Boulevard St-Germain. During the Revolution, the area was abandoned to the people, and the Marais's graceful *hôtels* fell into disrepair.

In the 19th and 20th centuries, the quarter became a centre for small industries and craftwork, and successive developers dug up and widened its picturesque streets. In 1962, André Malraux, President de Gaulle's arts minister, set wide-scale renovation work in motion to preserve what had by then become a very run-down area. By the 1990s, the Marais had regained its status as one of the most fashionable – and costly – places to live in Paris.

The Jewish and working-class communities that once occupied the area have been marginalised by the relentless gentrification process. The character of the Marais is now defined by its designer boutiques,

trendy bars and cafés, and a thriving gay community.

A TOUR OF THE OLD *HÔTELS*

Most of the *hôtels particuliers* have been converted into luxury apartments or offices, but several have been left intact and now house museums. A good place to begin a Marais tour is at the Hôtel de Ville (City Hall), on Rue de Rivoli, which marks its western boundary. Behind it is the 17th-century church of **St-Gervais-St-Protais** ❾ (daily; free) with a triple-tiered facade, Italianate steps and monstrous-looking gargoyles. The church is renowned for its 18th-century organ, and concerts are held here frequently.

Rue François-Miron leads from Place St-Gervais into the heart of the Marais. By the 1950s the houses here were practically derelict, but they have been carefully restored. At the corner of Rue Cloche-Perce is a half-timbered medieval house, and at No.

68 stands the **Hôtel de Beauvais** , built by Catherine Beauvais in 1654 with money from Louis XIV, who had greatly enjoyed her favours. She is also said to have entertained archbishops here. A more innocent young Mozart stayed here on his first visit to Paris, at the tender age of seven.

Neighbouring Rue de Jouy contains **Hôtel d'Aumont** , designed by the Versailles architect Louis Le Vau, renovated and enlarged by François Mansart (1598–1666) and decorated by Charles Le Brun (1619–90). With a formal garden by Le Nôtre, the mansion now functions as the city's administrative court.

Hôtel de Sens

Address: 1 rue du Figuier
Tel: 01 42 78 14 60
Opening Hrs: Tue, Fri, Sat 1pm–7.30pm, Wed, Thur 10am–7.30pm
Entrance Fee: free
Transport: Pont Marie

Built in the late 15th century for the Archbishop of Sens, this turreted mansion is one of Paris's few surviving medieval residences, with immaculate gardens. Henri IV lodged his first wife Marguerite de Valois (Reine Margot) here when he could no longer stand her promiscuity. She continued to leave a trail of broken hearts, and when a jealous ex-lover killed her current beau, she had him beheaded. It now houses the Bibliothèque Forney, devoted to graphic and applied arts.

THE VILLAGE ST-PAUL

Opposite the Hôtel de Sens, the Rue de l'Avé-Maria intersects with the Rue des Jardins St-Paul, a block away. This leads into the Village St-Paul past two towers and ramparts, the remnants of the city wall built for King Philippe-Auguste around the year 1200, and which now shadow the antics of local school children. The restored "village" consists of a series of small courtyards and fountains, sheltering bustling antique shops and second-hand stalls. At night, it is tranquil beneath the halo of old street lamps.

On Rue Charlemagne, wooden walkways running between the buildings have been restored to the way they were in the Middle Ages. Left along Rue St-Paul is an ancient

BELOW: relaxing in the delightful Place des Vosges.

passageway leading to the church of **St-Paul-St-Louis** , an amalgamation of two parishes, constructed by Jesuits in 1627 copying the Gesù church in Rome. Here, the hearts of Louis XIII and Louis XIV were kept as embalmed relics until the Revolution, when they were removed and sold to an artist, who crushed them to mix with oil for a varnish for one of his pictures. Later he gave what was left of Louis XIII's heart to the newly installed King Louis XVIII, in return for a golden snuffbox.

PLACE DES VOSGES

Rue St-Antoine is the ancient Roman road that led east out of the city. Built wide and straight in typical Roman fashion, it became a site for jousting tournaments until, in 1559, Henri II was fatally injured by a sliver from the shattered lance of Gabriel Montgomery, his Scottish Captain of the Guard. In a drastic bid to save his life, Henri's physician, Ambroise Paré, ordered the immediate decapitation of every prisoner awaiting execution and had their heads rushed to the surgery so that he could experiment

ABOVE: equestrian statue of Louis XIII.
BELOW: Victor Hugo lived on Place des Vosges.

on them in a bid to rescue his king. Needless to say he didn't succeed, and Henri died 10 days later. The unfortunate Montgomery lost his head, too.

At 62 rue St-Antoine, roughly halfway between Métro St-Paul and Place de la Bastille, stands the **Hôtel de Sully** (www.monuments-nationaux.fr; courtyards open daily 9am-7pm), one of the finest mansions in the Marais, and which is appropriately the HQ of Monuments Nationaux, the public organisation that looks after the country's most important historical buildings. Under the courtyard's grumpy statues, Voltaire was beaten with clubs by followers of the Count of Rohan, following a slanging match between the two at the Comédie Française. The cosy garden with clipped privet hedges *à l'anglaise* is an unexpected surprise. A door in the back right corner leads to the **Place des Vosges** . Initially called the Place Royale prior to the Revolution, this enchanting 17th-century square, with a garden surrounded by 36 arcaded residences, was built by Henri IV as a showcase for his court. Here courtiers

Victor Hugo – Man of Many Words

Poet, dramatist, novelist and politician, Victor Hugo (1802–85) lived at 6 place des Vosges from 1832 to 1848. His salon – now a museum – drew great luminaries of the day, including Balzac and Dumas. The museum traces Hugo's life: before exile, during exile and after exile. In 1841 he was elected to the Académie Française, and accepted political posts under King Louis-Philippe. During the 1848 Revolution, he became a leader of democratic opposition to Louis-Napoleon. In 1851 he went into exile in the Channel Islands, where he wrote much of *Les Misérables* (1862). At the fall of the Second Empire in 1870 Hugo returned to Paris.

paraded, preened and pranced. After the Revolution, when the melted-down statue of Louis XIII had been reforged and replaced, the square was named after the Vosges, the first *département* to have paid Napoleon's war taxes promptly.

Today, this is the most beautiful square in Paris, and one of the capital's most sought-after addresses; it was recently in the spotlight for being the location of the family home of Dominique Strauss-Kahn, the controversial former head of the International Monetary Fund. The arcades house chic cafés and boutiques, and in summer play host to classical concerts – in the same place that Mozart gave one of his first recitals in 1763.

Maison de Victor Hugo ⑯

Address: 6 place des Vosges
Tel: 01 42 72 10 16
Opening Hrs: Tue–Sun 10am–6pm
Entrance Fee: free

Transport: St-Paul
In the southeast corner of the square stands the house that was the Romantic writer's Paris home for 15 years. It's now a museum to the great man, containing portraits of his family, manuscripts, accomplished pen-and-ink drawings and pieces of furniture knocked together by Hugo in his spare time.

THE JEWISH QUARTER

Between the northwestern corner of Place des Vosges and Rue Vieille-du-Temple runs the Rue des Francs-Bourgeois, a shopper's paradise crammed with boutiques and curiosity shops, many of which have retained the shop signs from their previous incarnations as butchers or bakers. A left-hand turning just past the Musée Carnavalet leads to Rue Pavée and the **Hôtel de Lamoignon** ⑰, built in 1584 for the Duchesse d'Angoulême. Sixty people were murdered here during the massacres

LEFT: try Sacha Finkelsztajn for its cheesecake, strudel and poppy-seed cakes.
RIGHT: Librairie du Temple in Rue des Rosiers specialises in Jewish publications.

SHOP

Rue des Rosiers, the main thoroughfare of the Jewish Quarter, tells the tale of its changing community. Amid the bakeries and falafel outlets of yore, several designer fashion boutiques have opened here during the last decade. The area is known as Pletzl in Yiddish which means "little place".

ABOVE: old signs at the Musée Carnavalet.
BELOW: Madame de Sévigné.

Research for the creation of the Wall of Names at the Mémorial de la Shoah took six archivists two years to complete. The names of 76,000 Holocaust victims are given by year of deportation and in alphabetical order.

of 2 September 1792. The *hôtel* now houses the city's historical library.

Rue des Rosiers, a little further on, is the hub of what remains of the Jewish Quarter. As the area has become increasingly popular with bar and boutique owners, the Jewish community has retreated to a small pocket centred on this narrow street lined with kosher delis, falafel stands and tiny shops packed with religious artefacts. Originally an Ashkenazi community, with its origins in Eastern Europe, the local Jewish population was depleted by the Holocaust. Numbers swelled again with an influx of Sephardic Jews from North Africa following the independence of Algeria in the 1960s, giving the area a Middle Eastern feel. Among the restaurants and bookshops around the synagogue, look out for Chez Marianne (tel: 01 42 72 18 86), the perpetually busy restaurant for Jewish specialities such as rollmops and falafels. Jewish history

and decorative arts are treated in the Jewish Museum (see page 99).

A few minutes south, behind St-Gervais-St-Protais, is the Mémorial de la Shoah.

Mémorial de la Shoah ⓳

Address: 17 rue Geoffroy l'Asnier
www.memorialdelashoah.org
Tel: 01 42 77 44 72
Opening Hrs: Mon–Wed, Fri, Sun 10am–6pm, Thur 10am–10pm, closed Jewish holidays
Entrance Fee: free
Transport: Pont Marie

The memorial has a permanent exhibition on the concentration camps, in which documents, photographs and personal artefacts are used to present an overview of Nazi deportation and extermination, and moving personal stories. As the most important centre in Europe devoted to the Holocaust, it also contains a research centre, archive and auditorium. In the crypt, within a black marble Star of David, an eternal flame burns for the Mémorial du Martyr Juif Inconnu (Memorial to the Unknown Jewish Martyr).

Rue des Rosiers leads on to the **Rue Vieille-du-Temple**, with one of the best and liveliest stretches of cafés and bars in Paris.

CARNAVALET AND PICASSO

Musée Carnavalet ⓳

Address: 23 rue de Sévigné
www.carnavalet.paris.fr
Tel: 01 44 59 58 58
Opening Hrs: Tue–Sun 10am–6pm
Entrance Fee: free
Transport: St-Paul

This is one of the most fascinating of the many Marais museums. Occupying two mansions, the main 16th-century Hôtel Carnavalet and the neighbouring 17th-century Hôtel Le Peletier, it covers the history of Paris chronologically from its beginnings as a Gallo-Roman settlement to its transformation into a modern-day metropolis. The evolution of the capital is traced through paintings, objets d'art, sculpture and costume. Madame de Sévigné, whose celebrated letters provide an insight into 17th-century Paris high society, lived in the Hôtel Carnavalet between 1677 and 1696, and there is a gallery here devoted to her life.

Rue de Thorigny leads to one of the Marais's finest mansions, now home to the Musée National Picasso.

Musée National Picasso ⓴

Address: 5 rue de Thorigny
www.musee-picasso.fr
Tel: 01 42 71 25 21
Opening Hrs: currently closed until summer 2013 for renovation
Entrance Fee: charge
Transport: St-Paul

The Hôtel Salé was constructed with the booty of a 17th-century tax collector. Three centuries later, the French tax authorities scored another coup. Following his death in 1973, Pablo Picasso's family was faced with an enormous inheritance tax bill, and so, in lieu of payment, they donated to the French nation a vast collection of his works: 200 paintings, over 3,000 drawings and 88 ceramics, along with sculptures, collages and manuscripts, as well as Picasso's own collection of works by other artists like Cézanne, Matisse and Modigliani.

ABOVE: on his way to the synagogue.
BELOW: the Hôtel de Sens, the oldest mansion in the Marais.

The Curious Cannonball

If you stand at the junction of Rue du Figuier and Rue de l'Hôtel-de-Ville, look up at the Hôtel de Sens in front of you and you'll see, remarkably buried in the gable stonework, right next to the left-hand turret, a cannonball the size of a fist with a date (28 July 1830) written underneath it. The iron sphere was fired on day two of the three-day-long July 1830 revolt, in which some 600 rioters and 150 soldiers died, from a besieged army barracks on nearby Rue Charlemagne. Was it a warning shot? Was the cannoneer aiming at the second-storey window just below? And when the fighting was over, did no one ever think to dig it out?

The museum shows all Picasso's periods, in chronological order, including the Blue, Pink, Cubist, classical and Post-Cubist phases. The famous beach pictures of the 1920s and 1930s are here, as well as remarkable portraits of his model mistresses, Marie-Thérèse and Dora Maar. There is also a lot of sculpture made of driftwood, scrap iron and bicycle parts, a reminder of Picasso's motto: "I do not seek, I find."

Currently closed for renovation, to make the building safer and more accessible, the museum will have three times as much exhibition space and around 500 works on show over four floors when it reopens in the summer of 2013.

A CLUSTER OF MUSEUMS

Musée Cognacq-Jay ㉑

Address: 8 rue Elzévir
www.cognacq-jay.paris.fr
Tel: 01 40 27 07 21
Opening Hrs: Tue–Sun 10am–6pm
Entrance Fee: free
Transport: St-Paul

The exquisite Hôtel Donon houses the art and antiques collection of Ernest Cognacq and his wife Louise Jay, founders of La Samaritaine department store. The collection, which includes works by Rembrandt and Canaletto, is displayed in a succession of salons and small rooms, which are furnished to give the feel of a private house.

Hôtel de Rohan ㉒

Address: 87 rue Vieille-du-Temple
Opening Hrs: during exhibitions, times and details as for Musée des Archives Nationales

Further west, this stunningly restored mansion is part of the national archives and hosts exhibitions relating to history. Even if you don't go inside, take a look in the courtyard at the superb sculpture of the horses of Apollo over the stables.

Musée des Archives Nationales ㉓

Address: 60 rue des Francs-Bourgeois
www.archivesnationales.culture.gouv.fr
Tel: 01 40 27 60 96
Opening Hrs: Mon, Wed–Fri 10am–5.30pm, Sat–Sun 2–5.30pm
Entrance Fee: charge

ABOVE: ancient relief at the Musée Carnavalet.
BELOW: Pablo Picasso.

A Spanish Genius

Born in Málaga in Spain, Pablo Picasso (1881–1973) settled in Paris at the age of 23, having studied art in Barcelona and Madrid. His career began to take off thanks to the patronage of wealthy American art collector Gertrude Stein and the promotion of his work by highly respected dealer Daniel-Henry Kahnweiler. However, he never lost touch with his Spanish roots: his works ooze life, humour and sex, in a career that could never be separated from his personal life. The leading figure in 20th-century art, he passed through many phases, including his early Blue Period, as in the 1901 *Self-Portrait*, and *Les Demoiselles d'Avignon*, painted in 1907, which is often regarded as the first work of Cubism. In the 1920s and 1930s he produced his most abstract work, but in 1937 he painted *Guernica*, on the Spanish Civil War. He stayed in Paris, in Rue des Grands-Augustins, during World War II, moving to the south of France afterwards. His last paintings were long considered a splashy, crude decline, but they have been rehabilitated as proof of his continuing inventiveness up to his death in 1973, in Mougins. He left behind a massive collection of paintings, sculpture, drawings and ceramics.

Transport: Rambuteau

The Hôtel de Soubise is an exquisite 18th-century mansion, with a superb arcaded courtyard and exuberant Rococo decor. It now houses the National Archives, in which over 6 million of France's most important historical documents are kept, on 290km (180 miles) of shelving. Also here is a collection of historical objects including a small replica of the Bastille and furniture from Soubise and Rohan. Across the street is the Crédit Municipal, the state pawnbroker. Nicknamed *"Ma Tante"* (My Aunt), it opened in 1777, and still functions.

Musée de la Chasse et de la Nature ㉔

Address: 62 rue des Archives
www.chassenature.org
Tel: 01 53 01 92 40
Opening Hrs: Tue–Sun 11am–6pm
Entrance Fee: charge
Transport: Rambuteau

The Hôtel Guénégaud houses a display of stuffed animals and hunting-related objects with enjoyably quirky touches, such as "hunted species" that include unicorns.

Musée d'Art et d'Histoire du Judaïsme ㉕

Address: 71 rue du Temple
www.mahj.org
Tel: 01 53 01 86 53
Opening Hrs: Mon–Fri 11am–6pm, Sun 10am– 6pm
Entrance Fee: charge
Transport: Rambuteau

The grand Hôtel St-Aignan is now a fascinating museum of Jewish art, culture, history and heritage. As well as the permanent and temporary exhibitions, there are often music concerts.

QUARTIER DU TEMPLE

To the north of the Marais, the Quartier du Temple was once the headquarters of the Knights Templar. A medieval order of soldiers, originally formed to protect pilgrims in the Holy Land, the Templars owned large properties in France and were in charge of the royal treasury until 1307, when Philippe the Fair burned their leaders at the stake, and the order was disbanded. During the Revolution, the Temple Tower was a prison for the royal family; it was from here that Louis XVI went to the guillotine. It was razed by a superstitious Napoleon, and Haussmann

ABOVE: the Marais teems with trendy bars and cafés, including La Belle Hortense, a literary wine bar (31 rue Vieille du Temple, 3rd).
BELOW: Ofr system bookshop and gallery (20 rue Dupetit-Thouars, 3rd).

At 47 rue Vieille-du-Temple stands the 17th-century mansion Hôtel Amelot de Bisseuil. The playwright Beaumarchais lived here in the 18th century and he used it as the base for a gun-running operation to help the American fight for independence. These days it's a popular (if small) Paris photo opportunity, famed for the carved Medusa heads that scream from its heavy wooden doors.

DRINK

Rue Vieille-du-Temple is the epicentre of the Marais's cosmopolitan café culture. Trendy young types frequent the arty L'Etoile Manquante and La Perle (see page 103), the picturesque Petit Fer à Cheval (see page 103), wine bar-cum-bookshop La Belle Hortense and artfully distressed cocktail bar Les Etages. During early-evening happy hour, the gay community heads to Le Cox and the Open Bar on nearby Rue des Archives.

replaced it with a wrought-iron covered market, the Carreau du Temple, which still sells second-hand and bargain clothes and cloth by the metre.

Along Rue Perrée lies all that remains of the Temple fortress, the **Square du Temple** ㉖, a tree-lined garden that echoes with the gentle sound of table tennis balls on its two outdoor tables. Not far from the Temple district, another 10 minutes along Rue Réaumur, is France's most prestigious technical college, the **Conservatoire National des Arts et Métiers**, and its museum, the oldest dedicated to science and technology in Europe.

Musée des Arts et Métiers ㉗

Address: 60 rue Réaumur
www.arts-et-metiers.net
Tel: 01 53 01 82 00

Opening Hrs: Tue–Sun 10am–6pm, Thur until 9.30pm
Entrance Fee: charge
Transport: Arts et Métiers

The best part of this fascinating museum of technology is the converted 11th-century chapel that houses, among other innovations, Foucault's pendulum (a copy of which hangs in the Panthéon, see page 207). There are also ancient cars and flying machines set on glass floors, and hands-on exhibits for children.

To end a visit to the Marais, head down Rue du Temple past the glitzy wholesale jewellery outfits to No. 41 and its courtyard. Once the headquarters of the Aigle d'Or, the last stagecoach company in Paris, it is a bustling corner, where the Café de la Gare theatre (tel: 01 42 78 52 51) puts on alternative comedy and musical performances.

SHOPPING

From up-and-coming designers to one of the city's oldest department stores, the Marais is one of Paris's most interesting shopping areas.

Bargains

L'Habilleur
44 rue Poitou, 3rd.
Tel: 01 48 87 77 12
There is up to 70 percent off designer brands for men and women including Paul and Joe and Antik Batik at this discount outlet.

Department Store

BHV
52 rue de Rivoli, 4th.
Tel: 0977 401 400
The Bazar de l'Hôtel de Ville has everything you'd expect to find in a department store, especially hardware, and what's

good about this one is that the ranges tend to be "high street" with affordable prices to match.

Food

Mariage Frères
30, 32, 35 rue du Bourg Tibourg, 4th.
Tel: 01 42 72 28 11
Rare teas, tea-making equipment and tea-flavoured products including cake and chocolate truffles are the order of the day here. There is a tearoom too to try before you buy.

Popelini
29 rue Debelleyme, 3rd.
Tel: 01 44 61 31 44
This cake shop specialises in just one thing – choux buns. It's hard to choose from all the flavours but salted caramel, rose and raspberry or

dark chocolate are winners.

Gifts

Fragonard
51 rue des Francs Bourgeois, 4th.
Tel: 01 44 78 01 32
www.fragonard.com
Here, one of France's most celebrated *parfumiers* sells cosmetics, table linen, books about perfume and, of course, the perfumes themselves – Sorenza captures the roses from Grasse, where the company is based.

Home

L'Air du Bain
69 boulevard Beaumarchais, 3rd.
Tel: 09 54 53 05 85
As well as a lovely range of high-quality bathrobes and nightwear, this little

shop also sells bath products by Bains Plus and luxurious towels.

Women's Clothing

Abou d'Abi Bazar
33 rue du Temple, 4th.
Tel: 01 44 61 37 24
This stylish boutique sells young and funky clothes by a wide range of up-and-coming international designers. There is also a shop at 125 rue Vieille-du-Temple.

Azzedine Alaïa
7 rue de Moussy, 4th..
Tel: 01 42 72 19 19
Clothes by this Tunisian designer, famed for his bandage dresses, have been worn by many high-profile celebs including Michelle Obama and Lady Gaga. Last season's collection is sold at a discount nearby at 4 rue de la Verrerie.

Café Life

If you've never nipped into a café to make a phone call or met your lover on a terrasse, you are not a true Parisian.

The neighbourhood café is the Parisian's decompression chamber, easing the transition between *Métro-boulot-dodo* – commuting, working and sleeping. It offers a welcome pause in which to savour a *p'tit noir* (espresso) or an *apéritif*, empty the mind of troublesome thoughts and watch people go by. The café is also the place to meet friends, have a romantic tryst or even do business in a relaxed atmosphere.

The first café in France was Le Procope (see page 217) in 1686, and the literati soon began to congregate there, keen to exchange ideas. More sprang up all over the country, and it wasn't long before there was at least one in every village. In the 19th century, the neighbourhood *zinc*, named after its metal counter, became part of the fabric of French life. In Paris, each café developed its own character, and with the widening of the boulevards, their tables spilled out onto the pavements. By 1910 there were 510,000 *zincs* in France.

Things are changing

But today café life is waning. While the invasion of fast-food restaurants is partly to blame (a nearby McDonald's can slash a café's profits by 30 percent), changes in the French way of life are also culpable. When customers move out to homes in the suburbs, they tend to "cocoon", staying in to watch TV, and the local café eventually has to close. Then there are the ageing proprietors to consider: a café is traditionally a family business, but today fewer sons and daughters are prepared to take on gruelling 16-hour days.

Sadly, even the atmosphere of remaining cafés is not what it was. There is formica where once there was marble. Piped muzak and the beep of video games have replaced accordionists and the furious volleys of players on *baby-foot* machines. Only the Gauloise-fed haze (attitudes to the 1992 smoking ban are casual) and the hazards of the lavatories (some still holes in the ground) are the same.

Yet all is not lost. Authentic *zincs* can still be found in Paris, and many are thriving. Try stylish Café de l'Industrie on Rue St-Sabin, La Palette on Rue de Seine or the tiny but lovingly restored Le Cochon à l'Oreille on Rue Montmartre. For literary atmosphere there's Les Deux Magots, home to almost every Paris intellectual from Rimbaud to André Breton. At nearby Café de Flore, Sartre and Simone de Beauvoir wrote by the stove. "My worst customer, Sartre," recalled the *patron*. "He spent the entire day scribbling away over one drink."

But go soon, before things change too much, for this is one Parisian experience that demands to be savoured.

ABOVE AND RIGHT: the café experience is an integral part of a visit to Paris.

BEST RESTAURANTS, BARS AND CAFES

Restaurants

French-Asian Fusion

Le Petit Marché
9 rue de Béarn, 3rd
Tel: 01 42 72 06 67
Open: L & D daily.
€€€ **7** [p336, D2]
The "little market" is one of the Marais's many hip bistros, and it pulls a matching fashion-conscious clientele without losing its friendly feel. The short, modern menu has a pronounced Asian slant: raw tuna flash-fried in sesame seeds and served with Thai sauce, or pan-fried scallops with lime. From the similarly laconic wine list, the house red is a good bet.

French

L'Ambassade d'Auvergne
22 rue du Grenier-St-Lazare, 3rd

Tel: 01 42 72 31 22
www.ambassade-auvergne.com
Open: L & D daily.
€€ (set menu) €€€ (à la carte)
8 [p336, C1]
Auvergne fare is famously hearty, so make sure you come here hungry. One of this cheerful, almost rustic restaurant's signature dishes is the lentil salad, made with Puy lentils, bacon and shallots. End with a regional eau-de-vie, available to buy to take home if you like it.

L'Ambroisie
9 Place des Vosges, 4th
Tel: 01 42 78 51 45
www.ambroisie-paris.co
Open: L & D Tue–Sat.
€€€€ **9** [p336, D2]
A superb haute cuisine restaurant worthy of its royal location on Place des Vosges. Sumptuous seasonal ingredients are turned into stunningly

sophisticated food by chef Bernard Pacaud – with prices to match. Still, the chance to sample his much-in-demand langoustines with a light curry sauce shouldn't be passed up if you can afford it.

Au Bascou
38 rue Réaumur, 3rd
Tel: 01 42 72 69 25
Open: L & D Mon–Fri.
€€ **10** [p336, D1]
Generous meals from the Pays Basque: squid, roast lamb, stuffed peppers, *pipérade* and smoked tuna are on the menu in this small, friendly place. Exceptional wine list.

Breizh Café
109 rue Vieille du Temple, 3rd
Tel: 01 42 72 13 77
www.breizhcafe.com
Open: L & D Wed–Sun
€ **11** [p336, D1]
Owned and run by a Bre-

ton, this popular crêperie offers a good selection of *galettes* (savoury pancakes) and *crêpes* (sweet pancakes) made with organic flour. Try one with *Andouille* (chitterling sausage) accompanied by Breton cola or *lait ribot* (buttermilk).

Le Dôme du Marais
53 bis rue des Francs-Bourgeois, 4th
Tel: 01 42 74 54 17
Open: L & D daily.
€€ (set menu) €€ (à la carte)
12 [p336, D2]
This quiet, airy 18th-century dining room, topped with a glass dome, is unique. It is hard to believe that such a romantic place was once a pawnbroker's shop.

Aux Vins des Pyrénées
25 rue Beautrellis, 4th
Tel: 01 42 72 64 94
Open: L & D daily.
€€ **13** [p336, D3]
A youthful bistro adorned with cheerful bric-a-brac. Food, such as squid risotto, fish tartare, lamb curry or satisfying steak, is a mix of mode and tradition, drawing a noisy young Parisian clientele.

Italian

L'Osteria
10 rue Sévigné, 4th
Tel: 01 42 71 37 08
Open: L & D Tue–Sat.
€€ **14** [p336, D2]
This 32-seat rustic Italian restaurant is a favourite with French cel-

LEFT: a vintage film poster in Au Petit Fer à Cheval, just one of the bar's interesting features.

ebs – check out the autographs on the walls. The place is best known for its gnocchi and risotto – try it with ginger or citrus fruit.

Mexican

Candelaria

52 rue de Saintonge, 3rd
Tel: 01 42 74 41 28
Open: L & D daily.
€ **15** [p336, D1]

From guacamole dips to freshly-made tortillas, you'll find most Mexican delights, including vegetarian options, in this unremarkable-looking *taqueria*. There is brunch at weekends and the cosy, dimly-lit cocktail bar is a popular drinking den.

North African

Chez Omar

47 rue de Bretagne, 3rd
Tel: 01 42 72 36 26
Open: L Mon–Sat & D daily. €€
16 [p336, D1]

Couscous is king here, in an old brasserie setting. Popular with artists and the chattering classes. No reservations and no credit cards.

Thai

Thai Spices

7 rue de l'Ave-Maria, 4th
Tel: 01 42 78 65 49
Open: L Mon–Fri D Mon–Sat
€ (set menu) €€ (à la carte) **17** [p336, D3]

Delicious food and smart surroundings are what makes this place special. The set menus at lunch and dinner are good value; try the "Gaing Dang Ped" – duck in red curry sauce. But there are plenty of options for vegetarians too.

RIGHT: al fresco lunch on Place des Vosges.

Bars and Cafés

Andy Wahloo

69 rue des Gravilliers, 3rd.
Tel: 01 42 71 20 38.
www.andywahloo-bar.com
Open: Tue–Sat 6pm–2am.
2 [p336, C1]

The name is Arabic for "I have nothing", and the Moroccan bar that bears it (founded by the people behind its neighbour 404 and London's Momo and Sketch) is a tiny little spot that's popular with a fashionable crowd. Expect mint-and-vodka concoctions and apple-flavoured hookahs. It gets really packed in the evening.

L'Apparement Café

18 rue des Coutures-St-Gervais, 3rd.
Tel: 01 48 87 12 22.
Open: Non-stop daily.
3 [p336, D2]

This relaxed spot – distressed armchairs, jazz soundtrack, parlour games, lots to read and a low hubbub of conversation – feels a bit like someone's artfully bohemian flat. That's the intention. There are salads, meat and cheese dishes to eat, and some nice wines at the bar. Come on your own and read a book – plenty of people do.

La Perle

78 rue Vieille-du-Temple, 3rd.
Tel: 01 42 72 69 93.
Open: Non-stop daily.
4 [p336, D2]

This bar, another new addition to the Marais line-up, is almost always open: it doesn't close until 2am, and on weekdays opens at 6am. It's straight-forward, non-exclusive and has a pleasant neighbourhood feel. DJs spin in the evenings; food consists of salads and generous omelettes.

Au Petit Fer à Cheval

30 rue Vieille-du-Temple, 4th.
Tel: 01 42 72 47 47.
Open: L & D daily (until 2am).
5 [p336, D2]

Fin de siècle café/wine bar where an eclectic mix of locals and foreigners

Price includes dinner and a half-bottle of house wine:

€ = under €25
€€ = €25–40
€€€ = €40–60
€€€€ = more than €60

gather around the original marble-topped horse-shoe bar. Particularly atmospheric and a great favourite with the bourgeois-bohemian crowd. Solid food, rushed but genial service. An excellent place to people-watch.

Stolly's

16 rue Cloche Perce, 4th.
Tel: 01 42 76 06 76.
Open: L & D daily.
6 [p336, D2]

This Anglo bar, part of the city's Hip Bars stable, has been going strong for years: a drinking den that's a firm favourite on the expat circuit. There are long happy hours and a terrace, good vodka tonics and, unsurprisingly, a steady party vibe.

BEAUBOURG AND LES HALLES

One of the world's most popular venues, the "inside-out" Pompidou Centre has given this area its modern identity. But nearby around Les Halles – though blighted by failed 1960s redevelopment – there remain many traces of Paris's historic market district, one of the most pungently atmospheric parts of the city.

Sandwiched between the Louvre and Palais Royal to the west, and the Marais to the east, this central chunk of the Right Bank is one of the city's most hyperactive commercial and cultural areas. Its epicentre is the Forum des Halles, a vast and unlovely shopping and leisure complex. Next to the monumental grandeur of the Louvre, Les Halles is a scruffy poor relation, an unsightly multistorey blot on the landscape. The other landmark building here is the Pompidou Centre, Paris's modern art museum. Unlike the 1970s monstrosity of Les Halles, this hulking mass of pipes, ducts and scaffolds painted in primary colours is strangely alluring, and one of the world's most visited sites.

Place du Châtelet, hard by the Seine, is a good starting point for exploring the area. Flanked by two theatres (Théâtre de la Ville and Théâtre du Châtelet, for opera and modern dance), it lies above one of Paris's biggest Métro and rer stations. To the northeast rises the Gothic **Tour St-Jacques**, a lone belfry once attached to a church that was destroyed during the Revolution. Look out for the statue of scientist and philosopher Blaise Pascal

(1623–62), who carried out pioneering experiments on atmospheric pressure from the top.

HÔTEL DE VILLE ㉘

Address: www.paris.fr
Tel: 01 42 76 43 43
Opening Hrs: visits by arrangement
Entrance Fee: free
Transport: Hôtel de Ville

Opening out at the eastern end of Avenue Victoria is the wide esplanade of the Hôtel de Ville (Mairie de Paris), ornate home of the city

Main Attractions
HÔTEL DE VILLE
CENTRE GEORGES POMPIDOU
FORUM DES HALLES
RUE MONTORGUEIL
EGLISE ST-EUSTACHE
EGLISE ST-GERMAIN-L'AUXERROIS

Maps and Listings
MAP, PAGE 76
SHOPPING, PAGE 113
RESTAURANTS, PAGE 114
ACCOMMODATION, PAGE 300

LEFT: turbines on Place Georges-Pompidou.
RIGHT: shoppers on Rue Montorgueil.

ABOVE: the Auberge
Nicolas Flamel
promises an "alchemy
of flavours" (51 rue de
Montmorency, 3rd).
BELOW: watching the
French tennis open on
a big screen in front of
the Hôtel de Ville.

roofs, carved facade and army of statues, was rebuilt after the original 17th-century Town Hall was burned down in the 1871 Commune. The majestic Salle des Fêtes (ballroom), a magnificent staircase and lots of chandeliers are the most notable features inside. Such grandeur and opulence are a fitting backdrop for the city's governing powers, and the grand halls are often used for banquets and ceremonial receptions.

At most times only an exhibition space is open to visitors, but the rest of the building can be seen on free guided tours, available by arrangement, tel: 01 42 76 50 49. In recent years the whole exterior has been cleaned, with the result that the building now looks thoroughly imposing outside and in. It's worth skirting around to Rue de Lobau at the rear of the Hôtel to see the two monumental bronze lions either side of the eastern entrance. These noble beasts are by the late 19th-century animal sculptor Alfred Jacquemart, who also made the colossal rhino in the square just west of the Musée d'Orsay (see page 250).

council. In medieval times, the square was the site of hangings and macabre executions. No traces of its horrific past remain; today, the pedestrianised Place de l'Hôtel de Ville, which overlooks the Seine, is a pleasant place to stroll through, especially in the evening, when the fountains and Town Hall are floodlit.

The elaborate neo-Renaissance building, with its splendid mansard

QUARTIER BEAUBOURG

This area may, thanks to the Centre Pompidou, be synonymous with avant-garde architecture, but it's also one of the oldest parts of the city. In fact, what is said to be the oldest house in Paris is at 51 Rue de Montmorency; on the ground floor is the Auberge Nicolas Flamel (tel: 01 42 71 77 78), a restaurant named after the house's original occupant, the famous alchemist who took in the poor and homeless here. Beaubourg's parish church of St-Merri was at the centre of a local building boom in the 16th century, as the old medieval houses were steadily replaced by grand private mansions; the district remained a seat of nobility until the Revolution. Little of this architectural heritage remains today, however: many of the historic residences were pulled down in the 1930s, and the quarter was transformed further by the renovation of Les Halles in the 1960s and 1970s.

St-Merri ㉙

Address: 76 rue de la Verrerie
www.saintmerri.org
Tel: 01 42 71 93 93
Opening Hrs: Mon–Sat 3–7pm
Entrance Fee: free
Trasnport: Châtelet

Off Rue St-Martin stands this richly adorned 16th-century church, built in Flamboyant Gothic style. Its bell, dating from 1331, is the oldest in Paris, and the organ used to be played by the composer Camille Saint-Saëns (1835–1921).

Between the church and the Centre Pompidou, the playful waterworks of the **Fontaine de Stravinsky** were inspired by the composer's ballet *The Firebird*. Created by artists Niki de Saint-Phalle and Jean Tinguely, the forms and figures in the fountain represent the story – a heart, a snake, a bare-breasted torso, pursed red lips and the firebird in the middle all spin and spit water in every direction. In

fine weather, this square is a favourite picnic spot (though it's infested with pigeons). Alternatively, take a seat at one of the handful of cafés looking out at the colourful ensemble.

CENTRE GEORGES POMPIDOU ㉚

Address: www.centrepompidou.fr
Tel: 01 44 78 12 33
Opening Hrs: Wed–Mon 11am–9pm
Entrance Fee: charge

ABOVE: the Fontaine de Stravinsky.
BELOW: homage to the great composer Igor Stravinsky.

Transport: Rambuteau

Above: the tubed escalators add to the "inside-out" allure of the Centre Pompidou.
Below: the east facade of the Centre and its colour-coded tubes.

Known locally simply as Beaubourg, the Centre National d'Art et de Culture Georges Pompidou welcomes more than 6 million visitors a year. The basic idea was first mooted in 1969 by the cultivated president of the day, Georges Pompidou; the initial tender was put out in 1972. No fewer than 681 designs were put forward by architects around the world, but the winning partnership was Italian Renzo Piano and British Richard Rogers. The Centre opened to the public on 31 January 1977.

Rogers and Piano had placed the infrastructure – escalators, lifts, ducts, etc – on the outside: this high-tech design caused uproar when it first opened, but its popular appeal soon silenced the critics.

As well as housing one of the world's most important modern art collections, the cavernous interior accommodates a large public library, an educational area, a performance space, auditorium and cinemas, and the neighbouring avant-garde music institute IRCAM. There's also an excellent art bookshop on the ground floor, and the swish restaurant **Georges** (see page 114) on the roof. The fifth-floor balcony and roof terrace enjoy magnificent views of the city, right across to Montmartre; the terrace also displays sculptures by Tinguely, Ernst and others.

Exhibits and activities

The **Musée National d'Art Moderne** is on the fourth and fifth floors. Incredibly, the works on display represent only a small proportion of the 50,000-strong collection, which is why the museum has regular rehangs, in order to rotate the works of art and give the public access to as many of them as possible.

The museum's permanent collection is arranged thematically, suggesting interesting confrontations and parallels between different periods and styles. Architecture and design are displayed alongside painting, sculpture and video art. Thus modern masterpieces by Matisse, Picasso, Kandinsky, Delaunay, Dalí and Grosz can be seen with post-war masters like Dubuffet, Johns, Warhol, Bacon and Merz, and works by contemporary artists like Boltanski, Sherman and Viola.

In recent years the Centre has boosted its cinematic presence, acting as another Cinémathèque, with comprehensive retrospectives of the likes of Martin Scorsese and Jacques Rivette. Hand in hand with such seasons is an active publishing programme, which produces attractive and scholarly books on the directors under examination.

Outside on the plaza are a reconstruction of Constantin Brancusi's studio, **l'Atelier Brancusi**, which he left to the state, and American sculptor Alex Calder's work *Horizontal*, which is recognisable by its black triangular base. The plaza itself is a bustling space popular with street performers, buskers, barrel organists and portrait painters.

LES HALLES

The Les Halles quarter gets its name from the historic food market that stood from 1183 to 1969 on the spot now occupied by a vast shopping complex. Large-scale construction has been a feature of the area since 1851, when Napoleon III ordered architect Victor Baltard to design 10 colossal cast-iron hangars to go over the market. "Iron, nothing but iron" and "Make me some umbrellas" were the emperor's two instructions, and the resulting construction was an elegant masterpiece of 19th-century design, widely copied throughout France and abroad.

Stallholders, restaurant owners, pickpockets, artists, prostitutes and

TIP

Rue des Lombards, between St-Merri and Les Halles, is a must-visit for jazz fans, with clubs such as Baiser Salé (No. 58), Au Duc des Lombards (No. 42) and Sunset/ Sunside (No. 60) all hosting live performances by fine musicians, from world-famous names to exciting new talent.

BELOW: the imposing Fontaine des Innocents.

Fontaine des Innocents

The Fontaine des Innocents, a Renaissance fountain decorated with water nymphs by Pierre Lescot and Jean Goujon, stands in the Square des Innocents, between Place du Châtelet and Forum des Halles, formerly the site of the notorious Cimetière des Innocents. In use since the 12th century, the graveyard, encircled by a high wall and covering just 130 metres x 65 metres, had become a putrid necropolis by the 18th century, as the dead – mostly paupers – were carried there among produce bound for the market at Les Halles. Gruesome tales are told about how people ground up bones for bread when Paris was under siege in 1590, and used the skeletons for firewood. By 1780, corpses were overflowing above street level and the area was teeming with rats, which started to gnaw their way into people's homes. It was recognised that something had to be done, so the cemetery was finally closed and its contents moved to the Catacombs, where the remains can still be seen (see page 223).

Today, the square and fountain are a meeting place for the city's youth, and the pedestrianised Rue des Lombards is a centre for nightlife with bars, restaurants and jazz clubs.

The Pompidou's primary-coloured pipes are not just for show: the blue convey air, the green transport water, the yellow contain electricity and the red conduct heating.

police inhabited this vast market, which novelist Emile Zola called "the belly of Paris". Unsurprisingly, the market had a strong presence in the literary output of the time. Zola set an entire novel here; Hugo described it in some detail in *Les Misérables*; and the area was a regular haunt of the Romantic poet and tormented bohemian Gérard de Nerval, who was born here and eventually ended his own life by hanging himself in a nearby cellar.

By the 1960s the site, already expanded in 1936, had become impractical – not least owing to traffic problems associated with bringing vast quantities of provisions to a site in the centre of the city. The market decamped to the suburbs of Rungis and the hangars were thoughtlessly pulled down, leaving a gaping hole that became a national joke. It was filled in the 1980s by the **Forum des Halles ③**, an underground shopping mall with shops, a multiplex cinema, the Forum des Images film archive and cinema and an Olympic swimming pool. Combined with a massive RER/Métro interchange, the Forum

ABOVE: gateway to Rue Montorgueil, a foodie's haven.
BELOW: the foyer inside the Centre Pompidou.

has acquired a dodgy reputation as a hang-out for gangs of youths from the suburbs. In 2004, the Mairie de Paris launched a competition for redeveloping the Forum and relandscaping the squares and gardens.

Paris's modern underbelly

Surrounding the market area are some remnants of a bygone age, with brasseries staying open around the clock (the early-hours clientele no longer formed by hard-working market porters, but exhausted partygoers) and sleazy Rue St-Denis, the age-old domain of prostitutes, albeit only in its northern reaches; the section adjacent to Les Halles is instead packed with small independent clothes shops, selling largely tacky streetwear and trainers.

The best place for a glimpse of the old Les Halles is **Rue Montorgueil**, a narrow, pedestrianised street packed with romantic cafés, wine and cheese merchants, garrulous butchers and colourful fruit and vegetable stalls. The street also contains the venerable *pâtissier* **Stohrer**, purveyor since 1730 of delectable cakes and tarts; its founder Nicolas Stohrer is said to have invented the rum baba. This short, attractive strip is one of a few places in Les Halles where it is easy to linger – even if you end up buying nothing more than a coffee.

St-Eustache ㉜

Address: Rue du Jour
www.saint-eustache.org

Tel: 01 42 36 31 05
Opening Hrs: Mon–Fri 9.30am–7pm, Sat 10am–7pm, Sun 9am–7pm
Entance Fee: free
Transport: Les Halles

North of the Forum des Halles, this colossal, beautiful church is a rose among thorns. Modelled on Notre-Dame (note the flying buttresses), it took over a 100 years to build (1532–1637). The interior is a Renaissance

ABOVE: greengrocer on Rue Montorgueil.
BELOW: ribbons for sale.

Rag Trade

Like any area not enshrined in administrative ink, Sentier has fuzzy boundaries: however, to most Parisians it is the top-right of the 2nd *arrondissement*, north of Rue Réaumur. This maze of narrow streets is the stronghold of the wholesale clothes industry. Most buildings are taken up by workshops and storerooms, and windows pour out a constant buzz of machinery. Sentier makes clothes and it makes fortunes: the secret of its success is not just its low-paid, often immigrant workforce but the ability of its workshops to take in the latest couture trends almost overnight. Check out Rue Réaumur with its architectural collage and the "Egyptian" Place du Caire (see page 147).

ABOVE: the Renaissance interior of St-Eustache.
BELOW: the Gothic gaze of St-Eustache.

SHOP

When it comes to fashion, the eternally crowded Forum des Halles is something of a wash-out: mostly chain stores like H&M. Far richer pickings are to be had in the much nicer setting of Rue Etienne Marcel, a major *mode* thoroughfare of labels like Sandro, Barbara Bui and smaller, seriously hip labels.

feast of majestic columns, arches and stained-glass windows. Berlioz and Liszt played here in the 19th century, and concerts are held regularly – often for free – using the church's 8,000-pipe organ; a recent restoration included the addition of electronic equipment allowing the organ to be played from ground-level consoles. St-Eustache also has a prestigious choir, and is the burial place of French composer Jean-Philippe Rameau, and another personage with a musical connection – Mozart's mother.

Outside the church, a sculpture of a giant head and cupped hand by Henri de Miller attracts both children and pigeons to its benign seat. The stretch of gardens between Les Halles and St-Eustache is peopled by dog-walkers, loitering teenagers and down-and-outs. The green space features glass pyramids full of palms, papayas and banana trees. Metal walkways pass through them to the **Bourse du Commerce** (tel: 01 55 65 55 65; Mon–Fri 9am–6pm; free), a circular building erected in the 18th century as a corn exchange, and now a busy commodities market for coffee and sugar.

LES HALLES TO THE BEACH

Head back towards the Rue St-Honoré, south of Les Halles, an elegant street with a rich history and upmarket shops. A little further on, facing the eastern facade of the Louvre, is the church of **St-Germain-l'Auxerrois** ❸ (tel: 01 42 60 13 96; Mon–Sat 8am–7pm, Sun 9am–8pm). At midnight on 24 August

1572, the church's bells rang as the signal to start the St Bartholomew's Day Massacre, when thousands of Protestants were butchered on the orders of the Catholic Catherine de Médicis. Behind the church on the banks of the Seine is the historic

La Samaritaine department store, which has been closed for major safety modifications since 2005 and is due to reopen in 2014.

Immediately in front of La Samaritaine is the Voie Georges Pompidou, the river front roadway that hosts much of the Right Bank portion of the annual **Paris-Plage** festivities. Every summer since 2002, the road has been shut to traffic, covered with tonnes of fine golden sand and kitted out with palm trees, deckchairs, refreshment kiosks, beach volleyball courts and a free lending library. The highly popular city-beach concept has been copied in other big cities, including Lyon, Toulouse, Berlin and Budapest. And in Paris, the holiday fun has now expanded to the Bassin de la Villette in the 19th arrondissement and Port de la Gare on the Left Bank.

LEFT: during Paris-Plage, the Voie Georges-Pompidou is shut to traffic and the beach takes over.
ABOVE: controversial colonial fresco on Rue Montorgueil.

SHOPPING

Beaubourg's shops have something to suit most tastes and ages.

Children

Apache
Forum des Halles, Niveau 2, 1st.
Tel: 01 44 88 52 00
As well as selling a wide variety of toys, furniture and accessories for children aged up to 12, this shop also organises regular in-store activities and events.

Clothing

Agnès B
2, 3, 4 and 6 rue du Jour, 1st.
Tel: 01 45 08 56 56
www.agnesb.com
The well-known Paris-born designer has four shops in this street: women's clothing, men's clothing, children's cloth-

ing and there's even one devoted to travel accessories.

Food

Bières Cultes
14 rue des Halles, 1st.
Tel: 09 81 98 93 32
Beer aficionados will love this place as the shelves are stacked with bottles of the best brews from around the world. There are also associated accessories including bar towels and trays.

Pralus
35 rue Rambuteau, 4th.
Tel: 01 57 40 84 55
www.chocolats-pralus.com
While this *chocolatier* produces delicious dark chocolate made from the world's finest cocoa beans, many people come here to buy the Praluline – a brioche

studded with pink pralines.

Gifts

Artoyz
45 rue de l'Arbre Sec, 1st.
Tel: 01 47 03 09 90
www.artoyz.com
From pink plastic aliens to splodgy T-shirts, everything in this shop is inspired by Japanese graphic art culture. There's even a little model of the Twitter bluebird.

Nuxe Spa
32, 34 Rue Montorgueil, 1st.
Tel: 01 42 36 65 65
Organic beauty products for the face and body are sold in the company's chic spa housed in an old stone building. Spoil yourself with some treatments while you're there.

Home

E. Dehillerin
18 rue Coquillère, 1st.
Tel: 01 42 36 5313
www.e-dehillerin.fr
Professional chefs have been coming to this Aladdin's cave for cooks since 1820. The place is packed to the rafters with top-quality French cookware including copper pans.

Ekobo
4 rue Hérold, 1st.
Tel: 01 45 08 47 43
www.ekobohome.com
This little boutique specialises in selling kitchen and bathroom accessories made from eco-friendly bamboo. The colourful *pouffes* for children are particularly cute.

BEST RESTAURANTS, BARS AND CAFES

Restaurants

American

Joe Allen
30 rue Pierre Lescot, 1st
Tel: 01 42 36 70 13
www.joeallenparis.com
Open: non-stop daily.
€€ (set menu) €€€ (à la carte)
18 [p336, C1]
The Paris outpost of the
Joe Allen chain has been
going for over 30 years,
and is still one of the better American eating
establishments in Paris.
In a decor of brick walls
and dark wooden floors,
contented Parisians dine
on things like Caesar
salad, quesadillas and
very good cheeseburgers.

French

Benoît
20 rue St-Martin, 4th
Tel: 01 42 72 25 76
www.benoit-paris.com
Open: L & D daily.

€€€ **19** [p336, C2]
This celebrated vintage
bistro (open since 1912),
noted for its excellent
cooking and very high
prices, fell into the Alain
Ducasse fold in 2004,
but Ducasse has prom-
ised not to change its
style. Forget fussy indi-
vidual dishes – waiters
will bring a whole terrine
to the table and cut you a
slab, or dish up beef and
carrot casserole, or *cassoulet*, then tempt you
with a slice of the igloo-
size prune-and-Arma-
gnac ice-cream *bombe*.
Best to book ahead.

Au Chien Qui Fume
33 rue du Pont Neuf, 1st
Tel: 01 42 36 07 42
Open: non-stop daily noon–2am.
€€ **20** [p336, B1]
The "smoking dog" has
an extensive brasserie
menu, including shrimp
and langoustine salad,

and duck *à l'orange*. All
the classic desserts are
on offer, including iced
nougat and chocolate
mousse. Not a bad place
to lap up the late-night
atmosphere.

L'Escargot Montorgueil
38 rue Montorgueil, 1st
Tel: 01 42 36 83 51
Open: L & D daily.
€€€ **21** [p336, C1]
Its heyday has passed,
but the "snail of Mon-
torgueil", its Second
Empire decor intact,
remains a glamorous,
tourist-friendly restau-
rant nonetheless. Sadly,
the cooking is no match
for the surroundings, but
if you stick to a dozen
plump garlicky snails,
you can still get a feel for
its past splendour.

La Fresque
100 rue Rambuteau, 1st
Tel: 01 42 33 17 56
Open: L & D Mon–Sat (until

midnight)
€ **22** [p336, C1]
Sitting elbow to elbow at
one of the big wooden
tables is part of the
charm here, as is the
decor (white faience tiles,
frescoes). Bistro fare like
beef stew and duck are
excellent, and the staff
are friendly if sometimes
harassed. There is
always one vegetarian
main course.

Georges
6th floor, Centre Georges Pompidou, place Beaubourg, 4th
Tel: 01 44 78 47 99
Open: L & D Wed–Mon (until
1am)
€€€ **23** [p336, C2]
The chic clientele don't
go to Georges's restau-
rant for the food but to
see and be seen in a
unique setting at the top
of the Centre Pompidou.
With globular, brushed-
aluminium pods, bright
Pop Art colours, transpar-
ent tables, hip DJs and
one of the finest restau-
rant views in the city,
Georges is an art installation in its own right.

Le Hangar
12 impasse Berthaud, 4th
Tel: 01 42 74 55 44
Open: L & D Tue–Sat.
€€ **24** [p336, C1]
Minimalist yet cosy, this
modern bistro is just
steps from the Pompidou,
hidden in an alley. Pan-
fried foie gras with puréed
potatoes is always on the
menu, as well as a tower-
ing chocolate soufflé. No
credit cards.

LEFT: L'Escargot Montorgueil is a good place to
have, you guessed it, snails.

Au Pied de Cochon
6 rue Coquillière, 1st
Tel: 01 40 13 77 00
Open: non-stop daily
€€ (set menu) €€€ (à la carte)
25 [p336, B1]
In its heyday, the legendary all-night brasserie catered for the market workers; now it's rather more upmarket, if a little touristy. But the house speciality remains the same: grilled pig's trotter with béarnaise sauce. If that isn't your thing, there are oysters and seafood. And the onion soup is a good cure for hangovers.

La Tour de Montlhéry
5 rue des Prouvaires, 1st
Tel: 01 42 36 21 82
Open: L & D daily.
€€€ **26** [p336, B1]
This long-standing, late-opening (until 5.30am) purveyor of solid French food, also known as Chez Denise, is great fun. Portions are copious, the red-checked dining room cosy and the atmosphere friendly. The traditional menu runs to steaks, great home-made chips, some game, some offal and a few fish dishes.

Saveurs Végét'halles
41 rue des Bourdonnais, 1st
Tel: 01 40 41 93 95
Open: L & D Mon-Sat.
€ **27** [p336, B1]
With a colourful, contemporary dining room, this restaurant is an oasis for vegans and vegetarians in an area that is best known for its meat offerings. From soya kebabs to crème brûlée, this place is popular with non-vegetarians too.

RIGHT: bistro on food-obsessed Rue Montorgueil.

Bars and Cafés

Bistrot Beaubourg
25 rue Quincampoix, 4th.
Tel: 01 42 77 48 02.
Open: L & D daily.
7 [p336, C2]
This designer café opposite the Centre Pompidou is a study in style over substance. Food is mediocre, considering what you pay, but it's fine for a light bite to eat and a spot of people-watching. Either gaze out from the terrace onto the Pompidou forecourt or turn your gaze inwards, to the café's habitués.

Le Café des Initiés
3 place des Deux-Ecus, 1st.
Tel: 01 42 33 78 29.
Open: Non-stop daily.
8 [p336, B1]
From crumbling old corner café comes trendy hangout: this fashionable drinks purveyor has ergonomic red bench seating, a long zinc bar, swish black lamps and elegant flower arrangements in glass vases. It's friendly, too.

Le Père Fouettard
9 rue Pierre-Lescot.
Tel: 01 42 33 74 17.
Open: L & D daily (noon–midnight).
9 [p336, C1]
A warm and cosy bistro, with cheerful service, a young clientele and its fair share of regulars. Totally relaxing, the café terrace is leafy in summer, heated in winter. Cheap prices, and good food if you stick to the standards such as *brochettes* of beef from the Aubrac region, roast suckling pig, chocolate tart or spice roasted apples. Vegetarian options as well. Good wines by the glass.

Le Petit Marcel
65 rue Rambuteau, 4th.
Tel: 01 48 87 10 20.
Open: L & D daily (until midnight).
10 [p336, C1]
In a great location, a stone's throw from the Centre Pompidou, this quaint café/bar is a real find. Art Nouveau tiles decorate the interior. Sal-

Price includes dinner and a half-bottle of house wine:

€ = under €25
€€ = €25–40
€€€ = €40–60
€€€€ = more than €60

ads, omelettes, steak frites, crumbles and brownies. Good drinks selection and very friendly service. No credit cards.

Le Tambour
41 rue Montmartre, 2nd.
Tel: 01 42 33 06 90.
Open: Non-stop daily.
11 [p336, B1]
There's nowhere else in Paris quite like this 24-hour bar. Inside it looks like a junk shop, its decor a mash-up of all manner of old Métro signs, stray statues, old books and even older customers (there are lots of students, too). The moustachioed owner is usually on hand, swapping animated barroom philosophies with the regulars. Priceless.

CENTRE POMPIDOU

The inside-out museum of modern art is a world icon of contemporary architecture. Its escalators, outside sculptures and roof-top restaurant are more reasons to visit.

Georges Pompidou, the President of France from 1969–74, was a moderniser – and had a lasting fondness for the arts. He compiled an anthology of French poetry and it was he who proposed the building of a major cultural centre in Beaubourg. The chosen design, by the then-unknown duo Richard Rogers and Renzo Piano, put the air-conditioning ducts and escalators on the outside, which made for an adaptable space within. When Rodgers was awarded the prestigious Pritzker Architecture Prize in 2007 for designing the Lloyd's Building in London, the jury said that his Pompidou Centre "revolutionised museums, transforming what had once been elite monuments into popular places of social and cultural exchange, woven into the heart of the city". Building started on the centre in 1972 at a cost of 993 million FF and it opened in 1977; its multi-disciplinary set-up – the largest museum of modern art in Europe, plus a public library and cinemas – was an instant hit. It had a revamp at the end of the 20th century, which included the opening of the fashionable Georges rooftop restaurant (see page 114). Entrance to the forum and library is free, but you have to pay to go up the escalators.

RIGHT: the vast and cavernous atrium.

BELOW: Georges, the Centre's swish rooftop restaurant (see page 114).

The Essentials

Address: www.centre pompidou.fr
Tel: 01 44 78 12 33
Opening Hrs: Wed–Mon 11am–9pm
Entrance Fee: charge
Transport: Rambuteau

INSIDE AND OUT

The collection at the Pompidou is far too large to be displayed, even in such a cavernous setting: there are 50,000 works of art in all, and only 600 or so can be exhibited at once. Level four contains post-1960s art: here you'll find architecture, design and sections on movements like Arte Povera and Anti-Form. On level five is work produced between 1905 and 1960 by Matisse, Picasso and Braque, as well as Klee, Kandinsky, Magritte, Miró, Ernst and more. Art isn't confined indoors; the outdoor terraces showcase various sculptures and on the plaza is Alexander Calder's *Horizontal*, a kind of giant mobile with a black triangular base supporting a silver arm with coloured "petals" dangling off it, while to the south of the Centre is the Fontaine Stravinsky by Niki de Saint-Phalle and Jean Tinguely. On Place Georges Pompidou, the studio of Paris-based Romanian sculptor Constantin Brancusi (1876-1957) has been recreated exactly as it was on the day he died.

ABOVE: the view from the panoramic roof walkway covers a huge swathe of the city, including Montmartre.

RIGHT: the turbines outside the Centre.

BELOW: the Centre has an avant-garde music institute (IRCAM).

ABOVE: the escalators are contained in glass tubes.

BELOW: Alexander Calder's *Horizontal* graces the entrance.

Louvre and Grands Boulevards

0   400 m
0   400 yds

Pl. de Prony   Monceau   Courcelles   R. de Chazelles   R. de Prony

Courcelles   Pl. de la République Dominicaine   Musée Cernuschi ③⓪

Pl. de la République de l'Equateur   PARC MONCEAU   Musée Nissim de Camondo   ②⑨

Avenue des Ternes   Boulevard   Ternes   Daru   Avenue Hoche   Pl. de Rio de Janeiro

Espace Wagram   St-Alexandre-Nevsky

St-Joseph   Avenue Hoche   Annonciation   Pl. de Téhéran   St-Augustin

Chambre de Commerce et d'Industrie de Paris   Friedland   Boulevard   Haussmann   Boulevard

Ch.-de-Gaulle-Étoile   Fondation Jerome Seycoux-Pathe   Rue de La Baume

Arc de Triomphe ②⑥   Ch.-de-Gaulle-Étoile   St-Sacrement   St-Philippe-du-Roule   Miromesnil

Pl. Charles-de-Gaulle   St-Philippe-du-Roule   Musée Jacquemart-André ②⑦

George V   Champs-   St-George's   Colisée

St-Pierre de Chaillot   Pl. H. Dunant   Champs-   ②③   Élysées   Palais de l'Élysée

CHAILLOT   Th. Marigny

American Cathedral in Paris   Church of Scotland   Champs-Élysées Clémenceau

St-Etienne   Crazy Horse   Th. des Champs Élysées   St-Jean Baptiste   Grand Palais ②④   Musée du Petit Palais ②⑤

Musée Guimet   Musée Galliera   Palais de la Découverte

Site de Création Contemporaine   Palais de Tokyo   Musée d'Art Moderne de la Ville de Paris   Pl. de l'Alma   Seine

Musée du Quai Branly   Les Egouts de Paris   Quai   d'Orsay   Aérogare des Invalides   Invalides

St-Pierre du Gros Caillou   ESPLANADE DES INVALIDES   Institut Géographique National

Tour Eiffel   PARC DU CHAMP-DE-MARS   La Tour Maubourg   Musée de l'Armée   Varenne

Hôtel des Invalides

THE LOUVRE AND QUARTIER DES TUILERIES

Royal Paris: the queen of all art museums, the gracious Tuileries gardens, a fascinating mix of smaller museums, the urban oasis of the Palais Royal and, tucked away, the world's most charming shopping arcades.

On the Seine's Right Bank beautifully laid-out gardens stretch into ostentatious squares, and wide tree-lined boulevards overflow with upmarket restaurants and designer boutiques. There are royal palaces, an opulent opera house and the world's most famous museum. Meticulously planned by Haussmann, the elegant buildings, boulevards and open spaces engulf the visitor in 19th-century grandeur.

This area covers the royal heart of Paris, from the Louvre and Palais Royal westwards to the Jeu de Paume gallery and the Musée de l'Orangerie at the far end of the Tuileries gardens. The grand squares – Place de la Concorde, Place Vendôme and Place de la Madeleine – with the Champs-Elysées, the Grands Boulevards and the Opéra are covered in the next chapter.

MUSÉE DU LOUVRE ❶

Address: www.louvre.fr
Tel: 01 40 20 50 50
Opening Hrs: Wed–Mon 9am–6pm, Wed, Fri until 9.45pm
Entrance Fee: charge
Transport: Palais Royal-Musée du Louvre

Once the seat of royalty, the Musée du Louvre has been the home of fine art since a colony of painters and sculptors moved into the empty halls after King Louis XIV left for Versailles in 1682. The Louvre's art collection goes back even further, to 1516, when François I invited Leonardo da Vinci to be his royal court painter, and he brought with him his masterpieces the *Mona Lisa* and *Virgin of the Rocks*.

Originally built as a fortress in 1190 by Philippe-Auguste to protect a weak link in his city wall, the

Main Attractions
MUSÉE DU LOUVRE
LOUVRE PYRAMID
JARDIN DES TUILERIES
MUSÉE DE L'ORANGERIE
RUE DE RIVOLI
COMÉDIE FRANÇAISE
PALAIS ROYAL
GALERIE VIVIENNE
PLACE DES VICTOIRES

Maps and Listings
MAP, PAGE 118
SHOPPING, PAGE 137
RESTAURANTS, PAGE 138
ACCOMMODATION, PAGE 300

LEFT: the Jousseaume bookshop in the splendid Galerie Vivienne.
RIGHT: the old palace seen under one of the smaller pyramids.

"I don't know how you visit museums, but for a long time I used to fall into the common trap of wanting to see everything."
François Mitterrand, at the inauguration of the Louvre Pyramid

Louvre was transformed into a royal château in the 1360s by Charles V, who established his extensive library in one of the towers. Successive monarchs demolished, rebuilt and extended various sections until Louis XIV moved out. The squatters who consequently took up residence in the palace included Guillaume Coustou, sculptor of the Marly Horses, now one of the Louvre's most prized exhibits. A fine artistic reputation grew out of the decaying passageways and galleries and, in the 18th century, the fine arts academy, which had joined the Académie Française and other academic bodies in the royal apartments, set up salons for artists to exhibit their work, a tradition which lasted for more than 120 years.

From palace to museum

After the Revolution, in a moment of creative fervour, the new regime decided to open the palace as a museum, thereby fulfilling the plans of Louis XVI, the king they had just beheaded. Opened in August 1793, the museum benefited from the collection of royal treasures, augmented by Napoleon's subsequent efforts to relocate much of Europe's artistic wealth, following his victorious military campaigns in Italy, Austria and Germany. After Napoleon was defeated at Waterloo in 1815, a large number of the stolen masterpieces were reclaimed by their rightful owners. But many more remained.

In 1981, the newly elected President Mitterrand commissioned a massive renovation of the Louvre, one of his *grands projets*, transferring in the process the Finance Ministry from the Richelieu Wing to Bercy, in eastern Paris, in order to free up more space for the vast collection. When it was finally finished, the *Grand Louvre*, already a vast museum, had doubled in size, making it the world's biggest.

The Pyramid

In 1989 the emphatically modern Louvre Pyramid, designed by Chinese-American architect I.M. Pei, opened above the Louvre's new main entrance. A celebration of angles, the pyramid's 666 panes of glass are held together by stainless-steel nodes and cables. The glass reflects and too many minds complements the lines of the surrounding building; however, to traditionalists, such modernism amid such historic beauty is a heresy – the same criticism that was levelled against the now-beloved Eiffel Tower when it was first erected. The Pyramid stands on the Royal Axis, or Triumphal Way, an alignment of monuments, regal and triumphal, leading from the Louvre's Cour Carrée all the way to the Grande Arche at La Défense.

Of course, it was not just designed to dazzle. The Pyramid also serves an important practical purpose, as it allows light to flood into the sunken court where you buy your ticket, along with three smaller pyramids that illuminate the area where a cluster of shops, restaurants, cafés and

an exhibition area are situated. This exhibition area, called the Medieval Louvre, shows the palace at different stages of its development. It is also a location for the twice-yearly Paris fashion shows.

However, the Pyramid entrance gets very congested, so try to avoid peak times such as Sundays. There's

ABOVE: mix style, culture and cuisine at the Louvre's Café Marly.
BELOW: the Pyramid is the main entrance to the museum.

The Denon wing at the Louvre, which houses the new Department of Islamic Art, is named after Domique Vivant, Baron de Denon (1747–1825), a diplomat and archaeologist who was appointed the museum's first director by Napoleon following his Egyptian campaign.

BELOW: the new Department of Islamic Art in its new home under Cour Visconti.

an alternative entrance at 99 rue de Rivoli, which takes you in via the swanky Carrousel du Louvre shopping centre (a treasure trove of chic and cheerful gifts and souvenirs), or you can enter directly from Palais Royal-Musée du Louvre Métro. There are special queues for museum pass-holders, who can also use the Porte des Lions entrance.

A tour of the treasures

From the central Hall Napoléon, escalators whisk visitors off to various parts of the complex, divided into three separate sections: Sully (east wing), Denon (south wing) and Richelieu (north wing), with the exhibits on three levels. Although star attractions are well signposted, the free map provided is essential.

A good exhibition to start your visit with is the Medieval Louvre, en route to the Crypte Sully under the Cour Carrée, where the remains of Philippe-Auguste's fort and keep, and some of the artefacts discovered in the excavations to build the underground complex, can be seen. Pieces of Charles VI's parade

helmet were found at the bottom of the well in the keep in 1984, and a replica of the helmet is on display in the Salle St-Louis.

Up on the ground floor of the Sully and Richelieu wings are Oriental Antiquities, including the Mesopotamian prayer statuette of Ebih-il (dating from approximately 2400 BC), with its striking lapis lazuli eyes, as well as the black basalt Babylonian *Code of Hammurabi* (1792–1750 BC), which is one of the world's first legal documents.

Greece to the Renaissance

On the south side of the Sully Wing you will find the graceful Hellenic statue *Venus de Milo* (2nd century BC), bought by the French government for a thousand francs in 1820 from the Greek island of Milos. Head on into the Denon Wing to see the Etruscan sarcophagus of a *Reclining Couple*. Continuing along the ground floor, you will reach the Italian Sculpture section and its famous masterpieces, such as Michelangelo's *Slaves* (1513–20), sculpted in marble for Pope Julius

Islamic Art Gets a New Home

In the autumn of 2012 the Louvre opened a new exhibition space, which is the museum's most ambitious project since I. M. Pei's Pyramid. The Department of Islamic Art, previously confined to a section of the Department of Near Eastern Antiquities, now has its own special home in (or rather, underneath) Cour Visconti. The courtyard was excavated to a depth of 12 metres (40ft) and the exhibition space, covering 2,800 sq metres (30,000 sq ft), is spread over two floors. With around 3,000 works in its collection, which span the globe from Spain to India, the first floor focuses on Islamic artworks from the 7th to 10th century while the ground floor, or basement, takes visitors on a journey through the Islamic civilisation from the 11th to 19th century. The most striking aspect of this new "wing", designed by Rudy Ricciotti and Mario Bellini, is its undulating roof that is made up of 2,350 glass triangles each measuring 2.4 metres (8ft) wide. Visitors can get a shimmering view of the courtyard buildings from underneath the roof while those looking down from Galerie Drau and Salle des États will see what the has been described as "a golden, iridescent cloud".

II's tomb but never finished, and Canova's neoclassical *Psyche Revived by the Kiss of Cupid* (1793).

In the Denon Wing, on the first floor, is the work of art that everyone wants to see for themselves, the *Mona Lisa* (1503) – *La Joconde* in French. The first incumbent in the Louvre, Leonardo da Vinci's small painting of a Florentine noblewoman rests securely behind bulletproof glass since her knife assault in the 1980s. It now hangs in pride of place in the restored Salle des Etats, along with Veronese's superb *The Wedding Feast at Cana* and other Venetian paintings by Titian and Tintoretto. The E4.7 million cost of the refurbishment was met, believe it or not, by Japan's Nippon Television Network, which also forked out E1.7 million to upgrade the gallery housing the *Venus de Milo*. Other Italian masterpieces include works by Fra Angelico, Raphael and Caravaggio.

Delacroix to Rembrandt

On the same floor is the Grande Galerie, starting at the top of the Escalier Daru opposite the *Winged Victory of Samothrace* (2nd century BC), a Hellenistic stone figure commemorating a sea victory. Here hang 19th-century French paintings, with Delacroix's *Liberty Leading the People*, Géricault's *Raft of the Medusa*

ABOVE: the Louvre's massive *Wedding at Cana* (1563), by Paolo Veronese.
BELOW: the Louvre's vast covered courtyards make a nice change from the crowded galleries.

and David's *Sabine Women*. Spanish Paintings, with masterpieces by El Greco and Goya, is close by.

The second floor of Richelieu and Sully Wings are entirely given over to paintings, including Rembrandt's masterly portrait of his second wife, *Bathsheba Bathing* (1654), and his Dutch compatriot Vermeer's telling portrayal of domestic life in the 1660s, *The Lacemaker*. The beautifully renovated Richelieu Wing houses a vast collection of French sculpture on the ground floor and is focused around two splendid sculpture courts, starring Guillaume Coustou's two giant Marly Horses.

Musée des Arts Décoratifs ❷

Address: 107 rue de Rivoli
www.ucad.fr
Tel: 01 44 55 57 50
Opening Hrs: Tue–Sun 11am–6pm
Entrance Fee: charge
Transport: Palais Royal-Musée du Louvre

In a separate wing of the Louvre are three other museums that complement the main collection. This one surveys interior design and applied art from medieval tapestries to extravagant Empire furniture and 20th-century design, including Art Nouveau and Art Deco. There are medieval and Renaissance galleries, a jewellery collection and period rooms such as the lavish bedroom of Baron William Hope.

Musée des Arts de la Mode et du Textile

Details and opening times as for Musée des Arts Décoratifs

In the same wing on Rue de Rivoli, this muscum covers Paris fashions and textiles from the 16th century until today. Each year it mounts a big display focusing on a different aspect of its collection (which comprises 16,000 costumes, 35,000 fashion accessories and 30,000 textile pieces) from the earliest existing dresses to the ground-breaking designs of big-name couturiers of the 20th century, such as Schiaparelli and Christian Dior.

Musée de la Publicité

Address: www.museedelapub.org; other details as for Musée des Arts Décoratifs

Upstairs in this wing, the "Advertising Museum" was designed for the millennium celebrations by French architect Jean Nouvel, who turned to the city for inspiration. It is home to a comprehensive collection of posters – around 100,000 in all, starting from as early as the Middle Ages – press, TV and radio adverts and promotional memorabilia, complemented by interactive displays, slide shows and videos. Only a fraction of the vast collection can ever be exhibited at one time.

LEFT: up the stairs to the headless *Winged Victory of Samothrace.*
BELOW: the enigmatic *Venus de Milo.*

Aristide Maillol (1861–1944) started sculpting at the age of 40, concentrating his efforts on large, bronze, nude women – 20 of which adorn the Tuileries.

A WALK IN THE TUILERIES

The **Jardin des Tuileries** ❸ offers shade, statues, fountains and a place in which to relax and pretend to read *Le Monde*. Once a rubbish tip and a clay quarry for tiles (*tuiles*, hence the name), the garden was initially created in 1564 for Catherine de Médicis in front of her palace, to remind her of her native Tuscany. Louis XIV's celebrated gardener André Le Nôtre redesigned it in 1664, giving free rein to his predilection for straight lines and neatly clipped trees.

Louis XIV, however, was far more interested in Versailles, and the Tuileries gardens were, surprisingly, opened to the public. They quickly became the first fashionable outdoor area in which to see and be seen, triggering the appearance of Paris's first deckchairs and public toilets. One of the earliest hot-air balloon flights was launched from here, in 1783.

The Tuileries Palace for which the gardens had been created – which "closed off" the two wings of the Louvre – burned down in 1871, during the Paris Commune, leaving the gardens as a permanent park.

ABOVE: the Arc de Triomphe du Carrousel.
BELOW: sitting by the hexagonal pool.

Sculpture, paths and ponds

The Tuileries were renovated in the 1990s, restoring Le Nôtre's original design and incorporating a sloping terrace and enclosed garden. The Passerelle de Solférino footbridge across the Seine, opened in 1999, provides a quick route from the gardens to the Left Bank and Musée d'Orsay.

Approaching the gardens from the Louvre, you pass through the Arc de Triomphe du Carrousel, the smallest of the three arches (the others being the Arc de Triomphe and the Grande Arche at La Défense) on the Triumphal Way. Erected in 1809 by Napoleon to commemorate his Austrian victories, this arch is a garish imitation of the great triumphal arches built by the Romans, and the four horses galloping across its top are copies of four bronze horses that were stolen by Napoleon from St Mark's Square in Venice to decorate his memorial. After his downfall in 1815, the originals were returned.

In front and a little to the right of the arch, where the Tuileries Palace once stood, is a collection of sculptures of sensuous nudes, produced between 1900 and 1938 by Aristide Maillol, adorning ornamental pools and hedge-lined pathways. More works by sculptors such as Rodin and Le Pautre, along with copies of ancient works and a selection of modern sculpture by, among others, Dubuffet, Etienne-Martin, Ellsworth Kelly, Laurens and David Smith, can be found scattered around the park.

Continue westwards along the Terrasse du Bord de l'Eau, where Napoleon's children played under the watchful gaze of their father, to

ABOVE: relaxing in the Jardin des Tuileries.
BELOW: old-fashioned carousel in the Tuileries.

ABOVE: under the arcades of Rue de Rivoli. **RIGHT:** the entrance to the Musée de l'Orangerie. **BELOW:** tempting window display at Angelina's.

the hexagonal pool – still a favourite spot for children with boats, and seagulls with attitude. Here, facing each other, are the twin museums of the Jeu de Paume and the Orangerie. These buildings are all that remain of the Palais des Tuileries, after the fire that engulfed the royal residence during the 1871 Commune.

Jeu de Paume (Site Concorde) ❹

Address: www.jeudepaume.org
Tel: 01 47 03 12 50
Opening Hrs: Tue 11am–9pm, Wed–Sun 11am–7pm
Entrance Fee: charge
Transport: Concorde
Once the real tennis court of the Tuileries Palace, the Jeu de Paume is now a light, airy exhibition space, which is the main base of France's national photography centre. Its approach is multi-disciplinary, featuring video, installation and film, documentary and art photography.

Musée de l'Orangerie ❺

Address: www.musee-orangerie. fr
Tel: 01 44 77 80 07
Opening Hrs: Wed–Mon 9am–6pm
Entrance Fee: charge
Transport: Concorde
The list of canvases here is impressive: 22 Soutines, 14 Cézannes – including one of *The Bathers* that was cut in

three, then stuck back together again (look for the joins) – 24 Renoirs, 28 Derains and a pile of Picassos, Matisses and Utrillos. The highlight, though, is the unforgettable, extraordinarily fresh series of water lilies by Claude Monet, conceived especially for two oval rooms upstairs. Donated by the artist in 1918, the eight vast curved panels hover between abstraction and decoration.

During extensive renovations at the Orangerie, workers uncovered a wall dating back to Charles IX's reign (c.1566).

RUE DE RIVOLI

The long Rue de Rivoli starts in the Marais and then runs past the Louvre and along the Tuileries – where its north side becomes a pedestrian arcade topped with Haussmannian apartments – to Place de la Concorde. It was built to commemorate Napoleon's victory over the Austrians at Rivoli, north of Verona, in 1797, but was completed well after the emperor's demise. Amid the souvenir shops, the presence of two English-language

bookshops (Galignani and an outpost of WH Smith) and shirtmaker Hilditch & Key are a legacy of the English, who often stayed here in the 19th and early 20th centuries, notably at the Hôtel Meurice. Nearby is Angelina (see margin).

Parallel to Rue de Rivoli is the ancient Rue St-Honoré. Once full of noble residences, it still has some elegant facades and ornate shop fronts, but the area, long considered staid and straight-laced, has been transformed by the arrival of influential designer boutiques and so-called concept stores, of which the first and still the best-known is Colette (see page 35).

St-Roch ❻

Address: 296 rue St-Honoré
Tel: 01 42 44 13 20
Opening Hrs: Tue–Sun 9am–7pm
Entrance Fee: free
Transport: Pyramides

This Baroque church contains the tombs of royal landscape gardener Le Nôtre, the playwright Corneille and philosopher Diderot. In 1795, Royalist insurgents were shot dead

BELOW: Claude Monet's *Water Lilies*.

ABOVE: a game of *pétanque* in the Palais Royal garden.
BELOW: The palatial dining room at Le Meurice.

on the church steps on the orders of a young general named Napoleon Bonaparte (the bullet holes are still visible). The church is slowly being renovated; its spotlessly clean, honeyed stone facade is particularly fine.

On nearby Place des Pyramides is a shiny equestrian statue of Joan of Arc (one of four statues of the Maid of Orléans in the city), wounded here in battle when fighting against the English in 1429.

Comédie Française

Address: 1 place Colette
www.comedie-francaise.fr
Tel: 08 25 10 16 80
Transport: Palais Royal-Musée du Louvre

The French national theatre overlooks two squares named after the writers Colette and Malraux. The company that started life with Molière and his acting troupe, was given the official stamp in 1680 by Louis XIV. It has been in the present building since 1799, and the plays of Racine, Molière, Corneille and Shakespeare continue to form the backbone of its classical repertoire.

Louvre des Antiquaires ❽

Address: 2 place du Palais-Royal
www.louvre-antiquaires.com
Tel: 01 42 97 27 27
Opening Hrs: Tue–Sun 11am–7pm (closed Sun July–Aug)
Entrance Fee: free

Hotel with History

The sumptuous Hôtel Meurice (228 rue de Rivoli, see page 300) is one of Paris's grandest hotels, with a spa, Michelin-starred restaurant, supremely elegant cocktail bar and sumptuous decor. During the Nazi Occupation, however, it was the German headquarters. It was here in August 1944 that General Dietrich von Choltitz, military governor of Paris (he was only promoted to the job on the 7th), received direct orders from Hitler to blow up most of the city in advance of the Allied liberation. Von Choltitz famously refused – an act of disobedience that earned him the sobriquet "saviour of Paris" and the presence of French generals at his funeral 22 years later.

Transport: Palais Royal-Musée du Louvre

On Place du Palais-Royal, now a popular spot for stunt-mad rollerbladers, is this massive building, built as a department store and now home to some 150 upmarket antique dealers. Specialists take in everything from fine art, porcelain and furniture to Chinese and Japanese ivories, antique jewellery and scientific instruments. The area was cleared by a paranoid Napoleon following an attempt on his life in 1800, when two Royalists planted explosives in a cart, but the bomb missed his carriage.

PALAIS ROYAL ❾

The Palais Royal is a timeless and tranquil spot. The palace was built on the site of a Roman bathhouse for Cardinal Richelieu, Louis XIII's chief minister from 1624. On Richelieu's death in 1642, it was passed to the Crown, and became the childhood home of Louis XIV. At the beginning of the 18th century, the dukes of Orléans, descendants of Louis XIV's younger brother, took up residence, and the palace turned into a den of

debauchery, with the infamous "libertines' suppers" thrown regularly by the Regent, Philippe d'Orléans.

In 1780, to compensate for his family's profligate spending, Louis-Philippe of Orléans, known as *Philippe-Egalité* due to his liberal ideas, enclosed the gardens at the back of the palace with an elegant three-storey arcade, spaces in which were let as shops, theatres, restaurants, cafés, sideshows and brothels. The Jardins du Palais Royal became a focal point of Parisian life, as a place where all classes could mingle freely; the duke forbade the police entrance to the palace precincts, and gambling and prostitution were rife.

Birthplace of revolution

It was also a hotbed of radical ideas, and it was

ABOVE: Buren's Columns has turned the Palais Royal courtyard into a modernist playground of sorts.
LEFT: browsing at the Louvre des Anitquaires.
BELOW: the Palais-Royal métro entrance.

ABOVE: lunch at Galerie Vivienne's Le Bougainville café-restaurant.
BELOW: Molière, one of the most famous French playwrights.

After the Revolution the complex continued to be one of the social hubs of Paris, until the Palais was reclaimed by the Orléans family after the demise of Napoleon. The Palais Royal was seriously damaged during the Commune (1871), but was faithfully reconstructed in the following years.

Today, the Palais Royal houses the Ministry of Culture. In the main courtyard stand 250 black-and-white-striped columns of varying heights, erected by artist Daniel Buren in 1986. At weekends it echoes with the squeals of delighted children, who love to play around them. The garden, once a meeting place for revolutionaries, is now a tranquil oasis – with some fine restaurants – while the eccentric mix of shops ranges from old-fashioned specialists in medals and lead soldiers to make-up, vintage couture and upmarket interior design. In more recent years some seriously glam fashion labels have boosted the arcades' pulling power considerably: newcomers include Marc Jacobs, Rick Owens and Didier Ludot.

famously from a café table in the Palais Royal that Camille Desmoulins made an impassioned speech on 12 July 1789 calling on the people of Paris to take arms against the royal government, which led directly to the storming of the Bastille two days later.

Master of Comedy

Born Jean-Baptiste Poquelin in Paris in 1622, Molière, playwright, actor, director and stage manager, wrote 12 enduring comedies, including *Tartuffe* (1669) and *Le Bourgeois Gentilhomme* (1671). After studying law, he formed an acting troupe with the Béjart family (including his lover, Madeleine Béjart). He also changed his name to Molière, perhaps to spare his father the embarrassment of an actor in the family. The troupe had an unsuccessful start, but after Molière polished up his act in the provinces, they became Louis XIV's court entertainers.

In 1673, at 51, Molière collapsed on stage with a haemorrhage while playing *Le Malade Imaginaire*, in which an old man feigns death; he died hours later. In 1680 the king merged his company with a rival's, creating the Comédie Française, which was originally situated at 14 rue de l'Ancienne Comédie on the Left Bank but later moved to the theatre, now known as the Comédie Française, in Rue de Richelieu near the Palais Royal where his plays are still produced. The great thespian lived at 40 rue de Richelieu, and is commemorated by a fountain close by. The giant chair in which he was sitting when he died is in a case in the theatre's foyer.

Bibliothèque Nationale de France (Richelieu) ⑩

Address: 5 rue Vivienne
www.bnf.fr
Tel: 01 53 79 59 59
Opening Hrs: exhibitions Tue–Sat 10am–7pm, Sun 1–7pm
Entrance Fee: charge
Transport: Bourse

North of the Palais Royal is the former mansion of Cardinal Mazarin, which became the royal library and so the foundation of France's national library. Most of the collection has been transferred to the massive building at Tolbiac (see page 227) – last (and least successful) of Mitterrand's *grands projets*. The book collection is one of the biggest in the world, and includes Charlemagne's illuminated Bible, as well as manuscripts by Rabelais, Hugo and Proust. The Richelieu building now houses the collections of prints, drawings, maps, music and manuscripts. The main reading room, designed by Henri Labrouste in 1863, is an architectural masterpiece. Downstairs, the **Cabinet des Médailles** (open afternoons; charge) contains coins and objets d'art from the royal collections that were seized during the Revolution.

Opposite the library, across Rue de Richelieu, the charming **Square Louvois** contains one of the most beautiful fountains in Paris, which represents the four "female" rivers of France – La Loire, La Seine, La Garonne and La Saône.

GLORIOUS *GALERIES*

The area between the Palais Royal and Rue du Faubourg-Montmartre is laced with picturesque covered shopping arcades. The 20 or so *galeries* represent a fraction of the number that existed in the early 19th century. By the 1840s there were over 100 such *passages*, built by speculators who snapped up the land of the dispossessed aristocracy that came onto the market after the Revolution, and making imaginative use of the new technologies of the era with their combination of iron and glass to create a light, airy, and yet enclosed space. They became the ideal places in which to discover novelties, inventions and the latest

BELOW: the graceful Fontaine Louvois.

fashions, while keeping out of the
city's mud-splashed, carriage-laden
thoroughfares.

Galeries Vivienne and Colbert

The best-preserved and most elegant
of these shopping arcades is **Galerie
Vivienne** ⓫, first opened in 1826,
which has a fine mosaic floor, intricate brass lamps, graceful glass

canopies and restored wooden shop
fronts. It has been colonised by art
galleries, upmarket clothes designers, restaurants and a very pretty tearoom, A Priori Thé. The adjoining
Galerie Colbert has a spectacular
glass dome. Formerly an annexe of
the Bibliothèque Nationale, it has
been renovated to house a variety of
art institutions.

Victory Square

Adjacent to these arcades is the **Place
des Victoires** ⓬, an archetypal royal
square designed in 1685 by Louis
XIV's architect Jules Hardouin
Mansart as a backdrop for the equestrian statue of his patron the Sun
King (a bronze copy from 1822 –
revolutionaries destroyed the original). The square became a model for
squares across France. It was designed
to give the impression of an entirely
enclosed space, but this effect was
destroyed by the opening up of Rue
Etienne Marcel in 1883. Nowadays

a large number of its surrounding mansions are occupied by designer boutiques (Apostrophe, Mercadel, Kenzo and more).

Heading south down Rue Croix-des-Petits-Champs for about five minutes, you reach the most beautiful and atmospheric passageway in Paris, **Galerie Véro-Dodat** ⑬ (opposite Rue Montesquieu), with polished mahogany facades, brass lamps and skylights all beautifully preserved. It is named after the duo of wealthy pork butchers who financed the arcade's construction in 1826, fitting it with the new technology of the day: gas lighting. One of its main attractions is the picture-perfect brasserie the Café de l'Epoque.

EAT

A Priori Thé (tel: 01 42 97 48 75), in the Galerie Vivienne, is an elegant *salon de thé* that spills out into the gallery's main passageway. As well as teas and coffees, it serves light snacks and a very good cheesecake.

LEFT: the Dalamain bookshop has been in its current location in front of the Comédie Française since 1906.

SHOPPING

The area around the Louvre has its fair share of designer names, a shopping mall underneath the said museum and a branch of one of France's most popular department stores.

Accessories

Antoine
10 avenue de l'Opéra, 1st.
Tel: 01 42 96 01 80
Opened in 1745, this small shop is primarily known for its wide selection of umbrellas but also sells canes with decorative tops, fans, scarves and gloves.

Department Store

Colette
213 rue St-Honoré, 1st.
Tel: 01 55 35 33 90
www.colette.fr
This "lifestyle boutique" or "concept store" sources the coolest prod-

ucts from around the world – from books to music and from clothes to food. Prices range from a few euros to a few thousand euros.

Monoprix
21 avenue de l'Opéra,1st.
Tel: 01 42 61 78 08
There is a good, affordable range of everyday clothes, beauty and bath products, food and household items in this national chain. You'll find a store in most parts of the city.

Food

Michel Cluizel
201 rue St-Honoré, 1st.
Tel: 01 42 44 11 66
www.cluizel.com
Michel Cluizel has been making chocolates since 1948 and his creations are now sold around the world. His *premier cru* chocolate bars made with the cocoa beans

from single plantations are especially good.

Gifts

Nature et Découvertes
Le Carrousel du Louvre, 99 rue de Rivoli, 1st.
Tel: 01 47 03 47 43
This French chain aims to reconnect city dwellers with nature and sells natural and environmentally-friendly products including walking gear, gardening items, children's toys, skincare and home decoration.

Serge Lutens
142 galerie de Valois, Jardins du Palais Royal, 1st.
Tel: 01 47 48 95 89
Serge Lutens used to work for Japanese brand Shiseido but now has his own range of luxury perfumes and make-up. *Jeu de peau* smells like freshly-baked bread while *Sa majesté la rose* lives up to its name.

Jewellery

Les Minéraux
Le Carrousel du Louvre, 99 rue de Rivoli, 1st.
Tel: 01 42 60 05 40
From turquoise to amethyst, this shop sells jewellery made with crystals from around the world and has something to suit most pockets. There is usually a good selection of fossils too.

Shoes

Pierre Hardy
156 galerie de Valois, Jardins du Palais Royal, 1st.
Tel: 01 42 60 59 75
www.pierrehardy.com
Paris-born Hardy has designed shoe collections for Dior, Hermès and Balenciaga as well as the first capsule shoe collection for GAP. His own much-coveted women's and men's ranges are found here.

BEST RESTAURANTS, BARS AND CAFES

Restaurants

Corsican

A Casaluna
6 rue de Beaujolais, 1st
Tel: 01 42 60 05 11
L & D daily.
€€ (set menu) €€€ (à la carte)
28 [p336, B4]
This little corner of Corsica, the French-owned island in the Mediterranean, offers regional specialities in rustic-yet-stylish surroundings. Try the *figatellu* (sausage) followed by goat cheese with fig jam. There is live traditional music on Sunday evenings.

Fast Food

La Ferme Opéra
55–7 rue St-Roch, 1st
Tel: 01 40 20 12 12
Open: daily until 8pm (Sat & Sun until 7pm).
€ **29** [p334, A4]

Most of the ingredients are organic. On the menu you'll find salads, sandwiches, soups, a hot *plat du jour* and savoury tarts with options for vegetarians.

Oh Mon Cake!
154 rue St-Honoré, 1st
Tel: 01 42 60 31 84
Open: daily 11.30am–8.30pm.
€ **30** [p336, B1]
This more-stylish-than-most fast-food outlet is a fun and funky place to have lunch. Choose from an all-day menu of homemade soup, sandwiches, salads and a few hot dishes before trying the yummy cakes. Vegetarians won't go hungry.

French

L'Absinthe
24 place du Marché, 1st
Tel: 01 49 26 90 04
www.restaurantabsinthe.com
Open: L Mon–Fri, D Mon–Sat.

€€€ **31** [p336, A1]
Although they don't serve absinthe here and it is more chic than bohemian, it is still a lot of fun. The well-prepared bistro-style food includes chestnut velouté, crayfish ravioli and pear tatin with walnut sauce and caramel. The terrace is one of the best in Paris, and there are exhibits of contemporary artists (works for sale).

L'Ardoise
28 rue du Mont-Thabor, 1st
Tel: 01 42 96 28 18
www.lardoise-paris.com
Open: L Tue–Sat, D Tue–Sun.
€€ **32** [p336, A1]
A successful, modern bistro, which offers a good-value menu written on a blackboard – the *ardoise* in question. The typical bistro cooking is careful, even if the surroundings are rather utilitarian.

Le Fumoir
6 rue de l'Amiral-de-Coligny, 1st
Tel: 01 42 92 00 24
Open: L & D daily, Br Sun.
€€ (set menu), €€€ (à la carte)
33 [p336, B2]
With an admirable location facing the eastern facade of the Louvre, spacious, sophisticated Le Fumoir is renowned for shaking some of the best cocktails in town, including a remarkable choice of martinis. Come lunch and dinner it morphs into a restaurant serving light pan-European cooking (monkfish with peas, sea bass with ginger, rack of lamb and polenta), with a popular Sunday brunch.

Le Grand Véfour
17 rue de Beaujolais, 1st
Tel: 01 42 96 56 27
Open: L & D Mon–Fri.
€€€€ **34** [p336, B1]
Hiding under the arches of the Palais Royal is one of the most beautiful restaurants in Paris. Le Grand Véfour opened its doors in 1784 and has fed the likes of Napoleon and Victor Hugo. Today it serves grand classic haute cuisine – lobster salad, oxtail parmentier and clever desserts – in the hands of imaginative chef Guy Martin.

Restaurant du Palais Royal
110 galerie de Valois, 1st
Tel: 01 40 20 00 27
Open: L & D daily

LEFT: The grand Le Nemours on Place Colette is a fabulous café for people watching.

Price includes dinner and a half-bottle of house wine:

€ = under €25
€€ = €25–40
€€€ = €40–60
€€€€ = more than €60

€€€€ ⑤ [p334, B4]
The most attractive terrace on the Palais Royal and the finest of the restaurants circling the inner gardens. The food is not wildly imaginative but lives up to the view. The menu features langoustine cappuccino and red mullet with polenta.

Japanese

Kinugawa
9 rue du Mont-Thabor, 1st
Tel: 01 42 60 65 07
Open: L & D Mon–Sat.
€€€ (set menu) €€€€ (à la carte)
㊱ [p336, A1]
Paris has some seriously good Japanese restaurants, and this is one of the best and longest-established – a firm favourite with film stars, too. Each of the set menus is a good introduction to its prowess: faultless quality and presentation in dishes like turbot sashimi and egg custard studded with gingko nuts and chunks of whitebait.

Takara
14 rue Molière, 1st
Tel: 01 42 96 08 38
Open: L & D Tue–Fri, D Sat–Sun.
€€€ (set menu) €€€€ (à la carte)
㊲ [p336, B1]
Another superb Japanese, this one is the city's oldest: it's been in business since 1958. The specialities here, not readily available at other addresses in Paris, are the communal hotpots shabu shabu and sukiyaki, in which diners cook the ingredients themselves at the table. Not cheap, but well worth the outlay.

Bars and Cafés

Café Marly
Palais du Louvre, Cour Napoléon, 93 rue Rivoli.
Tel: 01 49 26 06 60.
Open: L & D daily (until 2am).
⑫ [p336, B1]
With views of the Louvre Pyramid, this designer museum café is abuzz with Parisian intelligentsia and tourists. The food, modern and light, is prepared to a high standard, but steeply priced. You may have to wait for a seat.

Jean-Paul Hévin – Chocolate Bar
231 rue St-Honoré, 1st.
Tel: 01 55 35 35 96.
Open: L Mon–Sat (noon–7pm).
⑬ [p336, A4]

The main reason to come here is to sample this master chocolate-maker's wonderful cake creations but there are omelettes and salads at lunchtime if you need something more substantial. Remember to buy some chocolates in the downstairs shop.

Juvéniles
47 rue de Richelieu, 1st.
Tel: 01 42 97 46 49.
Open: Mon–Sat noon–11pm.
⑭ [p336, B1]
Popular wine bar run by British ex-pat Tim Johnston, who offers a truly special selection of wines as well as tapas, simple *plats du jour* and a cheeseboard that celebrates the great British Stilton.

ABOVE: having lunch in Galerie Vivienne.
RIGHT: celebrated restaurant Le Grand Véfour.

THE LOUVRE

The largest museum in the world is a matchless treasure trove of paintings, sculpture, decorative art and antiquities - with an architecturally-stunning new wing.

The Musée National du Louvre has something for everyone. The palace that houses it is in itself a building of breathtaking beauty, and its galleries form a labyrinth of corridors. Getting lost may be a good way to find unexpected gems, but wander for too long without direction and you might miss even the major collections. Use the map on the right, or pick up one showing current exhibitions at the information desk on your way in. If it all gets too much, you can leave the museum and return on the same day, or you can rest and get a bite to eat at one of the Louvre's cafés and restaurants (one of the best is Café Marly, with a terrace overlooking the pyramid, see page 139). The museum also has some excellent shops selling souvenirs – but don't try to see everything in one day; go back again, and get lost in a different place.

ABOVE: the most famous painting of all: the *Mona Lisa*.

The Essentials

Address: www.louvre.fr
Tel: 01 40 20 50 50
Opening Hrs: Wed–Mon 9am–6pm, Wed, Fri until 9.45pm; closed Tues
Admission Fee: charge
Transport: Palais Royal-Musée du Louvre

Ground Floor

Near Eastern Antiquites

Islamic Art (open mid 2012)

Sculptures

Egyptian Antiquities

Greek, Etruscan and Roman Antiquities

History of the Louvre, The Medieval Louvre

Arts of Africa, Asia, Oceania and the Americas

Lower Ground Floor

THE HIGHLIGHTS

The Seated Scribe (2500–2350 BC)
This Ancient Egyptian figure is made from painted limestone and alabaster, with eyes of rock crystal (Sully, 1st floor).
Persian Winged Bull glazed tiles (c.500 BC)
A glazed, moulded relief from the palace of the Persian king Darius I at Susa (present-day Iran).
The Venus de Milo (c.2nd century BC)
The iconic Greek marble statue is on display in a gallery parallel to the Galerie des Antiquités.
Virgin and Child in Majesty (c.1270) by Cimabue
This Early Renaissance masterpiece was acquired by Napoleon (Denon, 1st floor).
Venus and the Graces Presenting Gifts to a Young Woman (c.1483) by Sandro Botticelli
One of a pair of frescoes from the Villa Lemmi near Florence, thought to have been commissioned for a wedding (Denon, 1st floor).
Mona Lisa (1503–6) by Leonardo da Vinci
The most famous Renaissance smile is better-displayed than ever, in a purpose-built new gallery.
The Rebellious Slave (1513–5) by Michelangelo
One of a pair of unfinished sculptures intended for the tomb of Pope Julius II (Denon, ground floor).
The Card Cheat (c.1635) by Georges de la Tour
A rich but unworldly young man falls in with a gang of card-sharps (French 17th-century painting; Sully, 2nd floor).
The Astronomer (1668) and *The Geographer* (1668–9) by Vermeer
Painted by Vermeer to celebrate the progress of science in Europe in the 17th century (Richelieu, 2nd floor).
The Bather (1808) by Ingres
This celebrated figure was reused by Ingres 50 years later for his painting *The Turkish Bath* (French 19th-century painting; Sully, 2nd floor).
Raft of the Medusa (1816) by Géricault
A stirring vision of suffering based on a true story of shipwreck and cannibalism (Denon, 1st floor).
Liberty Leading the People (1830) by Delacroix
Iconic painting of the July Revolution by the leader of Romanticism (Denon, 1st floor).

ABOVE: The *Martyrdom of St Sebastian* (c.1495), by Pietro Perugino.

The Main Collections

Egyptian antiquities
The collection spans the period from the 4th millennium BC to the 4th–6th centuries AD.
Oriental antiquities and Islamic arts
The collection is mainly from the eastern Mediterranean, and holds the oldest item in the museum – a 7,000-year-old neolithic statue from Ain Ghezal.
Greek, Roman & Etruscan antiquities
A comprehensive collection that includes the mythical *Venus de Milo* and the *Three Graces*.
French painting 17th–19th century
Works are arranged in chronological order, from the Late Gothic period to the mid-19th century.
French sculpture
French sculpture dominates the collection in the courtyards of the Richelieu wing.
Italian and Spanish painting
The Italian galleries contain early masterpieces, but the Spanish collection is patchy.
Northern Schools
Six new rooms show Northern European paintings of the 18th and 19th centuries.
Decorative arts
One of the least-known aspects of the Louvre is the extensive decorative arts collection.
Graphic arts
The Louvre has a vast stock of drawings and engravings by Michelangelo, Raphael, Dürer and more, which are shown in changing exhibitions.

Below: an Egyptian relief.

Second Floor

	French Paintings		Objets d'Art
	French Drawings & Prints		Paintings
	German, Flemish and Dutch Paintings		Prints and Drawings
	German, Flemish and Dutch Drawings		
	Egyptian Antiquities		
	Greek, Etruscan and Roman Antiquities		

First Floor

EGYPTIAN ANTIQUITIES AND ISLAMIC ARTS

The museum's spectacular Egyptian collection is very popular. Its core originates from the victory spoils of Napoleon's Egyptian campaign of 1798. The collection was subsequently expanded, largely through the efforts of the famous Egyptologist Jean-François Champollion (1790–1832), the first person to decipher hieroglyphics. Beyond the pink granite *Giant Sphinx*, insights into Egyptian life and the Nile culture are given through a thematic presentation on the ground floor, followed by a chronological presentation on the first floor. The later rooms follow religion and funerary rites.

The oriental antiquities collection (essentially from the eastern Mediterranean) may be overshadowed by the Egyptian collection, but it is no less important. The most spectacular items are the reconstructions of palaces at Susa and Khorsabad. The palace of Persian king Darius I at Susa (in present-day Iran) was constructed in around 510 BC. Other highlights include Cypriot terracotta figures and stag-shaped vessels, Mycenaean pots with geometric decoration, carved ivory, chalcolithic vessels from the Negev and the Neolithic statue from Ain Ghezal, discovered in 1985.

RIGHT: dating probably from the 2nd century BC, the marble *Venus de Milo* with its serene gaze, soft curves and naturalistic drapery rivals the *Mona Lisa* as an icon of female beauty. She was discovered, minus her arms, on the island of Melos in 1820 and promptly purchased by the French government for 6,000 francs. Various authorities have suggested that her left hand might have been holding the golden apple that was presented to Venus by Paris of Troy.

GRANDS BOULEVARDS AND CHAMPS-ELYSÉES

This area is a paradise for shoppers and strollers, with giant stores and grand fashion houses, glittering gourmet palaces and chic modern cafés, celebrated monuments and intimate mansion-museums, all amid some of Paris's most magnificent vistas.

North of the Palais Royal lie the Grands Boulevards, a string of wide avenues running from east to west. Their oldest sections date from the 17th century, when Louis XIV tore down the medieval walls around Paris and created wide, open spaces bordered with trees for his subjects. In the 19th century, Baron Haussmann extended the string westwards along Boulevard Haussmann. The western boulevards became the preserve of the rich, while the east was the playground of the city's industrial workers, lined with vaudeville theatres, restaurants, bars, brothels and, later, cinemas. Today the boulevards are dominated by mass-market clothing chains and discount outlets, but if you look up, the plate-glass traces of Second Empire extravagance can be seen in the ornate balconies and facades.

THE GRANDEST AVENUE

To the west, at a haughty distance from the populist strip, is the grandest of Parisian avenues, the Champs-Elysées, begun by Le Nôtre in 1667 as an extension of the Tuileries.

Initially the promenade reached only as far as the Rond-Point des Champs-Elysées; over 100 years passed before the rest, stretching up to the Arc de Triomphe, was completed. Its reputation has ebbed and flowed with the centuries: today, chic restaurants, cafés and nightclubs are joining the fashion and luxury goods shops that appeared there through the 1990s, heralding the monumental avenue's comeback as one of the world's premier shopping destinations.

Main Attractions
PALAIS GARNIER
GRANDS MAGASINS
PLACE VENDÔME
LA MADELEINE
RUE DU FAUBOURG-ST-HONORÉ
PLACE DE LA CONCORDE
THE CHAMPS-ELYSÉES
GRAND PALAIS
PETIT PALAIS
ARC DE TRIOMPHE

Maps and Listings
MAP, PAGE 118
SHOPPING, PAGE 156
RESTAURANTS, PAGE 158
ACCOMMODATION, PAGE 301

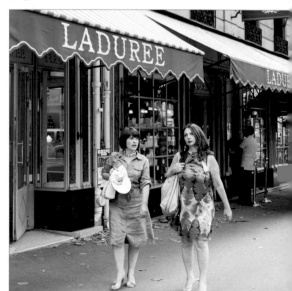

LEFT: the Champs-Elysées is often referred to as the most beautiful avenue in the world. **RIGHT:** Ladurée tearoom, a true Parisian institution.

ABOVE: the opulent
Opéra Garnier.

*When it was built, the
Palais Garnier was the
largest performance
venue in the city. It has
1,991 seats, 334 boxes,
1,606 doors, 7,593
keys, 450 fireplaces
and 6,319 steps.*

ALONG THE BOULEVARDS TO THE OPÉRA

Traces of the Grands Boulevards' early pomp can be seen in one of the easternmost sections, Boulevard St-Denis (around Strasbourg St-Denis Métro), in the two triumphal arches erected by Colbert in the 1670s in honour of Louis XIV's military victories, the **Porte St-Denis** and **Porte St-Martin**. When they were built they stood on the very edge of the city, and greeted new arrivals from the north.

Musée Grévin ⓮

Address: 10 boulevard Montmartre
www.grevin.com
Tel: 01 47 70 85 05
Opening Hrs: opening times vary throughout the year
Entrance Fee: charge
Transport: Grands Boulevards

Heading westwards, the first place of interest, especially if you have kids in tow, is Paris's venerable wax museum. It's full of cheerfully incompatible figures – from Marie-Antoinette and Gandhi to virtual heroine Lara Croft, Elton John and of course national football hero Zinédine Zidane – and a hall of mirrors. The lavish decor of this century-old establishment is a confection of Venetian Rococo, rosewood and marble, and the staircase by Rives is an architectural gem.

To the left of the Grévin is the **Passage Jouffroy**, with a shop selling cinema books (many in English and/ or out of print) and memorabilia, antique silver and the old-fashioned, affordable Hôtel Chopin. Next door is the soothing **Café Zephyr**, one of few cafés with style on the Grands Boulevards.

Across the busy boulevard is the **Passage des Panoramas ⓯**, one of the earliest of the covered arcades. It was opened in 1800 on the site of a former aristocratic mansion, and Parisians flocked here to see the giant painted panoramas of different cities that were exhibited in two great rotundas. The shop **Stern Graveur** has been engraving fine notepaper and wedding invitations since 1840; other shops sell lingerie, floaty clothes, vintage vinyl and old postcards, but above all this *passage* is a haven for philatelists, with half a dozen specialist stamp dealers.

La Bourse 16

Address: place de la Bourse
www.palaisbrongniart.com
Tel: 01 83 92 20 20

Emerging from the arcades, head south to Paris's imposing former stock exchange, also known as **Palais Brongniart** after its architect Alexandre Brongniart. Built in 1808, the grand colonnaded building is one of the most distinctive neoclassical constructions of the Napoleonic era. It now hosts events and conferences and is not open to the public.

Rue du Quatre-Septembre leads from here to Place de l'Opéra. This broad square is lined by elegant shops, luxury hotels and cafés, notably **Café de la Paix**, where you can join the chic clientele enjoying coffee and croissants, or a glass of

wine and oysters later in the day. Just remember, the prices match the luxurious setting.

Palais Garnier – Opéra National de Paris 17

Address: place de l'Opéra
www.operadeparis.fr
Tel: for visits 08 92 89 90 90
Opening Hrs: daily 10am–5pm, guided tours in English Wed, Sat, Sun 11.30am, 2.30pm (daily July–Aug)
Entrance Fee: charge for guided tours
Transport: Opéra

Soaring above the square is Paris's celebrated, now fully restored opera house, the Palais Garnier. It is now only part of the Opéra National de Paris with the Opéra Bastille, which has taken charge of larger, more ambitious opera and ballet productions, but the newcomer can never challenge the original "Paris Opera" in the style stakes. In 1860 architect Charles Garnier was commissioned by Napoleon III to build an opera house for the imperial capital, and his lavish designs were wholly in tune with the pomp and opulence that characterised the

A short walk from the Palais Garnier is another, smaller opera house, the Opéra Comique (Place Boieldieu, tel: 01 42 44 45 40, www.operacomique.com). This very pretty venue hosts a mixture of chamber orchestras and musicals.

BELOW: Place du Caire.

Egypt-sur-Seine

Place du Caire, in the Sentier garment district – just north of Sentier Métro, up rue d'Aboukir – is one of Paris's curios, off the tourist trail. This was the site of the so-called *Cour des Miracles* in the 1600s, home to beggars who spent their days around the city, apparently disabled, blind or deaf. At night they returned here, and immediately shed their wooden legs and eye patches – hence the "miracles". Not until 1667 did Louis XIV's police chief La Reynie clean up this notorious den of iniquity of all kinds. Today the square is notable for the bustle of multiracial porters lugging rolls of cloth or racks of finished clothes between workshops, as well as its mementoes of Napoleon's campaign in Egypt: the north side is covered with sphinxes and hieroglyphics. On the facade of 2 place du Caire are three sculpted heads of Hathor, the goddess of love, music, dance and fertility, who is remarkable by her cow's ears; and in the middle of the panel of hieroglyphs just below the roofline is the face of a man with an enormous nose – not Gérard Depardieu, but a local 19th-century scoundrel called Bouginier; Hugo mentions him in *Les Misérables*.

Rue St-Honoré, and its even more elegant continuation west of Rue Royale, Rue du Faubourg St-Honoré, form the traditional heartland of Parisian high fashion. St-Honoré, beginning at the Palais Royal, has cutting-edge boutiques as well as big names like John Galliano; the really grand fashion houses (Dior, Guy Laroche, Hermès) are clustered together on Rue du Faubourg. The concentration of chic is just dazzling.

ABOVE: pomp and lavishness at the Opéra.
BELOW: fashion emporium Galeries Lafayette.

Second Empire, creating a style in themselves.

The facade and exterior are covered in sculptures of great composers and allegorical figures representing spirits of music and dance, including voluptuous nudes that caused a scandal when first unveiled. The profusion of marble and gilt inside is almost oppressive in its excess, but the glamour of the Opéra's foyers is undeniable. The grand staircase was conceived by Garnier as the ultimate celebrity catwalk: "Everything is designed so that the parade of spectators become themselves a performance." The five-tiered auditorium, dripping in red velvet and gilt, is dominated by a 6-tonne chandelier, which famously crashed down on the audience during a performance in 1896. The auditorium ceiling was painted by Marc Chagall in 1964, commissioned by André Malraux. The visit also takes in the **library** and **museum**, with scores, portraits, costumes and sets.

Behind the Opéra is the **Musée du Parfum Fragonard** ⓲ (9 rue Scribe; www.fragonard.com; tel: 01 47 42 04

56; Mon–Sat 9am–6pm, Sun until 5pm; charge), a compact museum tracing 5,000 years of perfumery. A heady fragrance permeates the air, in a beautifully restored 19th-century town house. Nearby at 39 boulevard des Capucines is the **Théâtre des Capucines** ⑲ (Mon–Sat 9am–6pm), where legendary music-hall singer and actress Arletty began her career in the 1930s, and which is now also owned by Fragonard and has a perfume museum.

Grands magasins

The area just behind the Opéra, along Boulevard Haussmann, is dominated by the *grands magasins* (department stores). **Galeries Lafayette** and **Printemps**, both established in the late 19th century, have remained rivals ever since. Galeries Lafayette is especially famed for its splendid Art Nouveau central hall, topped with a vast stained-glass dome (see pages 59).

THE LUXURY QUARTER

One essential side of Paris: the streets and squares southwest of the Opéra are the number-one home of the fine foods, high fashion and exquisite jewellery that have made the city world capital of luxury for two centuries.

Place Vendôme ⑳

Centre of a grand vista between Palais Garnier and Rue de Rivoli, octagonal Place Vendôme is perhaps the smartest square in Paris. Laid out in 1699 by Colbert to glorify Louis XIV – whose equestrian statue was subsequently replaced in the centre by an imitation of Trajan's Column, glorifying Napoleon's exploits – it is now home to luxury jewellers and designers such as Boucheron, Van Cleef & Arpels, Bulgari, Cartier, Chaumet and Dior. Here, too, are big financial institutions such as the J.P. Morgan merchant bank, and of course the Ritz, at No. 15. The luxury hotel

ABOVE: the Opéra's five-tiered auditorium.
BELOW: Printemps, along with its rival Galeries Lafayette, are the two behemoth department stores on Boulevard Haussmann.

It's only natural that the jewellery shops on Place Vendôme should attract the interest of the criminal fraternity. A famous robbery took place in 1970, not in real life but on film: the heist in Jean-Pierre Melville's gangster classic Le Cercle Rouge, carried out by Alain Delon, Yves Montand and Gian Maria Volontè, is one of the best ever filmed.

is now most famous as the place where Princess Diana had her last meal before her fatal car crash in August 1997.

Eglise de la Madeleine ㉑

Address: place de la Madeleine
Tel: 01 44 51 69 00
Opening Hrs: daily 9.30am – 7pm
Entrance Fee: free
Transport: Madeleine

From just south of Place Vendôme chic, boutique-laden Rue St-Honoré leads to the church of **Sainte-Marie-de-la-Madeleine**, rising up amidst roaring traffic and expensive shops. This giant neoclassical temple was commissioned as a self-aggrandising exercise by Napoleon, but more recently has become a favourite venue for celebrity weddings and funerals. In the square around it the mouth-watering displays at foodstores **Fauchon** and **Hédiard** are tourist attractions in their own right.

Place de la Concorde ㉒

Rue Royale runs from La Madeleine to Place de la Concorde, designed for

Louis XV by Jacques-Ange Gabriel as a hub of spectacular vistas to north, south, east and west. The square has been the site of many historical events since its completion in 1763, notably the decapitation of Louis XVI by the Revolutionaries in 1793. Majestic in the middle of the traffic chaos, the central obelisk was a gift from the Viceroy of Egypt in 1829; the 3,300-year-old column, weighing 220 tonnes, took four years to reach Paris. On the north side of the square is a pair of grand neoclassical mansions, flanking the Rue Royale: the one on the right is the French Navy Ministry, the other is the opulent Hôtel de Crillon, where Benjamin Franklin signed the Treaty of Friendship between the newly formed United States of America and King Louis XVI in 1778.

THE CHAMPS-ELYSÉES ㉓

Initiated by Louis XIV in 1667, the Champs-Elysées was originally laid out by landscape architect Le Nôtre to create a visual extension of the Tuileries gardens running west from the Louvre. The broad avenue, lined

BELOW: the glitzy Ritz hotel on Place Vendôme.

Vedettes of Vendôme

Place Vendôme was home to two movers and shakers from the worlds of music and fashion. Although in Paris since 1831, the Polish composer Frederic Chopin spent the last year of his life – 1849 – in an apartment at 12 place Vendôme where he died aged just 39; the luxury Italian jeweller Bulgari occupies this building today. On the opposite side of the square is The Ritz, where fashion designer Coco Chanel lived from World War II until her death at the age of 87 in 1971; the suite she occupied, consisting of two bedrooms, two bathrooms and a living room, is available to guests for almost €10,000 per night.

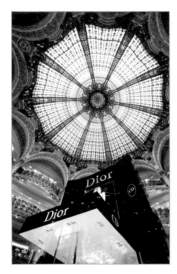

with elegant gardens and rows of trees, was continued after the completion of the Arc de Triomphe in 1836. By the 1900s the Champs, in contrast to the rather downmarket Grands Boulevards, had reached a zenith of popularity and elegance, attracting stylish and moneyed types from all over the world to linger on its animated café terraces.

The sophisticated spectacle on the avenue evaporated in World War I, but made a brief and giddy comeback during the 1920s. This was followed by the Depression, World War II and, post-war, traffic problems, as the Champs shifted from a luxury address to a commercial one distinguished by cinemas and airline offices in the 1950s, '60s and '70s. By the 1980s it was quite dowdy, with an atmosphere comparable to a tatty shopping mall.

Determined to resurrect the area, Jacques Chirac, then Mayor of Paris, budgeted the equivalent of E75 million to renovate, modernise and beautify the Champs: street parking was replaced by underground car parks; new street furniture was added, including handsome teak benches and retro Art Nouveau newspaper kiosks; dove-grey granite paving stones were laid; and the number of trees doubled. Parisians gave the avenue a second look. Today, the Champs is considered not only elegant again, but a cool place to hang out.

The two fountains designed by German architect Hittorf on the left and right of the central obelisk in Place de la Concorde are modelled after those of St Peter's Square in Rome.

ABOVE: the stunning Art Nouveau stained-glass dome of the Galeries. **BELOW:** Place Vendôme at dusk.

ABOVE: the Place de la Concorde fountains are at their resplendent best at night.
BELOW: the Eglise de la Madeleine's bronze doors bear reliefs representing the Ten Commandments.

Between the Champs-Elysées and Boulevard Haussmann at 2 rue Lamennais, the Fondation Jerome-Seydoux Pathé (tel: 01 71 72 31 26), of Pathé News fame, is a must visit for fans of cinema history. It houses a collection of film-related items including posters, scripts, photographs and cameras – in the 1900s Pathé was the world's leading maker of film equipment –and is open to visitors by appointment only.

Browsing the Champs

The main shopping stretch of the Champs-Elysées runs from the Rond-Point to the Arc de Triomphe. Landmark stores are the **Virgin Megastore** at Nos 52–60, where you can sample CDs until midnight; **Guerlain** (No. 68), with its Rococo facade and sumptuous interior; the Aladdin's cave of beauty products, **Sephora** (No. 70); and **Louis Vuitton**, at No. 101.

In the last few years a number of swanky concept stores have opened up as well, including one from luxury leather goods purveyor **Lancel** at No. 127, and a couple, bizarrely enough, by car manufacturers Toyota and Renault. The latter, the **Atelier Renault** at No. 53, features a swish café that serves a good choice of cocktails and light meals and has a fine view of passersby. Most of the grander designer outlets are concentrated around Avenue Montaigne and Avenue George V. This is fashion land, where prices for the majority are prohibitive, but window shopping is free. Most of the brands here are

established megastars – the likes of Dior, Chanel and Prada – but in the last few years they've been joined by younger, hipper labels **Paul & Joe**, at 2 avenue Montaigne; **Jimmy Choo**, at No. 34; and upmarket children's brand **Bonpoint**, at No. 49. The Montaigne Market, at No. 57, is the avenue's sole multi-brand emporium, stocking an ever-changing selection in different price brackets.

On Rue François 1er (No. 18) is a deluxe branch of boutique **Zadig &**

decorated with Art Nouveau motifs. Since reopening, it has been the venue for all manner of events and activities: DJs, a light installation, a Christmas funfair and fashion shows, as well as major art exhibitions.

The Grand Palais is also home to the **Palais de la Découverte** (www. palais-decouverte. fr; tel: 01 56 43 20 20; Tue–Sat 9.30am–6pm, Sun 10am–7pm; charge), the city's original science museum. It covers astronomy, biology, chemistry, physics and earth sciences through interactive experiments. Sadly, there's very little labelling in English.

Musée du Petit Palais ㉕

Address: avenue Winston Churchill
www. petitpalais.paris.fr
Tel: 01 53 43 40 00
Opening Hrs: Tue–Sun 10am–6pm
Entrance Fee: free

Above: the Grand Palais, a Belle Epoque masterpiece, hosts several major art exhibitions every year.
Left: the Hermès flagship store on Rue du Faubourg St-Honoré, a street so chic that one of the luxury brand's fine fragrances, 24 Faubourg, is named after the exclusive address.
Below: the Champs-Elysées seen from the top of the Arc de Triomphe.

Voltaire, with limited-edition pieces not found in its other stores.

Galeries Nationales du Grand Palais ㉔

Address: 3 avenue du Général Eisenhower
www.grandpalais.fr
Tel: 01 44 13 17 17
Opening Hrs: Wed–Mon 10am–8pm, Wed until 10pm
Entrance Fee: charge
Transport: Champs-Elysées-Clémenceau

Between the Champs and the Seine stands the huge, glass-domed **Grand Palais,** built for the 1900 World Fair, but which for decades has served as central Paris's largest exhibition centre. The building's grand nave closed in 1993 after a metal rivet fell from its roof, but after more than a decade of work it reopened in 2006 as good as new: a glorious Belle Epoque masterpiece of glass and iron, covering a vast open space collection of fine and decorative arts, and it too reopened in 2006 after being thoroughly refurbished. The renovation work has brought in a lot of extra natural light, which greatly benefits the eclectic collection that lives here. Its main strengths are paintings of the 19th and early 20th centuries, including works by Bonnard, Cézanne, Courbet and Sisley; but there are also Greek and Roman antiquities, icons, tapestries, ceramics and sculpture, and some fabulous Art Nouveau furniture.

Arc de Triomphe

Address: place Charles-de-Gaulle
www.monuments-nationaux.fr
Tel: 01 55 37 73 77
Opening Hrs: Apr–Sept daily 10am–11pm, Oct–Mar until 10.30pm
Entrance Fee: charge
Transport: Charles de Gaulle-Etoile

Transport: Champs-Elysées-Clémenceau

Across Avenue Winston Churchill from the Grand Palais is its smaller neighbour, inspired by the Grand Trianon at Versailles with its polychrome marble, magnificent long gallery and arcaded garden. The Petit Palais houses the municipal

ABOVE: under the Arc at dusk.
RIGHT: Baron Haussmann.

Crowning the Champs-Elysées is this great memorial to megalomania. The Arc de Triomphe was commissioned by Napoleon in 1806, but the arch, ornately carved with heroic images of Revolutionary

Haussmann's Handiwork

Because they're so often described as "Haussmannian", it's frequently assumed that the buildings that went up in the French capital's mammoth restructuring between 1853 and 1870 were actually designed by Baron Georges-Eugène Haussmann (1809–91) himself. But Haussmann, then Prefect of Paris, was just the project's coordinator; he was not an architect by any means. Landscape architect Jean-Pierre Barrillet-Deschamps was responsible for designing the city's new parks while another architect, also called Deschamps, from Paris Map Services, designed the new avenues. In a curious twist of fate, his plans entailed the demolition of the building he was born in, to make way for the elegant boulevard that bears his name.

battles and the emperor's victories, was not completed until long after his death, in 1836. Napoleon's only chance to pass under it came when his body was triumphantly returned to Paris for reburial in Les Invalides in 1840. Beneath the arch is France's Tomb of the Unknown Soldier, laid to rest in 1920. Since 1923 an eternal flame has been here too, rekindled each evening at 6.30pm with a wreath-laying ceremony. The platform above the arch can be reached via a lift, and offers one of the finest Paris views.

BELLE EPOQUE MANSIONS

Much of the old Paris that was swept away by Haussmann around his Grands Boulevards was replaced by opulent mansions typical of France's Belle Epoque, several of which now house intriguing small museums.

Musée Jacquemart-André ㉗

Address: 158 boulevard Haussmann
www.musee-jacquemart-andre.com

Tel: 01 45 62 11 59
Opening Hrs: daily 10am–6pm
Entrance Fee: charge
Transport: Miromesnil

This collection of art and furniture once belonged to wealthy collector Edouard André and his wife, erstwhile society portrait painter, Nélie Jacquemart. It includes a small Uccello masterpiece, *St George and the Dragon*, and works by Bellini, Donatello, Rembrandt, Titian, Boucher and David. The house and its ornate decor are also a magnificent example of Belle Epoque taste.

Parc Monceau ㉘

Opening Hrs: daily 7am–8pm, May–Aug until 10pm
Entrance Fee: free
Transport: Monceau

A 19th-century version of a theme park, with an English-style garden and lake, a fake Egyptian pyramid, Venetian bridge and Greek colonnade.

ABOVE: fine art at the Musée Jacquemart-André.
BELOW: the grand spiralling staircase of the Musée Jacquemart-André.

SHOPPING

This upmarket area has attracted some of the world's biggest designer names but there are still affordable shopping opportunities along the *Grands Boulevards*.

Louis Vuitton
101 avenue des Champs-Elysées, 8th.
Tel: 01 53 57 52 00.
www.louisvuitton.com
The luxury luggage specialist has a bag, trunk or suitcase for every occasion but also clothes and shoes for men and women designed by Marc Jacobs.

Children

Pain d'Epices
29, 31, 33 Passage Jouffroy, 9th.
Tel: 01 47 70 08 68
From traditional wooden toys to dolls' houses and from teddy bears to chris-

tening gifts, this shop in one of the city's covered arcades will delight young and old.

Clothing

Chanel
31 rue Cambon, 1st.
Tel: 01 44 50 66 00.
www.chanel.com
The original store of France's most famous designer where the famous boxy jackets and quilted bags were dreamed up. Nowadays, with Karl Lagerfeld in charge, you'll also find shoes, jewellery and beauty products here.
Christian Dior
30 avenue Montaigne, 8th.
Tel: 01 40 73 73 73.
www.dior.com
Now presided over by Belgian designer Raf Simons, Dior, famous for its post-war "new look", is still one of the world's

most coveted labels. The flagship store has both men's and women's fashion plus jewellery.
Promod
60 rue Caumartin, 9th.
Tel: 01 45 26 01 11.
www.promod.com
Similar to Spanish brand Zara, this French chain sells affordable women's fashions and swimwear. There are branches in most areas of the city.

Department Stores

Galeries Lafayette
40 boulevard Haussmann, 9th.
Tel: 01 42 82 34 56.
www.galerieslafayette.com
An entire floor devoted to lingerie and a food hall that stocks dozens of luxury brands as well as fine wines are just a couple of reasons to visit this massive department store.
Printemps
64 boulevard Haussmann, 9th.
Tel: 01 42 82 50 00.
www.printemps.com
The store is situated in three buildings on separate themes: L'Homme (men's fashion), La Maison (home) and La Mode (women's fashion) where there is a floor dedicated to the coolest brands, often featuring "pop-up" stores by various designers.

Food

Fauchon
24–26 place de la Madeleine, 8th.

Tel: 01 70 39 38 00.
www.fauchon.com
This luxury food store sells everything you'd need for a gourmet feast and even does ready-made meals and "executive lunchboxes" to take away. There are four in-house places to eat including a caviar bar.
La Maison du Chocolat
8 boulevard de la Madeleine, 9th.
Tel: 01 47 42 86 52.
www.lamaisonduchocolat.com
As well as pralines and ganaches, this top-notch chocolate maker also sells chocolate-flavoured *macarons*, *éclairs* and cakes. There are other branches in the city.

Gifts

FNAC
74 avenue des Champs-Elysées, 8th.
Tel: 0825 020 020
Books, music, DVDs, computers, MP3s, TVs and gaming equipment are all sold in this megastore, one of several in the city. You can also buy tickets for concerts here.

Jewellery

Cartier
13 rue de la Paix, 1st.
Tel: 01 58 18 23 00.
www.cartier.com
One of the world's finest jewellers and watchmakers also has a selection of accessories including bags, pens and sunglasses. Great for window shopping.

LEFT: a stunning creation from chocolatier La Maison du Chocolat.

Musée Nissim de Camondo 29

Address: 63 rue de Monceau
www.lesartsdecoratifs.fr
Tel: 01 53 89 06 40
Opening Hrs: Wed–Sun 10am–5.30pm
Entrance Fee: charge

Transport: Monceau

Overlooking the park, this stately home modelled on the Petit Trianon at Versailles was built for a wealthy Jewish banking family. Its remarkable collection of 18th-century tapestries, porcelain, objets d'art, furniture and paintings was left to the state in 1935 by the passionate collector Count Moïse de Camondo in memory of his son Nissim, killed in action in 1917.

Musée Cernuschi 30

Address: 7 avenue Velasquez
www.cernuschi.paris.fr
Tel: 01 53 96 21 50
Opening Hrs: Tue–Sun 10am–6pm
Entrance Fee: free

This is one of the most important collections of oriental art in Europe, thanks to financier Henri Cernuschi, who amassed his holdings in China and Japan in 1871–3 and then built this residence beside Parc Monceau to house them. Extensive renovation, completed in 2005, has brought more space and natural light to the army of terracotta tomb figures, bronze vessels, Buddhist statues and fine ceramics.

North of the Champs-Elysées at 55 rue du Faubourg Saint-Honoré is the Elysée Palace, the official home of the President of the French Republic; although President Hollande prefers to live in his own apartment in the 15th arrondissement and just has his office here. The building dates from 1722 and was designed by Armand-Claude Mollet for the Count of Evreux. Around the corner at 13 avenue de Marigny is the Hôtel de Marigny, which is used to house visiting dignitaries.

ABOVE: the Petit Palais's ornate Belle Epoque style.
BELOW: Parc Monceau's Greek colonnade.

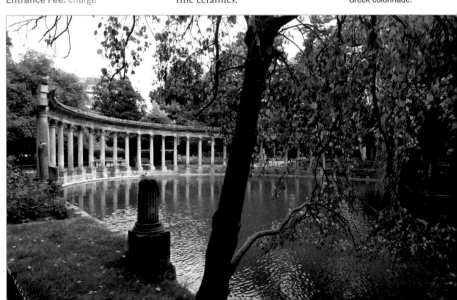

BEST RESTAURANTS, BARS AND CAFES

Restaurants

Danish

CPH
142 avenue des Champs-Elysées
Tel: 01 44 13 86 26
Open: L & D Mon–Fri.
€€€€ ❸ [p332, B2]
In a stylish dining room in the Maison du Danemark (Visit Denmark's office), chef Joël Veyssière serves up gourmet versions of Scandinavian specialities including rollmops and smoked salmon. There is a cheaper restaurant, Flora Danica, in the building too with breakfast and brunch on the menu.

French

Alain Ducasse au Plaza Athénée
25 avenue Montaigne, 8th
Tel: 01 53 67 65 00
www.plaza-athenee-paris.com
Open: L Thur–Fri, D Mon–Fri.
€€€€ ❸ [p332, C3]
Cooking elevated to art from France's first recipient of six Michelin stars (three apiece for two restaurants), in the hands of his acolyte, Christophe Moret. Expect truffles in abundance, but also superb vegetables from Provence, where Ducasse first made his name. The listed neo-Rococo decor has been rejuvenated with a shower of glittery crystals to match the scintillating cuisine and graceful service. Reservations essential.

L'Atelier de Joël Robuchon
133 avenue des Champs-Elysées, 8th
Tel: 01 47 23 75 75
www.joel-robuchon.net
Open: L & D daily.
€€€ (set menu) €€€€ ❹ (à la carte) [p332, B2]
The second 'atelier' from this Michelin-starred chef (the other is in St-Germain) is in the ultra-fashionable surrounds of the Publicis Drugstore, which also houses shops and a cinema. As well as sitting at a table, diners have the option of eating at the counter to watch the chefs at work. The meat, fish or vegetable skewers are quite affordable.

Brasserie Printemps
6th Floor, Printemps, 64 boulevard Haussmann, 9th
Tel: 01 42 82 58 84
www.printemps.com
Open: L & D (Thur until 10pm).
€€ (set menu) €€€ (à la carte)
❹ [p334, A3]
The main reason to come here is for the location –

LEFT: Ladurée is famed for its mouthwatering macaroons.

underneath the department store's listed glass dome. On the seasonal menus is a mix of traditional French and Italian dishes plus a good variety of ice creams and desserts.

Drouant
16–18 place Gaillon, 2nd
Tel: 01 42 65 15 16
www.drouant.com
Open: non-stop daily.
€€ (Sun brunch), €€€€ (à la carte) **42** [p334, A4]
This old stalwart has recently had a makeover, and it's now one of the most talked-about places in town. Star Alsace chef Antoine Westermann has revived the humble hors d'œuvre tradition here, so you can eat the food in more or less any order you feel like, and friendly sharing is encouraged. Dishes include Thai beef salad and a modish deconstructed version of eggs in mayonnaise.

Guy Savoy
18 rue Troyon, 1/th
Tel: 01 43 80 40 61
www.guysavoy.com
Open: L Tue–Fri, D Tue–Sat.
€€€€ **43** [p332, B2]
Savoy's imaginative haute cuisine has (belatedly) earned the highest Michelin rating. The son of a gardener, Savoy has an obsession with vegetables that anticipated the recent trend by more than a decade. He doesn't hesitate to pair truffles with lentils or artichokes.

Ladurée – Salon de Thé
16 rue Royale, 8th
Tel: 01 42 60 21 79
www.laduree.com
€ **44** [p332, C2]
This oh-so-civilised tearoom is a true Paris institution and a wonderful

place to start the shopping day. World-famous for its melt-in-the-mouth macaroons.

Lavinia
3 boulevard de la Madeleine, 1st
Tel: 01 42 97 20 27
Open: L Mon–Sat.
€€ **45** [p332, E3]
A restaurant/bar on the first floor of Paris's largest wine emporium. You can drink anything you buy with no corkage fee. The best approach is to order the simpler dishes and select a different glass of wine for each one with a little help from the expert sommeliers.

Aux Lyonnais
32 rue St-Marc, 2nd
Tel: 01 42 96 65 04
www.auxlyonnais.com
Open: L & D Tue–Fri, D only Sat.
€€€ **46** [p334, B3]
This pretty vintage bistro (opened 1890), with its *banquettes* and Belle Epoque floral tiles, has been transformed by superchef-entrepreneur Alain Ducasse to bring a modernised take on Lyonnais cooking. The iron casserole of slow-cooked seasonal vegetables is a must. Other specialities include crayfish and frogs' legs from the Dombes.

Market
15 avenue Matignon, 8th
Tel: 01 56 43 40 90
Open: L & D daily.
€€€ **47** [p332, D3]
Popular contemporary restaurant, run by globe-trotting star chef, Jean-Georges Vongerichten, next to the glamorous new Parisian headquarters of Christie's auctioneers. East-meets-West style preparations and an international crowd against a slick backdrop.

Savy
23 rue Bayard, 8th
Tel: 01 47 23 46 98
www.chezsavy.com
Open: L & D Mon–Fri.
€ (set menu), €€€ (à la carte) **48** [p332, C3]
Amid all the fashionable designer haunts around the Champs-Elysées, Savy remains resolutely traditional. The food focuses on the meaty, rustic cuisine of the Auvergne and Aveyron in central France, although excellent fish is brought in daily from Brittany.

Lebanese

Al Ajami
58 rue François 1er, 8th
Tel: 01 42 25 38 44
L & D daily.
€–€€ (set menu) €€€ (à la carte) **49** [p332, C3]
A vegetarian-friendly restaurant where diners are taken on a tour of flavours from the Middle East. Lamb (from Sisteron in Provence) features heavily – the *kefta* and *shish kebab* are particularly good – while the homemade ice cream – milk with pistachios – is a favourite for dessert. The dining room is smart and traditional and there's a terrace too.

Bars and Cafés

Café Jacquemart-André
158 boulevard Haussmann, 8th.
Tel: 01 45 62 04 44.
Open: Daily 11.45am–5.30pm.
15 [p332, D2]
This sumptuous café pulls in local residents as well as museum-goers. While waiting for your lunch salad to arrive (served with smoked salmon, breast of duck, etc.), look up at the *trompe l'œil* ceiling by Tiepolo, and a gal-

Price includes dinner and a half-bottle of house wine:

€ = under €25
€€ = €25–40
€€€ = €40–60
€€€€ = more than €60

lery of 17th-century faces staring down at you.

Café Le Nôtre
Pavillon Elysée, Carré Marigny, 10 avenue des Champs-Elysées, 8th.
Tel: 01 42 65 85 10.
Open: L & D daily.
16 [p332, D3]
This pretty, wedding-cake-style pavilion in the gardens of the Champs-Elysées offers lunch, dinner, afternoon tea and snacks. Famous for its pastries.

Café de la Ville
34 boulevard Bonne-Nouvelle, 10th.
Tel: 01 48 24 48 09.
Open: Non-stop daily.
17 [p334, C3]
The gang behind fashionable Oberkampf Café Charbon have expanded and refurbished their western outpost. The place now has a trendy clubbing area, a lounge and exhibition space. The mood is relaxed and buzzy, drinks are affordable and varied.

Kitty O'Shea's
10 rue des Capucines, 9th.
Tel: 01 42 96 02 99.
Open: L & D daily.
18 [p334, A4]
Lively Irish bar with traditional music on Sunday nights, a quiz on Wednesdays and screenings of Six Nations' rugby and Premiership football matches. Authentic decor and Irish bar staff. There is also a branch at 17 boulevard Gouvion St-Cyr, 17th.

THE ARC DE TRIOMPHE

Built by Napoleon to celebrate all of his military successes, the Triumphal Arch is the focal point of French national pride and visited by millions.

It's the most recognisable Paris landmark after the Eiffel Tower and, in the words of its website, "the most illustrious symbol of French history"; victory parades flowed through it in 1919 and 1944 (a few weeks later, aviator Charles Godefroy flew his biplane through the middle); Victor Hugo lay in state beneath it in 1885. Every year since 1880, the Bastille Day Military Parade has taken place on the morning of 14 July, starting at the Arc (bar for a few years in the 1970s when President Valéry Giscard-d'Estaing varied the route) and heading down the Champs-Elysées to the Place de la Concorde. However, it is not possible to march through the arch these days as the Tomb of the Unknown Soldier has lain beneath it since Armistice Day 1920; the tomb is marked by an eternal flame. Access for visitors is via an underpass; such is the traffic chaos encircling it at all times that crossing the road would be tantamount to suicide. The roof of the Arc is reached by a narrow staircase or a small lift (so not for those with claustrophobia), and the view from the top, out over Paris in all directions, is simply glorious.

ABOVE: carved on the inside of the monument are the names of the Generals who fought in the Napoleonic wars.

RIGHT: two of the four main sculptural groups on the exterior base of the Arc, *Le Triomphe de 1810* by Jean-Pierre Cortot (left) and *La Marseillaise* by François Rude (right).

BELOW: the view from the top is breathtaking; here the Eiffel Tower and Tour Montparnasse are visible in the distance.

The Essentials

Address: Place Charles-de-Gaulle www.monuments-nationaux.fr
Tel: 01 55 37 73 77
Opening Hrs: L daily 10am–10.30pm, Apr–Sept until 11pm
Entrance Fee: charge
Transport: Charles de Gaulle-Etoile

STANDING TALL

In conception, the Arc de Triomphe was a typical piece of Napoleonic self-advertisement, intended to honour the military triumphs of his armies. Although the monument was designed by Jean Chalgrin in 1806, inspired by the Arch of Titus in Rome, work didn't begin on it until 1809. It wasn't finished until 27 years later (laying the foundations alone took two years, and work was halted several times) – by which time Napoleon was dead. For all that, the names of his 128 major battles were carved on its sides, along with the names of the 660 generals who took part in them, and the entire structure is richly adorned with sculptures depicting battle scenes and allegories, of which the most famous is Rude's *Le Départ des Volontaires* (also known as *La Marseillaise*). It stands 50 metres (164ft) tall, set on the axis that runs from the Louvre, through the Arc du Carrousel and out west to the Grande Arche de la Défense.

ABOVE: an eternal flame burns above the Tomb of the Unknown Soldier, buried here in 1920 and honoured every Armistice Day.
LEFT: viewed from the air, it's easy to appreciate why the square around the Arc de Triomphe is called L'Etoile ("Star") – no fewer than 12 avenues radiate out from it.
BELOW: on major national festivities, such as Bastille Day and Armistice Day, an enormous tricolour is flown underneath the main arch.

MONTMARTRE

One of the great birthplaces of bohemia, cabaret and modern art, Montmartre threatens to surrender to its own clichés, without ever quite doing so. The maze of steep, narrow streets around the hill still have a unique atmosphere, and even seedy Pigalle has reinvented itself with a new sense of cool.

The "village" of Montmartre occupies the highest point of Paris, nestling on a hillside in the 18th *arrondissement*, north of the city centre. Extending from sometimes seedy yet always vibrant Place Pigalle in the south to the sugar-white cupolas of Sacré-Cœur, this urban village is an alluring huddle of small steep streets and hidden steps.

In parts Montmartre resembles a country hamlet, with ivy-clad cottages and cobbled squares. Elsewhere, neon, fast food, sex shows and tourist buses set the tone. Follow the golf caps up to Place du Tertre, filled with tourist bistros, tatty gift shops and would-be artists, and Montmartre will seem brash and commercial. Enter a narrow side street, veer down a deserted flight of steps and you will be alone, wandering in one of the city's most charismatic quarters.

MONTMARTRE'S BEGINNINGS

Montmartre has always stood slightly apart from the rest of Paris. Legend has it that in AD 250 the Romans decapitated St Denis, first bishop of Paris, and two priests on the hill. St Denis picked up his head and walked off with it to where the Basilica of St-Denis now stands (see page 280). The hill became known as *Mons Martyrium* (Martyrs' Mound). As local bar owners point out, people have been picking their heads out of the gutters of Montmartre ever since.

In the 12th century a Benedictine convent settled on the hill, and 400 years later Henri IV took shelter in it when laying siege to Paris in 1589. His only conquest of the campaign, it appears, was the 17-year-old abbess. The last Mother Superior here was guillotined during the Revolution at

Main Attractions
MOULIN ROUGE
PIGALLE
SACRÉ-CŒUR
PLACE DU TERTRE
ESPACE SALVADOR DALÍ
MUSÉE DE MONTMARTRE
AU LAPIN AGILE
CIMETIÈRE DE MONTMARTRE

Maps and Listings
MAP, PAGE 164
SHOPPING, PAGE 177
RESTAURANTS, PAGE 178
ACCOMMODATION, PAGE 303

LEFT: a breakdancing group entertain tourists on the steps of the Sacré-Cœur.
RIGHT: stylish Montmartre locals.

ABOVE: concert venue La Cigale.

the age of 82, despite her deafness and blindness, and the convent buildings were destroyed.

Revolution has been the district's speciality ever since. In 1871, its inhabitants seized 170 cannons to defend themselves after the fall of Paris to the Prussians. The Thiers government sent troops to recapture them, but the generals were overwhelmed, lined up on the hill and shot – so beginning the Paris Commune (see page 36).

For much of the 19th century, Montmartre was mined for gypsum, and retained a country charm with its vineyards, cornfields, flocks of sheep and 40 windmills. This charm and the hill's lofty isolation attracted artists and writers. Painters and their models frequented Place Pigalle, and people flocked to the Moulin Rouge. Impressionism, Fauvism and Cubism were conceived in the lofts, bars and dance halls of Montmartre.

When the bohemians migrated to Montparnasse, Montmartre was left to sex-shop owners, pawnbrokers and cheap hotels, and for many years afterwards it was synonymous with sleaze. Yet today, the village is fashionable once more. Dingy strip bars have been transformed into chic rock clubs and the narrow streets are lined with buzzing cafés, quirky design shops, offbeat second-hand shops and hippy-chic boutiques. A new generation of bohemians is reclaiming Montmartre.

THE CHARMS OF PIGALLE

The traditional gateway to Montmartre, at the foot of the *Butte* or hill, Pigalle is also the place where modern nightlife was invented.

Moulin Rouge ❶

Address: 82 boulevard de Clichy
www.moulinrouge.fr
Tel: 01 53 09 82 82

ABOVE: the Moulin Rouge – you can't miss it.

Opening Hrs: shows daily 9pm, 11pm
Entrance Fee: charge
Transport: Blanche

The kitschy Moulin Rouge with its signature neon windmill still does a roaring trade as tourists flock to see the high-kicking cabaret girls in feathers strut their stuff. Of all the glitzy Parisian floor shows it is probably the most tame and traditional (children are welcome here), but the club's history is gloriously scandalous. Toulouse-Lautrec sat here sketching the working girls' energetic cancan; in 1896, the annual Paris Art School Ball at the Moulin Rouge was the scene of the first all-the-way strip-teases, by one of the school's prettiest models. She was arrested and imprisoned, and students went to the barricades in the Quartier Latin, proclaiming "the battle for artistic nudity" – two died in subsequent scuffles with police.

Modern Pigalle

Next door to the Moulin Rouge, **La Machine du Moulin Rouge** (tel: 01 53 41 88 89), a huge disco, has live music concerts and club nights ranging from swing to soul. A few doors away at 100 boulevard de Clichy, the **Théâtre des Deux Anes** (tel: 01 46 06 10 26) offers a dose of typical Parisian cabaret (in French, naturally).

A little further east along Boulevard de Clichy lies sprawling **Place Pigalle ❷** itself. Less artistic attractions abound in Pigalle (or "Pig Alley", as it was once known to American soldiers), for this has been the core of the Paris sex trade for decades. In the surrounding streets, tassled curtains provide glimpses of smoky interiors, signs promote live sex shows and aggressive bouncers attempt to entice tourists into "naked extravaganzas". But, Pigalle's reputation has been changing from sleaze centre to trendy nightspot. The cabarets that occupied

SHOP

Some of the finest breads and most irresistible *pâtisseries* imaginable can be found just south of Pigalle at the shop of Arnaud Delmontel, 39 rue des Martyrs (closed Tue). Specialities include beautifully subtle cinnamon and raisin bread, and fabulous fruit tarts. He has another shop on the north side of the Butte Montmartre at 57 rue Damrémont (closed Mon).

ABOVE: the environs of the Sacré-Cœur teem with street performers.
BELOW: dancing the night away at the Bus Palladium.

half the houses on Rue des Martyrs in the 18th century are being taken over by hip clubs – such as **Le Divan du Monde** at No. 75 – and bars.

Nothing symbolises the revival of Pigalle better than the state of the **Elysée Montmartre** ❸. Founded in 1807, rebuilt by Eiffel in 1889, frequented by Lautrec and used to host wrestling and boxing in the 1950s, this historic music and dance hall has been reborn yet again as one of the city's best live rock and club venues, hosting both big names and the up-and-coming. However, it's currently closed following a fire in 2011.

CLIMBING THE *BUTTE*

The wide esplanade at the foot of the Butte Montmartre, above Anvers Métro, is Square Willette.

Halle St-Pierre ❹

Address: 2 rue Ronsard
www.hallesaintpierre.org
Tel: 01 42 58 72 89
Opening Hrs: Mon–Fri 10am–6pm, Sat until 7pm, Sun 11am–6pm
Entrance Fee: charge
Transport: Anvers

Just off the square is this former market hall designed by Victor Baltard, the original architect of Les Halles (see page 109), which is now a cultural centre housing a museum of "outsider" and Naïve art. The highly individual works are by artists from over 30 countries, many of them self-taught. Several shops in the area specialise in cheap textiles, which often attract professional designers.

Impossible to miss from Square Willette, overlooking the tide of

Pigalle Nightspots

Popular venues in Pigalle include: **Le Divan du Monde** (75 rue des Martyrs, tel: 01 40 05 06 99), an old establishment full of memories of the 1890s that's now a cool, relaxed nightclub and music venue with an eclectic programme; **La Cigale** (120 boulevard de Rochechouart, tel: 01 49 25 89 99), an old vaudeville house that now hosts big-name acts, both French and international; and the **Bus Palladium** (6 rue Fontaine, tel: 01 45 26 80 35), an iconic 1960s disco hall, now a fashionable venue (Serge Gainsbourg mentioned it in a song, and Dalí, Roman Polanski and the Beatles all hung out here); it was refitted and reopened in 2006 with an all-new sound system.

human activity that ebbs and flows beneath it is the vast white bulk of the Sacré-Cœur. To reach it, you can either walk up through the square, laid out in terraces in 1929, or take the *funiculaire* (funicular railway – Métro tickets are valid for travel).

Sacré-Cœur ⑤

Address: 33 rue du Chevalier-de-la-Barre
www.sacre-coeur-montmartre.com
Tel: 01 53 41 89 00
Opening Hrs: basilica daily 6am–10.30pm, crypt and dome daily summer 9am–7pm, winter 10am–6pm
Entrance Fee: charge for crypt and dome
Transport: Anvers

This domed basilica was conceived by a group of Catholics in 1871, who vowed to build a church to the Sacred Heart if Paris was delivered from the Prussian siege, and to expiate the sin represented by the atheist Commune, which had begun in Montmartre. The heart of one of the men, Alexandre Legentil, is preserved in a stone urn in the crypt. The Church took responsibility for the project in 1873,

and work started two years later. Paul Abadie, the chief architect, based his design on the Romano-Byzantine cathedral of St-Front in Périgueux.

The bone-white colour of the building comes from its Château-Landon stone, which secretes calcite when it rains, bleaching the walls. Its mediocre architecture, added to its symbolic censure of a popular uprising, has made the Sacré-Cœur one of Parisians' least favourite monuments.

Completed in 1914 but not consecrated until after the war in 1919, the dome offers a stunning view over Paris, up 237 spiral steps (the second-highest vantage point over the city, after the Eiffel Tower). From the stained-glass gallery beneath there is a good view of the cavernous interior which, apart from a massive mock-Byzantine mosaic of Christ (1912–22) by Luc Olivier-Merson on the chancel ceiling, has little to offer.

Outside on the terrace, crowds gather in the early evening to drink wine, strum guitars and watch the glittering lights of Paris, overlooked by statues of Joan of Arc and St Louis on horseback.

Montmartre's first funicular railway was built in 1900, driven by a water-filled counterweight; the current system, put in place in 1991, is electric. Bus and Métro tickets are valid for the short and dramatic ride up or down the steep slope.

BELOW: the Sacré-Cœur was built in 1876, much later than its architectural style implies.

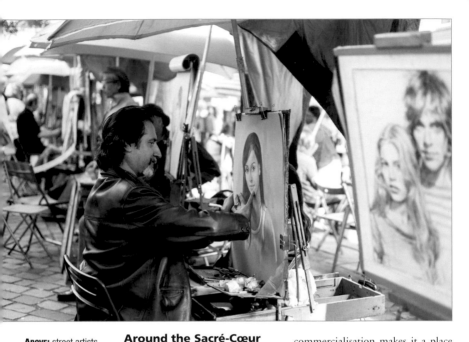

ABOVE: street artists conjure up quick portraits in Place du Tertre.
BELOW: St-Pierre-de-Montmartre is Paris's second oldest church.
RIGHT: selling nudes on Place du Tertre.

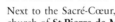

Around the Sacré-Cœur

Next to the Sacré-Cœur, the simple church of **St-Pierre de Montmartre** ❻ (daily 9am–7pm) is the second-oldest in Paris (after St-Germain-des-Prés, see page 213), dating from 1133, and the only remaining vestige of the Abbey of Montmartre, where the nuns used to live. After the Revolution the church was abandoned, until it was reconsecrated in 1908. If you are here on Toussaint (All Saints' Day – 1 November), visit the small, romantic graveyard behind the church, as this is the only day of the year when it opens.

To the west, **Place du Tertre** ❼ is the tourist trap of Montmartre, laden with kitschy overpriced bistros and craft shops selling junk. The square, once the site of the village hall, now throngs with coach loads of tourists. Artists began exhibiting here in the 19th century, and now there are legions of mediocre (and sometimes aggressively pushy) painters on the square. This oppressive commercialisation makes it a place best avoided by day. It's far more appealing at night, when the square is lit up by fairy lights and retains an animated charm.

Just off the square on place du Tertre, **La Mère Catherine** (tel: 01 46

06 32 69) lays claim to being Paris's first bistro. Originally a revolutionary drinking den (where Danton pronounced the immortal words, "Eat, drink, for tomorrow we shall die"), the story goes that during the Allied occupation of 1814, the old inn greeted Russian soldiers. As they ordered their drinks (forbidden by the Russian military authorities) they shouted "*bistrot*", meaning "quickly", thereby founding a Paris institution.

Don't be put off by the masses on the square; escaping them is easy. From Place du Tertre, winding Rue Poulbot leads through Place du Calvaire – the smallest square in Paris, with a spectacular view, and a cosy magnet for lovers and drinkers – to another kitschy artistic attraction.

Espace Montmartre Salvador Dalí ⑧

Address: 11 rue Poulbot
www.daliparis.com
Tel: 01 42 64 40 10

Opening Hrs: daily 10am–6pm, July–Aug until 8pm
Entrance Fee: charge
Transport: Abbesses

Over 330 sculptures and drawings by the Catalan Surrealist painter are exhibited in unusual settings, including his famous clocks, intended to represent "the fluidity of time".

A few minutes' walk to the north, **Rue des Saules** crosses **Rue St-Rustique**, a quiet, rustic street leading away from the buzz of Place du Tertre, which contains the **Auberge de la Bonne Franquette** (tel: 01 42 52 02 42). It was originally called Le Billard en Bois; Vincent Van Gogh and Auguste Renoir both painted here, and the crossroads outside and other street scenes nearby were immortalised by the paintings of Maurice Utrillo. Other frequent visitors to the auberge were Cézanne, Toulouse-Lautrec, Monet, Pissarro and Sisley, and novelist Emile Zola.

ABOVE: the Sacré-Cœur offers one of the best views of the French capital.

According to the writings of Saint Ignatius Loyola (1491–1556), the church of Saint-Pierre-de-Montmartre was where the Society of Jesus was founded in 1543. The Roman Catholic male religious order, whose members are known as Jesuits, carries out its work in the fields of higher education, social justice and human rights.

ABOVE: Le Clos Montmartre, Paris's only remaining vineyard.
BELOW: Dalí in Montmartre in 1956.

OLD MONTMARTRE

The further you move from the Sacré-Cœur and Place du Tertre, the easier it is to get a scent of the days when Montmartre really was just a village.

Musée de Montmartre ❾

Address: 12 rue Cortot
www.museedemontmartre.fr
Tel: 01 49 25 89 37
Opening Hrs: daily 10am–6pm
Entrance Fee: charge
Transport: Lamarck-Caulaincourt

This charming museum chronicles the life and times of Montmartre and the artists' quarter in a 17th-century manor, the oldest house on the *Butte*. It was originally the country home of Rosimund, an actor in Molière's theatre company who suffered the exact same fate as his master: in 1686 he died during a performance of *Le Malade Imaginaire*, just as Molière had done 13 years earlier (see page 134). Many artists had studios here, including Renoir, Dufy and Utrillo; the composer Erik Satie (1866–1925) lived in the same street. The museum is an evocation of past simplicity, gaiety and bohemian living, with

pictures by Kees van Dongen (1877–1968) and Dufy, Toulouse-Lautrec posters, reconstructions of Utrillo's favourite café, complete with zinc counter top and absinthe bottles, and an artist's studio, with yellowing photographs and a wonderful view over Paris.

Nearby on Rue St-Vincent is Montmartre's famous vineyard, **Le Clos Montmartre**, planted in 1933 in memory of the vines cultivated here since the Middle Ages. In early October, the grape harvest attracts hundreds of volunteers, and the streets host processions and parties. Around 300 litres of wine are sold at auction, with the proceeds going to Montmartre pensioners.

Au Lapin Agile ❿

Address: 22 rue des Saules
www.au-lapin-agile.com
Tel: 01 46 06 85 87
Opening Hrs: Tue–Sun 9pm–2am
Entrance Fee: charge
Transport: Lamarck-Caulaincourt

Opposite the vineyard stands this legendary cabaret. It was the headquarters of the avant-garde around 1900, a

Salvador Dalí

A true eccentric, Catalan painter Salvador Dalí (1904–89) was desperate to go to Paris in the 1920s, for it was the world's art capital, already conquered by fellow Spaniards Picasso and Joan Miró. After studying art in Madrid at the Real Academia de Bellas Artes de San Fernando where he befriended the poet and dramatist Federico Garcia Lorca and the future film director Luis Buñuel, with whom he went on to cowrite the film *Un Chien Andalou* (An Andalusian Dog, 1929), he reached Paris in 1926. With the help of introductions from the two older Spanish artists, and motivated by his "Catalan sense of fantasy", Dalí held his first Surrealist exhibition the same year. Through Miró, Dalí met other Surrealists, many of whom he was to quarrel with later. Picasso said that Dalí's imagination reminded him of "an outboard motor continually running", and the painter himself wanted to "systematise confusion". As well as painting, Dalí produced films and books, including an autobiography. "Every morning when I wake up," he stated, "I experience an exquisite joy – the joy of being Salvador Dalí – and I ask myself in rapture, 'What wonderful things is this Salvador Dalí going to accomplish today?'"

Cubist Fernand Léger – and cabaret every evening.

TRANQUIL MONTMARTRE

Far from the helter-skelter animation of Pigalle and Place du Tertre, the west of Montmartre, on the other side of St Vincent cemetery, is a puzzle of little old streets and tumbledown houses. Take the steps from Place Constantin-Pecqueur, off Rue Caulaincourt, to **Square Suzanne-Buisson** ⑪, a quiet, dusty square that has a children's play area. The square occupies the former garden of the Château des Brouillards, an 18th-century folly inhabited at different times by Renoir and the mad poet Gérard de Nerval (who hanged himself in Les Halles in 1855, leaving a note saying, "Don't wait for me, for the night will be black and white"), and which was later turned into a dance hall. During the 19th century, the "château" could only be seen when the *brouillards* (thick fogs) of Montmartre lifted, hence the name. In the middle of the square, a statue of St Denis washes the blood off his head while watching the old men playing *pétanque*.

ABOVE: Place Dalida honours the *chanteuse* who lived in Montmartre.
LEFT: the Auberge de la Bonne Franquette was frequented by all the famous Impressionists in its heyday.
BELOW: La Maison Rose bistro on Rue de l'Abreuvoir was the subject of a lithograph by French painter Maurice Utrillo.

restaurant-cabaret where Renoir and the Symbolist poet Paul Verlaine laid tables, and Guillaume Apollinaire sang with fellow poet Max Jacob. Picasso paid for a day's meals at the Lapin with one of his *Harlequin* paintings – now worth millions. Today a tourist attraction, the smoke-stained inn still has its old wooden tables, original paintings by Gill and

Avenue Junot, beside the square, is one of the widest, most expensive streets in Montmartre. Constructed in 1910, the avenue cut through the ancient maquis scrubland that used to cover the hillside, where windmills turned their graceful sails and goats scampered among the trees.

The street's 1920s Art Deco elegance has attracted the cream of Montmartre society – singer Claude Nougaro lived in the big ochre house. **Le Hameau des Artistes** (No. 11) still provides artists' studios. **Maison Tristan Tzara** (No. 15) is named after the eccentric Romanian Dadaist who once lived here, and was designed especially for him by the Austrian architect Adolf Loos.

Below, between Avenue Junot and Rue Lepic, is the last of the great windmills of Montmartre, the **Moulin de la Galette ⑫**. Built in 1604, the mill became an illustrious dance hall in the 19th century. Artists and writers living in Montmartre often hosted parties here, and it was on one such occasion that Auguste Renoir began sketches for his famous painting *Le Moulin de la Galette*

ABOVE: the Moulin de la Galette was immortalised by Renoir in his 1866 painting of the same name.
RIGHT: tranquil Square Suzanne-Buisson.
BELOW: the Lapin Agile's popularity has not waned.

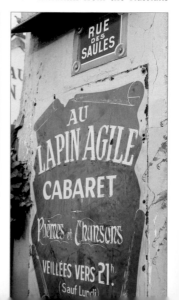

(1866). Emile Zola held a party here to celebrate the success of his novel *L'Assommoir* (1877), set in La Goutte d'Or, just to the east. The novelist lived below the village, on Boulevard de Clichy.

Much earlier, in the 1814 siege of Paris, its owners the four Debray brothers had fought fiercely to save their windmill from the Russians

A Happy Bunny

The tiny Lapin Agile ("Nimble Rabbit") on Rue des Saules is the oldest surviving cabaret from Montmartre's high-kicking heyday. When it first opened in 1855 it was known as the Cabaret des Assassins, according to tradition because a gang of robbers had once broken in and killed the owner's son; but in 1875 it acquired the name it still bears today, when the painter André Gill painted a sign showing a rabbit escaping from a copper saucepan. The word "agile" described the bunny's nifty getaway, but was also a pun on the painter's name: A Gill. By the early 20th century, the cabaret was a popular spot in which painters and artists met and talked; Utrillo depicted it more than once, and Picasso's 1905 painting *Au Lapin Agile* cemented its renown; both lived and worked nearby at Le Bâteau Lavoir in Place Emile Goudeau along with other luminaries of the age, including Georges Braque, Raoul Dufy and Amedeo Modigliani (see page 174). The fame still holds good: US comedian Steve Martin wrote a successful play, *Picasso at the Lapin Agile*, in the 1990s, and visitors still flock to the Lapin to hear old-fashioned French songs from as far back as the Middle Ages.

Vincent Van Gogh and his brother Theo, an art dealer, at No. 54 for two years in the late 1880s. During that time Van Gogh is said to have exhibited his paintings at Le Tambourin, a seedy cabaret on Boulevard de Clichy, until the owner demanded that he remove them as they disturbed her customers.

Further down the hill, Rue Lepic turns into a quaint but slightly grubby market street, lined with mouthwatering shops selling pastries and exotic produce. Grab a drink at **Les Deux Moulins** (No. 15), where Amélie Poulain worked as a waitress in the eponymous movie.

A surreal sculpture of the writer Marcel Aymé (1902–68) stands in a square named after him in Montmartre; his shorts stories convey a vivid sense of the fantastic.

– one of them was subsequently crucified on its sails. Today, the windmill is better-protected, as a notice proclaims, "Residence under electronic, radar and guard-dog surveillance".

Picturesque Rue Lepic, leading from the windmill and past the Moulin du Radet, descends to Place Blanche. This old quarry road housed

Cimetière de Montmartre 🔞

Address: 20 avenue Rachel
Tel: 01 53 42 36 30
Opening Hrs: mid-Mar–Oct Mon–Fri 8am–6pm, Sat 8.30am–6pm, Sun 9am–6pm, Nov–mid-Mar closes daily at 5.15pm
Entrance Fee: free
Transport: Blanche

Just west of Rue Lepic, the area's artistic bias is reflected in

ABOVE: bust of Parisian-born Emile Zola in the Cimetière de Montmartre.
BELOW: Cimetière de Montmartre.

ABOVE: typical Haussmannian building in Montmartre.
BELOW: café society.

DRINK

Rue des Abbesses is a hub of Montmartre's boho bar scene. Le Sancerre (see page 179) bursts at the seams every night; further along is the slightly calmer Le Chinon (No. 49); and the wine shop Caves des Abbesses (No. 43) has a tiny wine bar. Down the hill, La Fourmi (see page 179) draws a young arty set, while weekend sunseekers head to the Butte's east side for the terrace at L'Eté en Pente Douce (23 rue Muller).

Montmartre's cemetery. The tombs are elegantly sculpted, and their inmates famous: here lie the 19th-century novelists Stendhal and Alexandre Dumas, poet and critic Théophile Gautier, the painter Edgar Degas, the dancer Vaslav Nijinsky, composers Hector Berlioz and Jacques Offenbach, and a bust of Emile Zola (his body was moved to the Panthéon). Film director François Truffaut was also laid to rest here, in 1984.

Heading back into Montmartre, cut left off Rue des Abbesses into Rue Ravignan, for a detour to **Place Emile-Goudeau** ⑭, a particularly attractive square. At No. 13, modern art studios have replaced the wooden ramshackle building called **Le Bateau-Lavoir**, so named because it resembled a floating laundry. This artists' den housed Picasso and fellow Cubists Braque and Van Dongen in its narrow, ship-like corridors. Picasso painted *Les Demoiselles d'Avignon* (1907) in his chaotic studio, recalling the prostitutes of Barcelona, and Apollinaire and Max Jacob liberated verse form in the rooms alongside. Unfortunately, the building burned

down in 1970, just as it was about to be renovated.

Turning left out of the square, take the Passage des Abbesses, a little further on, down to pretty **Place des Abbesses** ⑮ and its remarkable Art Nouveau Métro station, designed by Hector Guimard. The brownstone church is Saint-Jean-de-Montmartre (Mon–Sat

9.30am–6pm, Sun 9am–7pm), which was built from 1894 to 1904 and has a definite Art Nouveau look about it. Rue des Abbesses is a focus of Montmartre life, with bustling cafés, grocery stores, wine merchants and trendy shops. The trio of streets east of the station – Rue de la Vieuville, Rue Yvonne-le-Tac, Rue des Trois Frères – are lined with designer boutiques, offbeat secondhand shops, little galleries supporting local artists and "boho" bars that are especially lively in the evenings.

AROUND MONTMARTRE

La Goutte d'Or ⑯

To the east of Montmartre is the old working-class district of La Goutte d'Or, centred on Barbès-Rochechouart Métro station. Vividly described by Zola in *L'Assommoir*, the district may still be one of the poorest and most run-down in the city, often marked by a heavy police presence, but it's also one of the liveliest. The conglomeration of Islamic butchers, African grocers, West Indian bakers, Jewish jewellers

and Arab tailors is a never-ending spectacle of sight, sound and smell. Over 30 nationalities live in the streets around Rue de la Goutte d'Or and Rue des Poissonniers. Cut-price clothes are sold at the huge flagship store of the Tati chain on Boulevard Rochechouart.

In an attempt to develop the area, the Fédération Française du Prêt à Porter (Ready-to-Wear Association) and the Mairie de Paris have tried to make Rue des Gardes a new centre of fashion. Ten couture boutiques of "emerging talent" have opened in the street (Métro Château-Rouge).

La Nouvelle Athènes

South of Pigalle, this area has been rediscovered in the last few years. In the early 19th century writers, artists and composers, among them Chopin and George Sand, as well as actresses and courtesans came to live here, leading it to be dubbed the "New Athens". Place St-Georges and the exclusive residential streets off Rue des Martyrs give an idea of its grander past, as do two museums: the **Musée Gustave Moreau** (14 rue de La Rochefoucauld; www.musee-moreau.fr; tel: 01 48 74 38 50; Mon,

ABOVE: greengrocer on Rue des Abbesses.
LEFT: Montmartre stairways are steep.
BELOW: the *Je t'aime* wall in Place des Abbesses, a mural that reads 'I love you' in 311 languages.

The Métro

Wandering through white-tiled tunnels following *Correspondance* signs is as essential a part of the Parisian experience as strolling the squares and boulevards.

Deep beneath the streets of Paris is another city, with its own shops, cafés, market stalls, hairdressers, banking facilities, musicians, artists, beggars and pickpockets, even its own police force and its own microclimate. Temperatures here occasionally exceed 30°C (86°F), while wind speeds through the tunnels can reach up to 40km (25 miles) per hour.

In Luc Besson's 1985 thriller, *Subway*, audiences had a glimpse of this surreal world and the characters who make the Métro their home. In real life, every night around 1,000 people take refuge underground, most because they have nowhere else to go.

A growing network

Construction of the Paris Métro began in 1898. The first line, 10.3km (6.4 miles)

long, between Porte de Vincennes and Porte Maillot, opened on 19 July 1900. Since then the Métro has extended in every direction, and is hailed as one of the world's cheapest and most efficient underground rail systems, carrying 3.5 million passengers daily on over 200km (124 miles) of track to 372 stations on 14 Métro, five RER and two railway lines. Two new stations – Mairie de Montrouge on Ligne 4 and Front Populaire on Ligne 12 – are due to open in 2013 and three more are due to open by 2019.

The massive station at Châtelet-Les Halles is the hub of the network. Five Métro lines and three RER lines meet here, disgorging millions daily into its labyrinth of corridors. As you search this nightmarish warren for an exit, you may wonder if you'll ever come up for air. Trudging the Métro's 75km (47 miles) of corridors, it seems unsurprising that the Parisian's average body weight is among the lowest in the industrialised world.

The architecture

At no point in the city are you further than 500 metres (550yds) from a Métro station. Some station entrances retain their elegant Art Nouveau features, designed by architect Hector Guimard, characterised by soft flowing lines and motifs evoking the growth of plants. Two that are still covered by his beautiful iron-and-glass pavilions are at Porte Dauphine and Abbesses.

Underground, walls are mostly covered in white tiles, apart from a few stations such as St-Michel, with a mosaic ceiling, and Bastille, with scenes from the Revolution.

In an attempt to make commuting slightly more bearable, the RATP (which runs the Métro and city buses) organises a variety of cultural events, from photography exhibitions to fashion shows, classical concerts to puppet theatre. Less organised but equally ubiquitous are the train-hopping buskers and beggars, hoping to profit from a captive audience – it's calculated that the average Parisian spends a year and four months of his or her life below ground.

LEFT: Art Nouveau Abbesses station.

Wed, Thur 10am–12.45pm, 2–5.15pm, Fri, Sat, Sun 10am–5.15pm; charge), which overflows with fantastical paintings and drawings that the symbolist painter left to the state, and the **Musée de la Vie Romantique** (16 rue Chaptal; www.vie-romantique. paris.fr; tel: 01 55 31 95 67; Tue–Sun 10am–6pm; charge; *see margin*).

Rue Clauzel is an enclave of retro clothing outlets, bric-a-brac and boho clothes shops, while the lower half of Rue des Martyrs has several good bakeries and delis.

Batignolles

West of Place de Clichy, this area developed in the 19th century with a very different atmosphere from that of the grand mansions and apartment blocks in the western half of the 17th *arrondissement*, around Parc Monceau. Sliced through by huge railway depots, it still retains its authentic urban fabric, with old workers' cafés, budget hotels, craft workshops and picturesque alleys and courtyards, but is also being colonised by quirky boutiques and arty bistros.

Square des Batignolles was once an empty space, where the Fêtes des Batignolles were held. Transformed in 1862 into Napoleon III's idea of a London park, it still has its 19th-century chalets, kiosks, glass-enclosed lookout and miniature river and waterfall. Black swans cruise its little lake. Towards the *Périphérique*, a great swathe of former railway land is being made into an all-new park, the **Parc Clichy-Batignolles**.

ABOVE: the reliable Parisian Métro.
BELOW: cutting-edge fashion on Rue Montmartre.

SHOPPING

The quaint, narrow streets of Montmartre house a variety of boutiques selling shoes and stylish clothes.

Clothing

Loft by Design
20 rue Yvonne Le Tac, 18th.
Tel: 01 42 51 39 10.
www.loftbydesign.com
A more upmarket, French version of GAP, this chain sells chic basics for women, men and children.

Department Store

Tati
5 rue Belhomme, 18th.

Tel: 01 55 29 50 00
This bargain department store sells everything from clothes, including wedding dresses, to home decoration and gardening equipment. Look out for the pink-and-white check plastic bags.

Shoes

Melle Montmartre
17 rue Vieuville, 18th.
Tel: 01 42 59 19 94
Quirky shoes and boots – check out the suede biker boots sporting a skull and crossbones – for women. There is also a selection of unusual bags and jewellery.

BEST RESTAURANTS, BARS AND CAFES

Restaurants

French

L'Auberge du Clou
30 avenue Trudaine, 9th
Tel: 01 48 78 22 48
Open: L & D daily.
€€ **50** [p334, B2]
This cosy *auberge* is particularly lovely in winter when a log fire crackles upstairs. Food is traditionally French – try onion soup to start followed by *confit de canard* then maybe, if you've got room, a peach crème brûlée. The set menus are good value, especially at lunchtime. Tables outdoors in summer.

Le Bouclard
1 rue Cavallotti, 18th
Tel: 01 45 22 60 01
Open: L Tue–Fri, D Mon–Sat.
€€ **51** [p334, A1]
Everything here is still cooked *façon grand-mère*, from the macaroni with foie gras to the braised chicken with tarragon and vanilla. Among the delicious desserts: chocolate mousse and mojito sorbet.

Chez Jean
8 rue St-Lazare, 9th
Tel: 01 48 78 62 73
www.restaurantjean.fr
Open: L & D Mon– Fri.
€€€ (set menu), €€€€ (à la carte) **52** [p334, B2]
This popular brasserie boasts a lovely, high-ceilinged dining room, a high staff-to-diners ratio and a set menu that's good value. Adventurous sorts should try smoked eel to start followed by rabbit, which is cooked in a variety of ways; the desserts are more traditional.

Chez Michel
10 rue de Belzunce, 10th
Tel: 01 44 53 06 20
Open: D Mon, L & D Tue–Fri.
€€€ (set menu) €€€€ (à la carte) **53** [p334, C2]
One of the flag-bearers of the wave of small, excellent regional restaurants that's been spreading across Paris in the last decade. Chef-proprietor Thierry Breton (from Brittany, of course) does fine, hearty food like marinated salmon with purple potatoes and rabbit braised with rosemary and Swiss chard. Blackboard specials, at extra cost, follow the seasons. The desserts are equally fabulous; choose from the St-Honoré or the typical, and perfect, *far breton*. Booking recommended.

Chez Toinette
20 rue Germain-Pilon, 18th
Tel: 01 42 54 44 36
www.cheztointte.com
Open: D Mon–Sat.
€€ (set menu), €€€ (à la carte) **54** [p334, B1]
Where many places in this part of town shamelessly fob off the unwitting tourist with overpriced fare, this amiable bistro has a good and good-value blackboard menu that might run to steaks, wild boar terrine, a lovely warm goat's cheese salad and prunes soaked in armagnac.

La Famille
41 rue des Trois-Frères, 18th
Tel: 01 42 52 11 12
Open: D only Tue–Sat.
€€€ **55** [p334, B1]
A welcome addition to the Montmartre restaurant scene, La Famille has immediately become one of the hippest. The interior is tastefully simple (powdery white walls and graceful, suspended lampshades) – a clean canvas on which to show off exciting creations

LEFT: lunch in Montmartre.

such as raw shrimps served with passion fruit, pan-fried tuna with grilled polenta, and pink grapefruit sorbet.

Pétrelle
34 rue Pétrelle, 9th
Tel: 01 42 82 11 02
Open: D Tue–Sat.
€€€ (set menu) **56** [p334, C2]
The no-choice set menu served at this haute cuisine restaurant is a stunning bargain – perhaps marinated sardines and tomato relish, rosemary-scented rabbit and poached figs – but that doesn't mean you should ignore the carte, which brings on tournedos Rossini or, in winter, various game dishes. The place is very popular with designers and movie actors.

Le Relais Gascon
6 rue des Abbesses, 18th
Tel: 01 42 58 58 22
Open: L & D daily.
€€ **57** [p334, B1]
This busy, good-value, bistro is a fine choice when you're on a Montmartre walkabout. Their speciality is a *salade géante*, which has a vegetarian option, served in a big earthenware bowl. Note that the place fills up quickly at weekends.

North African
Wally le Saharien
36 rue Rodier, 9th
Tel: 01 42 85 51 90
Open: L & D Tue–Sat
€€€ **58** [p334, B2]
Step out of Montmartre and into a Saharan encampment, where couscous – served without vegetables, which is the custom in the south of Algeria – is the order of the day; the other spe-

ciality is sardines. Desserts are of the Middle Eastern variety and they also do takeaway.

World Food
Just Be
46 rue de Caulaincourt, 18th
Tel: 01 42 55 14 25
www.justbe-paris.com.
Open: L & D Tue–Sun.
€ (set menu) €€ (à la carte) **59** [p334, A1]
Feeling more like a New York loft with its brick walls, this hip restaurant's menu takes diners on a tour of world flavours. The burgers are the reason to come here (there's even a vegetarian one) and the apéro shots are a nice idea. There are regular art exhibitions and also brunch at the weekend.

Bars and Cafés

Le Café qui Parle
24 rue Caulaincourt, 18th.
Tel: 01 46 06 06 88.
Open: Daily 8.30am–11pm.
19 [p334, A1]
A young chef who has worked in some of the finest restaurants in Paris and New York now brings his touch of class to a neighbourhood café, done out in a stylish grey and white theme with retro furniture. The place is renowned for its excellent brunch at weekends.

L'Etoile de Montmartre
26 rue Duhesme, 18th.
Tel: 01 46 06 11 65.
Open: Daily 7.30am–2am.
20 [p334, A1]
Café à *la française* and genuine Montmartre charm are to be found in this archetypal Parisian restaurant with friendly staff. A classic hang-out

for Parisians living in the heart of the 18th arrondissement. The epitome of a local neighbourhood café.

La Fourmi
74 rue des Martyrs, 18th.
Tel: 01 42 64 70 35.
Open: Non-stop daily.
21 [p334, B1]
This retro-industrial bar was once a bistro, now given a modish modern makeover. The big windows pour light into the sand-coloured interior, and the attractive zinc bar counter is lit by industrial lamps. They play good music, and the piles of flyers for local gigs and club nights make it a good source of nightlife tips.

Le Sancerre
35 rue des Abbesses, 18th.
Tel: 01 42 58 08 20.

Price includes dinner and a half-bottle of house wine:

€ = under €25
€€ = €25–40
€€€ = €40–60
€€€€ = more than €60

Open: Non-stop daily.
22 [p334, B1]
Le Sancerre is one of the cornerstones of the Montmartre bar scene. The terrace is always packed, the music (sometimes live) always loud, the crowd largely young, hip, arty and eclectic. There's a good choice of beers, wines and the standard cocktails; food-wise, there are decent salads and a variety of daily specials. Pavement chairs allow you to enjoy the scene.

CABARET LIFE

Cabaret used to be high kicks, frou-frou and unbridled revelry; today, it's high kicks, sequins, tasteful nudity and good behaviour.

It wasn't until the Revolution that costumed masquerades and dancing became a democratic phenomenon; previously they'd been confined to the powdered world of the aristocracy. But by the 19th century, every stratum of Paris society had its *bals*, *café-concerts* and cabarets, though the different classes stuck to separate parts of the city: the chic crowd frequented establishments on the Grands Boulevards and Champs-Elysées, while the bohemians and lower classes whooped it up in Montparnasse. Another populist hotspot, especially in the 1890s, was the hill of Montmartre, with iconic cabarets Le Moulin Rouge (famously painted by artist Henri de Toulouse-Lautrec and where dancer "La Goulue" aka Louise Weber invented the Can-Can), Le Chat Noir (considered to be the first modern cabaret and whose iconic poster by Théophile-Alexandre Steinlen is still a striking image around the city) and Au Lapin Agile (see page 170). Cabaret's heyday didn't last beyond the 1920s, and today's surviving examples are too expensive to qualify as populist entertainment, their tightly choreographed routines only occasionally catching the atmosphere of yesteryear. Still, they're good fun: the best are Le Lido (see page 308) and Le Moulin Rouge (see page 164) while French speakers might enjoy the ultra-camp Cabaret Michou (80 rue des Martyrs; tel: 01 46 06 16 06). Some of the original 19th-century cabaret premises have now been turned into hip nightclubs.

ABOVE: the iconic Mistinguett performed her risqué routines at the Folies Bergère, the Moulin Rouge and Eldorado.
RIGHT: the short-lived Montmartre cabaret Le Divan Japonais is still remembered today thanks to this poster by Toulouse-Lautrec.

ABOVE: the Crazy Horse cabaret (12 avenue Georges V, 8th) elevates striptease to a form of art.

ABOVE: the Moulin Rouge still trades on the image of Toulouse-Lautrec.

HIGH KICK HIGHLIGHTS

Cabaret wouldn't be cabaret without its dancers – female dancers, that is. The first cancan performers were often part-time courtesans, but the leading lights of cabaret's Belle Epoque heyday – figures such as La Goulue and Jane Avril – were purely entertainers. Avril and La Goulue were huge stars and made a lot of money, though La Goulue lost hers in unlucky business ventures. Another hugely popular dancer in later years was Josephine Baker, a Missouri dancer who made her Paris premiere in 1925 and wowed the capital with her frenetic dancing and the briefest of costumes: a skirt made of bananas and little else. Soon she was a fixture at the Folies Bergère and one of the most popular entertainers in France; Hemingway described her as "the most sensational woman anyone ever saw". Baker recorded the iconic Paris song "J'ai deux amours" in 1931.

ABOVE: Aristide Bruant, shown on this advertisement by Toulouse-Lautrec, was an entertainer who flourished in the Montmartre cabarets: his act was largely song, with some comedy thrown in. He later became a cabaret owner.

RIGHT: Joséphine Baker.

w: the Belle Epoque cabarets of Montmartre were especially popular the writers and artists of the day – figures such as Pierre-Auguste ir, who painted this famous view of revellers at the Moulin de la Galette.

BASTILLE AND EAST PARIS

St-Germain and Montmartre may have the fame, but the tree-lined avenues, grungy alleyways, canalside walks and bohemian-chic streets east from the Bastille form one of the most vibrant parts of the modern, multicultural city.

Traditionally, Paris has been divided into the Right and Left Banks (north and south), but these days the division between the east and west is more marked. The eastern side of Paris has long been associated with the workers and – unsurprisingly – social rebellion, beginning with that most famous revolutionary act of them all, the storming of the Bastille. This was the heartland of the Paris Commune, and today trade unions still begin their May Day marches and other big demonstrations at Place de la Bastille.

Architecturally, the east of the city suffered under the reforming drive of the 1960s and 1970s. However, it is the tantalising whiff of a less salubrious past, of a grittier, less conventional Paris, that makes the most appealing areas in the east – namely Bastille, Oberkampf and, to a lesser extent, République – intriguing alternatives to the bourgeois conservatism prevailing in the western *arrondissements*. The east is certainly very run down in parts, but however much sophistication and glamour may be lacking, creativity and youthful energy abound.

QUARTIER DE LA BASTILLE

Once a fearsome symbol of royal strength, the Bastille and its surroundings fell into disrepair after the prison was destroyed during the Revolution. On 14 July 1789, when crowds stormed the prison, freeing the inmates – all seven of them – Louis XVI was unimpressed, recording in his diary, "Today – nothing." Following the dismantling of the Bastille, an enterprising workman made sculptures of the prison from the rubble and sold them to local

Main Attractions

PLACE DE LA BASTILLE
OPÉRA BASTILLE
OBERKAMPF
CANAL ST-MARTIN
CIMETIÈRE DU PÈRE-LACHAISE
BERCY VILLAGE
PARC DE BERCY
CINÉMATHÈQUE FRANÇAISE

Maps and Listings

MAP, PAGE 185
SHOPPING, PAGE 192
RESTAURANTS, PAGE 194
ACCOMMODATION, PAGE 303

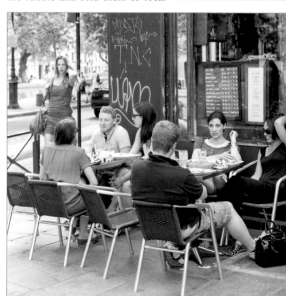

LEFT: the tree-lined Canal St-Martin is a delightful place to amble. **RIGHT:** watching the world go by at Chez Prune.

In Place de la Bastille, be sure to look down at the pavement: marked in the paving slabs – wherever possible, between the multiple lanes of cars – is the outline of the old fortress, demolished within five months of its storming in July 1789.

RIGHT: Faubourg St-Antoine played an important role in the French Revolution.
BELOW: busy Place de la Bastille.

councils, who were denounced as anti-Republican if they refused the price demanded.

The medieval Bastille covered present-day **Place de la Bastille** ❶ and the Arsenal to the south, at the junction of the Seine and Canal St-Martin. The modern square is a wide, busy traffic hub, with the Colonne de Juillet in the middle. The tall column was erected to commemorate the victims of the 1830 and 1848 revolutions, who are buried underneath it.

Opéra National de Paris – Bastille ❷

Address: box office 130 rue de Lyon
www.operadeparis.fr
Tel: 08 92 89 90 90
Opening Hrs: guided tours, days and times vary, tel: 01 40 01 19 70
Entrance Fee: charge for tours
Transport: Bastille

Dominating the square, this giant structure is now Paris's primary venue for opera and ballet, having taken over pride of place from its opulent predecessor the Palais Garnier (see page 147). Ever since it was opened by Mitterrand in 1989, the "new" opera has been the subject of much polemic from politicians, critics, musicians and public alike. Aside from its appearance (half a goldfish bowl attached to a black triumphal arch), the opera house is actually coming apart, and nets are in place to keep the concrete tiles on its outer walls from falling on people's heads.

The district to the east has changed enormously over the past 20 years. Old crumbling streets have been gentrified, and old crumbling inhabitants have moved out. Some of the rebellious charm remains in streets such as Rue de Lappe and Rue de Charonne, but the influx of the upwardly mobile has led to an epidemic of dimly lit bistro-bars. Designer boutiques and trendy cafés have sprouted up, particularly on Rues Keller, Charonne and de Lappe, and clothes shops have replaced many of the furniture stores on Faubourg-St-Antoine. Rue de la Roquette is a buzzing night-life centre.

Le Balajo (www.balajo.fr) and **La Chapelle des Lombards** (tel: 01 43 57 24 24) are two Latin clubs on Rue de Lappe that attract a mix of local

Latinos and tourists. **Théâtre de la Bastille** (76 rue de la Roquette; tel: 01 43 57 42 14) offers Paris's most challenging dance works.

At 17 rue de la Roquette, **La Rotonde** is a chic bar – a far cry from its past life as a brothel, whose owner was shot dead by a blind accordion player. Off Rue du Faubourg-St-Antoine, you can wander through passages of workshops producing furniture, rugs and jewellery, as they have for centuries. **Passage du Cheval Blanc** leads off from the Bastille, with courtyards named after the months of the year. **Passage de la Main d'Or**, further east, is equally intriguing.

OBERKAMPF AND RÉPUBLIQUE

As a rule, Paris is a city that doesn't change that quickly, but recent history has proved Oberkampf the exception. This area just north of Bastille has come a long way from the slums of Edith Piaf's childhood. Even ten years ago this was just another run-down district, but these days it is one of the hippest neighbourhoods in town. Remember, though, this is the east, so we're talking urban rather than glamour. The vanguard

WHERE

On Canal St-Martin is one of the city's foremost alternative cultural venues, Point Ephémère (200 quai de Valmy; tel: 01 40 34 02 48). A 1930s former warehouse, it has been converted into artists' studios, a gig and nightclub venue, music studios, a gallery and a café.

Bastille and the East

ABOVE: canal views.
BELOW: the Canal
St-Martin is still used
by a surprising amount
of boat traffic today.

may have moved on, but the bars, restaurants and clubs that make it so vibrant still remain.

Rue Oberkampf is the hippest limb of the 11th *arrondissement*, especially at the upper end, east of Avenue de la République, where there's a high concentration of cafés and bars and unusual shops. Look out for trendy bars **Le Mécano** (tel: 01 40 21 35 28) and **Café Charbon** (tel: 01 43 57 55 13), with its club venue alongside, the **Nouveau Casino**.

If you're looking for some of the old flavour of the area, wander down the side streets off Rue Oberkampf. Rue St-Maur, which crosses Rue Oberkampf, and Rue Jean-Pierre Timbaud are lined with tiny Middle Eastern food stores and cafés.

Canal St-Martin ❸

The Canal St-Martin begins at Pont Morland by the Seine, disappears undergound at Bastille (supposedly to allow troops faster access to subdue potential uprisings), then re-emerges in the 10th *arrondissement* near Place de la République and leads up to Place Stalingrad, before continuing eastwards as the Canal de l'Ourcq through the Parc de la Villette (see page 259). The canal was dug in 1821 as a transport link for the area's factories and warehouses, many of which now house art galleries and small shops.

The canal is shielded by trees, dotted with small squares and crossed by iron bridges. It is a popular strolling and busking ground, particularly on balmy summer evenings. The bend in the canal is where you'll find the trendy **Chez Prune** café (see page 194), and a row of pastel-coloured shop fronts belonging to **Antoine et Lili**. On

BELLEVILLE AND MÉNILMONTANT

More than 60 nationalities make Belleville the melting pot of Paris. It is gradually becoming gentrified, which adds yet another layer of complexity. There are no major tourist attractions, five-star hotels or three-star restaurants, but it is a fascinating neighbourhood for an off-the-beaten-path excursion. In the 19th century, Belleville was a fertile country village whose springs were tapped to channel water into Paris. There are still a few old stone *regards* left – control stations for the aqueducts, particularly in the little lanes that wind around **Parc de Belleville ❹**.

The park is a terraced crescent of green atop a hill with a panoramic view of Paris. An "air" museum occupies one of the terraces. The **Maison de l'Air** (27 rue Piat; tel: 01 71 28 50 56; Wed 1.30–5pm, Sat until 5.30pm; charge) is an air-measuring station hooked up to a weather satellite, with amazing views over the city. A permanent exhibition demonstrates the alarming levels of air pollution in Paris.

the opposite bank is the **Hôtel du Nord** (**tel: 01 40 40 78 78**), subject and title of a 1930s French movie classic and now a stylish bar and restaurant. With its nine locks, the canal also makes for an attractive boat trip (Paris Canal; tel: 01 42 40 96 97; www.pariscanal.com).

Marcel Carné's classic film Hôtel du Nord was not filmed on the bank of the Canal St-Martin at all, but in a superb reconstruction of the hotel and the lock in front of it, built by the great set designer Alexandre Trauner in the suburban film studios at Boulogne in southwest Paris.

ABOVE: the canal was completed in 1825 to improve the supply of drinking water to the city.
BELOW: the canal is just as atmospheric at night.

ABOVE: statue of a praying girl in Père Lachaise.
BELOW: reminiscing in the Parc de Belleville.

Legend has it that Edith Piaf was born under a lamp-post in the Rue de Belleville, outside No. 72. There is now a plaque over the doorway that claims: "On the steps of this house, on 19 December 1915, was born, in the greatest poverty, Edith Piaf, whose voice would later take the world by storm."

The tiny **Musée Edith Piaf** (5 rue Crespin-du-Gast; tel: 01 43 55 52 72; by appointment only; donations requested), run by some of her true fans, is a touching tribute to the diminutive queen of French *chanson*.

Incorporating part of Rue Ober-kampf, the eastern district of **Ménilmontant** is another hotbed of alternative culture. The area is home to a large number of the city's immigrants, forming an ethnic pastiche of cultures. It's not unusual to find a kosher butcher shop, Chinese DVD store and a Turkish snack kiosk on the same corner.

Cimetière du Père-Lachaise ❺

Address: boulevard Ménilmontant
www.pere-lachaise.com
Tel: 01 55 25 82 10
Opening Hrs: mid-Mar–Oct Mon–Fri 8am–6pm, Sat 8.30am–6pm, Sun 9am–6pm, Nov–mid-Mar closes daily at 5.15pm
Entrance Fee: free
Transport: Père Lachaise

The great tourist draw in the east is this giant cemetery, an oasis of peace in Paris. The list of famous people buried here reads like a who's who of the city's history – Abélard and Héloïse, Apollinaire, Balzac, Edith Piaf, Oscar Wilde, Molière, Proust, Gertrude Stein, Sarah Bernhardt, Chopin and, of course, Jim Morrison, the cemetery's most visited grave, manned by a stony-faced attendant. You can get a free map at the entrance, or purchase a better one from shops that border the cemetery or sellers by its gates.

The cemetery was the site of the last battle of the Paris Commune (see page 36) against the troops of the right-wing Versailles government on 27 May 1871. At dawn the next day, the remaining 147 Communards were lined up against a wall and shot. They were buried in a ditch where they fell, and the **Mur des Fédérés** (Federates' Wall) has become a socialist shrine. Nearby are monuments to both world wars.

SOUTH OF THE BASTILLE

The area south of Place de la Bastille has become a potent symbol of urban regeneration in the 21st century. A disused railway viaduct and dilapidated wine-warehouse district have been brought back to life, and are now thriving commercial and recreational centres.

Viaduc des Arts ❻

Address: 15–121 avenue Daumesnil

www.leviaducdesarts.fr
Tel: 01 44 75 80 66
Transport: Gare de Lyon

Built in 1859, during the golden age of the railways, the Viaduc de Paris supported a railway that ran from Bastille to the Bois de Vincennes, at a time when the area between Gare de Lyon and Bastille was a thriving den of artisan workshops. But, as the railways declined in the 20th century, the viaduct fell into disrepair.

ABOVE: Oscar Wilde's tomb in Père Lachaise was designed by Modernist artist Jacob Epstein.
BELOW: view over Paris from the Parc de Belleville.

ABOVE: Edith Piaf is buried in Père Lachaise, under a simple polished marble slab next to her last husband Theophanis Lamboukas.
BELOW: the winding cobbled lanes of Père Lachaise.

Cruises along the Canal de l'Ourcq to La Villette leave from the Quai de la Loire, parallel to the Bassin de La Villette, and are organised by Canauxrama (13 quai de la Loire; tel: 01 42 39 15 00; www. canauxrama.com) and Paris Canal (see page 187).

Thankfully, it was saved from demolition, and reopened in 1998 as the Viaduc des Arts. The arches beneath the viaduct have been converted into glass-fronted *ateliers* (workshops) and craft boutiques.

After exploring the shops under the viaduct you can take one of the city's most unusual walks along the former tracks on top, all the way across the south of the Bastille quarter. The railway tracks have been replaced by the **Promenade Plantée**, a leafy walkway planted with herbs and roses that provides a welcome green breathing space amongst the urban regeneration. Stretching for some 4km (2.5 miles) along the viaduct, and continuing at ground level through the Jardin de Reuilly and eastwards to the Bois de Vincennes, the promenade is accessible via staircases from the street.

It makes a very pleasant walk and an excellent way to see the city from a completely different angle.

BERCY

For centuries, wine was brought to Paris by boat from Burgundy to the river port of Bercy. Today, it's Paris's

Cour St-Emilion for the park and village, and Bibliothèque François Mitterrand for the New Left Bank; line 6 also goes to Bercy and Quai de la Gare on the Left Bank). The two areas were linked in 2006 by a new footbridge, the elegant **Passerelle Simone de Beauvoir**.

Old stone-walled warehouses and cobbled streets have been given a new lease of life in the shape of **Bercy Village** ❼ (www.bercyvillage. com). The car-free village, centred on the cobbled Cour St-Emilion, is full of boutiques, restaurants and cafés. Parisians visit its Club Med complex to enjoy a themed meal or drink designed to inspire them to book a holiday. The futuristic ugc Ciné Cité is Paris's biggest multiplex cinema, with 18 screens showing both mainstream and arthouse films, usually in their original language with French subtitles.

Musée des Arts Forains ❽

Address: 53 avenue des Terroirs de France
www.pavillons-de-bercy.com
Tel: 01 43 40 16 22

newest neighbourhood. The city is busy reclaiming the old river port, while creating a "new" Left Bank across the river, around the glass towers of the National Library (see page 227). A fully automated, driverless "Meteor" Métro line was opened in 1998 (line 14, the first new Métro line since 1935), linking both areas to central Paris (stops at Bercy and

(see page 227)

EAT

The Marché d'Aligre (Rue d'Aligre; Tue–Sun until 1pm) is one of Paris's best and cheapest open-air food markets. Sharing the same square at the end of the street, the covered market hall the Marché Beauveau (Place d'Aligre; Tue–Sat 9am–1pm, 4–7.30pm, Sun 9am–1pm) sells a wealth of oysters, foie gras, cheeses and, in season, wild boar and venison.

ABOVE: artist painting on fine porcelain at Le Tallec workshop in the Viaduc des Arts.
BELOW: the Cimetière de Picpus, where the victims of the French Revolution are buried.

Relics of Revolution

Père Lachaise is atmospheric, tranquil, and packed with the mortal remains of the great and good. But a little to the south is another graveyard that's much less known, yet just (in its way) as interesting: the **Cimetière de Picpus** (35 rue de Picpus, 12th; tel: 01 43 44 18 54; Tue–Sun 2–6pm; Métro Picpus). It's part of a still functioning convent, so privately owned, and houses the bones of thousands guillotined in the Revolutionary years: 1,298 of 1,306 people executed in nearby Place du Trône (now Place de l'Ile-de-la-Réunion) in July 1794 are here; the plots still belong to the families of the original victims. Off a lovely walled garden is "the cemetery of nobility", with family plots belonging to the Chateaubriands, La Fayettes (the tomb of the general is draped with an American flag due to his involvement with the American Revolutionary War), Montalamberts, Crillons, La Rochefoucaulds and more. There are also two mass graves, discovered in 1929, in one of which are the bones of the poet André Chénier. As you walk around, or sit in the little chapel, you may encounter nuns in white lace bonnets – and feel as if Paris is very far away.

ABOVE: students in Parc de Bercy.
BELOW: Antoine et Lili, a favourite with the girly girls.

Opening Hrs: by appointment
Entrance Fee: charge
Transport: Cour St-Emilion

Another less obvious attraction is this delightful collection of antique fairground attractions. The beautifully crafted carousels, amusement stalls, organs and mechanical figures are displayed in the Pavillons de Bercy, a former wine depot. It's officially only open to groups, but individuals can call ahead to join a group tour.

SHOPPING

From cool labels to everyday shoes, the east of Paris caters for its working-class population as well as incoming hipsters.

Clothing

Antoine & Lili
95 quai de Valmy, 10th.
Tel: 01 40 37 41 55.
www.antoineetlili.com
Colourful clothes, shoes and accessories for women and children in an equally colourful shop on the Canal St-Martin. There is a small range of toys and home decoration too.
Isabelle Marant
16 rue de Charonne, 11th.
Tel: 01 49 29 71 55.

www.isabelmarant.fr
A hip location for a hip French designer who purveys boho chic for the effortlessly fashionable, such as actress Charlotte Gainsbourg. Think tailored jackets with skinny jeans.

Shoes

La Halle aux Chaussures
76 rue du Faubourg St-Antoine, 12th.
Tel: 01 44 68 88 17.
Affordable smart and casual shoes for men, women and children from a variety of brands, including French ones. There are other branches in the city including 35 boulevard de Belleville, 11th.

Parc de Bercy ❾

The busy road running down Quai de Bercy is backed by this vast park, graced by centuries-old chestnuts and plane trees. This charming belt of green has nine themed sections, among them Le Jardin Romantique and Le Jardin du Philosophe. The Maison du Jardinage (House of Gardening) is an 18th-century building where green-fingered people share their secrets. The park has a lake filled with water from the Seine, neoclassical ruins and a trio of ornate bridges.

On the north side of the park, the former American Center juts out among the houses and offices around the park. According to architect Frank Gehry, it expresses the spirit of a "younger country with fewer laws and fewer constraints" than Europe. It's now the magnificent and long-awaited new home for the **Cinémathèque Française** ❿ (51 rue de Bercy; tel: 01 71 19 33 33; www.cinematheque.fr).

The reclaimed area is also the site of the vast new Ministry of Finance, whose edifice extends out over the Seine as if it were intended to be a bridge. Its architects, Paul Chemetov

and Borja Huidobro, claim it is "the monumental entrance which the east of Paris had always lacked".

The neighbouring structure, the **Palais Omnisports de Paris-Bercy**, is a state-of-the-art sports hall seating 17,000 spectators, which offers a varied menu of concerts and sporting events from Thai boxing to opera recitals and reggae festivals. For the current programme, see www.bercy.fr or tel: 01 40 02 60 60.

ABOVE: the pyramid-shape POPB (Palais Omnisports de Paris-Bercy).
BELOW: Frank Gehry's cubist building now houses the iconic Cinémathèque Française.

Screens on the Green

Paris loves its cinema, and so loves its cinemas: here you'll find some of the best in the world, with some of the best programming. The big story has been the reopening in 2006 of its most prestigious picture house, the **Cinémathèque Française**: bigger, more streamlined and more ambitious than ever. Frank Gehry's Cubist building in Bercy went up in 1992 for another customer, but was cleverly re-purposed (a monthly guided tour shows how) to give the CF its fifth home in 70 years. Four screens under one roof replace the previous two under two; there are digital and traditional projectors; a museum, guarded by the robot from Metropolis; an exhibition space for temporary shows; and a bookshop and a restaurant with two different dining rooms and an outdoor terrace. The feel is light, airy and inviting, and the parkside location is lovely.

Though the setting is spacious, the programme barely fits into the quarterly 112-page booklet. There are retrospectives of film-makers contemporary, vintage, underprized and forgotten, themed seasons, B-movie strands, kids' screenings, a new emphasis on art and avant-garde cinema, shorts, even dance films… and a lively programme of conferences, talks and classes. A truly inspiring place.

BEST RESTAURANTS, BARS AND CAFES

Restaurants

French

Astier
44 rue Jean-Pierre Timbaud
Tel: 01 43 57 16 35
Open: L & D daily.
€€ ⑥⓪ [p334, E4]
A traditional, well-known bistro in the north of Paris. Home cooking with an inventive touch and a few classics, all for a modest price. Try the escargots, beef with morels or chocolate pra-line pots. Alternatively, test out the famous cheese and wine lists.

Booking is advised.
Auberge Pyrénées-Cévennes
106 rue de la Folie-Méricourt, 11th
Tel: 01 43 57 33 78
Open: L Mon–Fri, D Mon–Sat.
€€€ ⑥① [p334, E4]
Bring an appetite for French soul food like *caviar du Puy* (green lentils in vinaigrette) or Lyonnais-style endive salads topped with chunky bacon. The humble *cassoulet* and earthy Sabodet sausage are richly satisfying. Good-value wines from Morgon. For

dessert, the *tarte tatin* takes pride of place.
La Bellevilloise
19-21 rue Boyer, 20th
Tel: 01 46 36 07 07
Open: D Wed–Sat, Br Sun
€€ ⑥② [p334, E3]
This historic arts venue, the home of the city's first cooperative, also houses a restaurant in a light, bright room filled with olive trees. Food is traditionally French albeit with a touch of spice and there are options for vegetarians. On Sundays, the jazz brunch is popular.

Bofinger
5 rue Bastille, 4th
Tel: 01 42 72 87 82
www.bofingerparis.com
Open: L & D daily.
€€ (set menu) €€€ (à la carte)
⑥③ [p336, E3]
A classic brasserie that claims to be the oldest in the city, with a stunning Art Nouveau interior. It serves excellent *fruits de mer* and some of the best Alsatian *choucroute* (sauerkraut) in Paris. The more creative dishes can sometimes disappoint.
Chez Prune
71 quai Valmy, 10th
Tel: 01 42 41 30 47
Open: L & D daily.
€ ⑥④ [p334, D3]
A cornerstone of the Canal St-Martin area. This is one of the best places in Paris to watch the world go by. Good food at lunch time and tapas-style snacks at night.
Comme Cochons
135 rue de Charenton, 12th
Tel: 01 43 42 43 36
Open: L & D daily.
€ (lunch menu) €€ (à la carte)
⑥⑤ [p336, E4]
The big terrace is a great place for people-watching and browsing an honestly priced range of wines. Eat here before or after walking the nearby Promenade Plantée, elevated railway tracks now planted with roses and shrubs.
Crêperie Bretonne Fleurie
67 rue de Charonne, 11th
Tel: 01 43 55 62 29

LEFT: the beautiful interior of the Bofinger brasserie.

Open: L & D Mon–Fri, D Sat.
€ ⑥⑥ [p336, E3]
For economy and speed,
it's hard to beat a crêpe.
This authentically Breton
spot near Bastille is one
of the best places in town
for that particular
regional staple – served
with a choice of fillings
that includes ham,
cheese, egg, onions and
mushrooms; there are
vegetarian options too.
The approved accompa-
niment is cider; you can
have a crêpe for dessert,
too, filled with chocolate
sauce and ice cream.

L'Encrier
55 rue Traversière, 12th
Tel: 01 44 68 08 16
Open: L & D Mon–Fri, D Sat.
€ (set menu), €€ (à la carte) ⑥⑦
[p336, E3]
One of those cosy restau-
rants that you dream of
stumbling across: amaz-
ing value, traditional
decor, an open kitchen,
bubbly local crowd,
cheerful staff and decent
food: fried rabbit kidneys
on salad dressed with
raspberry vinegar, home-
made terrine or goose
magret with honey – but
there are also vegetarian
options. Finish up with
the delicious profiteroles.
No reservations.

Paris Main d'Or
133 rue du Faubourg-St-
Antoine, 11th
Tel: 01 44 68 04 68
Open: L & D Mon–Sat.
€€€ ⑥⑧ [p336, E3]
This is an authentic slice
of Corsica in Paris. The
food displays a charac-
teristic mix of sea and
mountain ingredients
and centuries of Genoan
influence: superb Corsi-
can charcuterie, auber-
gine baked with
ricotta-like *brocciu*
cheese, herby stews, fish

soups and superb roast
kid. It's also a good place
to discover the island's
wines and unusual *eaux-
de-vie*. Liveliest at night.
The lunch menu provides
more standard bistro
fare, with a few Corsican
elements thrown in.

Le Train Bleu
Gare de Lyon, 12th
Tel: 01 43 43 09 06
www.le-train-bleu.com
Open: L & D daily.
€€€€ ⑥⑨ [p336, E4]
Climb the main station
staircase, busy with com-
muters and pigeons, and
suddenly you're in the
glittering confines of a fabulous Belle Epoque res-
taurant. The menu offers
traditional dishes (including foie gras, *sole
meunière* and profiter-
oles) that are a bit pricey,
but for atmosphere this
place is hard to beat.

Le Janissaire
22–24 allée Vivaldi, 12th
Tel: 01 43 40 37 37
Open: L Mon–Fri, D Mon–Sat
€–€€ (set menu) €€€ (à la carte)
⑦⓪ [p336, E4]
A warm and welcoming
restaurant where the
food is beautifully pre-
sented in a dining room
decorated with cream
walls and dark wood.
Lamb is the speciality but
there are also options for
vegetarians and a good
selection of Turkish
wines. The lunchtime
menu is good value.

Bars and Cafés

Bistrot à Vins Mélac
42 rue Léon-Frot, 11th.
Tel: 01 43 70 59 27.
www.melac.fr.
Open: L & D Tue–Sat (until midnight).
㉓ [p336, E3]
Wine bar/shop/"vine-

yard" (there are a few
vines on the exterior wall)
crowded with workers at
lunchtime. Cheese and
specialities from the
Auvergne region are
paired with a wide choice
of wines.

Café Cannibale
93 rue Jean-Pierre Timbaud,
11th.
Tel: 01 49 29 95 59.
Open: Daily until 2am.
㉔ [p334, E3]
A hip bar-brasserie where
the waiting staff are
sometimes too cool or
too busy to be nice but
the shabby-chic sur-
rounds and buzzy atmos-
phere still make it a fun
place to enjoy a drink.
There's brunch on Sun-
days and regular DJ sets
or live music.

Café Charbon
109 rue Oberkampf, 11th.
Tel: 01 43 57 55 13.
Open: L & D daily (9am–2am,
until 4am Thur–Sat).
㉕ [p334, E4]
The former coal (*char-
bon*) shop with its *fin-de-
siècle* atmosphere – lofty
ceilings, ornate mirrors
and red-leather sofas –
is a fixture of east Paris's
café culture.

Le Café Noir
15 rue St-Blaise, 20th.
Tel: 01 40 09 75 80.
Open: L Tue–Fri, D Tue–Sat until
11pm.
㉖ [p334, E3]
The 1930s-style interior
is the main reason to
come here but arty locals
like it for a civilised cup of
coffee or glass of wine.
Food is typically French.

Au Chat Noir
76 rue Jean-Pierre Timbaud,
11th.
Tel: 01 48 06 98 22.
Open: Daily until 2am.
㉗ [p334, E3]
A high-ceilinged, typically
French café frequented

Price includes dinner
and a half-bottle of
house wine:

€ = under €25
€€ = €25–40
€€€ = €40–60
€€€€ = more than €60

by an older crowd who
come here to read the
paper during the day or
listen to live music or
poetry readings in the
evening. There are board
games available too.

Le Jemmapes
82 quai des Jemmapes, 10th.
Tel: 01 40 40 02 35.
Open: Non-stop daily.
㉘ [p334, D3]
Unusual flavoured vod-
kas are the speciality at
this ever-popular canal-
side café-bar; it's packed
at weekends, especially
the terrace. Good beers
and a relaxed vibe are
two more reasons to pay
a visit.

Plein Soleil
90 avenue Parmentier.
Tel: 01 48 05 41 06.
Open: D 7.30am–2am.
㉙ [p334, E4]
Trendy bar-café with a
cosy sun-filled terrace
and DJ nights on Thur, Fri
and Sat. There is brunch
on Sundays and live
music on the first Sunday
of the month.

Au P'tit Garage
63 rue Jean-Pierre-Timbaud,
11th.
Tel: 01 48 07 08 12.
Open: Sun–Mon 6pm–2am.
㉚ [p334, E4]
Rue Jean-Pierre-Timbaud
is bar-hopping heaven –
the street is one string of
largely good drinking
dens. This one's possibly
the best: a jumble of
assorted junk-shop furni-
ture, cool crowd, nice
cheap drinks and good
choices of music.

THE LATIN QUARTER AND ST-GERMAIN-DES-PRÉS

Writers, artists and thinkers have made these districts their home since Roman times. Nowadays, fashion rules as much as philosophy on the Left Bank, but the literary legacy lives on in its historic colleges, cafés, theatres, book stalls and street markets.

The Latin Quarter and St-Germain-des-Prés, side by side, make up the heart of the Left Bank. Once the home of artists and intellectuals, they have changed over the past few decades, with high fashion replacing high art. Nevertheless, the *Rive Gauche* maintains its charm in its beautiful tree-lined boulevards, narrow streets, manicured parks and imposing monuments. This is the place to stroll, imbibe and look cool. Sit in the shaded parks and on café terraces by day, and scan the menus in the fairy-lit streets by night.

THE DIVIDING BOULEVARD

What is generally referred to as the Latin Quarter lies east of Boulevard St-Michel, which runs from Place St-Michel on the banks of the Seine, to cross Boulevard St-Germain in front of the ancient Roman baths of Cluny – a reminder that this was once part of the Roman city of Lutetia. This maze of ancient streets and squares has been the stamping ground of students for nearly eight centuries, and Latin was virtually its mother tongue until Napoleon put a stop to it after the Revolution.

To the west of the Boulevard St-Michel is St-Germain-des-Prés, the historical centre of literary Paris and Existentialism, with the oldest church in Paris at its heart, but now chock-a-block with designer boutiques. If St-Germain's literary credentials remain intact it is thanks to Flammarion, Gallimard, Grasset and smaller publishers, who have refused to be tempted by luxury groups' lucrative offers for their premises. As for the three monuments to the district's literary heyday – the Café

Main Attractions

MUSÉE NATIONAL DU MOYEN AGE
LA SORBONNE
LE PANTHÉON
MOSQUÉE DE PARIS
JARDIN DES PLANTES
INSTITUT DU MONDE ARABE
JARDIN ET PALAIS DU
   LUXEMBOURG
ST-SULPICE
EGLISE ST-GERMAIN-DES-PRÉS

Maps and Listings

MAP, PAGE 198
SHOPPING, PAGE 215
RESTAURANTS, PAGE 216
ACCOMMODATION, PAGE 304

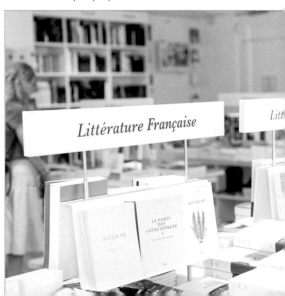

Littérature Française

LEFT: the legendary Left Bank Café de Flore. **RIGHT:** La Hune, the city's best-known bookshop, keeps St-Germain's literary credentials alive and well.

Latin Quarter, St-Germain-des-Prés and Montparnasse

des Deux Magots, Café de Flore and Brasserie Lipp – they are certainly thriving, even if their current clients are more likely to have Cartier than Camus on their minds.

THE LATIN QUARTER

Settled by the Romans in 53 BC and a cradle of philosophy and art since the Middle Ages, the Quartier Latin conjures up contradictions and delights in paradox, epitomised by the words of student and poet François Villon in 1456, as he declared "I laugh in tears." Villon debated with professors at the Sorbonne by day, and drank with thieves in the brothels of St-Michel by night.

Villon's legacy of rebellion survived him. In 1871, Place St-Michel was the headquarters of the Commune. Then in May 1968 – a turning point in the history of post-war France – demonstrations at conditions in the Nanterre faculty led to students tearing up the old cobblestones of Boulevard St-Michel to hurl at riot police. Hundreds of students were arrested, but a year later General de Gaulle relinquished power.

The Latin Quarter had been the centre of academic life in France since the 13th century, and the university had enjoyed immense privileges (included that of obliging all who entered it to speak Latin). After 1968, however, the University of Paris was decentralised to the suburbs, and the ancient cobblestones were buried under concrete. Protests, albeit far more subdued, still take place these days, and roads are sometimes blocked by squatting students, but the academic-hothouse atmosphere of the old Quartier has gone.

Nevertheless, the Latin Quarter remains a place of happy incongruity, where countless Greek souvlaki vendors stand amid traditional cafés spilling over the pavements, and arthouse cinemas occupy buildings with ancient academic facades.

ALONG THE BOUL' MICH

Now called Hôtel Belloy Saint Germain, the Hôtel des Etrangers, on the corner of Boulevard Saint Michel and Rue Racine in the Latin Quarter, was a meeting place in the 1870s for a group of poets including Arthur Rimbaud and Paul Verlaine.

Place St-Michel ❶ revels in recklessness, across the river from the palaces of justice and salvation (the Préfecture de Police and Notre-Dame). Its fountain depicting St Michael and a surprised dragon often seems buried under scooters, lovers and *clochards* (tramps), sitting philosophically amid the youthful chaos. Extending south from the square, the grand Boulevard St-Michel (Boul' Mich to the locals) will nourish the senses, the mind as well as the stomach, with an eclectic assortment of stalls, bookshops, alternative cinemas and fast-food joints.

Musée National du Moyen Age – Thermes de Cluny ❷

Address: 6 place Paul-Painlevé
www.musee-moyenage.fr
Tel: 01 53 73 78 16
Opening Hrs: Wed–Mon 9.15am–5.45pm
Entrance Fee: charge
Transport: Cluny-La Sorbonne

At the crossroads of Boul' Mich and Boulevard St-Germain stands

ABOVE: cheap eateries abound near the Boulevard St-Michel.
BELOW: St-Michel locals.

the fine Hôtel de Cluny, built in 1485–98 and a rare example of a late-medieval urban mansion. Once the residence of the Abbots of Cluny, these Flamboyant Gothic walls house one of the world's finest collections of medieval artefacts. Many of its treasures reflect life in religious communities, such as illuminated manuscripts, embroideries, stained glass, liturgical vestments and various church furnishings.

Among the numerous tapestries is the exquisite 15th-century *La Dame à la Licorne* (The Lady and the Unicorn) on the first floor of the rotunda. The six panels are beautifully worked in the millefleurs style of design, using rich, harmonious colours to create a delicate allegory on the worth of the five senses. The museum also holds 21 of the original heads of the kings of Judah, sculpted in 1220 for the facade of Notre-Dame but vandalised during the Revolution.

The Hôtel de Cluny was constructed on the remains of a huge Gallo-Roman bathhouse complex, believed to have been built in ad 200 by the guild of *nautae* (boatmen) – ships' prows are carved on the arch supports of the *frigidarium* (cold bathhouse). As elsewhere in their empire, the Romans living in Lutetia regarded bathing as the essence of civilisation.

Cluny's medieval garden is not a reproduction of a medieval garden but an imaginative modern evocation of the Middle Ages, taking its inspiration from objects in the collection and evoking the two spheres of the spiritual and the profane that governed the medieval world.

Latin lanes

Heading east along Boulevard St-Germain you'll reach Place Maubert, a bustling market square at the centre of a network of small, medieval streets lined with a jumble of boutiques revealing their shadowy interiors to the curious. The **Musée de la Préfecture de Police ❸** (4 Rue de la Montagne-Ste-Geneviève; tel: 01 44 41 52 50; Mon–Fri 9am–5.30pm, Sat 10.30am–5.30pm; free), on the

ABOVE: romanesque columns in the Musée de Cluny.
BELOW: a section of the six-panel, 15th-century tapestry *La Dame à la Licorne*, in the Musée de Cluny.

ABOVE: English bookshop Shakespeare and Company.

Most of the striking stained-glass windows in the side chapels of church St-Séverin are by 19th-century Chartres master Emile Hersch.

second floor of a pretty bleak police station, houses an intriguing collection of macabre objects, weapons and documents, including many relics of Napoleon's much-feared police chief Joseph Fouché.

St-Julien-le-Pauvre ❹

Address: 1 rue St-Julien-le-Pauvre
Tel: 01 43 54 52 16
Opening Hrs: daily 9.30am–1pm, 3–6.30pm
Entrance Fee: free
Transport: Cluny-La Sorbonne

Back on the banks of the Seine, quiet repose is to be found in this tiny 12th-century church, in the shadow of Notre-Dame. The Italian poet Dante is said to have prayed here in 1304. In the garden you can sit under a 300-year-old false acacia. Behind it is Rue du Fouarre, named after the bales of hay on which students used to perch during open-air lectures in the Middle Ages.

La Huchette

The streets around St-Julien and across Rue St-Jacques make up the Quartier de la Huchette, remarkably missed by Haussmann's 19th-century boulevard-building and today one of the most engaging and liveliest parts of the Left Bank.

Shakespeare and Company (37 rue de la Bûcherie, www.shakespeare andcompany.com) follows in the footsteps of Paris's most famous English bookshop founded in 1921 by Sylvia Beach in Rue de l'Odéon, which published the first edition of Joyce's *Ulysses*. It closed down during World War II, and the present shop was founded in 1956 by the late George Whitman, an American, who passed it on to his daughter Sylvia. It stocks a wide range of literature, from the Bard to the Beatniks, and famous expatriate writers such as William Burroughs and James Baldwin were frequent

Trial by Revolutionary council has been replaced with jazz at the **Caveau de la Huchette** (5 rue de la Huchette, see page 310). Danton and Robespierre selected guillotine victims in the cellars where musicians now jam. At No. 10, a young Napoleon dreamed of power.

St-Séverin ❺

Address: 3 rue des Prêtres-St-Séverin
Tel: 01 42 34 93 50
Opening Hrs: Mon–Sat 11am–7.30pm, Sun 9am–8.30pm
Entrance Fee: free
Transport: Cluny-La Sorbonne

This beautiful flamboyant Gothic church is famous for its palm-tree vaulting and twisting spiral columns, fine stained glass, mighty organ loft and the oldest bell in Paris in its bell tower, dating from 1412.

La Sorbonne ❻

Address: 17 rue de la Sorbonne
www.sorbonne.fr
Tel: 01 40 46 22 11
Opening Hrs: tours by appointment
Entrance Fee: free
Transport: Cluny-La Sorbonne

visitors. Today, it still stays open until midnight.

Le Petit Pont close by is a perfect spot from which to see the lights of the Seine shimmer at night. Here, the Quais St-Michel and Montebello offer picture-book views of the Ile de la Cité. By day, ancient bookstalls line the river banks, offering expensive antique volumes.

SHOP

Bookworms can find an abundance of material in the famously learned 5th and 6th *arrondisse-ments*. The Boulevard St-Michel is full of bookshops catering to students; Gibert Joseph (at No. 26) also has good second-hand titles, some in English. Two anglophone bookshops worth finding are tiny Abbey Bookshop (29 rue de la Parcheminerie, 5th); and San Francisco Book Company (17 rue Monsieur-Le-Prince, 6th).

ABOVE: fresh sardines for sale on Rue Mouffetard.
BELOW: the daily market on Rue Mouffetard.

TIP

The Latin Quarter boasts many arthouse cinemas; film buffs will enjoy the three cinemas in the Action mini-chain: Grand Action, Action Ecoles (5 and 23 rue des Ecoles, 5th) and Action Christine (4 rue Christine, 6th): all screen a rich variety of international arthouse fare, classic and modern.

ABOVE: Mouffetard bowling alley.
BELOW: Léon Foucault's pendulum inside the Panthéon.

when it began to attract thinkers from all over Europe.

In 1469, France's first printing press was set up here by three Germans summoned by Louis XI, which encouraged the growth of intellectual life. Sorbonne alumnus Cardinal Richelieu rebuilt the university in the 1630s, but it was closed down during the Revolution, and allowed to become dilapidated. Napoleon then reopened, revitalised and expanded it to become once more the most important university in France. Since decentralisation in 1970, though, there are 13 universities in Paris, and the Sorbonne has lost its force, if not its reputation.

The 17th-century chapel, commissioned by Richelieu and containing his marble tomb, overlooks the university's main courtyard. Above the tomb, beautifully carved by François Girardon, hangs a hat believed to be the cardinal's. Legend has it that the hat will fall when Richelieu's soul is released from hell.

Across Rue St-Jacques is the **Collège de France** (www.college-de-france.fr; tel:

Continue south along Rue St-Jacques and you'll come to the vast complex of the Sorbonne. Established in 1253 by King Louis IX (St Louis) and his confessor Robert de Sorbon, France's oldest university has been rebuilt many times since its inception as a dormitory for 16 theology students,

The Illustrious Dead

The Panthéon is one of the world's most exclusive clubs. To take up residence, you need to be a high achiever, French – and dead. It also helps if you're a man, as all but two of the 73 people interred within are men; the two women are Marie Curie and Sophie Berthelot, who only got in with her husband, chemist Marcellin Berthelot. One of the world's most famous artworks – *The Thinker* by Rodin – was based here too from 1906–22 (albeit outside in the square).

Here are some of France's greatest writers, Rousseau, Voltaire, Hugo and Zola; scientists, like the Curies; and politicians, including a president, Sadi Carnot, who was assassinated in 1894.

Others took longer to get to the Panthéon, as if their membership took a while to be ratified: André Malraux was reinterred here in 1996, 30 years after his death; and Alexandre Dumas *père* only joined the illustrious throng in 2002 – in a coffin draped in blue velvet with the motto of the Three Musketeers, "One for all, all for one". A lapse between death and national consecration was also the lot of the man who designed the Panthéon, J. G. Soufflot: he had to wait 59 years.

01 44 27 12 11; Oct–June Mon–Fri and Sat am; free), set up by François I in 1530 on the inspiration of the great humanist Guillaume Budé, to offer a more liberal education unfettered by the intolerance and dogmatism of the Sorbonne.

Today the college still has its academic independence, even though financially dependent on the state; lectures are open to the public without charge. Next door, the Lycée Louis-le-Grand is the school from which the 19th-century poet Charles Baudelaire was expelled, and in which Jean-Paul Sartre taught.

Montagne Ste-Geneviève

Further along Rue St-Jacques the ground rises to the top of Montagne Ste-Geneviève, site of the hermitage of the devout woman credited with saving the city from destruction by Attila the Hun in AD 451 (see page 30). She became the city's patron saint and the hilltop her shrine.

St-Etienne-du-Mont ❼

Address: place Ste-Geneviève
Tel: 01 43 54 11 79
Opening Hrs: Tue–Fri 8.45am–7.30pm, Sat 8.45am–noon, 2–7.45pm, Sun 8.45am–12.15pm, 2.30pm–7.45pm
Entrance Fee: free
Transport: Cardinal Lemoine

Built in a mixture of late Gothic and Renaissance styles in the 16th century, this beautiful church was part of the abbey of Ste-Geneviève, closed by the Revolution. Inside, the remains of the saint are buried in an ornate shrine. Playwright Jean Racine (1639–99) and the scientist and philosopher Blaise Pascal (1623–62) are also buried here, and a marble slab near the entrance marks the spot where the Archbishop of Paris was stabbed to death by a priest in 1857.

Le Panthéon ❽

Address: place du Panthéon
www.monuments-nationaux.fr

ABOVE: the mosque's tranquil main courtyard.

TIP

The bowling alley (tel: 01 43 31 09 35) on Rue Mouffetard offers a pleasant alternative for an evening out to the line of cheap bistros and souvenir shops.

RIGHT: the mosque has a delightful tearoom.
BELOW: playing *boules* in the Arènes de Lutèce.

Tel: 01 44 32 18 00
Opening Hrs: daily Apr–Sept 10am–6.30pm, Oct–Mar 10am–6pm
Entrance Fee: charge
Transport: Cardinal Lemoine

St-Etienne shares its commanding hilltop site with this monumental edifice. It was intended to be a new church to Ste-Geneviève, rashly promised by Louis XV when he recovered from a serious illness in 1744. Money was short, however, so public lotteries were organised to raise funds. Designed by neoclassical architect Jacques-Germain Soufflot (1713–80), who drew inspiration from Rome's Pantheon, the building was only finished just in time for the Revolution. The Revolutionaries had no use for a vast new church, however, so in 1791 it was designated a pantheon or resting-place for the "Founders of Liberty", a monument to rival the royal mausoleum at St-Denis (see page 280). Thus Voltaire, who was transferred from the country, and Jean-Jacques Rousseau came to lie in the crypt, to be joined later by Victor Hugo, Emile Zola and Louis Braille. Nobel Prize-winning

scientists Pierre and Marie Curie joined them in 1995, and the remains of World War II Resistance hero Jean Moulin were reburied here in 1964; the man who read his eulogy at the ceremony, André Malraux, did not join him until 1996.

After the Revolution, the use of the Panthéon yo-yoed from church to necropolis to church to headquarters of the Commune, until it finally became a lay temple and tomb in 1885. The interior is in the shape of a Greek cross, with the iron-framed dome towering above the centre. Frescoes by Puvis de Chavannes on the life of St Geneviève line the south wall; her glorification is portrayed on the upper section of the dome. Foucault's 67-metre (220ft) pendulum hangs from the centre of the dome, returned here from the Musée des Arts et Métiers in 1995; the one hanging there today is a replica.

Rue Mouffetard

Rue Mouffetard, originally the road to Rome, is one of the oldest streets in Paris; narrow, crowded, and full of cheap and cheerful places to eat. Hidden beneath it, now flows the River Bièvre, whose stench in medieval times, known as *moffettes*, gave the street its name. In its lower half is a street market (Tue–Sat, Sun am) around the Gothic church of **St-Médard**. Walk there via the picturesque **Place de la Contrescarpe** (a few minutes from Place du Panthéon eastwards), a lively place

to sit and people-watch with students skipping class, amid a maze of surrounding streets.

In the corner house (No. 1) Rabelais (1494–1553) composed his risqué rhymes, as had François Villon a century earlier. At No. 122, towards the bottom of the hill, the well carved onto the facade dates from Henri IV's reign.

THE JARDIN DES PLANTES

East of Rue Mouffetard is a quieter section of the Left Bank, the site of one of Paris's oldest parks, a distinguished mosque and intriguing museums and other attractions.

Mosquée de Paris ❾

Address: 2 place du Puits-de-l'Hermite
www.mosquee-de-paris.org
Tel: 01 45 35 97 33
Opening Hrs: tours Sat–Thur 9am–noon, 2–6pm
Entrance Fee: charge
Transport: Monge

This green-and-white mosque was built in Hispano-Moorish style in 1922 by French architects to

BELOW: skeletons inside the Grande Galerie de l'Evolution, Muséum d'Histoire Naturelle.

ABOVE: beautiful flower display in the Jardin des Plantes; in the background the stunning Grande Galerie de l'Evolution.
BELOW: moving some plants around in the Jardin des Plantes.

commemorate North African participation in World War I. Incorporating the Institut Musulman, the complex of buildings includes a museum of Muslim art, a patio inspired by the Alhambra in Granada, and an impressive selection of carvings and tiles. There is also a library, a restaurant, a delightful Moroccan tearoom and a Turkish bath.

Arènes de Lutèce ⑩

Address: rue Monge
Opening Hrs: daily summer 9am–9.30pm, winter 8am–5.30pm
Entrance Fee: free
Transport: Cardinal Lemoine

Behind a nondescript wooden doorway is the ancient gladiatorial arena of Roman Lutetia. The 15,000-seat arena – destroyed by barbarians in

Exotic Imports

When the Jardin des Plantes was expanding in the early 18th century, the royal doctor, Fagon, and botanists such as Tournefort and the three Jussieu brothers travelled far and wide bringing back seeds from around the world. The wild and wonderful collection of flora that resulted includes a 2,000-year-old American sequoia, a Ginkgo biloba and a Persian iron tree. A laricio pine was grown from a seed brought back from Corsica in 1774, and the pistachio tree is almost 300 years old. The oldest Lebanese cedar in France, planted in 1734, was brought from Kew Gardens in England by the Jussieu brothers' nephew, Bernard de Jussieu. The story goes that after dropping and breaking the pot containing the young plants, he nurtured the seedlings in his hat. The oldest tree in Paris, a false acacia or Robinia brought from America in 1635, is also here. The most attractive features for children are the zoo (founded by botanist Bernardin de Saint-Pierre with animals from the royal menagerie at Versailles in 1795), the 18th-century maze, the model of a stegosaurus in his garden of ancient plants and the Grande Galerie de l'Evolution, part of the Muséum National d'Histoire Naturelle.

AD 280 – was unearthed during the construction of Rue Monge in 1869; Victor Hugo led the campaign to preserve it. Today, the arena where gladiators fought serves as a children's playground, and on a fine day echoes with the clink of *pétanque* balls.

Jardin des Plantes ⑪

Address: rue Geoffroy-St-Hilaire
Tel: 01 40 79 56 01
Opening Hrs: daily summer 7.30am–7.45pm, winter 8am–5.30pm
Entrance Fee: free
Transport: Gare d'Austerlitz

Paris's botanical garden was inaugurated in 1640 as a medicinal herb farm for Louis XIII. The oldest tree in Paris, a false acacia planted in 1635, is here. The garden expanded in the 1700s, with the addition of a maze, amphitheatre and exhibition galleries. In 1889, the Galerie de Zoologie opened in the grounds, to display and study the millions of specimens brought back by globe-trotting naturalists and explorers.

Opened in 1794, the **Ménagerie** or zoo (daily 9am–6pm; charge) is popular with children, with its panthers, monkeys, orang-utan, flamingoes, reptile house and petting zoo.

Muséum National d'Histoire Naturelle ⑫

Address: 36 rue Geoffroy-St-Hilaire www.mnhn.fr
Tel: 01 40 79 54 79
Opening Hrs: Wed–Mon 10am–6pm
Admission Fee: charge
Transport: Gare d'Austerlitz

France's official natural history museum – one of many institutions created just after the Revolution, in 1793 – has galleries on palaeontology, mineralogy, geology and even a micro-zoo, but its great attraction is the lavishly restored **Grande Galerie de l'Evolution**. Its objective is to illustrate principles of evolution and dramatise the impact of human behaviour on the natural environment. The hall has retained elements of a 19th-century museum – parquet floors, iron columns, display cases – but has been completely modernised and equipped with the latest audiovisual techniques and interactive displays (mostly in French). The museum's *pièce de*

ABOVE: literary St-Germain.
BELOW: the new futuristic pavilion in the courtyard of the Institut du Monde Arabe.

ABOVE: the shuttered
windows inspired by
the screens of Moorish
palaces at the Institut
de Monde Arabe.
BELOW: basketball
game in the Jardin du
Luxembourg.

head west to this park-cum-modern sculpture exhibit. It's not the prettiest space, and noisy by day, but it takes on a whole new character on summer evenings, when it's a venue for free salsa and tango sessions.

Institut du Monde Arabe ⑭

Address: 1 rue des Fossés-St-Bernard
www.imarabe.org
Tel: 01 40 51 38 38
Opening Hrs: Tue–Thu 10am–6pm,
Fri until 9.30pm, Sat–Sun until 7pm
Entrance Fee: charge
Transport: Jussieu

One of the most striking buildings on the Seine is this high-tech blend of modern and traditional Arab styles, symbolic of the Institute's *raison d'être* – to deepen cultural understanding between the Western and Islamic worlds. A cultural centre and museum of Arab-Islamic art and civilisation, the nine-storey palace of glass, aluminium and concrete was designed by Jean Nouvel: its southern facade is a flat patterned wall of gleaming symmetry that recalls traditional Arab latticework. Its

résistance is the great herd of stuffed African animals that sweeps through the atrium.

Musée de la Sculpture en Plein Air (Jardin Tino Rossi) ⑬

Address: quai St-Bernard
Opening Hrs: Mon–Fri 8am–dusk,
Sat–Sun 9am–dusk
Entrance Fee: free
Transport: Gare d'Austerlitz

For a riverside stroll, leave the Jardin des Plantes at Place Valhubert and light-sensitive camera-like irises are supposed to open and close according to the movement of the sun, but have been plagued with problems, and most stay fixed at one setting. Fully redesigned and renovated, the museum reopened to the public in early 2012 after three years' work. In 2011, a futuristic pavilion designed by Iraqi-born architect Zaha Hadid 'landed' in the museum's main courtyard, bringing some curves to the very linear main museum. Views from the roof terrace restaurant, Noura, are breathtaking.

ODÉON AND LUXEMBOURG

The Odéon district acts as a buffer between the boisterous Latin Quarter (5th *arrondissement*) and the more refined St-Germain-des-Prés (6th *arrondissement*). From St-Michel Métro, walk along Rue St-André-des-Arts to the **Cour de Rohan**. It's worth popping in to admire the picturesque courtyards with Renaissance facades. Turn left into **Rue de l'Ancienne-Comédie**, the next street along, where **Le Procope**, the first-ever café in Paris and credited with introducing coffee

to the city in 1686, is still doing good business (see page 217).

At Carrefour de l'Odéon, a statue of the Revolutionary leader Georges Danton marks the spot where his old house once stood. Fellow Revolutionary Camille Desmoulins lived at No. 2 before storming the Bastille in 1789. Others plotted in neighbouring streets, which now shelter some of the most bourgeois boutiques and apartments in Paris.

From here, Rue de l'Odéon – first street in Paris to have gutters and pavements – leads to Place de l'Odéon and the neoclassical **Odéon-Théâtre de l'Europe** ⑮ (www.theatre-odeon. fr; tel: 01 44 85 40 40), founded by the Comédiens Ordinaires du Roi in 1782. Recently restored, this is one of France's leading public theatres, and as the "Theatre of Europe" hosts many international productions – albeit mostly performed in French.

Jardin du Luxembourg ⑯

Address: rue de Vaugirard
Opening Hrs: daily 8am–dusk
Entrance Fee: free
Transport: Odéon/rer Luxembourg

LEFT: stained-glass window, St-Sulpice.
BELOW: inside St-Sulpice.

Beautifully landscaped, this is the quintessential Paris park, a haven of manicured greenery where young couples rendezvous under plane trees by the romantic Baroque Fontaine de Médicis, while children sail boats across the carp-filled lake in the middle. Statues of queens of France gaze down from the terrace, while the thwack of tennis balls disturbs the quiet reverie of sunbathers and smartly clad nannies push babies in expensive prams.

On Wednesdays and weekends, the famous Guignol puppet show is performed in the **Théâtre des Marionnettes** (tel: 01 43 29 50 97). More serious entertainment is found by the corner with Rue de Vaugirard, where people play chess under the fragrant orange trees. There are 200 varieties of apple and pear trees in the garden, and an apiary that produces hundreds of kilos of honey a year. The **Musée du Luxembourg** (19 rue de Vaugirard,

www. museeduluxembourg.fr; tel: 0140 13 62 00; daily 10am–7.30pm, Fri until 10pm; charge) puts on crowd-pulling major exhibitions.

Palais du Luxembourg ⓱

Address: www.senat.fr
Tel: 01 44 54 19 49
Opening Hrs: guided tours by appointment
Entrance Fee: free
Transport: Odéon/RER Luxembourg

The palace that presides over the gardens was built for Marie de Médicis after the murder of her husband Henri IV, on the site of a mansion that had belonged to Duke François of Luxembourg. Its Italianate style, modelled on the Pitti Palace in Florence, was intended to remind her of home. The widowed queen moved into the palace in 1625, but was forced into exile by Richelieu before its completion. During the Revolution it was used as a prison, and in

World War II it was the German headquarters. Today it is the seat of the French Senate, and the adjacent Petit Luxembourg is the residence of its president.

St-Sulpice ⑱

Addess: place St-Sulpice
www.paroisse-saint-sulpice-paris.org
Tel: 01 46 33 21 78
Opening Hrs: daily 7.30am – 7.30pm
Entrance Fee: free
Transport: St-Sulpice

From the Petit Luxembourg, Rue Garancière leads to this imposing church. Apart from one of the finest organs in Europe (used for many recitals) and Delacroix's *Jacob Wrestling with the Angel*, inspired by the painter's own struggle with art, the great cavern of a church has little to offer, but attracted worldwide attention after featuring in the 2003 book *The Da Vinci Code*.

In front of the huge colonnaded facade, with mismatching towers, is a square with an amusing fountain made by Joachim Visconti in 1844.

ST-GERMAIN-DES-PRÉS

Historic heart of literary Paris, St-Germain-des-Prés covers an area roughly from St-Sulpice to the Seine. Its elegant streets now house chic boutiques, yet it retains a sense of animation, with cafés spilling out onto the pavements. In the 1940s the area became a breeding ground for literature and ideas. Existentialists, inspired by Jean-Paul Sartre, Simone de Beauvoir and Albert Camus, gathered in local cafés such as Les Deux Magots and Café de Flore.

The days of black sweaters and beret-clad Existentialists locked in debate are well and truly over; the area has been colonised by designers and antique dealers. The **Marché St-Germain** shows how things have changed. Tastefully restored, the old stone market hall now contains fashion shops, a swimming pool and an auditorium, as well as a local market.

The hub of St-Germain is the junction of Boulevard St-Germain and Rue Bonaparte, with, opposite each other, **Café de Flore** and **Les Deux Magots**, which serve some of the best hot chocolate in Paris – and some of the most expensive. Once favourite haunts of the literati, these cafés are now packed with tourists. Also here is the sleek **La Hune** bookshop, crammed with literature and books on art, architecture and performing arts, in French and English. It stays open until midnight, and feels most "St-Germain" after dark.

Eglise St-Germain-des-Prés ⑲

Address: www.eglise-sgp.org
Tel: 01 55 42 81 33
Opening Hrs: daily 9am – 7pm
Entrance Fee: free
Transport: St-Germain-des-Prés

Overlooking the crossroads is the oldest church in Paris, begun in AD 542, when it was built as a basilica for holy relics. It is named after St Germain, cardinal of Paris, who is

ABOVE: street art depicting Van Gogh. **BELOW:** waiter at Les Deux Magots.

ABOVE: the Pont des Arts leads to the imposing Institut de France.
RIGHT: *bouquiniste* along the Quai des Grands-Augustins.
BELOW: Café de Flore was a favourite haunt of writer Jean-Paul Sartre.

Tel: 01 44 41 86 50
Opening Hrs: Wed–Mon 9.30am–5pm
Entrance Fee: charge
Transport: St-Germain-des-Prés

Heading east down Rue Jacob, filled with fascinating antiques and design shops, you pass Place Furstenburg, with the studio where Romantic painter Eugène Delacroix (1798–1863) lived from 1857 to his death, while he painted the murals in St-Sulpice. Now a museum, it has engaging sketches and memorabilia.

Ecole Nationale Supérieure des Beaux-Arts ㉑

Address: 14 rue Bonaparte
www.ensba.fr
Tel: 01 47 03 50 00
Opening Hrs: exhibitions Tue–Sun 1–7pm
Admission Fee: charge
Transport: St-Germain-des-Prés

Paris's finest art school fills the *hôtels* fronting the Quai Malaquais. Begun in 1608, the main building was a monastery until the Revolution; the School of Fine Arts moved here in 1816, and today holds

buried here. Ransacked and rebuilt over centuries, the heavily restored 11th-century building is a blend of simple Romanesque, Early Gothic, Baroque tombs and 19th-century wall paintings. In the small square alongside stands Picasso's tribute to his friend, the poet Apollinaire.

Musée National Eugène Delacroix ⑳

Address: 6 place Furstenberg
www.museedelacroix.fr

Left Bank Rendezvous

Cafés have played a huge part in Paris's intellectual, political and artistic development. In the 18th century, Café Voltaire (1 place de l'Odéon), named after its most famous regular, was the place where he met fellow philosopher Diderot to discuss their Enlightenment theories. The tormented 19th-century poets – Verlaine and Mallarmé – threw Symbolist ideas at each other here and, much later, in the 1920s, American writers Ernest Hemingway and F. Scott Fitzgerald extolled the café's "sudden provincial quality". Other writers in Paris between the world wars spent hours in Le Procope (see page 217), and Jean-Paul Sartre and Simone de Beauvoir favoured Les Deux Magots (6 place St-Germain-des-Prés) in the 1940s.

exhibitions of students' work and works from its extensive collection, notably of French and Italian Old Master drawings.

Close by is the imposing **Institut de France** ㉒, seat of the Académie Française, established in 1635. The select members of the illustrious institution are guardians of the French language, protecting it from the insidious onslaught of English.

Musée de la Monnaie ㉓

Address: 11 quai de Conti
www.monnaiedeparis.fr
Tel: 01 40 46 56 66
Opening Hrs: Tue–Fri 11am–5.30pm, Sat–Sun noon–5.30pm
Entrance Fee: charge
Transport: Pont Neuf

Next door is the neoclassical **Hôtel des Monnaies**, designed by Jacques Antoine for Louis XV to replace an earlier royal mint, and completed in

1775. The *hôtel* now houses a comprehensive museum of France's money and medals.

Quai des Grands-Augustins is the oldest quay on the Seine, and is lined with antiquarian bookshops and antique dealers. Picasso lived for 20 years on Rue des Grands-Augustins, which branches off the quay.

One of the most popular bridges in Paris is the cast-iron Pont des Arts – an appropriate name for a footbridge that spans the river between the Institut de France and the Louvre. It was built in 1804, but by the 1970s had been severely damaged by three boat collisions and was closed to the public. It was rebuilt from the original plans and reopened in 1984; today it's a popular spot for picture-taking and picnics.

SHOPPING

From designer boutiques to gourmet food shops, St-Germain has plenty to offer those who love the finer things in life.

Children

Eveil et Jeux
19 rue Vavin, 6th.
Tel: 0892 350 666
Educational and fun games, toys, books, crafts and multimedia for children aged up to 12. There is also a range of cute furniture.

Clothing

Petit Bateau
26 rue Vavin, 6th.
Tel: 01 55 42 02 53
Famous for its stripy cotton T-shirts, this chain now stocks clothes for all the family including

babies. There are other branches in the city.
Plein Sud
29 rue du Dragon, 6th.
Tel: 01 45 48 79 29
Sexy fashion for women, including evening wear, by Moroccan designer Fayçal Amor. He does an equally sexy collection of spiky heels and leather boots.
Sonia Rykiel
175 boulevard St-Germain, 6th.
Tel: 01 49 54 60 60
The orange-haired Parisian designer sells chic, wearable clothes for women and girls at her flagship store. The handbags are pretty snazzy too.

Food

Gérard Mulot
76 rue de Seine, 6th.

Tel: 01 45 26 85 77
Some of the finest cakes, chocolates and macaroons in Paris are the reason to visit this wonderful patisserie. There is also a shop at 6 rue du Pas-de-la-Mule in the Marais.

Gifts

Diptyque
34 boulevard St-Germain, 5th.
Tel: 01 43 26 77 44.
www.diptyqueparis.com
Gorgeous candles, perfumes, body care and home fragrance from this luxury French brand. There is also a range of smaller-sized products, which are ideal to take travelling.

Home

Alexandre Biaggi
14 rue de Seine, 6th.
Tel: 01 44 07 34 73.
www.alexandrebiaggi.com
Amid the art galleries and antique shops on Rue de Seine, this place specialises in new and classic 20th-century furniture. There are many easily portable items but everything comes at a price.

Markets

Le Marché St-Germain
14 rue Lobineau, 6th.
Tel: 01 43 26 01 44
Near St-Sulpice, this covered market houses a range of fashion boutiques for men, women and children (including GAP) as well as several bars and restaurants.

BEST RESTAURANTS, BARS AND CAFES

Restaurants

Cambodian

Bayon
121 rue Monge, 5th
Tel: 01 43 36 67 43
Open: L daily, D Tue–Sat.
€ **71** [p336, C4]
This new restaurant specialises in the cuisine from one of France's former colonies, either to eat on site or take away. Try *tear bom pong empile thom* (duck fried in tamarind sauce) or *khor trey* (caramel fish stew). There are options for adventurous vegetarians too.

French

L'Alcazar
62 rue Mazarine, 6th
Tel: 01 53 10 19 99
www.alcazar.fr
Open: L & D daily, Br Sun.

€€€ **72** [p336, B2]
Sir Terence Conran's contribution to the Paris restaurant scene was to transform this old music hall into a designer brasserie. A *réussite* with Parisians and tourists alike. The atmosphere is easygoing and the menu competitively priced.

Les Bouquinistes
53 quai des Grands-Augustins, 6th
Tel: 01 43 25 45 94
www.lesbouquinistes.com
Open: L Mon–Fri, D Mon–Sat.
€€ (set menu) €€€€ (à la carte)
73 [p336, B2]
Guy Savoy's stylish Seine-side bistro continues to draw a fashionable crowd. Chef Stéphane Perraud's modernised take on bistro cooking is seen in

dishes such as langoustines roasted with citrus butter, courgette and lemon confit or pheasant with sauerkraut and foie gras.

Chez René
14 boulevard St-Germain, 5th
Tel: 01 43 54 30 23
Open: L & D Tue–Sat.
€€ (set menu) €€€ (à la carte)
74 [p336, C3]
Classic French bistro, one block from the Seine with a small outdoor terrace. It serves groaning plates of daily specials such as an excellent coq au vin, a perfectly aged entrecôte Bercy for two, and a fine selection of cheeses and charcuterie.

Le Comptoir du Relais
9 carrefour de l'Odéon, 6th
Tel: 01 44 27 07 97
Open: non-stop daily.

€€ (set menu), €€€ (à la carte)
75 [p336, B3]
One of the biggest stories in the restaurant world in recent years, Yves Camdeborde's bistro serves a no-choice €40 meal in the evening that's so good you have to book months ahead. The brasserie dishes served at lunch are no mean fare, either: iced cream of chicken soup, or rolled saddle of lamb.

Lapérouse
51 quai des Grands-Augustins, 6th
Tel: 01 43 26 68 04
www.laperouse.com
Open: L & D Mon–Fri, D Sat.
€€€ (set menu), €€€€ (à la carte) **76** [p336, B2]
Diners at this 17th century institution have included Hugo and

BELOW: St-Germain is all about café culture.

Proust. Its run of self-contained individual dining rooms used to lock on the inside, hence Lapérouse's rumoured popularity with ministers and their mistresses; the main dining room is hardly less romantic. The refined classical cooking is as elaborate as the decor. Prices reflect the riverside setting. Lunch times are relatively quiet, and the lunch set menus are less pricey.

Moissonnier
28 rue des Fossés-St-Bernard, 5th
Tel: 01 43 29 87 65
Open: L & D Tue–Sun.
€€ **77** [p336, C3]
A Parisian institution serving specialities from the Jura and the Rhône. Dishes include a *saladier lyonnais* (salad served with crisp bacon, hard-boiled eggs and chicken livers) and *quenelles de brochet* (pike dumplings).

L'Ourcine
92 rue Broca, 13th
Tel: 01 47 07 13 65
Open: L & D Tue–Sat.
€€ **78** [p336, B4]
Talented young chef Stéphane Danière produces updated versions of French regional dishes, combining seasonal produce with more cosmopolitan flavours. Tables are tightly packed into a minimalist but attractive room in a 17th-century building.

Pierre Gagnaire à Gaya Rive Gauche
44 rue du Bac, 7th
Tel: 01 45 44 73 73
www.pierre-gagnaire.com
Open: L & D Mon–Sat.
€€€€ **79** [p336, A2]
Food at this clever reworking of a famous fish restaurant costs far less than at Gagnaire's

HQ in the 20th. The piscine stars run from illustrious langoustine and sole to more humble cod; there are some nicely inventive dishes, too, such as red snapper daubed with peppered caramel.

Le Voltaire
27 quai Voltaire, 7th
Tel: 01 42 61 17 49
Open: L & D Tue–Sat.
€€€€ **80** [p336, A2]
Not the least of this vintage bistro's attractions is its riverside setting; others include the polished service and the food, which runs the gamut from elegant salads and rustic grub like sautéed rabbit to luxury dishes like lobster omelette. Cosy, but chic at the same time.

Ze Kitchen Galerie
4 rue des Grands-Augustins, 6th
Tel:01 44 32 00 32
www.zekitchengalerie.fr
Open: L & D Mon–Fri, D Sat.
€€€ **81** [p336, D2]
Former Guy Savoy protégé William Ledeuil, who used to run Les Bouquinistes around the corner, branched out on his own in this arty modern bistro. The successful fusion fare is bursting with ideas, but centred round sushi-style raw fish preparations, spicy condiments and main course meat and fish speed-cooked *a la plancha* and served with Asian-style condiments.

Le Grenier de Notre-Dame
18 rue de la Bûcherie, 5th
Tel: 01 43 29 98 29
Open: L & D daily.
€ **82** [p336, C2]

This no-frills vegetarian and macrobiotic restaurant has been going strong since 1978 and around 80 per cent of the produce it uses is organic. The dishes, which include vegetarian couscous and tofu quiche, are not only delicious but huge and are excellent value for money.

Le Bar Dix
10 rue de l'Odéon, 6th.
Tel: 01 43 26 66 83.
Open: Daily 6pm–2am.
31 [p336, B3]
A favourite with students and the economy-minded for decades, this bar has a cramped upper bar done out with old Jacques Brel record sleeves, and a basement romantically lit by candles. The drinks of choice are cheap reds by the glass or the home-made sangría.

Café de Flore
172 boulevard St-Germain, 6th.
Tel: 01 45 48 55 26.
Open: Non-stop daily.
32 [p336, A3]
Of the two celebrated "intellectual cafés" on Boulevard St-Germain, this (the other being Les Deux Magots) is the better. Prices are just as steep, but the prevailing language among customers here is French, not English; and you do see the occasional student writing an essay on a table.

Café de la Mairie
8 place St-Sulpice, 6th.
Tel: 01 43 26 67 82.
Open: Non-stop daily.
33 [p336, A3]
This place is always packed. Strangely, given its ringside view of St-

Sulpice church, there never seem to be many tourists – stranger, when you remember it was frequented by Camus and Miller. Perhaps it's the low-marks food or rather gruff service.

Le Pousse au Crime
15 rue Guisarde, 6th.
Tel: 01 46 33 41 91.
Open: Tue–Wed 11pm–2am, Thur–Sat 11pm–dawn.
34 [p336, A3]
With no fewer than three bars, you can request your favourite music to dance to. A must in St-Germain-des-Prés. Two floors with just one motto: party! 15-euro entry on Fri and Sat.

Le Procope
13 rue de l'Ancienne-Comédie, 6th.
Tel: 01 40 46 79 00.
Open: Sun-Wed 11.30am–midnight, Thur–Sat 11.30am–1am.
35 [p336, B3]
Founded in 1686 by Francesco dei Coltelli, this is the city's oldest café. Enjoy lunch or dinner in the very place where Voltaire, Danton, Robespierre, Marat and Benjamin Franklin once sat.

La Rhumerie
166 boulevard St-Germain, 6th.
Tel: 01 43 54 28 94.
Open: Daily noon–2am.
36 [p336, A3]
This 77-year old café serves delicious cocktails and rums with *accras* (fritters), crab toasts and other exotic specialties.

JARDIN DU LUXEMBOURG

The quintessential Paris park has leafy pathways, statues, boules, a bandstand, a boating pond and a lovely, civilised atmosphere.

The Jardin du Luxembourg is one of the largest parks in Paris: 25 hectares (63 acres). It's also one of the loveliest, with its atmosphere of quiet panache and relaxed bonhomie. Its regulars, a mongrel crowd of smart locals, students, artists, joggers, and nuns from the nearby convents, refer to it by the affectionate nickname "Luco", a short-ening of the Roman name for the area, Lucotitius. As well as an art museum (the Musée du Luxembourg, see page 212), the park contains an apiary, an orangery, a bandstand, both tennis and basketball courts, *boules* pitches, a puppet theatre, tables for chess, as well as a small café. The grand Palais du Luxembourg, located on its northern edge, was constructed in 1615 for Queen Marie de Médicis, the widow of Henri IV of France, who ordered a building in Florentine style to remind her of the Pitti Palace of her childhood; she also commissioned Florentine engineer Tomasso Francini in 1630 to design her a fountain, which looks like a grotto and is a popular place to head on a warm day thanks to its shady trees. Since 1958, the palace has been home to the French parliament's upper house, the Senate.

The Essentials

Address: rue de Vaugirard www.senat.fr/visite/jardin/index.html
Opening Hrs: daily summer 8am–dusk, winter 9am–dusk
Entrance Fee: free
Transport: Odéon/RER Luxembourg

ABOVE: many people come to the tranquil gardens simply to read.

BELOW: chess players meet regularly in the park.

ABOVE: the Palais du Luxembourg, centrepiece of the park.

ART AND LITERATURE IN THE PARK

The park is studded with nearly 100 sculptures, of varying styles, eras and subject matters. Famous artists are a dominant group: Baudelaire, Flaubert, Verlaine and George Sand to name but a few. *Le Marchand de masques* features a young boy holding the face of Victor Hugo and the sculpture also features the faces of Balzac and Berlioz. Historical figures, including French queens and saints, are also present: Blanche de Castille, St Geneviève and Marie de Médicis, among others; and allegorical subjects include a scaled-down version of the Statue of Liberty (although the original scale model was cleaned up and moved to the Musée d'Orsay in 2012). The park has also featured in some famous works of literature: the two lovers, Cosette and Marius Pontmercy, first meet here in Victor Hugo's *Les Misérables* while Lambert Strether, the main protagonist in *The Ambassadors* by Henry James, has a pivotal moment in the gardens; the place also provide the backdrop to the final chapter in William Faulkner's controversial 1931 novel *Sanctuary*.

ABOVE: colourful toy sailing boats are available for hire on the ornamental pond directly in front of the Palais.

LEFT: the park is dotted with sculptures of varying size and theme.

BELOW: the gilded Salle du Livre d'Or inside the Senate.

MONTPARNASSE AND BEYOND

Once a backwater, Montparnasse has a unique place in modern culture – at some point between 1910 and 1939, Picasso and Matisse, Lenin and Stravinsky, Hemingway and Joyce could all be found here. Their legacy lives on amid tower blocks and redevelopment schemes, in a thriving café and nightlife scene.

Main Attractions
MUSÉE DU MONTPARNASSE
MUSÉE BOURDELLE
MUSÉE ZADKINE
TOUR MONTPARNASSE
CIMETIÈRE DU
  MONTPARNASSE
LES CATACOMBES
BIBLIOTHÈQUE FRANÇOIS-
  MITTERRAND

Maps and Listings
MAP, PAGE 198
SHOPPING, PAGE 225
RESTAURANTS, PAGE 228
ACCOMMODATION, PAGE 306

The once-rural area southwest of the Jardin du Luxembourg was christened Mount Parnassus – after the classical home of Apollo and his Muses – by a local poetry society in the 17th century, when they gathered on quarry mounds to recite verses. In the early years of the 20th century, the area became a magnet for artists, composers and revolutionaries, including Chagall, Léger, Soutine, Picasso, Modigliani, Lenin and Stravinsky. Some decamped from Montmartre because of the inflated rents; others were émigrés in search of refuge or a new beginning, drawn to a place that embraced freethinkers and the avant-garde. They rented studios in the newly built-up area, and gathered in cafés and brasseries such as Le Select, Le Dôme, La Rotonde and La Coupole. Their bohemian lifestyle is as much a part of the Paris myth as the era's legacy of artworks (see page 226).

After World War II, writers and philosophers such as Jean-Paul Sartre, Simone de Beauvoir, Henry Miller and Louis Aragon moved in, patronising the same cafés clustered around the lively **Carrefour Vavin**, where the district's inescapable artery, the **Boulevard Montparnasse**, crosses Boulevard Raspail. Now relabelled Place Pablo Picasso, the Carrefour still throbs with life well into the early hours. Further east, the Closerie des Lilas was another favourite artistic haunt (see page 228).

AROUND MONTPARNASSE

Above the Carrefour on Boulevard Raspail stands Rodin's dramatic **Statue de Balzac**. This sculpture so shocked the Société des Beaux-Arts when unveiled at the 1898 Salon – by showing the great writer in a

LEFT: the Tour Montparnasse looming behind the Edgar Quinet Métro station.

dressing gown – that it was turned down, and only finally cast and installed here in 1939.

Musée du Montparnasse ㉔

Address: 21 avenue du Maine
www.museedumontparnasse.net
Tel: 01 42 22 91 96
Opening Hrs: Tue–Sun 12.30–7pm
Entrance Fee: charge
Transport: Montparnasse-Bienvenüe

Tucked away down one of the small alleys of artists' studios that formerly littered Montparnasse, this museum was once a studio and art school run by Russian avant-garde artist Marie Vassilieff. Exhibitions focus on different aspects of the area's artistic heritage, with photos and art works.

Musée Bourdelle ㉕

Address: 16–18 rue Bourdelle
www.bourdelle.paris.fr
Tel: 01 49 54 73 73
Opening Hrs: Tue–Sun 10am–6pm
Entrance Fee: free
Transport: Montparnasse-Bienvenüe

A showcase for the work of Modernist sculptor Antoine Bourdelle spread over his former apartment and studio. A pupil of Rodin, Bourdelle is best known for his friezes on the Théâtre des Champs-Elysées.

Musée Zadkine ㉖

Address: 100bis rue d'Assas
www.zadkine.paris.fr
Tel: 01 55 42 77 20
Opening Hrs: Tue–Sun 10am–6pm
Entrance Fee: free
Transport: Vavin

Among the influx of émigrés from Russia was Cubist sculptor Ossip Zadkine, who moved into this tiny house and studio in 1928. His sculptures are displayed around the house and garden, along with his drawings and engravings, and paintings by his wife Valentine Prax.

Tour Montparnasse ㉗

Address: 33 avenue du Maine
www.tourmontparnasse56.com
Tel: 01 45 38 53 16
Opening Hrs: daily 9.30am–11.30pm, winter until 10.30pm
Entrance Fee: charge
Transport: Montparnasse-Bienvenue

The Fondation Henri-Cartier-Bresson opened in 2003. Its mission is "to preserve the independence and keep alive the spirit" of the photographer. The Fondation is located at 2 impasse Lebouis, 14th arrondissement. Métro: Gaîté. Tel: 01 56 80 27 00; www.henricartierbresson.org.

BELOW: Musée Zadkine sculpture garden.

ABOVE: the fabulous view from the top of Tour Montparnasse.
BELOW: street art.

The district, however – and the whole southern skyline – is dominated by this lumbering 59-storey tower, built in 1974 and the only skyscraper in central Paris (as no more have been allowed since then). If you've a head for heights and the stomach for a lightning-fast lift, the roof terrace offers superb views of Paris. At the foot of the tower, by an ugly shopping centre, is **Place du 18 Juin 1940**, commemorating the day when General de Gaulle sent his famous bbc radio message urging the French to carry on resisting German occupation: "We have lost a battle, but not the war."

Behind the tower is the **Gare Montparnasse**, which serves northwestern France. In the mid-19th century, thousands of Bretons emerged from this station, fleeing rural poverty and famine in Brittany, hence the many crêperies in the area.

Cimetière du Montparnasse ㉘

Address: boulevard Edgar-Quinet
Tel: 01 44 10 86 50
Opening Hrs: mid-Mar–Oct Mon–Fri 8am–6pm, Sat 8.30am–6pm, Sun 9am–6pm, Nov–mid-Mar closes daily at 5.15pm

morning market on Wednesdays and Saturdays, contains the third of Paris's giant cemeteries, with Père Lachaise and Montmartre. Among those buried here are artists Antoine Bourdelle and Man Ray, composer Saint-Saëns and writers Charles Baudelaire, Guy de Maupassant, Jean-Paul Sartre and Irish writer and long-term local resident Samuel Beckett.

Les Catacombes ㉙

Address: 1 avenue Colonel Henri Rol-Tanguy
www.catacombes.paris.fr
Tel: 01 43 22 47 63
Opening Hrs: Tue–Sun 10am–5pm (last entry at 4pm)
Entrance Fee: charge
Transport: Denfert-Rochereau

If you're still in macabre mood after the Cimetière, visit this labyrinth beneath Place Denfert-Rochereau, where the neatly stacked skulls, femurs and tibias of some 6 million departed souls line long passageways. The former Roman quarries were converted into ossuaries in 1785, when cartloads of skeletons were

Baudelaire, one of the star residents of Montparnasse cemetery, has two memorial stones: the first is his grave, in the sixth division; the second is the cenotaph on Avenue Transversale, an eerily lifelike recumbent sculpture of the poet watched over by a brooding figure representing Ennui.

Entrance Fee: free
Transport: Raspail

Boulevard Edgar-Quinet, as well as some nice cafés and a lively

LEFT: La Butte-aux-Cailles has a village atmosphere.
BELOW: the floating Piscine Joséphine-Baker.

Place d'Italie is the traffic hub of the 13th *arrondissement*, where old districts alternate with soulless 1960s tower blocks. The square is dominated by the modern Centre Commercial Italie, but more down to earth is the food market on Boulevard Auguste-Blanqui (Tue, Fri, Sun am).

Les Gobelins is the oldest part of the neighbourhood. Traces of a Gallo-Roman necropolis were discovered here, and the tomb of the first Archbishop of Paris, St-Marcel. The district's name stems from the **Manufacture Nationale des Gobelins** (42 avenue des Gobelins; tel: 01 44 0853 49; Tue-Sun 11am–6pm; charge), the tapestry factory founded in 1662. Visitors can watch weavers at work.

Hidden just south of Place d'Italie is the tranquil, villagey *quartier* of **La Butte-aux-Cailles**. In the 1900s the hill was still covered with working windmills and water mills. Its narrow, cobbled streets offer some of Paris's friendliest, cheapest bars. The hub of activity is around the Rue de la Butte-aux-Cailles and Rue des

ABOVE: restaurant in La Butte-aux-Cailles.
BELOW: Paris-Plage in full swing.

removed from the overflowing cemeteries at Place des Innocents and other areas. Take a torch, and someone to hold your hand, as the inscription on the door reads: "Stop. You are entering the empire of the dead."

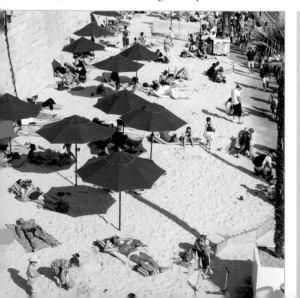

Off the Waterfront

The "New" Left Bank is one of the locations for Paris-Plage, which brings the beach to the city in July and August (see page 113). Since 2006 the fun on the Left Bank has revolved around a new floating swimming pool, Piscine Joséphine-Baker, that's moored up by the Bibliothèque Nationale. It's a purpose-built barge that also features a huge sun deck, cafeteria and children's play area. Water is pumped from the river before being treated to crystalline cleanliness. A huge, sliding glass roof covers the pool, and when the sunshine's hot enough, it's pulled back to let in the open air. There's even a packed programme of exercise classes.

Cinq-Diamants. A few trendy restaurants have opened here, but it's still an unassuming, delightful area to visit.

Chinatown is a close neighbour, roughly bordered by Avenue d'Italie and Avenue d'Ivry – a mini-city of skyscrapers where streets are lined with kitsch gift shops, Thai groceries, Vietnamese pho noodle bars and Chinese *pâtisseries* and tearooms.

THE "NEW" LEFT BANK

The "new" *Rive Gauche* is Paris's biggest urban renewal project since the 1860s, when Baron Haussmann sliced up the city's medieval heart to carve out his tree-lined boulevards. New streets and buildings are going up in a zone of rusty factories and disused railway tracks extending south for 130 hectares (320 acres) from Gare d'Austerlitz; work is due to be completed in 2015. With the new national library as its centre-piece, the area is gradually taking shape as new offices, apartments and schools go up, and the **MK2-Bibliothèque** multiplex cinema draws in the public at weekends; it is estimated that 15,000 people work in the area and that there are 5,000 residents here. A new garden has been created, the Jardin des Grands-Moulins Abbé-Pierre, which is split into three areas: a sports section, a green space and a children's playground. Art galleries, upmarket cafés, restaurants and boutiques have cropped up, and the **Rue Louise-Weiss** is the focus of a small gallery scene. In an unusual display of

ABOVE: La Butte-aux-Cailles graffiti.
BELOW: shopping for shoes.

SHOPPING

Better known for its café life than its shopping, Montparnasse nonetheless has a large mall and a few individual boutiques.

Children

Les Cousins d'Alice
36 rue Daguerre, 14th.
Tel: 01 43 20 24 86
A true wonderland for children with card games, puppets, jewellery plus old-fashioned and modern toys.

Gifts

Au Nom de la Rose
1 boulevard de Montparnasse, 6th.
Tel: 01 40 56 05 15.

www.aunomdelarose.com
This French chain of florists sells gorgeous bouquets of roses in every colour as well as perfumes, soaps and rose-flavoured foodstuffs, including honey, chocolate and tea.

Malls

Centre Commercial Montparnasse
22 rue du Départ or 11 rue de l'Arrivée, 15th.
Next to the Montparnasse Tower, this shopping mall has a branch of Galeries Lafayette and many chain stores including Naf Naf, Etam, André (shoes) and Kookaï.

Paris Schooling

"Paris was where the 20th century was," said Gertrude Stein, and for a time all the fads and fashions, the art and ideas of modernity came together in Montparnasse.

Today the name "Ecole de Paris" still conjures up the incredible artistic momentum of Paris between the wars, the mood of intellectual ferment, of artistic and literary debate, and the arrival of cocktails, jazz and the tango. It was neither a school nor a movement, nor an organised group – rather it is a label that has come to designate those mostly foreign-born artists who congregated around Montmartre in the first years of the 20th century and, after World War I, in the cafés and studios of Montparnasse.

A magnet for artists

Paris was an intellectual and cultural magnet; a bold city, where academic tradition had been challenged by the Impressionists, Cézanne and the Fauves; a city open to avant-garde currents like Cubism, Expres-

sionism and Dadaism. Paris was a magnet also for foreign artists, in search of refuge or a new beginning, be they Jews escaping the ghetto, Russians fleeing the Revolution or Americans after adventure escaping from Prohibition.

Though not a style, the Ecole de Paris is associated with figuration, not abstraction, a form of expressionism and a certain relationship to the contemporary world, not Surrealism. At its centre were Chagall, Soutine, Modigliani, Foujita, Pascin, Kisling and Van Dongen. More peripheral figures include Picasso, Chana Orloff, Marie Vassilieff and Maurice Utrillo.

Life imitates art

The Ecole de Paris, though, was as much to do with lifestyle as artistic style. Artists rented studios at La Ruche, Cité Falguière, Villa Seurat and countless other studio courtyards around Montparnasse. Exchanges also took place in the area's cafés and brasseries, such as Le Dôme, La Rotonde and the glamorous La Coupole.

The artists painted each other, but also writers, critics and poets like Apollinaire, Max Jacob, Gertrude Stein and Henry Miller. Their paintings captured drinkers, dancers and prostitutes, Parisian icons like the Eiffel Tower, and themes like clowns and the circus.

The queen of Montparnasse

Curiously, though, the figure that best epitomised the spirit of artistic Montparnasse was not an artist, but model and muse Kiki de Montparnasse. Born Alice Prin in 1901, she arrived in Paris during World War I and became part of the artistic circle who met at La Rotonde. Painted by Soutine, Van Dongen, Kisling and Foujita with her characteristic black fringe, she also entered the Surrealist pantheon, as mistress and model of Man Ray; she starred in several of his experimental films and in his photo *Le Violin d'Ingres*. Beautiful, charming, outrageous, Kiki painted, danced, sang lewd songs at Le Jockey and published her memoirs at the age of 28.

LEFT: multi-talented Kiki de Montparnasse.

solidarity, the galleries have synchronised openings.

Bibliothèque Nationale François-Mitterrand ③

Address: quai François-Mauriac
www.bnf.fr
Tel: 01 53 79 59 59
Opening Hrs: Tue–Sat 10am–7pm, Sun 1–7pm
Entrance Fee: charge
Transport: Bibliothèque François Mitterrand

Designed by Dominique Perrault and opened in 1997, the library cost over €1 billion to build. Its 90-metre (300ft) -high glass towers are meant to evoke open books on end, set on top of a plank-covered plinth 305 metres (1,000ft) long. Like it or not, the library is undeniably impressive.

Nightlife on the Seine

The new Left Bank is to have its own "Latin Quarter", with 30,000 students on a new campus around a giant rehabilitated grain store. Streets have been extended to the Seine and the river banks landscaped, and this is Paris's hottest new nightlife area, with boats and barges where you can eat, drink and dance: the **Batofar**, **La Dame de Canton, and El Alamein**, to name but a few, are all moored by Quai de la Gare near the Bibliothèque.

ABOVE: the barges along the Seine have become a nightlife hotspot.
BELOW: the imposing Bibliothèque Nationale François-Mitterrand.

BEST RESTAURANTS, BARS AND CAFES

Restaurants

French

L'Assiette
181 rue du Château, 14th
Tel: 01 43 22 64 86
Open: L & D Wed–Sun.
€€€ **33** [p336, B4]
Lulu, the cigar-smoking longtime owner, might have retired but her restaurant is still going strong in the capable hands of David Rathgeber, a protégé of Alain Ducasse. Dishes, although not quite as fancy as his creations at the Plaza Athénée, lean towards the southwest and include foie gras, roast lamb, sausage from the Landes region and home-made caramel ice cream. Everything is cooked to perfection.

L'Avant-Goût
26 rue Bobillot, 13th
Tel: 01 53 80 24 00
Open: L & D Tue–Sat.
€€€ **34** [p336, C4]
Great value for money, the inventive cuisine of chef Christophe Beaufront draws an appreciative crowd. The house speciality is roast pork *pot-au-feu* or, in season, *sanglier* (wild boar). The wine list is intelligent and affordable. This is probably the neighbourhood's best restaurant, and everyone knows it, so book ahead. There's also a takeaway menu.

La Cagouille
10 place Constantin-Brancusi, 14th
Tel: 01 43 22 09 01
Open: L & D daily.
€€€ **35** [p338, E4]
Gérard Allemandou learned to love seafood on the Atlantic coast where he grew up. Grilled, roasted or fried, his seafood has an exquisite flavour. His tasty specialities include red mullet in olive oil and black sea bream grilled with cumin. Service is attentive, the wine list extensive and desserts are good. In warm weather, go for the pleasant outdoor seating – it makes up slightly for the somewhat plain interior.

La Closerie des Lilas
171 boulevard du Montparnasse, 6th
Tel: 01 40 51 34 50
www.closeriedeslilas.fr
Open: L & D daily (piano bar until 1.30am).
€€€ (brasserie) €€€€ (restaurant) **36** [p336, A4]
The historic brasserie retains its charm and offers richly satisfying fare, though it does cash in on its reputation as a famous 1920s watering hole, favoured by the likes of Hemingway, Lenin and Modigliani. For dining, choose from the reliable brasserie or the expensive restaurant, which serves great French classics such as frogs' legs and crêpes Suzette.

La Coupole
102 boulevard du Montparnasse,14th
Tel: 01 43 20 14 20
www.lacoupole-paris.com
Open: L & D daily (until midnight).
€€ (set menu) €€€ **37** (à la carte) [p338, E4]
This vast, legendary Art Deco brasserie remains an eternal favourite with Parisians as well as tourists. Waiters offer elegant service in a 1920s dining hall. Hot dishes can be hit and miss, but the oysters and shellfish platters are superb. The terrace is a great place for people-watching on sunny days.

L'Entrepôt

7 rue Francis-de-Pressensé, 14th
Tel: 01 45 40 60 70
Open: non-stop daily.
€€ **88** [p336, B4]
This used to be a paper warehouse, but now it's a three-in-one: bar, restaurant and arthouse cinema. The dining side of the operation serves fairly standard brasserie fare like *magret de canard*, beef tartare or fillet of salmon, with choices like crème brûlée for dessert. The place also does live music at weekends.

Le Parc aux Cerfs

50 rue Vavin, 6th
Tel: 01 43 54 87 83
Open: L & D daily.
€€ (set menu) €€€ (à la carte)
89 [p338, E3]
This former artist's atelier has a cosy mezzanine and an interior courtyard that's a delight in summer. The Mediterranean menu is short but full of flair, and there's an excellent wine list. The ice creams are home-made.

Le Select

99 boulevard du Montparnasse, 6th
Tel: 01 45 48 38 24
Open: non-stop daily.
€€€ **90** [p338, E3]
No shortage of history or artistic associations at this Montparnasse stalwart: Hemingway, Cocteau, Man Ray and all used to frequent the place. Local intellectuals still hang out at the bar. The food, for what you get, is no bargain, but there's a very good choice of cocktails and spirits,

especially whiskies.

Wadja

10 rue de la Grande-Chaumière, 6th
Tel: 01 46 33 02 02
Open: L Mon–Fri, D Mon–Sat. (set menu), €€€ (à la carte) **91** [p336, A4]
The friendly owner serves up a market-fresh menu with personally chosen wines in a dining room that hasn't lost its 1930s atmosphere. A la carte takes over in the evening, with imaginative starters and hearty meat or fish mains. The daily menu is less expensive.

Thai

Paradis Thaï

132 rue Tolbiac, 13th
Tel: 01 45 83 22 26
Open: L & D daily.
€€ **92** [p336, C4]
The exotic yet understated mood in this restaurant is set by the enormous elephant in the entrance. The discreet decor offsets beautifully presented Vietnamese and Thai

specialities, and the varied menu indicates levels of spiciness.

Vietnamese

Bambou

70 rue Baudricourt, 13th
Tel: 01 45 70 91 75
Open: L & D Tue–Sun
€ **93** [p336, C3]
A buzzy, busy restaurant where it's advisable to come early to try the house speciality, *pho*; the caramelised pork is pretty good too. Desserts are based around coconut milk and they also do takeaway. Service can be brusque.

Bars and Cafés

Café de l'Atelier

95 boulevard du Montparnasse, 6th.
Tel: 01 45 44 98 81.
www.cafelaterlierparis.com.
Open: Non-stop daily.
37 [p338, E3]
This pleasant café has a youthful crowd, friendly staff, a useful terrace (with heaters when

required) and a range of snacks. The fact that it's open round the clock is an added bonus.

Les Tontons

38 rue Raymond-Losserand, 14th.
Tel: 01 43 21 69 45.
Open: Non-stop Mon–Sat.
38 [p336, A4]
This pleasant café boasts late opening hours and a traditional zinc counter. Its food offerings have a regional theme – the southwest – and run to large salads and 10 different varieties of tartare. The two owners are fans of French gangster movie *Les Tontons Flingueurs* (1963), hence the name of the place and all the posters and other memorabilia.

> Price includes dinner and a half-bottle of house wine:
>
> € = under €25
> €€ = €25–40
> €€€ = €40–60
> €€€€ = more than €60

LEFT: poised for service at La Coupole. **RIGHT:** café life in La-Butte-aux-Cailles.

THE EIFFEL TOWER AND LES INVALIDES

Vital Paris experiences: the views from the top of its great iron tower, and in the dark depths of its sewers. At ground level, there are gracious boulevards, imperial splendour at Les Invalides and a grand art buffet: Impressionists at Musée d'Orsay, exotic artefacts at Quai Branly and new creativity at Palais de Tokyo.

The Eiffel Tower looms up above the Seine like a giant playing hide-and-seek among the grand apartment blocks of the 7th *arrondissement*. At its foot is the **Champ de Mars**. This stretch of parkland, once a military exercise ground, now teems with tourists all year-round. Facing the tower at the southern end of the Champ de Mars is the **Ecole Militaire**, the military academy where Napoleon learned his trade. Glimpses through the shuttered security are rare, but occasional open doorways reveal fountains, statues and soaring stairways. To the east, the **Esplanade des Invalides** is another splendid carpet of green that rolls from the gleaming gilt-domed church of the **Hôtel des Invalides** to the Seine and the Pont Alexandre III.

Drift away from the crowd-filled Champ de Mars and savour the gracious tree-lined streets bordered by *hôtels* (mansions), whose sumptuous apartments are occupied by senior civil servants, captains of industry and rich, retired Americans.

THE TROCADÉRO

Across the river lies the 16th *arrondissement*. This takes up a sizeable slice of western Paris and, like the 7th, it is full of smart residences occupied by wealthy inhabitants. Not for those in search of the arcane or the avant-garde, this is the bastion of BCBG (*bon chic, bon genre*), a never-never land of big hair, Burberry plaid, diamond rings, pedigree dogs and Berthillon ice cream. The reason most tourists and Parisians venture here is to visit one of the museums around Place du Trocadéro, or to gaze at the magical views across the Seine to the Eiffel Tower.

Main Attractions

TROCADÉRO
MUSÉE D'ART MODERNE DE LA
  VILLE DE PARIS
PALAIS DE TOKYO
EIFFEL TOWER
MUSÉE DU QUAI BRANLY
LES EGOUTS (THE SEWERS)
LES INVALIDES
MUSÉE RODIN
MUSÉE D'ORSAY

Maps and Listings

MAP, PAGE 232
SHOPPING, PAGE 244
RESTAURANTS, PAGE 246
ACCOMMODATION, PAGE 306

LEFT: the Eiffel Tower, world symbol of the French capital. **RIGHT:** the Musée Rodin's beautifully landscaped garden.

Eiffel Tower and Les Invalides

Begin by crossing the Pont d'Iéna to the Trocadéro. From here, framed by the cascading fountains and gold statues of the **Jardins du Trocadéro** , the Eiffel Tower can be seen at its most magnificent. Dominating the Place du Trocadéro is the **Palais de Chaillot**, built for the Paris International Exhibition of 1937. The imposing pseudo-classical palace was designed in the shape of an amphitheatre, with its wings following the original outline of the old Trocadéro, built for Paris's 1878 Exhibition. The building holds three museums and the Théâtre National de Chaillot.

Musée de la Marine ❷

Address: www.musee-marine.fr
Tel: 01 53 65 69 69
Opening Hrs: Mon–Fri 11am–6pm (closed Tue), Sat–Sun 11am–7pm
Entrance Fee: charge
Transport: Trocadéro

In the west wing, this museum charts the history of France as a seafaring nation. Hundreds of models, often of extraordinary craftsmanship, cover everything from historic battleships and three-masted schooners to langoustine fishing boats and primitive canoes. A fine painting collection includes Vernet's series of the ports of France, but the centrepiece of the museum is the carved and gilded imperial barge built for Napoleon. Other displays include navigational instruments, sections on shipbuilding and ropemaking, carved whale teeth and giant lighthouse lenses.

Musée de l'Homme ❸

Address: www.mnhn.fr
Tel: 01 44 05 72 72
Opening Hrs: Mon, Wed–Fri 9.45am–5pm, Sat, Sun 10am–6pm
Entrance Fee: charge

In the same wing, the "Museum of Mankind" is somewhat reduced since its collection of tribal art was transferred to the Musée du Quai Branly (see page 237). Currently under renovation, it is due to reopen in 2014.

Cité de l'Architecture et du Patrimoine ❹

Address: www.citechaillot.fr

ABOVE: gilded statue on the terrace of the Place des Droits de l'Homme, in front of the imposing Palais de Chaillot.
BELOW: view from the Eiffel Tower.

The Musée du Vin (Rue des Eaux, 16th; tel: 01 45 25 63 26, www. museeduvinparis.com), with its inappropriate address, is a sweet little museum devoted to all things related to the vine: tools, bottles, corkscrews and more. Visits conclude, naturally, with a glass of wine.

Tel: 01 53 58 51 52 00
Opening Hrs: Mon, Wed, Fri, Sat, Sun 11am–7pm, Thur 11am–9pm
Entrance Fee: charge
Transport: Trocadéro

Located in the east wing, this museum and research centre hosts large-scale exhibitions on related topics. A state-of-the-art audiovisual centre is open to the public.

AROUND THE TROCADÉRO

Against the backdrop of the Palais de Chaillot, the terraces and grassy banks of the garden play host to flamboyant skateboarders and rollerbladers. At night, when the ornamental pool's huge fountains are lit up, the sight is spectacular.

West of Chaillot, villagey **Passy** is an upmarket residential area around busy shopping streets, on Rue de Passy and Rue de l'Assomption.

Maison de Balzac

Address: 47 rue Raynouard
www.balzac.paris.fr
Tel: 01 55 74 41 80
Opening Hrs: Tue–Sun 10am–6pm
Entrance Fee: free

Transport: Passy

Wealthy Passy also hides the atmospheric house where the great writer Honoré de Balzac penned much of his massive *Comédie Humaine*, furnished as at the time and with a rich collection of Balzacian manuscripts and memorabilia, including the

RIGHT: young skaters enjoy the vast, smooth open spaces of the Trocadéro.
BELOW: striking an Eiffel Tower pose for the camera.

coffee pot that sustained his legendary 15-hour writing sessions.

PLACE D'IÉNA

Between the Trocadéro and the Champs-Elysées, this busy boulevard-hub is the site of an unusual mix of museums and culture centres.

Musée d'Art Moderne de la Ville de Paris ❺

Address: 11 avenue du Président-Wilson

www.mam.paris.fr

Tel: 01 53 67 40 00

Opening Hrs: Tue–Sun 10am–6pm

Entrance Fee: free, charge for special exhibitions

Transport: Iéna

To the east, another of the 1937 Exhibition buildings, the Palais de Tokyo, contains the city of Paris's own, underrated modern art collection. It gives a coherent survey of 20th-century art, especially relating to Paris, with strong holdings of

the Fauvists, the *Ecole de Paris* (see page 226) and conceptual art from the 1970s. Its masterpieces include works by Picasso, Matisse (among them *La Danse*, 1932), Modigliani, Van Dongen and Soutine, and Raoul Dufy's gigantic mural *La Fée Electricité* (Electricity Fairy), a celebration of light and energy commissioned for the 1937 Exhibition; displayed in an oval room, it serves as a reminder of the building's original purpose as the Electricity Pavilion.

Palais de Tokyo – Site de Création Contemporaine ❻

Address: 13 avenue du Président-Wilson

www.palaisdetokyo.com

Tel: 01 81 97 35 88

Opening Hrs: Wed–Mon noon–midnight

Entrance Fee: charge

Transport: Iéna

ABOVE: the Musée d'Art Moderne de la Ville de Paris.

SHOP

Maison Baccarat (11 place des Etats-Unis; tel: 01 40 22 11 00, www. baccarat.com), the showcase of illustrious glass manufacturer Baccarat, is an *hôtel particulier* transformed by Philippe Starck into a cocoon of soft brushed concrete, crystal chandeliers and handmade carpets. As well as an elegant showroom, it contains the Cristal Room restaurant and the Galerie-Musée Baccarat, with a display of precious items made for world exhibitions and maharajahs.

ABOVE: wall relief at the Musée d'Art Moderne de la Ville de Paris.
BELOW: tribal art at the Musée du Quai Branly.

focuses on young artists through a dynamic mix of exhibitions, performances and workshops, and its fresh atmosphere, the hip "Tokyo Eat" restaurant-café, a stylish souvenir shop and the unique late-night opening hours have made it hugely popular.

Musée Galliera/Musée de la Mode de la Ville de Paris ❼

Address: 10 avenue Pierre 1er de Serbie
www.galliera.paris.fr
Tel: 01 56 52 86 00
Opening Hrs: during exhibitions Tue–Sun 10am–6pm
Entrance Fee: charge
Transport: Iéna

In the east wing of the Palais, this state-funded contemporary arts centre, opened in 2002, is intended to serve as a laboratory for current art production. In 2012 it reopened after increasing its size from 8,000 sq metres (86,111 sq ft) to 22,000 sq metres (236,806 sq ft), making it one of Europe's largest contemporary art centres. An adventurous, multi-disciplinary programme

The imposing Italianate Palais Galliera is hard to miss. It houses the municipal collection of some 12,000 outfits and 60,000 accessories dating from the 18th century to the present day. To rotate these rich holdings, only a fraction of which can be displayed at a time, two exhibitions are held each year focusing on a historic period, a theme or a designer. It is currently closed for renovations and due to reopen in 2013.

Musée Guimet ❽

Address: 6 place d'Iéna
www.museeguimet.fr
Tel: 01 56 52 53 00
Opening Hrs: Wed–Mon 10am–6pm
Entrance Fee: charge
Transport: Iéna

One of the world's finest museums of Asian art, the Guimet reopened in 2001 after five years of renovation. Begun as the private collection of industrialist Emile Guimet but later taken over by the French state, the once-dusty museum has been enlarged and rejuvenated with spacious day-lit galleries that give its collections new visibility. The superb collection includes oriental art, statuary and textiles from China, Japan, India, Tibet, Nepal, Pakistan, Afghanistan, Korea and Vietnam – a reflection of France's colonial past. The prize exhibits are the Cambodian Buddhist sculptures from the temples of Angkor.

ACROSS THE PONT DE L'ALMA

Cross the Pont de l'Alma to discover two very different but equally fascinating museums.

Les Egouts de Paris – The Paris Sewers ⑨

Address: entrance by 93 quai d'Orsay
www.paris.fr/culture
Tel: 01 53 68 27 81
Opening Hrs: Sat–Wed May–Sept 11am–5pm, Oct–Apr 11am–4pm
Entrance Fee: charge
Transport: RER Pont de l'Alma

For a surprisingly entertaining experience, descend into the bowels of Paris for an excursion into the sewer system, and a museum full of interesting facts about waste and water. Described by Hugo in *Les Misérables* as the "other Paris", this network of tunnels follows the well-known streets above ground. Accompanied by a film and, unsurprisingly, a strong odour, this is the alternative tour of Paris.

Musée du Quai Branly ⑩

Address: 37 quai Branly
www.quaibranly.fr
Tel: 01 56 61 70 00

The branches of the city's sewers, which follow the road network almost exactly, are signposted with the same names (and the same blue-and-white plaques) as the streets above them. There are 2,050km (1,274 miles) of sewers inside the Paris ringroad; the first public tours took place in 1867, during that year's Paris Exhibition.

ABOVE: the Musée du Quai Branly was designed by French architect Jean Nouvel. **BELOW:** view of the Musée du Quai Branly from the Eiffel Tower.

Opening Hrs: Tue, Wed, Sun 11am–7pm, Thur, Fri, Sat until 9pm
Entrance Fee: charge
Transport: RER Pont d'Alma

Unlike his predecessor François Mitterrand, President Jacques Chirac was not known for his *grands projets*, but in his last years in office he sponsored this new museum of world cultures, in a multicoloured building by architect Jean Nouvel. It houses a fabulous collection of tribal art, including African, Aztec and Mayan artefacts, many formerly in the Musée de l'Homme or other museums but which can now be seen in a whole new light.

THE EIFFEL TOWER

ABOVE: taking in the spectacular view from the top of the tower.
BELOW: view up from the tower's second floor.

It's a short walk from the Musée du Quai Branly to Paris's trademark.

Tour Eiffel ⓫

Address: www.tour-eiffel.fr
Tel: 01 44 11 23 23

Opening Hrs: daily mid-June–Aug 9am–midnight, Sept–mid-June 9.30am–11pm
Entrance Fee: charge
Transport: RER Champ de Mars-Tour Eiffel

When Gustave Eiffel's icon of iron girders was chosen as the centrepiece to the Exhibition of 1889, he was delighted. But his designs were met with a barrage of opposition. Opéra architect Charles Garnier and novelist Guy de Maupassant were the most vocal opponents; Maupassant organised a protest picnic under the tower's four legs – "the only place out of sight of the wretched construction".

However, the Parisian public loved their new tower, and only a few years later it was being lauded by writers and artists such as Apollinaire, Jean Cocteau, Dufy and Utrillo. Surviving a proposal for it to be dismantled in 1909, when the placing of a radio transmitter at the top saved the day, the tower is now swarmed over by some 6 million visitors a year.

The first two floors are negotiated on foot or by lift, and then another

Eiffel Statistics

At 321 metres (1,054ft) high, including the masts, the Eiffel Tower was the tallest structure in the world until the Chrysler Building was constructed in New York in 1930. On hot days, the ironwork expands, enabling it to grow as much as an incredible 15cm (6ins).

A masterpiece of engineering, Gustave Eiffel's tower, world symbol of Paris, is held together with 2.5 million rivets, and the 10,100 tonnes of iron exert a pressure of 4kg per sq cm (57lb per sq inch), equivalent to the weight of a man sitting on a chair. Even in the strongest winds, the tower has never swayed more than 12cm (4ins). Up to 40 tonnes of paint are used when it is painted, every seven years. There are 360 steps to the first level, where there's an audiovisual presentation of the tower's history, and another 700 to the second. There's always a queue for the lifts, which travel 100,000km (62,137 miles) a year. On the third level is Gustave Eiffel's sitting room. On a clear day panoramas of over 65km (40 miles) can be seen; enjoy a tipple in the champagne bar while taking in the view.

diamond-studded jewellery, as 20,000 flashbulbs start firing on the hour to create a stunning five-minute display.

Along the Champ de Mars

Stretching beneath the Eiffel Tower are the ever-crowded gardens of the Champ de Mars. For centuries this was a market garden supplying vegetables to Parisians, but after the Ecole Militaire was built in 1752 it became a parade ground, with capacity for 10,000 men. The first balloon filled with hydrogen rather than hot air was launched from here in 1783, and it was the venue for the first-anniversary celebration of the storming of the Bastille – a miserable Louis XVI was forced to attend.

At the far end of the gardens is the imposing **Ecole Militaire** ⑫ (closed to the public). Louis XV commissioned the military college to help men of little means learn the art of soldiering, and a young

ABOVE: strolling in the Parc du Champ de Mars.
LEFT: no less than 12kg (26 lb) of gold were needed when the Eglise du Dôme was regilded in 1989.
BELOW: Napoleon's tomb inside the Eglise du Dôme.

lift goes up to the top which, as well as a weather station and air navigation point, is an observation platform with space for up to 800 people at a time. The view is awesome. At night, the tower is transformed into a giant piece of

ABOVE: the interior of the dome was painted by Charles de la Fosse.
RIGHT: statue of Napoleon in his coronation robes.

Napoleon studied here for a year in 1784. The splendid 18th-century academy, designed by Jacques-Ange Gabriel, is still the foundation stone of French military expertise. With its Cour d'Honneur enclosed by colonnades, the main facadeborders Avenue de Lowendal.

UNESCO ⑬

Address: 7 place Fontenoy
www.unesco.org
Tel: 01 45 68 03 59
Opening Hrs: visits by reservation
Entrance Fee: free
Transport: Ségur

Behind the Ecole Militaire is the foundation for reconciliation and understanding, the headquarters of the United Nations cultural organisation. The graceful, Y-shaped building was designed by an alliance of American, French and Italian architects, and engineers led by Bauhaus member Marcel Breuer. Inside, 142 countries cooperate on educational,

scientific and cultural projects. A temple of modern art, its decoration is equally cosmopolitan: Joan Miró ceramics, Henry Moore sculptures, an Alexander Calder mobile as well as a huge Picasso mural. The Japanese garden displays a spine-chilling relic: a stone angel found after the atomic bomb blast at Nagasaki in 1945.

LES INVALIDES ⑭

Address: www.invalides.org
Tel: 01 44 42 38 77
Opening Hrs: daily Apr–Sept 10am–6pm, Oct–Mar 10–5pm; closed 1st Mon of each month except July–Sept
Entrance Fee: charge, includes Dôme and museums
Transport: Invalides

The gleaming dome of the **Hôtel des Invalides** is a masterpiece of French Baroque architecture and one of Paris's most prominent landmarks. Behind it is a remarkable set of 17th-century buildings commissioned by Louis XIV to house and care for retired and wounded soldiers. It also served as the royal arsenal, and it was from here, in 1789, that revolutionaries comandeered 30,000 rifles for the storming of the Bastille. Napoleon, whose wars kept the hospital full, restored the institution to its former glory, making the church a necropolis and regilding its dome. The **Eglise du Dôme**, built as a royal chapel for Louis XIV, now contains Bonaparte's tomb. The emperor's body was returned to the city from St Helena in 1840, with much pomp and ceremony, and eventually laid to rest in the church crypt.

Spread across either side of the Cour d'Honneur, the large **Musée de l'Armée** offers an extensive view of man's inhumanity to man and skill at warfare from the Stone Age to Hiroshima, with a terrifying selection of weapons and armour, and poignant displays on the two world wars. In a separate wing, the **Musée de l'Ordre de la Libération** commemorates the Resistance fighters who received the Order of Liberation, created by De Gaulle in 1940.

Stretching to the Seine, the grassy **Esplanade des Invalides** is much loved by strollers, joggers, dog-walkers and rollerbladers. On its west side is a series of *pétanque* courts, and nearby is a small airport coach terminal, by the Métro-RER station.

Around Les Invalides

Heading east along the Seine towards the Musée d'Orsay, you immediately pass the august colonnades of France's parliament, the **Assemblée Nationale (Palais Bourbon)** ⑮ (www.assemblee-nationale.fr; tel: 01 40 63 60 00, ring for details of guided tours). The extravagant neo-Grecian columns facing the river were grafted onto the earlier 18th-century palace by Napoleon, to complement his Madeleine across the river, and they now shelter an armed guard in charge of protecting the *577 députés* (Members of Parliament).

Musée Rodin ⑯

Address: Hôtel Biron, 79 rue de Varenne
www.musee-rodin.fr

ABOVE: bronze casts of Rodin's work are displayed in the lovely rose garden.
BELOW: the 7th is a smart, residential neighbourhood.

occupant. Auguste Rodin's first critically acclaimed sculpture was *The Age of Bronze* (1877), depicting a naked youth caressing his hair, modelled by a Belgian soldier. The establishment was shocked, maintaining that the statue was too lifelike to be regarded as art. Eventually, the French government bought the statue, and Rodin's reputation was confirmed.

Rodin came to live in the Hôtel Biron in 1908, and stayed here until his death in 1917. He paid his rent with his best works, which form the basis of the museum's exquisite collection. Here you can admire *The Kiss* (removed from the Chicago World Fair of 1893 for being too shocking), *The Thinker* (reputedly Dante contemplating the Inferno), *The Burghers of Calais*, *The Hand of God* and many other works.

Restored to their white marble finish, the statues ripple with life. Bronze casts of many of Rodin's major works are displayed outside in the beautiful rose garden, amid the lawns, hedged enclosures, pools, mature trees and topiaried yews,

Tel: 01 44 18 61 10
Opening Hrs: Tue–Sun 10am–5.45pm, Wed until 8.45pm
Entrance Fee: charge
Transport: Varenne

ABOVE: open tour bus on its way to Les Invalides.
BELOW: Rodin's *The Thinker*.

Just next to Les Invalides stands the **Hôtel Biron**, a charming 18th-century *hôtel particulier* that's now forever linked to its most famous

Solid Genius

François-Auguste-René Rodin was born in the Quartier Latin in 1840 to a working-class family, and grew up wandering the markets of Rue Mouffetard (see page 207). Trained at the Petite Ecole from age 14, but rejected by the Ecole des Beaux-Arts, he worked as an assistant for ornamental artists and the sculptor Carrier-Belleuse, training himself while visiting the zoo at the Jardin des Plantes and horse markets on Boulevard St-Michel for inspiration. A trip to Italy in 1876, where he discovered Michelangelo, transformed his career. Further stimulus came from his incessant love affairs, notably with the now internationally acclaimed fellow artists Camille Claudel and Gwen John, interrupted only for a while when he took holy orders as a reaction to the death of his sister in a convent, after she had been rejected in love by one of his own close friends. Chastity did not suit him, though, and he soon returned to his mistresses and his art. Among his masterpieces are *The Kiss, The Thinker, The Burghers of Calais* and the unfinished *Gates of Hell*, on which he worked from the 1880s until his death from influenza in 1917. Many of his sculptures were criticised during his lifetime.

providing a context for the studies and smaller works around the house. Also in the garden is one of Paris's most atmospheric museum cafés. The museum, still open to the public, is currently undergoing renovation to comply with accessibility and health and safety regulations, which is due to be completed in 2013.

Faubourg St-Germain

The area lying east of Les Invalides is well worth exploring, an elegant, aristocratic extension of St-Germain-des-Prés built up in the 18th century. Begin with Paris's most interesting cinema and teahouse, **La Pagode** (tel: 01 45 55 48 48) ⓱ in Rue de Babylone. The tea is strong, the gardens tropical and the films up to date, and the building itself is simply stunning, a 19th-century replica of a Far Eastern pagoda whose main auditorium is lined with golden dragon motifs.

When the nobility moved out of the Marais in the 18th century, the rich and famous built new town houses across the river from the

Tuileries. Beautifully preserved, they are now mostly shut away behind heavily secured gates, since only French ministries and foreign governments can afford the rent. On Boulevard Raspail (at No. 45) stands the **Hôtel Lutétia** ⓲, its extravagant statued facade fronting a deluxe four-star hotel where Charles de Gaulle enjoyed his first night of married life. When the hotel was requisitioned by the Gestapo in 1940, the owner bricked up the vintage wine cellar and, even though the hotel staff were interrogated to reveal the whereabouts of the *cave*, no one talked.

Continue walking along Boulevard Raspail towards the Seine until you come to Rue de Grenelle on the left, a narrow street stacked with beautiful buildings, including the Swiss and Dutch embassies, the Ministry of Education and the National Geographic Institute.

ABOVE: the clocks are vestiges from the museum's past as a railway station.
BELOW: the Musée d'Orsay's architecture is as impressive as the collections inside.

Musée Maillol – Fondation Dina Vierny ⑲

Address: 61 rue de Grenelle
www.museemaillol.com
Tel: 01 42 22 59 58
Opening Hrs: daily 10.30am–7pm, Fri until 9.30pm
Entrance Fee: charge
Transport: Rue du Bac

The Hôtel Bouchardon is a distinguished 18th-century residence where the poet Alfred de Musset lived between 1824 and 1839, before going on an oriental voyage of discovery with George Sand. Since 1995 it has housed this museum displaying the works of sculptor Aristide Maillol, along with art by contemporaries Cézanne and Degas, drawings by Matisse, multiples by Duchamp, and works by Russian and Naïve artists. Dina Vierny, its founder and owner, was an art dealer and model for Maillol, whose sculptures adorn the Tuileries.

Rue de Varenne, one street over, has a collection of fine old houses, the most famous being the Paris residence of the French Prime Minister, **Hôtel Matignon** ⑳, which has the biggest private garden in the city.

MUSÉE D'ORSAY ㉑

Address: 62 rue de Lille,
www.musee-orsay.fr
Tel: 01 40 49 48 14

SHOPPING

Paris's chic southwest offers plenty of great shopping opportunities for food, clothes and shoes.

Clothing

Paul and Joe
64-66 rue des Saints Pères, 7th.
Tel: 01 42 22 47 01.
www.paulandjoe.com
Loved by Parisian fashionistas, this upmarket brand sells shabby-chic, seventies-style designs. Think flared, halterneck jumpsuits for women and skinny jeans for men.
Princesse Tam Tam
70 rue St-Dominique, 7th.
Tel: 01 45 51 43 91
Stylish and affordable underwear, swimwear and homewear for women. There are other branches in the city including nearby at 23 rue de Grenelle.

Department Store

Le Bon Marché
24 rue de Sèvres, 7th.
Tel: 01 44 39 80 00
One of Paris's most stylish *grands magasins* is housed in a building designed by Gustave Eiffel. Highlights include the Theatre of Beauty and the men's section, Balthazar. All the top designers are here so bring your credit card.

Food

Debauve & Gallais
30 rue des Saints Pères, 7th.
Tel: 01 45 48 54 67
Founded in 1800, the chocolates made here were a favourite of French kings. The packaging is as beautiful as you'll ever see and the prices as high.
Fromagerie Barthélemy
51 rue de Grenelle, 7th.
Tel: 01 45 48 56 75
Arguably the finest cheese shop in Paris, you'll smell this place before you see it. There are cheeses from all around France but the creamy Fontainebleau is the house speciality.
La Grande Epicerie de Paris
38 rue de Sèvres, 7th.
Tel: 01 44 39 81 00
Le Bon Marché's gourmet grocery store sells every delicacy under the sun, with plenty of everyday items including biscuits and chocolate. There is also a good wine section and freshly prepared takeaway meals.

Gifts

Editions de Parfums Frédéric Malle
37 rue de Grenelle, 7th.
Tel: 01 42 22 76 40.
www.fredericmalle.com
Malle, the grandson of the founder of Parfums Christian Dior, gave seven of the world's leading "noses" carte blanche to create a fragrance under their own names. Judge the results for yourself in his elegant boutique.

Shoes

Christian Louboutin
38-40 rue de Grenelle, 7th.
Tel: 01 42 22 33 07.
www.christianlouboutin.com
This tiny shop is usually packed with women from around the world trying on the coveted red-soled heels. There are a couple of other branches in the city including a men's store at 17 rue Jean-Jacques-Rousseau in the 1st.
Mephisto
78 rue des Saints Pères, 7th.
Tel: 01 45 44 03 04.
www.mephisto.com
Walking shoes and sandals for men and women, which are perfect for getting around Paris in comfort. There are other branches in the city.

Opening Hrs: Tue–Sun 9.30am–6pm, Thur until 9.45pm
Entrance Fee: charge
Transport: RER Musée d'Orsay

No visit to Paris is complete without a pilgrimage to this spectacular former railway station, crammed full of the finest art spanning the period from 1848 to World War I. Built in two years in 1898–1900, it was almost torn down to make way for a hotel in 1970. Prompted by public outcry, the government fulfilled the prophecy of painter Edouard Détaille, who said at the opening ceremony in 1900 that the station would make a better museum. Its glass-and-iron construction was a triumph of modernity, rivalling Eiffel's tower, while the facade reflected the Louvre across the river. Redesigned as a museum by Italian architect Gae Aulenti, it opened in 1986.

The museum is arranged on five levels around a vast central aisle, a grand setting for sculpture by artists such as Rudé, Cavalier and Guillaume. The best pieces are by Carpeaux, the Second Empire's foremost sculptor, including his controversial *La Danse* for the Opéra Garnier.

Other artworks are displayed in chronological order; starting on the ground floor, there are famous works by Ingres (notably *La Source*), Romantic painting by Delacroix, like the colourful *La Chasse aux Lions (Lion Hunt)*, and Manet's nude *Olympia* (1863), pronounced pornographic at the 1865 Paris salon and considered the first "modern" painting.

The museum's biggest draw, its Impressionist paintings, hang on the crowded top floor, bathed in soft light from the glass-vaulted roof. The galleries are full of paintings by Monet, Manet, Renoir, Pissarro, Degas and Cézanne. At the end is a small café with great views of Paris.

On the mezzanine is the gallery of neo and Post-Impressionists which includes the work of Van Gogh, Gauguin, Seurat and Signac. There is also a fine collection of Art Nouveau decorative arts here.

Next door, the **Musée National de la Légion d'Honneur** ❷ (www.legiondhonneur.fr; tel: 01 40 62 84 25; Wed–Sun 1–6pm; charge), with a pleasant courtyard, tells the story of France's most celebrated award.

BELOW: the Palais de Chaillot, built for the Paris International Exhibition of 1937.

Fair's Fair

Paris owes many famous buildings and monuments – even its most famous, the Eiffel Tower – to the series of World Fairs, *Expositions universelles*, it staged in the 19th and 20th centuries. The first Trocadéro was built for the Exhibition of 1878, and demolished to make way for the Palais de Chaillot, centrepiece of the city's last big fair in 1937, an event that also produced the Palais de Tokyo. Other durable constructions are the Grand and Petit Palais, built for the *Exposition* of 1900 – as was the Gare d'Orsay, now the Musée d'Orsay.

World Fairs were grand jamborees of national pride, a chance to show the world a catalogue of French triumphs in technology and the arts. The idea came from London, but Paris took to it with verve, staging its first fair in 1855; the second, in 1867, gave its patron Napoleon III great popular prestige. The 1937 fair was very different, a symbolic face-off between Nazi Germany and Soviet Russia, whose grandiose pavilions were opposite each other. Notably, the Spanish pavilion featured Picasso's famous *Guernica* – while the Exhibition jury awarded a Grand Prix to Hitler's architect Albert Speer, for his design for the Nazi rally grounds at Nuremberg.

BEST RESTAURANTS, BARS AND CAFES

Restaurants

French

L'Affriolé
17 rue Malar, 7th
Tel: 01 44 18 31 33
Open: L & D Tue–Sat.
€€ **94** [p332, C4]
One of the most appealing bistros in the area, with colourful mosaic tables and decorated with traditional *objets de cuisine*. The menu is seasonal and changes daily, and dishes are artfully presented with little *amuse-bouches* (appetisers). Reservations recommended.

L'Ami Jean
27 rue Malar, 7th
Tel: 01 47 05 86 89
Open: L & D Tue–Sat.
€€€ (set menu) €€€€ (à la carte)
95 [p332, C4]
Chef Stéphane Jégo has taken over this longstanding Basque restaurant, and he sends out some fine food from his kitchen: dishes like veal shank with the bones removed and served with onions and broad beans, or salted cod that's drizzled with a nice vinaigrette.

L'Arpège
84 rue de Varenne, 7th
Tel: 01 47 05 09 06
Open: L & D Mon–Fri.
€€€€ **96** [p338, D1]
Chef Alain Passard, one of the heavyweight stars of French cuisine and an accomplished musician, hit the headlines when he turned his haute cuisine restaurant vegetarian, though he has since started serving seafood and poultry again. Much of the produce comes from his kitchen garden. Beetroot baked in Guérande sea salt and the 12-flavours tomato confit dessert are among his famed inventions. The wine list hits the stratosphere. There's also a *prix fixe* lunch menu.

Au Bon Accueil
14 rue Montlessuy, 7th
Tel: 01 47 05 46 11
Open: L & D Mon–Fri.
€€ (set menu) €€€ (à la carte)
97 [p338, C1]
The Eiffel Tower can be seen looming from the pavement tables of this neighbourhood favourite. Inside is a sleek, contemporary dining room. The daily menu is based on market-fresh produce and the *prix fixe* menu is great value. The wine list is excellent (if expensive).

L'Esplanade
52 rue Fabert, 7th
Tel: 01 47 05 38 80
Open: L & D daily (until 1am).
€€€ **98** [p332, D4]
This bar-restaurant has it all: breathtaking views of Les Invalides from the terrace, opulent decor by Jacques Garcia, a fashionable crowd and good, if expensive contemporary food.

La Fontaine de Mars
129 rue St-Dominque, 7th
Tel: 01 47 05 46 44
www.fontainedemars.com
Open: L & D daily.
€€€ **99** [p338, C1]
The menu changes depending on the market, but southwest fare takes pride of place at this 1930s neighbourhood bistro. The house speciality, *cassoulet au canard confit*, is the real thing and so is the *île flottante*.

Jules Verne
Eiffel Tower, 7th
Tel: 01 45 55 61 44
www.lejulesverne-paris.com
Open: L & D daily.

BELOW: rustic cuisine with an elegant twist.

€€€€ **100** [p332, B4]
Now overseen by the great Alain Ducasse, enjoying lunch or dinner half way up the Eiffel Tower is a "must do" experience on at least one visit to Paris, particularly for a special occasion. Food is traditionally French and beautifully presented while the wine cellar is well stocked with all the top marques.

Le Vin de Bellechasse
20 rue de Bellechasse, 7th
Tel: 01 47 05 11 11
Open: L & D Mon–Fri.
€€–€€€ **101** [p338, E1]
A lovely restaurant with red *banquettes* and caricatures of loyal clients and stars on the wall. The menu and the wine list are well priced, and the setting is both intimate and lively. A popular locale among low-key fashion types and other creative or literary souls.

French-Asian
Tokyo Eat
Palais de Tokyo, 13 avenue du Président-Wilson, 16th
Tel: 01 47 20 00 29
Open: L & D Wed–Mon.
€€€ **102** [p332, B4]
The restaurant inside the Palais de Tokyo art gallery is an airy space with open kitchen, artist-customised chairs and funky lighting. The food, which skips from global *satays*, *tandooris* and unusual *carpaccios* to old faves like roast chicken, is generally OK, drawing the bright young things of western Paris as well as the art world. In fine weather, the restaurant migrates outside onto the terrace.

Russian
Petrossian
144 rue de l'Université, 7th
Tel: 01 44 11 32 32
Open: L & D Tue–Sat
€€€€ **103** [p332, D4]
Founded in the 1920s by the Petrossian brothers, this smart, bright restaurant is the place to go for caviar – ideally washed down with a shot or two of vodka. As you'd imagine, the menu has a fishy focus but meat lovers won't be disappointed.

Bars and Cafés
Bellota-Bellota
18 rue Jean-Nicot, 7th.
Tel: 01 53 59 96 96.
Open: Tue–Fri 11am–11pm (Sat until midnight).
39 [p332, C4]
A gem of a tapas bar specialising in the fine Iberian ham after which it is named, as well as Spanish cheeses, wine and seafood. Great for grazing or a light, romantic dinner. You can stop in and dine at the bar if you're early; otherwise reserve one of the handful of tables.

Le Café Constant
139 rue St-Dominique, 7th.
Tel: 01 47 53 73 34.
Open: daily 8.30am–10.30pm.
40 [p338, C1]
It's a buzzy place, this café – hardly surprising given the quality of the food and the light price tag. There's a blackboard menu that changes regularly, lining up dishes like salmon-folded poached eggs with salad or steak tartare that's been cooked under the grill. Nice wines, too.

Le Café du Marché
38 rue Cler, 7th.
Tel: 01 47 05 51 27.
Open: Non-stop Mon–Sat.
41 [p338, C1]
Rue Cler is a market street, hence the name of this ever popular café – ideal for a break in the middle of a bit of shopping, which is exactly what most of the clientele are doing. The house wine, served by the carafe, is as good as the food.

Price includes dinner and a half-bottle of house wine:

€ = under €25
€€ = €25–40
€€€ = €40–60
€€€€ = more than €60

BELOW: bistro La Fontaine de Mars is not too far from the Eiffel Tower.

THE EIFFEL TOWER

It's the thing that, more than any other, says "Paris" – a true icon that was originally intended to stand for a mere 20 years.

ABOVE: the tower took two years to build. The first man to climb it was the Prince of Wales (later Edward VII).

It's the most famous monument in the world – or at least, a member of a very select club: only the Pyramids and the Statue of Liberty (whose framework was also designed by Eiffel) enjoy similar renown.

Built for the 1889 Exposition Universelle, it took over two years to build; it remained the world's tallest building until 1930, when it was overtaken by the Chrysler Building in New York (though the tower gained another 20 metres (65ft) in 1957, with the addition of television aerials). Not everyone liked it at first, but today the tower is the most visited attraction in Paris. It has three platforms open to the public, at 57, 115 and 276 metres from the ground as well as three lifts (although not all are in operation concurrently). There are two restaurants: Le 58 Tour Eiffel on the first level, and the haute cuisine Jules Verne (see page 246) on the second plus a champagne bar at the top. Highlights of any visit include an exhibition on the history of the tower on the first level and the view from the terrace on the second level. Whatever you do, don't leave without buying an Eiffel Tower clock, keyring or snowdome.

ABOVE: this stamp dates from 1939 and commemorates the 50th anniversary of the Eiffel Tower.

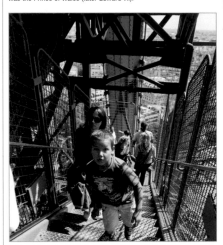

ABOVE: the walk from the ground to the first level is over 300 steps.

The Essentials

Address: www.tour-eiffel.fr
Tel: 01 44 11 23 23
Opening Hrs: daily mid-June–Aug 9am–midnight, Sept–mid-June 9.30am–11pm
Entrance Fee: charge
Transport: RER Champ de Mars-Tour Eiffel

ABOVE: view over the Champ de Mars from the tower.

ABOVE: the Trocadéro esplanade and gardens, built for the 1937 World Fair, offer a splendid view of the Eiffel Tower.

LEFT: even after nightfall, the tower is an unmissable landmark: thousands of flashbulbs fire in a dazzling diamond-like frenzy every hour.

THE MAN OF IRON

"Gustave Eiffel epitomises all that is best of 19th-century architecture, heralding the Modern movement: inventiveness, lightness, structural expression, movement… The [Eiffel Tower] still inspires us today." So says Richard Rogers, and he's not alone. Born in Dijon in 1832, Eiffel was a prolific engineer who made a lasting mark: his bridge designs, for instance, were exported all over the world, including to Portugal where his viaduct still crosses the river Douro. He was also responsible for designing a bridge over the river Truyère in the Massif Central region of France, Pest railway station in Hungary and the dome of the observatory in Nice. When his most famous creation was finished, he drew some heavy fire for its design, but always argued that the structure's curves had been chosen more for their structural benefits than for their looks. Like his works, the man was an enduring figure: he died in 1923, aged 91.

RIGHT: Gustave Eiffel.

MUSEE D'ORSAY

The national museum of 19th-century art is best-known for its French Impressionist paintings, but it also contains key pieces from other artistic movements.

When the Gare d'Orsay was built to coincide with the 1900 World Fair, painter Edouard Détaille said it looked like a palace of fine art – and that, over eight decades later, is exactly what it became. For all that, the Musée d'Orsay is the museum that very nearly didn't happen. It was no longer a railway station by 1950 (its platforms were too short for modern trains) and was lined up for demolition. However, after a short spell as a theatre, President Giscard d'Estaing had it turned into a museum devoted to art – painting, sculpture and decorative works – from the period between 1848 and 1914, and since then it has been one of the city's three most important museums. The building itself is an impressive sight.

ABOVE: the museum is dotted with reminders of its former life as a railway station.

The Essentials

Address: www.musee-orsay.fr
Tel: 01 40 49 48 14
Opening Hrs: Tue–Sun 9.30am–6pm, Thur until 9.45pm
Entrance Fee: charge
Transport: RER Musée d'Orsay

Upper Level

Up to Level 6

40   39   Café

41   38
41   37

Down to Level 4
49 Photographs
50 Kaganovitch Collection

Temporary Exhibitions

45
46   47

Middle Level

54   52   53   56
51   55

Restaurant

72

Ground Floor

Temporary Exhibition

A   B

Bookshop

Seine Gallery

4

Front Square   Tickets and Information

Bookshop

1

C

Cloakroom

Lille Gallery

Open-air Terrace

33 | 32 | 31 | 30 | 29

Bookshop

Down to
"Pavillon Amont"
Rooms 24 to 27

60 | 62 | 63 | 66
59 | 61 | 64 | 65

Seine Terrace

Rodin Terrace

Lille Terrace

70 | 69 | 68 | 67

16 | 20 | 23
7 | 17 | 21 | 24 to 27 Pavillon Amont
15 | 19 | 22

Seine Gallery

Direct access
to Upper Level

14 | 18

Central Aisle

"Opera"
Room

11 | 12 | 13

Lille Gallery

9 | 10

Sculpture
Painting
Architecture
Decorative Arts

Exhibitions
Drawings and Pastels
Photography

THE HIGHLIGHTS

The Musée d'Orsay fol-
lows a chronological
route, from the ground
floor to the upper level
and then to the mezza-
nine, thereby showing
links between the Impres-
sionist painters and their
forerunners.

Ground Floor

In the central sculpture
aisle, there are several
works by Carpeaux

ABOVE: admiring the smaller
works.

including the charming *The imperial prince and his
dog Nero*; lifelike busts of proud citizens of the African colonies by Cordier; and a sensuous, naturalistic *Eve after the fall* by Delaplanche. To the rear of
the aisle is a superb model of the Opéra Garnier.
The decorative arts galleries on the ground floor
and mezzanine parallel developments in fine art:
on the lowest level, don't miss the wardrobe by
Diehl and Brandoly. The ground floor also has a
number of paintings: the scandalous *Olympia* by
Manet; the even more scandalous *Origin of the
World* by Courbet; Daumier's expressive *Scène de
Comédie* and his 24 painted clay heads, *Célébrités
du Juste Milieu*, and Ingres's *La Source*, are also
worth looking out for on this floor.

Middle Level

The Rue de Lille side houses a gallery of neo and
Post-Impressionists including the major works by
Van Gogh and also a terrace with sculptures by
Rodin, Bourdelle and Maillol.

BELOW: Edouard Manet's *Le Déjeuner sur l'Herbe* caused a scandal
when it was first exhibited in 1863.

ABOVE: Renoir's *The Bathers* (1818–19). The theme of the bathers dominates the final season of the painter's work.

ABOVE: the Gare d'Orsay was converted into a museum between 1977 and 1986. From the museum's upper level, visitors get a strong sense of the original railway station layout: the platforms ran either side of what is now the central sculpture aisle. The vast, curved glass-and-iron roof is also shown to advantage, as is the elaborate decoration over the side arches. The glorious gilded clock at the far end is original.

ABOVE: Claude Monet's wife Camille is the *Woman with a Parasol* (1886).

RIGHT: Hippolyte Moulin's *Secret from on High* (1879) depicts a life-size nude Mercury (Hermes) whispering a secret to a herm, knowing that it will never repeat what he tells it.

THE HIGHLIGHTS (CONTINUED)

Upper Level
Most visitors come to see the Impressionist paintings in the Galerie des Hauteurs. In the first room (29) is Manet's masterpiece *Le Déjeuner sur l'Herbe*; his pastels are exhibited in rooms 39 and 40. Room 30 mainly has works by Sisley but also contains Monet's *The Poppies*, an image that went on to sell thousands of greetings cards. Next along (rooms 31 and 33) are Degas's elegant bronze dancers, which were originally created in wax then cast in bronze after his death, and also his beautifully lit paintings of dance classes and performances; interestingly, although one of the founders of the movement, Degas considered himself to be a "realist" and not an "impressionist". Monet and Renoir (rooms 32, 34,36) stuck closest to the Impressionist ideal of pure colour and modelling through light, while the 3D, still lifes of Cézanne (room 35), who originally exhibited with the Impressionists but differed from them in his search for underlying structure, pave the way for Cubism and modern art. The Impressionists would have been proud of Café Campana, the eaterie here named after the Brazilians who designed it; the shimmering walls and lights transport diners to a watery, dreamlike environment that Monet himself could have conjured up. Before leaving, step out onto the terrace and take in the view over the Seine.

ABOVE: take a break from all the art at the museum's Café Campana.

ABOVE: *L'Absinthe* by Edgar Degas (detail). In its first showing in 1876, the picture was panned by critics, who called it ugly and disgusting.

RIGHT: snapping the masters.

PARIS PARKS

Paris may often have seen itself as the quintessential city, but even born-and-bred Parisians feel a yearning for open spaces – and in the past few decades highly inventive, all-new parks have been added alongside the city's charming gardens and historic woodland.

I n 1759 Voltaire wound up his famous novel *Candide* with the line "We must cultivate our garden", but it was not until the 19th century that Paris began to make parks and gardens a touchstone for the health of the capital. While the 1980s may be remembered as the decade of the *grands projets* and monumental building, the 1990s and the new millennium have seen the city's parks and gardens flourish. Politicians have realised that improving the urban environment is a vote-winner, and thus derelict industrial sites are flowering and blossoming into suburban parks with a fervour not seen since Haussmann's day. More than ever, Parisians are looking to their green spaces as an escape from the increasing congestion and stress of urban living.

BOIS DE BOULOGNE ❶

Transport: Porte Maillot, Porte Dauphine, Porte d'Auteuil, Les Sablons
Past the *Périphérique* ringroad to the west of Paris, the Bois de Boulogne is one of the reasons why the 16th *arrondissement* alongside it is preferred by the wealthy as a place to live – Avenue Foch, perhaps the most expensive residential street in the capital, leads straight to its park gates. Cradled by an elbow of the Seine, this 860-hectare (2,125-acre) expanse of woods and gardens has been the Sunday afternoon playground for generations of Parisian families. Historically, it has also had a reputation for love, as successive kings used to house their mistresses here, and after Louis XIV opened the woods to the public in the 17th century, it was noted that "marriages

Maps and Listings
MAP, PAGE 259

PRECEDING PAGES: achieving almost perfect symmetry in the Jardin du Luxembourg. **LEFT:** a lovely summer's day in the Bois de Boulogne. **RIGHT:** boating in the Bois.

On 19 October 1906, the Bois de Boulogne was the setting for France's first powered flight, when Brazilian aviator Alberto Santos-Dumont flew 60 metres (200ft) in his box biplane 14bis.

from the Bois de Boulogne do not get brought before the Right Reverend".

In 1852, Napoleon III had the surrounding wall of the royal hunting ground, built by Henri II, demolished and the park remodelled following the example of Hyde Park in London. Today it offers gardens, wild woods, horse racing at two of France's most famous racecourses, Longchamp and Auteuil, a sports stadium, boating, museums, restaurants and theatre.

Discovering the Bois

The best way to explore the Bois is by bicycle, which can be rented (May–Sept daily, Oct–Apr Sat–Sun) opposite the Porte des Sablons entrance. A network of cycle paths and nature trails criss-crosses the woods, giving easy access to the vast park and its lakes and waterfall. Note that walking around the park at night is a risky undertaking.

Near the Porte des Sablons is the **Jardin d'Acclimatation** (www.jardin-dacclimatation.fr; tel: 01 40 67 90 82; daily Apr–Sept 10am–7pm, Oct–Mar until 6pm; charge), an amusement park for children, with a hall of mirrors, zoo, go-kart racing, a wooden fort, theatre and puppet show (Wed, Sat–Sun at 3pm and 4pm). Further west, the **Parc de Bagatelle** (charge) surrounds a small château built by the Count of Artois, later Charles X, who bet Marie-Antoinette he could build a house in three months. The bet was won at great cost, hence the ironic name *bagatelle* (meaning "paltry sum"). The gardens are magnificent, with 8,000 roses blooming from June to October, a walled iris garden flowering in May and a display of water lilies in August. Art exhibitions and classical concerts are held in the Trianon and Orangerie during the summer season.

In the centre of the Bois is the **Pré Catalan**, the most romantic spot in western Paris. In spring, narcissi, tulips and daffodils carpet the manicured lawns, bathing the foot of the colossal copper beech, over 200 years old, whose branches span over 500 metres/yds. **Le Pré Catalan** (tel: 01 44 14 41 00) restaurant offers sumptuous fare in elegant Belle Epoque surroundings.

Nearby, the **Jardin Shakespeare** (tel: 01 40 19 95 33; daily for guided tours 3–3.30pm, 4–4.30pm; charge; no credit cards) is planted with flowers, trees and shrubs that feature in Shakespeare's plays: there's *Macbeth's* heather, Mediterranean herbs from *The Tempest* and Ophelia's stream. In summer, open-air productions of the Bard's plays (usually in French) are presented in the leafy theatre.

Musée Marmottan ❷

Address: 2 rue Louis Boilly, www.marmottan.com
Tel: 01 44 96 50 33
Opening Hrs: Tue–Sun 10am–6pm.

Thur until 8pm
Entrance Fee: charge
Transport: La Muette

Just inside Passy by the eastern border of the park is this dazzling little museum, with 65 paintings by Monet that were donated by his son Michel in 1971, among them his celebrated *Impression Soleil Levant* (1872), which gave its name to the Impressionist movement. Once home to avid art collector Paul Marmottan, this beautiful 19th-century mansion also exhibits works by Pissarro, Renoir, Gauguin and Berthe Morisot, as well as a superb collection of First Empire furniture.

PARC DE LA VILLETTE ❸

Transport: Porte de Pantin, Porte de la Villette

In northeast Paris, nestling against the *Périphérique*, this multi-purpose park and leisure area was one of the most spectacular 1980s *grands projets*. Built on the site of a huge abattoir,

---

TIP

Every June and July, the lovely Orangerie de Bagatelle, in the Bois de Boulogne, hosts candlelit recitals of the music of Chopin. For information, tel: 01 45 00 22 19 or see www.frederic-chopin.com

---

Paris Parks

TIP

From mid-July to the end of August every year, the Parc de la Villette stages a popular free film season, Le Cinéma en Plein Air; seating is on one of the park's big lawns, and the huge screen is inflatable. The park also holds a 10-day jazz festival each September. For information about both events, tel: 01 40 03 75 75 or log on to www. villette.com.

BELOW: model boat on one of the lakes within the Bois de Boulogne.

rendered obsolete by improved refrigeration techniques and poor design (the cows could not even get up the steps), its 55 hectares (136 acres) of futuristic gardens surround a colossal science museum, the **Cité des Sciences et de l'Industrie** (www. cite-sciences.fr; tel: 01 40 05 70 00; Tue–Sat 10am–6pm, Sun until 7pm; charge). It's not a museum for academics: exhibits are interactive, with buttons, levers, keyboards and screens to keep mind and body alert. There's even a Mirage jet fighter to inspire budding aviators.

Begin at *L'Univers*, with a spectacular planetarium and explanation of the inexplicable Big Bang. *La Vie* is an eclectic mix of medicine, agriculture and economics. *La Matière* reproduces a nuclear explosion and lets you land an Airbus 320, and *La Communication* has displays of artificial intelligence, three-dimensional graphics and virtual reality.

La Géode (www.lageode.fr; tel: 01 40 0579 99; Tue–Sun 10.30am–8.30pm; charge) is a giant silver ball housing an imax cinema; there is also L'Argonaute, a retired submarine,

and Cinaxe (charge), a flight simulator-cum-cinema, which is definitely not for the queasy. The refurbished Planétarium (charge) boasts digital projectors that bring new visual panache to its virtual journeys through space.

Music and *Folies*

The former cattle market now houses a cultural and conference centre in the immense 19th-century **Grande Halle**. Next to it, the **Cité de la Musique** (www.cite-musique.fr; tel: 01 44 8444 84; Tue–Sat noon–6pm, Sun 10am–6pm; charge) is an edifice of sharp angles designed by Christian de Portzamparc, which includes the **Musée de la Musique**. It charts the development of classical, jazz and folk music, and houses an impressive collection of over 4,500 musical instruments. Portzamparc also designed the music and dance conservatory, another part of the Cité, east of the Grande Halle. The Cité's large auditorium hosts concerts by some of the world's most illustrious visiting performers, and nearby is the

Zénith, one of Paris's biggest rock and pop venues.

The gardens of La Villette are the biggest built in Paris since Haussmann's time. Designed by Bernard Tschumi and opened in 1993, they comprise several thematic areas, such as the **Jardin des Frayeurs Enfantines** (Garden of Childhood Fears), with a huge dragon slide, and the **Jardin des Vents** (Garden of Winds), home to multicoloured bamboo plants. Abstraction continues in the form of Tschumi's *folies*: red, angular tree houses – minus the trees – that are scattered throughout the park, each with a special function, such as play area, workshop, day-care centre or café. After dark, blue strip lighting gives the gardens a strange, otherworldly aspect.

South of La Villette towards Belleville, this charmingly eccentric park was built by Haussmann in the 1860s on the site of a rubbish dump and gypsum quarry. The uneven ground provided a perfect setting for some wooded, rocky landscaping, and a lake was created around an artificial 50-metre (165ft) "mountain", capped by a Roman-style temple, with a waterfall and a cave containing artificial stalactites. It's a little like a picturesque fantasy, and children love to explore here. Ice-skating, boating and donkey rides are also on offer down below, and the puppet show or "Guignol" in the open-air theatre has been a popular attraction for over 150 years.

ABOVE: blue skies reflected in La Géode in the Parc de la Villette.
BELOW: Cité de la Musique exhibit.

PARC DES BUTTES-CHAUMONT ❹

Opening Hrs: daily 7.30am–dusk
Transport: Botzaris, Buttes-Chaumont

BOIS DE VINCENNES ❺

Transport: Château de Vincennes, Porte de Charenton,

The "Chaumont" in Buttes-Chaumont is a corruption of monts chauves, which means bald mountains. The park created there under Napoleon III was, in the 20th century, highly popular with the Surrealists: André Breton and Louis Aragon averred that it was the home of the "city's subconscious", and regularly used to stroll there in the evening.

RIGHT: fun and games at the Cité des Sciences.
BELOW: Cité de la Musique posters.

Porte Dorée

On the southeast edge of Paris lies this expanse of wood and parkland, another former royal hunting ground, which Philippe-Auguste enclosed in the 12th century with a 12km (7-mile) wall to protect its forests from poachers. Renowned for its château, racecourse and zoo, the Bois de Vincennes has other modern attractions such **La Cartoucherie**, which was once an ancient arsenal, but now a complex of theatres where plays are staged by some of France's most avant-garde companies.

Château de Vincennes

Address: www.chateau-vincennes.fr
Tel: 01 48 08 31 20
Opening Hrs: 21 May–22 Sept 10am–6pm, 23 Sept–20 May 10am–5pm
Entrance Fee: charge

King Charles V built much of this medieval fortress in the 1360s, and Henry V of England died here in 1422. Over the centuries it has had many uses: it has served as a prison – incarcerating among

others the philosopher Diderot and Revolutionary Mirabeau – a porcelain factory and, under Napoleon I, an arsenal. Napoleon III began a restoration programme, but the château was severely damaged by the Germans in 1944. Restoration is now complete, and there is a museum in the 14th-century keep.

Parc Floral de Paris

Address: www.parcfloraldeparis.com
Tel: 01 49 57 24 84
Opening Hrs: daily 9.30am–dusk
Entrance Fee: charge

Just south of the château, this park within the Bois is a favourite with families, who wander the Vallée des Fleurs, in bloom all year-round, the pine wood and the water garden, and take advantage of the adventure playground. At weekends in summer it puts on an excellent season of jazz and classical concerts by the lake, which are free for visitors already inside the park.

Parc Zoologique de Paris

Tel: 01 44 75 20 00
Opening Hrs: Mon–Sat 9am–6pm,
Sun 9am–6.30pm
Entrance Fee: charge

On the western side of the Bois is Paris's main zoo, although it is currently closed for renovation until 2014. It was all the rage when it opened in 1934, because its animals roamed free. Each enclosure is different, inspired by the animals' natural environment, and a giant artificial mound is home to 60 species of animals, including monkeys, gazelles and goats.

Palais de la Porte Dorée – Aquarium Tropical

Address: www. aquarium-portedoree.fr
Tel: 01 53 59 58 60
Opening Hrs: Tue–Fri 10am–5.30pm,
Sat–Sun 10am–7pm
Entrance Fee: charge

A few minutes' walk from the zoo is the city's aquarium, which has tropical fish and also a crocodile pit, in the basement. The Palais is a masterpiece of Art Deco design, built as a "Museum of the Colonies" at the height of the colonial era; its sculpted facade celebrates the *"Gloire"* of the French Empire in Africa, Asia and the South Pacific. It was formerly also home to a museum of tribal art, but this collection has been absorbed by the **Musée du Quai Branly** (see page 237). The Palais also houses a museum dedicated to the history of immigration in France (same opening hours for aquarium; charge).

NEW-AGE EXPERIMENTS AND ORIENTAL GARDENS

Parc Montsouris ❻

Transport: Porte d'Orléans,
RER Cité Universitaire

In the south of Paris, this 19th-century park is made up of 16 hectares (40 acres) of gently undulating grass and trees. It was much loved by Cubist Georges Braque and the exiled Lenin, who both used to live close by. On the day the park opened in 1878, the lake suddenly and inexplicably drained dry, and its engineer committed suicide.

ABOVE: Roman-style temple at les Buttes. **BELOW:** high spirit in the Parc des Buttes-Chaumont.

Parc Georges-Brassens ❼

Transport: Porte de Vanves

The far-flung southwest of Paris is the capital's most populated district and home to two of its newest parks. Parc Georges-Brassens was opened in 1982 on the site of another old abattoir, and is now a child's playground paradise, with playhouses, rock piles, rivers and mini-lakes. It includes a garden designed for the blind: close your eyes and follow the trickling of fountains and smell the fragrant foliage. Braille signs give relevant information on herbs and shrubs. Along Rue des Morillons there are also 700 vines, which produce a few hundred bottles each year of the red Clos des Morillons (full-bodied, fine bouquet). It is sold at the wine shop **Le Repaire de Bacchus** at 75 rue des Morillons, and proceeds go to charity. At weekends, the ancient market halls host a giant antiquarian book market.

Parc André-Citroën ❽

Transport: Balard, Javel-André Citroën, RER Boulevard Victor

Further west on the banks of the Seine, the once-derelict site of the Citroën car factory has been turned into this stunning modern park, designed by Gilles Clément and Alain Prévost, where futuristic formal gardens mix with spacious lawns and a wild garden; two huge glasshouses glisten next to the esplanade, and children leap in and out of spurting fountains.

Beyond the glass greenhouses lie two themed gardens – one "black" and

ABOVE: playing *boules*.
BELOW: amongst the ferns and flowers at the Parc Floral.

one "white" – and on the park's north-east side a series of six more colourful gardens have been planted to a different colour scheme – gold, silver, red, orange, green and blue. Each garden is linked to a metal, a planet, a day of the week, and a sense: thus gold is linked to the sun, Sunday and the intangible sixth sense. The tethered **Eutelsat** hot-air balloon (charge) lifts 135 metres (440ft) into the air at weekends to give visitors a stunning panoramic aerial view over the capital.

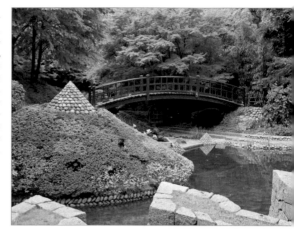

Jardins Albert Kahn ❾

Address: 14 rue du Port, Boulogne-Billancourt
www.albert-kahn.fr
Tel: 01 55 19 28 00
Opening Hrs: Tue–Sun May–Sept 11am–7pm, Oct–Apr until 6pm
Entrance Fee: charge
Transport: Boulogne-Pont St-Cloud

More traditional horticulture is found beyond the city limits in the suburb of Boulogne-Billancourt, where the legacy of financier Albert Kahn (1860–1940) takes the form of an extraordinary park, created between 1895 and 1910. Japanese, English and French gardens lie alongside an Alpine forest and North American prairie. The grass is cut at different levels, from "beatnik" style to "sailorboy". Kahn called the gardens "the plant expression of my thoughts concerning a reconciled world", an idea complemented by 72,000 photographs of world landscapes taken between 1910 and 1931, and exhibited on permanent rotation.

ABOVE: the Japanese garden on Jardins Albert Kahn.
BELOW: Parc des Buttes-Chaumont.

Green-Fingered Emperor

It was Napoleon III who gave Paris its first public gardens; before that, the only landscaped green spaces in the city were owned by noblemen, who sometimes let ordinary citizens have the use of them, and sometimes didn't. His motives had as much to do with a desire to improve the city's hygiene as with philanthropy. The Parcs et Plantations department, created by Haussmann to carry out the emperor's gardening zeal, created the majority of the parks and gardens visible in the city today: some 1,834 hectares (4,532 acres) in all. Although, the gardens were actually designed by Jean-Pierre Barillet-Deschamps, who was inspired by the "English garden" style, and built by the engineers Jean-Charles Alphand and Eugène Belgrand; the latter's other major achievement was to improve the Parisian sewerage system. Napoleon took a close interest in the work; he had acquired a taste for English landscape gardening styles during his years of exile in London, and he oversaw the laying out of the Bois de Boulogne personally. Other notable green spaces landscaped during his rule included the Bois de Vincennes, the Parc de Montsouris and, one of the greatest triumphs of the Parcs et Plantations designers, the Parc des Buttes-Chaumont.

LA DÉFENSE

West of the capital, just outside the city ringroad, is a brave new world of glass-faced skyscrapers and architectural daring.

Named after a 19th-century statue called *La Défense de Paris*, which commemorated the French soldiers who defended Paris during the Franco-Prussian war, La Défense was a business district from the outset, and its visitor attractions are understandably few: mainly a shopping mall and a multiplex cinema. That said, it's worth visiting for the buildings themselves: from the 1950s, when the first landmark edifice went up (the vast, parachute-shaped CNIT), La Défense has been an architectural playground. The most iconic sight is La Grande Arche, a 110-metre (360ft) rectangular arch that once housed a couple of techy museums and a gourmet restaurant as well as offices. However, following problems with the lifts, the Arche is now closed permanently to the public. To the west of here is the Musée de la Défense (15 place de la Défense; Sun–Fri 10am–6pm, Sat until 7pm; free) which exhibits the designs and scale models of the buildings. Plans are afoot for two major new edifices to be completed by 2017: Le Phare (300 metres/984ft), conceived by Los Angeles-based Thom Mayne, and the Norman Foster-designed Hermitage Plaza, two skyscrapers that will reach 320 metres/1050ft and will be the tallest buildings in the European Union.

The Essentials

Address: www.grandearche.com
Tel: 01 49 07 27 27
Opening Hrs: daily Apr–Aug 10am–8pm, Sept–Mar 10am–7pm
Entrance fee: charge
Transport: La Défense

ABOVE: office workers running on their lunch break near the Quatre-Temps shopping centre.

BELOW: : the glass-clad sphere of the IMAX theatre.

ABOVE: the Arche was designed as a 20th-century version of the Arc de Triomphe, with which it aligns along the Axe Historique that runs through Paris.

SKYSCRAPERS, CAMERA, ACTION!

With such a striking alternative to the classic Paris topography right on their doorstep, it's surprising that relatively few French film-makers have brought their cameras to La Défense: this is, after all, the nearest thing France has to Manhattan. When it does come to the screen, the districts' emphatically 21st-century urban scenery is used either for sheer dramatic impact, or as visual shorthand for the soullessness of modern life, as in Bertrand Blier's social satire *Buffet Froid*. With similar intentions, Jacques Tati set his 1967 comedy *Play Time* (pictured) in a concrete jungle clearly intended to represent La Défense – although it was all built on a studio back lot in Joinville, some distance from Paris. In the 2007 British film *Mr Bean's Holiday*, the hapless protagonist ends up by accident at La Grande Arche instead of the Gare de Lyon. The area has also appeared in several French music videos, notably the 2007 song *Ding Dang Dong* by Les Rita Mitsouko where the band drives through the streets of Paris.

ABOVE: Jacques Tati in *Playtime*.

BELOW: the extensive use of glass on many of the buildings at La Défense fosters a certain futuristic feel – and the multiple reflections make for some interesting photo opportunities.

ABOVE: La Défense isn't only concrete and glass – there are fountains, gardens and sculptures like *Red Spider* (1976), by Alexander Calder.

DISNEYLAND PARIS

A fairy-tale castle, classic Disney fantasy and eye-popping rides, plus a full-scale hands-on movie studio, crashing cars and state-of-the-art special effects – Walt's vast dream world promises fast fun for the entire family.

Maps and Listings
MAP, PAGE 279

With twice as many visitors a year as the Eiffel Tower or the Louvre, **Disneyland Paris ❶** (www.disneylandparis.com; tel: 08 25 30 02 22; for more details, see box) is the most popular tourist attraction in Europe. Located at Marne-la-Vallée, 32km (20 miles) east of Paris, on an 83-hectare (205-acre) site, this is, as Disney put it, the land "where dreams come true".

According to the Disney marketing machine, Disneyland Paris was something of a homecoming – Walt's family originally came from Isigny-sur-Mer in Normandy, and their name d'Isigny (from Isigny) became Disney in America. But generous financial incentives from the French government rather than family history were behind the final decision to bring Disneyland to Europe.

This complex is in fact properly named **Disneyland® Resort Paris**, and it has three parts: the main park, the hotels and shops of **Disney Village** and, the most recent addition, **Walt Disney Studios**, a self-contained park that offers a behind-the-scenes look at the history of animation, film and television. But it doesn't end there. If present plans are maintained, the whole site will not be fully developed until 2017, by which time there will be another new golf course and 13,000 more hotel rooms.

GETTING YOUR BEARINGS

Disneyland Paris theme park is divided into five main areas, or "lands", each with attractions, restaurants and shops on a particular theme – the same floor plan as in other Disneylands in California, Florida and Tokyo. Designed by "Imagineers", the artistic and mechanical wizards who spend their lives thinking up weird and wonderful attractions, this is Disney's

LEFT: Sleeping Beauty's castle.

most technologically advanced park, benefiting from state-of-the-art robotics and audio-animatronics, so that life-size, lifelike figures speak, sing and dance with gusto.

Decide what you want to do in order of priority, and get there early, as queues at popular rides soon get pretty long – up to 45 minutes. The circular train chugs clockwise so heading round the park in an anticlockwise direction cuts down crowds.

Main Street USA

Once through the Victorian turnstiles you enter this trademark Disney souvenir and shopping area, replicating one idea of 19th-century, small-town America. **City Hall**, on the left, is the central information centre and contact point for lost children and property. Here, too, is **Main Street Station**, from where the Disneyland train circles the park. The Disney Train leaves the Central Plaza at 1.30pm, 2.30pm and 3.30pm each day. The station is often quite crowded, so it's a good idea to board the train at one of the other stations en route, such as Frontierland.

The bandstand in Main Street square is the best place to view the parades that traverse the park at least once every day, passing around the bandstand and out through the large green gates. The Disney Magic Parade takes place at 7pm while Disney Dreams is a dinner-show (charge), which takes place at the end of the day in the Central Plaza. Winnie the Pooh and Duffy the Disney Bear are around here throughout the day.

Frontierland

To the left of Main Street, Frontierland evokes dreams of the Wild West (at least that's the idea). Its centrepiece, **Big Thunder Mountain**, is a towering triumph of red rock reminiscent of a Western movie. The small town of Thunder Mesa surrounding the mountain represents a pioneer settlement, including Cavalry Fort and Lucky Nugget Saloon, where Miss Lil entertains on a vaudeville stage. **Phantom Manor**, home to some spectacular animatronics, provides a high-tech rollicking ride through a haunted house. The house itself was copied from Norman

ABOVE: Indiana Jones and the Temple of Peril, the first ever 360-degree roller-coaster. **BELOW:** take a trip down the Rivers of the Far West on this paddle steamer.

Disneyland Made Easy

Disneyland Paris is open every day of the year. Times vary slightly, but in general from Sept–mid-July the main park is open 10am–7pm, Walt Disney Studios 10am–6pm, often with later hours at weekends; mid-July–Aug, the main park opens daily 10am–11pm, the Studios 10am–7pm. For all details, including bookings, current prices and places where you can buy tickets, tel: 08 25 30 02 22 or visit www.disneyland paris.com.

A standard Disney ticket is valid for one day's entry to either the main park or Walt Disney Studios; there are several ticket types available to save money. Staying in one of the Resort hotels can also cut costs.

ABOVE: fans of the *Cars* movies will enjoy Cars Race Rally.

TIP

Disneyland is easy to reach from central Paris, via RER line A to Marne-la-Vallée-Chessy (from Châtelet-Les Halles). The trip takes about 35 minutes. A combined RER and single Disney ticket is available from many RER stations and tourist offices. Disneyland Paris also has its own train station, with direct Eurostar services from London and fast TGV connections from Roissy airport and many other destinations. It's also possible to take a bus, the Disneyland Express (www.disneylandparis-express.com), from Paris.

Bates's abode in Hitchcock's *Psycho*. Inside are singing cowboy skeletons and holographic ghosts.

The **Rivers of the Far West**, an artificial lake in the middle of Frontierland, can be enjoyed by Mississippi paddle steamer, keelboat or Indian canoe. The Indian canoe station, verdant and full of birdsong (taped, but it fools the real birds) is a tranquil contrast to the roller-coaster ride. Also in Frontierland you'll find the Pocahontas Indian Village, inspired by the Disney film of the same name, and the Rustler Roundup Shootin' Gallery. An hour-long show, The Tarzan Encounter, takes place in The Chaparral Theater several times each afternoon.

Adventureland

Paths lead on to Adventureland: sparse scrub gives way to bamboo and flowers, and the twang of guitar fades into the beat of African drums. Here is another unforgettable attraction, **Pirates of the Caribbean** (queues generally move fast). As you descend, the air cools, water drips

and the darkness is punctuated only by flickering firelight. The water ride, through tropical swamp to the open sea, is orchestrated by jovially barbaric Disney workers. For the six-minute journey you are spellbound by animated pirates invading a treasure-rich port – here, a singing donkey, there, an inebriated pig that taps its trotters in time to the music. Jack Sparrow can usually be found lurking near the Blue Lagoon Restaurant in the afternoons.

Rival to Big Thunder Mountain, the first-ever 360-degree looping roller-coaster created by Disney is **Indiana Jones and the Temple of Peril**, near Explorers' Club Restaurant. Hold on to your stomach as the ore-carts plunge through rainforest and turn upside down above a mock archaeological dig inspired by the Indiana Jones saga. As with other top rides, get here early.

Elsewhere, Adventureland offers the ultimate treehouse, **La Cabane des Robinson**, home of the Swiss Family Robinson; an **Adventure Isle** based on *Treasure Island*, with a rope bridge and Ben Gunn's cave; and **Captain Hook's Pirate Ship** that, with Skull Rock, acts as a playground.

Fantasyland

The most popular land for younger children, with Disney's emblem **Le Château de la Belle au Bois Dormant** (Sleeping Beauty's Castle), centrepiece of the park, where Sleeping Beauty's tale is told through rich tapestries and stained-glass windows. Underneath lies **La Tanière du Dragon** (The Lair of the Dragon), hiding a 27-metre (88ft) -long creature that roars, curls its claws and hisses smoke. Next door, **Blanche-Neige et les Sept Nains** (Snow White and the Seven Dwarfs) leads children through the classic fairytale in cars from the dwarfs' mine, and terrifies them with a holographic floating witch's head.

Peter Pan's Flight is another one to visit early in the day, before the tour buses arrive; here you can take a pirate galleon into the skies above London, as far as Never-Never Land. More sedate amusement is found in **It's a Small World**, a cheerful puppet kingdom of singing children, a real Disney classic. Mickey Mouse and Princess Daisy are around and about here throughout the day.

Discoveryland

The futuristic high-tech experiences in Discoveryland are great for older kids. **Space Mountain** is a rollercoaster ride into outer space inspired

TIP

When you get to the park (as early as possible!) go straight to the Fastpass desks by the most popular rides, such as Space Mountain or Buzz Lightyear Laser Blast. For no extra charge, Fastpass allows you to book a time for the ride later in the day; so when you go back at the right time, you don't have to queue. Resort hotel guests also cut queues, as they can enter the parks an hour early.

ABOVE: the Hollywood Tower Hotel attraction will spook you out.
BELOW: the Mad Hatter's Tea Cups ride.

Disney Village

Open every day, for several hours after the main park and Walt Disney Studios have closed – so that visitors needn't fear having nothing to do once they've left their last ride – the "Village" between the park and the hotels buzzes with shops, restaurants, nightclubs and a huge cinema complex. Family entertainment takes the form of **Buffalo Bill's Legend**, a 90-minute Wild West show with Indian chiefs, buffaloes and carousing cowboys.

For places to eat, **Planet Hollywood** offers burgers, salads and pasta while surrounded by movie memorabilia; **King Ludwig's Castle** is a fairytale Bavarian castle, the kind that inspired the Disney castle, where diners can enjoy Bavarian and European food in a beamed dining hall. With tropical forests, giant aquariums and life-size model animals, the **Rainforest Café** has a more exotic menu. Slightly more low-key, **Annette's Diner** is well priced and entertaining, and fills up early with young families; taking the theme of an American 1950s diner, it serves burgers, fries and beer, brought by roller-skating waiters. Across the strip, **Billy Bob's** presents simple chicken dishes with a background of country tunes. The area around the lake is more sedate and more expensive, and appeals to couples on a romantic night out.

of cinema, opened in 2002. The park is supposedly arranged around a working film studio, and guests learn about the movie-making process and can step into the action themselves. Instead of "Lands", this park is made up of four zones.

Front Lot

As you walk through the majestic Studio Gates, the first thing you see are palm trees, a Mickey Mouse "Sorcerer's Apprentice" water fountain and a 33-metre (110ft) water tower, the traditional symbol of a Hollywood film studio. Strolling down the 1940s Hollywood Boulevard and watching starlets in veiled hats pose for the cameras, you soon realise this is all an elaborate set, complete with hundreds of movie props. Don't be surprised when "producers" try to recruit you as an actor.

Toon Studio

This is Disney's homage to the art of film animation – from its origins in Europe to the greatest animated pictures of the 21st century. Movie highlighting moments from Disney's cartoon classics is followed by a cartooning demonstration, and guests can try out their own animation skills at interactive play stations.

Animagique is a colourful show in the tradition of Czech "black light" theatre, bringing to life scenes from pictures like *The Lion King* and *Pinocchio*. The genie from *Aladdin* invites kids of all ages onto a film set called **Flying Carpets over Agrabah** – the mayhem begins when the actor-turned-director tries to organise a film shoot, with guest actors whizzing round a giant lamp on magic carpets. For the resort's 15th anniversary this was expanded with two high-excitement new attractions: **Crush's Coaster**, a spinning rollercoaster based on the film *Finding Nemo*, and **Cars Race Rally**, an interactive ride based on the film *Cars*.

by Jules Verne's *From the Earth to the Moon*, and **Star Tours** offers a trip with George Lucas's *Star Wars* characters. To get there, you walk past hard-working robots complaining about the trials of life. On the ride itself, the five minutes spent in the flight simulator are riveting as the spaceship crashes through meteors and engages in a laser battle. Captain EO is a futuristic film starring, and with the music of, Michael Jackson.

Discoveryland also has **Buzz Lightyear Laser Blast**, based on the *Toy Story* films, which launched in 2006. Allow plenty of time for queuing: it's rather like a giant video game, in which participants use their laser pistols to shoot down baddies, all under the guidance of Buzz. A photo is taken of players as they end the ride, with their score printed in the corner.

WALT DISNEY STUDIOS PARK

Walt Disney Studios, built alongside the main park, is a new park of rides and attractions inspired by the world

Production Courtyard

This is the heartbeat of the studio production facilities, with productions and shows almost every day. The **Walt Disney Television Studios** is the European home of Disney Channel. You get a glimpse of a busy production facility, and there's even a chance guests may be chosen to appear in one of the shows. Combining live performers and special effects, **CinéMagique** is a magical journey through 100 years of the moving image.

The **Studio Tram Tour** takes you on a tour of the studios, offering a peek behind the scenes at sets, movie props, special effects, decor and costumes. When the tram visits **Catastrophe Canyon**, a dam bursts, releasing a deluge of recycled water.

The Twilight Zone **Tower of Terror** takes you on a gravity-defying 13-storey drop and will delight all thrill seekers. Kids will enjoy a live encounter with **Stitch**.

Back Lot

This is home to some of the biggest thrills – the special effects facility, recording stages and the stunt workshops. The **Rock 'n' Roller Coaster**, starring Aerosmith, gives you the chance to "ride the music" in a sight-and-sound spectacular, featuring hairpin turns, loops and heart-stopping drops (it is too scary for small children). **Armageddon** takes guests on a voyage through the history of special effects, and into a full-sized set of a Mir Russian space station (from the Bruce Willis sci-fi hit *Armageddon*). Wind tunnels howl, meteors crash and guests dodge fireballs until an explosion in the heart of the ship brings the action to a climax.

Highlight of the Back Lot is the **Stunt Show Spectacular**. This live-action show trashes cars, motorcycles and jet-skis in a crescendo of movie stunts performed in a Mediterranean village seaside set.

Where to Stay

The wider resort – **Disney Village** and the hotels – is a celebration of "Americana". **Hotel Cheyenne** is the most imaginative: a film-set Western hotel, with saloon, sheriff's jail and wooden-planked stores. At the other "moderately priced" hotel, **Santa Fe**, Clint Eastwood grimaces down from a mock drive-in movie screen above the reception. The hotel style recalls Mexican villages.

The more expensive **Sequoia Lodge** and **Newport Bay Club** hotels overlook Lake Disney. One recalls Hitchcock's *North by Northwest* in its pine surroundings, and the other is a New England mansion. Across the lake, **Hotel New York** offers luxury rooms in a Manhattan-style skyscape designed by Michael Graves.

The jewel of the resort's hotels is naturally the four-star **Disneyland Hotel**, its Victorian style whispering 19th-century elegance. In a forest 5km (3 miles) from the main park is **Davy Crockett Ranch**, with 97 camping and caravan places, 498 fully equipped cabins in "pioneer village" style and sports facilities.

SHOP

There is a new shop, World of Disney, at the entrance to Disney Village whose Art Deco design mirrors the elegant department stores of Paris. Five minutes away from the park is the designer shopping outlet La Vallée Village (daily 10am–7pm; www.la valleevillage.com), which has more than 95 boutiques for men, women, children and the home.

BELOW: there's no shortage of places to eat at Disneyland Paris.

TRIPS OUT OF TOWN

Within easy reach of Paris can be found the grand
palaces beloved of Louis XIV and Napoleon,
medieval gems such as Chartres or St-Denis,
and the natural world that has inspired so
many artists, at Barbizon and Monet's fabulous
garden at Giverny.

Many of the fascinating places
beyond the city limits
are just a train ride away.
Alternatively, you can hire a car (see
page 297) to venture off the beaten
track – your meanderings may
lead to quaint old *auberges* serving
hearty evening meals by the fire or
lunch on a riverside terrace. If time
is limited, then a trip to Versailles or
Disneyland Paris ❶ (see page 268)
is an obvious choice, but you could
take a day or two to visit towns such
as Rouen or Chartres further away,
stopping at sights along the way. The
forests of the Ile-de-France and surrounding regions are dotted with
châteaux and monuments.

   SNCF trains are generally fast and
efficient, and, on arrival at your destination, you'll find the needs of visitors well catered for, with a plentiful
supply of maps and information on
tourist sights, hotels, restaurants and
taxis. Some places, such as St-Denis,
St-Germain-en-Laye and Versailles
itself, are stops on Paris's speedy RER
suburban train network (see page
295). Tours to all the main destinations are also available from hotels
and many agencies in Paris.

PRECEDING PAGES: Monet's lily pond at
Giverny. **LEFT:** view of the gardens at
Versailles. **RIGHT:** ornate lampstands inside
the Château de Versailles.

THE SHORTEST HOPS

Château de Versailles ❷

Address: www.chateauversailles.fr
Tel: 01 30 83 78 00
Opening Hrs: Tue–Sun Apr–Oct
9am–6.30pm, Nov–Mar until
5.30pm; other parts of the estate have
separate opening times
Entrance Fee: charge
Transport: RER C5 to Versailles-Rive
Gauche

The RER line C5 from St-Michel-
Notre-Dame will drop you very near

Main Attractions

CHÂTEAU DE VERSAILLES
CHÂTEAU DE MALMAISON
CHÂTEAU DE ST-GERMAIN-EN-LAYE
BASILIQUE DE ST-DENIS
CHANTILLY
VAUX-LE-VICOMTE
CHÂTEAU DE FONTAINEBLEAU
CHARTRES
ROUEN
FONDATION MONET, GIVERNY

Maps and Listings

MAP, PAGE 279

the Sun King's magnificent château and gardens. You will have to pick and choose what you most want to see, as you need much more than a day to take in everything.

Apart from the main palace there is the **Grand Trianon** in the north of the park, the **Petit Trianon** and the nearby **Hameau de la Reine**, Marie-Antoinette's fantasy farmhouse, where she played at being a shepherdess. In the vast gardens (open daily dawn until dusk), the fountains dance to music every Saturday and Sunday afternoon from April to September (extra charge), while on most Saturdays in July and August the gardens stay open at night for a superbly lit repeat performance, the dazzling *Grandes Eaux Nocturnes*.

Musée National de Céramique – Sèvres ❸

Address: www.sevrescitececeramique.fr
Tel: 01 46 29 22 00
Opening Hrs: Wed–Mon 10am–5pm
Entrance Fee: charge
Transport: Pont de Sèvres

Half a day will suffice for a visit to Sèvres, set on the edge of the lovely wooded Parc de St-Cloud, laid out by Le Nôtre around a château that no longer exists. The suburb has been famous for its porcelain for more than 200 years, and the ceramics workshops, set in a wooded park, contain this beautiful museum.

Château de Malmaison ❹

Address: www.chateau-malmaison.fr
Tel: 01 41 29 05 55
Opening Hrs: Apr–Sept Mon–Fri 10am–12.30pm, 1.30–5.45pm, Sat–Sun 10am–12.30pm, 1.30-6.15pm, Oct–Mar Mon–Fri 10am–12.30pm, 1.30–5.15pm, Sat–Sun 10am–12.30pm, 1.30–5.45pm
Entrance Fee: charge
Transport: RER A to La Défense, bus 258

Further west in Rueil-Malmaison, this château was the favourite home of Napoleon Bonaparte's first wife, Empress Joséphine, and he allowed her to live on here after their divorce; she died here in 1814. Before the break-up, Napoleon used to retreat here between battles. Along with the neighbouring little **Château de Bois-Préau**, it forms an important

museum of the First Empire, with period interiors that include Joséphine's bedroom and other Napoleonic memorabilia. The magnificent rose garden looks much as it did in Joséphine's day.

Château de St-Germain-en-Laye – Musée des Antiquités Nationales ❺

Address: www.ot-stgermainenlaye.fr
Tel: 01 39 10 13 00
Opening Hrs: Wed–Mon 10am–5pm
Entrance Fee: charge
Transport: RER A1 to St-Germain-en-Laye

The wealthy suburb of St-Germain-en-Laye has perched above Paris since the 12th century, and was once a royal retreat. Its château, which has a lovely Gothic chapel, was rebuilt for François I (his royal salamander and "F" can be seen in the courtyard). Inside, you won't find period furnishings or portraits, but a museum of prehistoric and ancient times. The

During the Revolution, the tombs in St-Denis were vandalised and the royal bodies thrown into a pit. However, they were secretly rescued and finally returned to their original resting places in restored tombs by Louis XVIII in 1816.

ABOVE: Chantilly curio.
RIGHT: the duchess's
blue bedroom in the
Château de Chantilly.
BELOW: admiring the
collection of paintings
in the Château de
Chantilly.

terrace gardens overlooking the Seine were designed by Le Nôtre and inspired Impressionist painter Alfred Sisley (1839–99).

Basilique de St-Denis ❻

Address: www.monuments-nationaux.fr
Tel: 01 48 09 83 54
Opening Hrs: Apr–Sept Mon–Sat 10am–6.15pm, Sun noon–6.15pm, Oct–Mar Mon–Sat 10am-5pm, Sun noon–5.15pm
Entrance Fee: charge
Transport: Basilique-St-Denis

Less than 4km (3 miles) north of Paris stands the final resting place of France's kings and queens. Revered as an early masterpiece of Gothic architecture, the basilica was mainly built by the charismatic Abbot Suger, close friend of Louis VII, in the 12th century on the site of an abbey church. According to legend, this is the spot reached by St Denis, first bishop of Lutetia, when he walked out of Paris carrying his head, after being

beheaded on Montmartre. Monarchs from as far back as Dagobert I (628–37) are buried here, and the medieval and Renaissance tomb sculptures are some of the finest in France.

NORTH TO CHANTILLY AND COMPIÈGNE

Chantilly, about 50km (30 miles) away from Paris, is famous for horse racing, but also has a sumptuous palace, a magnificent park created by Le Nôtre and the splendidly palatial 18th-century **Grandes Ecuries**, stables built by Prince Louis-Henri de Bourbon, who believed that he would be reincarnated as a horse.

The Château de Chantilly ❼

Address: www.chateaudechantilly.com
Tel: 03 44 27 31 80
Opening Hrs: Apr–Oct Wed–Mon (daily July–Aug) 10.30am–6pm, Nov–Mar Wed–Mon 10.30am–5.30pm
Entrance Fee: charge

Transport: SNCF from Gare du Nord

This fairytale castle is nestled in a forest grove, its white walls topped by a blue-slate roof, and wild ducks bustling around the moat. Inside, the **Musée Condé** holds works by Botticelli, Raphael, Giotto and Holbein.

You don't have to be a horse-racing enthusiast to enjoy the **Musée Vivant du Cheval** (Wed–Mon Mar–Nov 10am–5pm, Dec 1.30–5pm; charge), under the impressive dome of the Grandes Ecuries, with various breeds on show and many exhibition rooms – these stables once housed 240 horses and 500 dogs. Riding displays are held on the first Sunday of each month. The Chantilly racecourse is the most fashionable in France, and high society gathers here in June for the prestigious flat-racing trophies.

Compiègne and its forest

The town of **Compiègne** ❽, 30km (20 miles) northeast of Chantilly and 80km (50 miles) northeast of Paris (SNCF from Gare du Nord), sits between the Oise River and one of France's largest forests. Its Hôtel de Ville has the oldest bell in the country in its clock tower, and picantins (little figures) strike every hour. The **Château de Compiègne** (www.musee-chateau-compiegne.fr; tel: 03 44 38 47 02; Wed–Mon 10am–6pm; charge) was once the favourite residence of Napoleon III and has three museums (one of vintage cars).

If you enjoy walking, make your way on foot to **Les Beaux Monts**, just outside the town, for a spectacular view of the château and the Oise. From here, a circular walk, lasting between one and two hours, has been marked out, guiding you through the beautiful **Forêt de Compiègne**, an ancient royal hunting forest full of old oaks and beech trees. By car or SNCF bus from Compiègne station, you can also visit the **Musée Wagon de l'Armistice** (tel: 03 44 85 14 18; Apr–mid-Sept daily 10am–6pm, mid-Sept–Mar Wed–Mon 10am–5.30pm; charge) in the Clairière de l'Armistice (Armistice Clearing), where the 1918 Armistice between Germany and the Allies was signed, and where Hitler humiliated the French by making them surrender in the same place on 22 June 1940.

On the eastern edge of the forest is Napoleon III's hunting lodge, the **Château de Pierrefonds** (www.monu-ments-nationaux.fr; tel: 03 44 42 72 72; May–Aug daily 9.30am–6pm, Sept–Apr Tue–Sun 10am–1pm, 2–5.30pm; charge). Entirely reconstructed in the 19th century in Romantic medi-eval style by Viollet-le-Duc, with drawbridge, moat and towers, it is a remarkable architectural oddity. Inside, the fanciful architect allowed his imagination free rein.

SOUTHEAST TO FONTAINEBLEAU

Vaux-le-Vicomte ❾

Address: www.vaux-le-vicomte.com
Tel: 01 64 14 41 90
Opening Hrs: late Mar–early Nov daily 10am–6pm, gardens open some weekends Nov–Mar

"Why have I been taken to Versailles seven times and never here?" A famous statement made by President of the United States Richard Nixon, during his official visit to Chantilly in 1968.

BELOW: inside the Gothic Basilique de St-Denis.

Entrance Fee: charge
Transport: SNCF from Gare de Lyon to Melun

Some 40km (25 miles) south of Paris outside Melun is this luxurious 17th-century château, built by Louis XIV's powerful treasurer Nicolas Fouquet, a devoted patron of the arts. The impeccable house, along with a beautiful garden *à la française* – the

first created by Le Nôtre – was his undoing: jealous advisers whispered to the king that Fouquet had paid for it with treasury funds. After a grand house-warming party for the young monarch, Fouquet was imprisoned at Vincennes, and the upstaged Louis set out to build something even more splendid – Versailles – using the very same architect and designers.

The château and grounds provide an intriguing visit. One room traces the history of its owners, others are decorated in sumptuous period style, with coffered, painted ceilings and Gobelins tapestries, and the kitchen equipment is fascinating. The candle-lit tour on Saturday evening (May–mid-Oct 8pm–midnight) gives an added atmospheric dimension.

Château de Fontainebleau ⑩

Address: www.musee-chateau-fontaine bleau.fr
Tel: 01 60 71 50 70
Opening Hrs: Wed–Mon Apr–Sept 9.30am–6pm, Oct–Mar until 5pm
Entrance Fee: charge
Transport: SNCF from Gare de Lyon to

first of France's purpose-built royal châteaux, residence of French sovereigns from François I to Napoleon III. Each one added something to the palace, creating a mixture of styles, but Napoleon I outdid them all by building an ornate throne room – his *grands appartements* are definitely worth seeing.

The artists' village: Barbizon

Barbizon, 7km (4 miles) away on the eastern edge of the forest, is a village that has attracted landscape painters since the 1840s, when Théodore Rousseau (1812–67) and Jean-François Millet (1814–75) fled to the woods to escape the Industrial Revolution and rediscover nature. The Office du Tourisme is set in Rousseau's former house, and his workshop is now a museum to the **Ecole de Barbizon** (www.barbizon-tourisme.fr; tel: 01 60 66 22 27; Wed–Mon 10am–12.30pm, 2–6pm; charge).

SOUTHWEST TO CHARTRES

A trip to **Chartres** ⓫ – 89km (55 miles) from Paris – can be taken

As well as designing some of the most famous gardens in France, his most celebrated at Versailles, André Le Nôtre (1613-1700) drew up designs for a parterre at Greenwich Park in London (uncompleted) and designed the gardens of the castle of Racconigi near Turin.

Fontainebleau-Avon, then bus

Melun sits on the edge of the **Forêt de Fontainebleau**, which was once a royal hunting ground and is now the haunt of cyclists, mushroom hunters, birdwatchers, picnickers and rock climbers, attracted by the giant rock formations. The town of Fontainebleau lies just 15km (9 miles) away, and is dominated by the

ABOVE: inside the Château de Fontainebleau.
BELOW: the majestic entrance to the Château de Fontainebleau.

The Musée des Impressionnismes has a café, Terra Café, where the menu focuses on regional specialities from Normandy; snacks and drinks are available too. There is a lovely garden terrace for fine days.

ABOVE: Claude Monet, the father of Impressionism.
BELOW: exquisite stained-glass window, Chartres cathedral.

slowly, stopping off at the châteaux of **Dampierre** and **Rambouillet** (see box) on the way, or you can go straight there by train (sncf from Gare Montparnasse). The two spires of the magnificent Gothic cathedral (www.chartres-tourisme. com; tel: 02 37 18 26 26; daily 8am–7.30pm; entrance charge for towers) soar above the surrounding fields. Originally Romanesque, the cathedral dedicated to the Virgin Mary was destroyed by fire in 1194, but everyone from peasant to lord contributed straightaway to the rebuilding, with labour or money. The famous rose windows, together with 170 more of Europe's finest original stained-glass windows, fill the cathedral with changing colours. Behind the cathedral is the **Musée des Beaux-Arts** (tel: 02 37 90 45 80; Nov–Apr Wed–Sat 10am–noon, 2–5pm, Sun 2–5pm, May–Oct until 6pm; charge), with Renaissance and 18th-century paintings and some fine tapestries.

La Maison Picassiette (22 rue du Repos; 02 37 34 10 78; Apr–Oct Wed–Mon 10am–noon. 2–6pm; charge) was built by Raymond

Isidore from broken bits of tile and glass from 1938-1962; it is considered a fine example of naïve art and is a listed building.

WEST TO MONET'S GIVERNY

For a longer break from Paris, head for **Rouen** ⑫, which is on the Seine about 110km (70 miles) along the N13 from Paris (or by SNCF from Gare St-Lazare). Once the capital of Normandy, Rouen has a wealth of picturesque timber-frame houses, narrow streets and many of France's finest Gothic buildings, both civic and religious, despite the damage it suffered during World War II. The city is centred on the impressive, soaring Gothic cathedral, which was much loved and much painted by Claude Monet. Joan of Arc was burned at the stake in the city in 1431, after a trial conducted by the bishop of Beauvais, who was in cahoots with the English occupiers, on a site that is now one of Rouen's liveliest squares.

The road to Rouen passes not far from **Giverny**. Set on a hillside just above the Seine, this small village is where Claude Monet lived and worked for 43 years until his death in 1926, at the age of 86.

Fondation Claude Monet ⑬

Address: www.fondation-monet.com
Tel: 02 32 51 28 21
Opening Hrs: Apr–Oct daily 9.30am–6pm
Entrance Fee: charge
Transport: SNCF from Gare St-Lazare to Vernon 6km/3 miles away, then bus

Monet's house is now a museum and memorial beautifully restored and redecorated in the same colours the painter loved. The gardens that the father of Impressionism designed and drew inspiration from are a living work of art – at their colourful best during May, June and July – with the Japanese bridge and the famous water lilies on the pond. Arrive early, though, to try to avoid the crowds, and if possible go on a weekday.

Only copies of Monet's works are on display at Giverny but, nearby, the **Musée des Impressionnismes** (www.mdig.fr; tel: 02 32 51 94 65; Apr–Oct daily 10am–6pm; charge), which opened in 2009, celebrates the work of the Impressionists and puts on temporary exhibitions.

You can also head for the **Forêt de Lyons**, northeast of Giverny (buses run from Rouen and Vernon). The centennial beech trees make a walk or cycle ride a particular pleasure, with fine views of Norman villages and their half-timbered houses.

ABOVE: Monet's garden in Giverny.
BELOW: Château de Sceaux.

Châteaux around Paris

The Ile-de-France region is rich in châteaux, many built in the wake of the Sun King's extravagance at Versailles. The **Château de Sceaux** (tel: 01 41 87 29 50), 7km (4 miles) south of Paris, was built in 1670 for Fouquet's successor Colbert, with a beautiful park and gardens by Le Nôtre. Rebuilt in 1856, it now hosts the Musée de l'Ile-de-France. More Le Nôtre gardens are found at the **Château de Dampierre** (tel: 01 30 52 53 24), 35km (22 miles) southwest, which has a touch of Versailles about it. The president's summer residence, **Rambouillet** (www.rambouillet-tourisme.fr; tel: 01 34 83 00 25), 15km (9 miles) further on, was once a feudal castle and is open when the president is away. The **Château d'Ecouen** (www.valdoise-tourisme.com; tel: 01 34 38 38 50), 19km (11 miles) north, is a masterpiece of Renaissance architecture, now the Musée National de la Renaissance, with the finest tapestries in France. **Maisons** (www.tourisme-maisonslaffitte.fr; tel: 01 39 62 01 49) at Maisons-Laffitte, near StGermain-en-Laye, is a small gem designed in 1641 by François Mansart for René de Longueil, future finance minister of Louis XIV; the town itself is well known for its horse racing.

VERSAILLES

Paris was not always the capital of France – for a while, the country was run from a sumptuous palace at Versailles, to the southwest of the city.

The Château de Versailles is the ultimate expression of the French monarchy's power and ostentation prior to the Revolution.

Built in 1624 as a hunting lodge for Louis XIII, the building was developed (as was the land surrounding it) by Louis XIV, who employed the celebrated creative trio of Le Vau, Le Nôtre and Le Brun, as well as the no less illustrious architect Mansart. Versailles became the capital of France, and, by 1774, following alterations by Louis XV and XVI, the palace had 2,143 windows and 67 staircases, and was home to 10,000 courtiers and servants. The gardens were designed by Le Nôtre on the same grand scale as the château itself, and adorned with statues and fountains. The Royal Family left Versailles for the Tuileries in 1789 and in 1790 it was emptied of its furniture, which was eventually sold off. After the arrest of Louis XVI in 1791, the palace was sealed by the National Constituent Assembly. In 1793 it became a depository for seized artworks and was

ABOVE: this beautiful gilded clock face is one of many Versailles adornments with the Sun King's effigy.

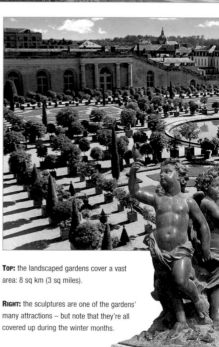

The Essentials

Address: www. chateauversailles.fr
Tel: 01 30 83 78 00
Opening Hrs: Château: Tues–Sun Apr–Oct 9am–6.30pm, Nov–Mar until 5.30pm
Entrance Fee: charge
Transport: RER C5 to Versailles-Rive Gauche

TOP: the landscaped gardens cover a vast area: 8 sq km (3 sq miles).

RIGHT: the sculptures are one of the gardens' many attractions – but note that they're all covered up during the winter months.

THE SUN KING

Louis XIV came to the throne at the age of five, in 1643, and his reign lasted 72 years – the longest in the history of France. He believed in the divine right of kings and it was because everything revolved around him that he later became known as The Sun King. It was a golden age of literature and art, and of French international expansion: Louis waged an aggressive foreign policy, built up a navy and reorganised the army into the most formidable fighting force on the Continent. His energy was prolific, and he served as his own prime minister – hence his famous comment *"L'Etat, c'est moi"* ("I am the state"). But for all the show of luxury and accomplishment, he was far from a benevolent monarch: in 1685 he revoked the Edict of Nantes, which brought about the bloody persecution of Protestants. He died aged 76 in 1715 and was succeeded by his five-year-old grandson, Louis XV.

TOP: Louis XIV, the Sun King.

ABOVE: the view northwest from the château along the gardens' central aisle. The fountain in the foreground is the centrepiece of the Bassin d'Apollon (Apollo's Pond).

BELOW: the scale and glory of the château are apparent right from its main entrance – the Cour de Marbre (Marble Courtyard).

ABOVE: there's an extra charge to enter the gardens on Saturdays and Sundays between April and September, when the fountains come to life and 17th-century music plays over the flower beds and pathways. But although it's fabulous to see the gardens in such watery splendour, Sunday is the worst day to visit the inside of the château, as it can become unbearably overcrowded.

then turned into a museum, which was closed when Napoleon came to power and reopened in the 1830s by Louis-Philippe. Its preservation for the nation has been ongoing since then.

The highlights

The château's main tour, plus the gardens, can be covered in a day; but to savour fully the wealth of historic and architectural heritage, allow two days.

TOP: Marie-Antoinette.

The main tour

The main part of the château, which can be accessed without a guide, includes the lavish State Apartments of the King and Queen (*Grands Appartements*), notably the King's State Bedroom. Also included are the Queen's bedchamber and the vast Hall of Mirrors. Other highlights of the main tour include, in the Hercules Room, François Lemoyne's fresco *The Apotheosis of Hercules*, and, in the Battle Gallery near the end, a copy of David's colossal *The Crowning of the Empress Joséphine at Notre-Dame*. For an extra fee, access is granted to Louis XIV's private bedroom and the apartments of the dauphin and dauphine.

ABOVE: as Premier Peintre, or Chief Painter to the King, Charles Le Brun (1619–90) directed the team of artists who decorated the ceilings at Versailles.

The Trianons and Hameau

The single-storey, Italianate Grand Trianon was built for Louis XIV as a miniature palace in which he could escape the formality of the château. The Petit Trianon was built as a retreat for Louis XV and his mistresses. A cluster of thatched cottages, the Hameau ("Hamlet") is associated with Marie-Antoinette; they were the queen's fairy-tale farm and dairy.

RIGHT: the magnificent Baroque Royal Chapel, adorned with carved white marble, gilding and murals. The royal family worshipped from the gallery.

BELOW: the impossibly lavish Galerie des Glaces (Hall of Mirrors). The unification of Germany was ratified here in 1871, as was the Treaty of Versailles in 1919.

The best ticket to purchase is the Passport, valid for one day, which allows entry to the main palace (with an audioguide), the Trianon palaces, Marie-Antoinette's farm and the gardens.

LEFT: the Hameau de la Reine ("Queen's Hamlet") was built in 1783 at the request of Marie-Antoinette, who wanted a refuge from the routines of the château. It was a working farm, with orchards and fields that produced food for the royal table.

THE UNLUCKY QUEEN

Marie-Antoinette has always had a bad press. On the one hand, there's the apparent heartlessness of her almost certainly fictitious comment "Let them eat cake"; on the other, the frivolity of her antics at her model farm, Le Hameau de la Reine, where she and her servants dressed as farm hands and milked carefully washed cows and goats into Sèvres porcelain buckets. What's more, she was Austrian, a lifelong handicap in the French court where she was known as *l'autre-chienne* (the other bitch) which was a pun on *l'autrichienne* (Austrian woman). For many courtiers, the unfortunate queen could do nothing right; Versailles was a vipers' nest of intrigue, and she was continually criticised – unfairly for the most part. In the 1780s, she was thought to be involved in a scheme to defraud the crown jeweller out of the fee for an elaborate diamond necklace (unproven), an incident which tarnished the monarchy in the eyes of the public and which led to the Revolution. Losing her life on the guillotine in 1793 was the crowning misfortune.

LEFT: bust of Marie-Antoinette.

BELOW: the King's State Bedroom, created in 1701 – a place for day-to-day business, not sleep.

INSIGHT GUIDES **TRAVEL TIPS**

PARIS

Transport

Getting There **292**
   By Air **292**
   By Sea or Tunnel **293**
   By Rail **293**
   By Bus **294**
Getting around **294**
   From the Airports **294**
   Public Transport **295**
   Private Transport **296**

Accommodation

Booking and Prices **298**
Holiday Flats **298**
Bed & Breakfast **298**
Hostels **298**
Ile de la Cité, Ile St-Louis
   and the Marais **299**
Beaubourg, Les Halles,
   Louvre and Tuileries ..**300**
Grands Boulevards and
   Champs-Élysées **301**
Montmartre, Bastille
   and East Paris **303**
Latin Quarter and
   St-Germain-des-Prés **304**
Montparnasse, the Eiffel
   Tower and Invalides ..**306**

Activities

The Arts **307**
   Theatre, Opera, Ballet
   and Concerts **307**
   Museums **308**
Nightlife **308**

Cabarets **308**
Nightclubs **309**
Music Venues **310**
Cinema **310**
For Children **311**
Sports **312**
   Participant **312**
   Spectator **312**
Courses **313**
Sightseeing Tours **313**

A – Z

Addresses **314**
Admission charges **314**
Budgeting for Your Trip ..**314**
Business Visitors **314**
Children **315**
Climate **315**
Complaints **315**
Crime and Safety **316**
Customs Regulations **316**
Disabled Travellers **317**
Electricity **318**
Etiquette **318**
Gay Travellers **318**
Health & Medical Care ..**318**
Internet **319**
Maps **320**
Media **320**
Money **321**
Opening Hours **321**
Postal Services **322**
Religious Services **322**
Student Travellers **322**
Study in France **322**
Telephones **323**

Time Zone **323**
Tour Operators **323**
Tourist Offices **324**
Useful Addresses **324**
Visas and Passports **324**
Weights & Measures **324**

Language

General **325**
   The Alphabet **325**
   Basic Rules **325**
Useful Words &
   Phrases **325**
   On Arrival **326**
   Emergencies **326**
   Shopping **326**
   Sightseeing **327**
   Dining Out **327**
   Breakfast and
   Snacks **327**
   First Course **327**
   Main Courses **327**
   In the Café **329**
   Days of the Week **329**
   Seasons **329**
   Months **329**
   Numbers **329**

Further Reading

History **330**
Art and Architecture **330**
Expat Memoirs **330**
Fiction **330**
Food **330**
Other Insight Guides **330**

Transport

Getting There and Getting Around

Getting There

By Air

Most major international airlines fly regularly to Paris's Roissy-Charles de Gaulle airport (Paris-CDG), northeast of the city. Air France naturally has the largest number of flights from North America and within Europe. British Airways have frequent flights from various UK airports, and the low-cost airlines easyJet, Flybe and Jet2 also fly to Charles de Gaulle from airports around the UK, including Belfast.

Travellers from the US and Canada can fly direct to Paris-CDG or to the larger provincial cities such as Nice and Lyon on Air France, Air Canada and many US airlines. Note, though, that a flight to London and then a train or local low-cost flight to Paris may prove cheaper.

Many French domestic, and some international flights, use Orly airport in the south of the city. Low-cost operator Ryanair fly to Beauvais, 88 km (55 miles) north of Paris, from Edinburgh, Glasgow Prestwick, Manchester, Dublin and Knock.

A big range of fare options can be found on the internet. For

Airlines

Aer Lingus: tel: 0871 718 5000 (UK), 0818 365000 (Ireland), 516 622 4222 (US), 0821 23 02 67 (France), www.aerlingus.com

Air Canada: tel: 0871 220 1111 (UK), 1 888 247 2262 (Canada/US), 08 25 88 08 81 (France), www.aircanada.ca

Air France: tel: 0871 663 3777 (UK), 800 237 2747 (US), 36 54 (France), www.airfrance.com

American Airlines: tel: 0844 499 7300 (UK), 800 433 7300 (US), 0826 460 950 (France), www.aa.com

British Airways: tel: 0844 493 0787 (UK), 800 247 9297 (US), 08 25 82 54 00 (France), www.ba.com

Delta Airways: tel: 0871 22 11 222 (UK), 800 221 1212 (US),

0892 702 609 (France), www.delta.com

United Airlines: tel: 0845 607 6760 (UK), 800 864 8331 (US), 01 71 23 03 35 (France), www.united.com

Budget Airlines

easyJet: tel: 0843 104 5000 (UK), 0820 420 315 (France), www.easyjet.com

flybe: tel: 0871 700 2000 (UK), 00 44 1392 268529 (UK no, for calls from France), www.flybe.com

Jet2: tel: 0871 226 1737 (UK), 0821 230 203 (France), www.jet2.com

Ryanair: tel: 0871 246 0000 (UK), 1520 444 004 (Ireland), 08 92 562 150 (France), www.ryanair.com

flights originating in the UK, check out Cheap Flights (www.cheap-flights.co.uk) or the Travel Super-market (www.travelsupermarket.com); from North America, try www.flightcenter.com or www.euro-vacations.com. In France, Nouvelles Frontières (www.nouvelles-frontieres.fr) or Last minute (www.last-minute.com) offer competitive fares on both scheduled and charter flights, and Opodo (www.opodo.com) is a

pan-European alliance of several major airlines that offers a broad range of fares.

Students and anyone under 26 can also get discount flights through specialist travel agencies. In the UK, try STA Travel, with over 46 branches, tel: 0871 230 0040, www.statravel.co.uk; in the US, STA Travel also has branches across the country, tel: 1 800 781 4040, www.sta travel.com.

By Sea or Tunnel

Ferries

Ferries from the UK, Ireland and the Channel Islands to France have cut prices since the Channel Tunnel opened. Catamaran-style "fast ferries" offer the quickest service, but are sometimes cancelled if the sea is really rough. Boulogne, Calais and Le Havre all have motorway links to Paris. Trains meet connecting ferries at Dover, Calais and some other Channel ports.

The following companies operate from the UK and Ireland:
Brittany Ferries, tel: 0871 244 0744 (UK), 08 25 82 88 28 (France), www.brittany-ferries.com. Portsmouth to Caen, Cherbourg and St-Malo: Poole to Cherbourg, and Plymouth and Cork to Roscoff.
Condor Ferries, tel: 0845 609 1024 (UK), 08 25 13 51 35 (France), www.condor-ferries.co.uk. Poole to St-Malo and Portsmouth to Cherbourg, via the Channel Islands.
Irish Ferries, tel: 0818 300 400 (Ireland), 01 70 72 03 26 (France), www.irishferries.com. Services from Rosslare to Cherbourg and Roscoff.
LD Lines, tel: 0844 576 8836 (UK), 08 25 30 43 04 (France), www.ldlines.com. Dover to Calais, Newhaven to Dieppe and Ports-

mouth to Le Havre.
DFDS, tel: 0871 574 7235 (UK), 20 81 27 83 03 (France), www.dfdsseaways.co.uk. Dover to Calais and Dunkerque.
P&O Ferries, tel: 08716 642121 (UK), 08 25 12 01 56 (France), www.poferries.com. Sails from Dover to Calais.

The Channel Tunnel

The alternative to ferries for those driving from the UK, **Eurotunnel** takes cars and passengers from Folkestone to Calais on a drive-on, drive-off service, known as *Le Shuttle*, taking 35 minutes platform to platform and about an hour from motorway to motorway. Payment is made at toll booths, which accept cash or credit cards, and the price applies to the car, regardless of the number of passengers. You can book in advance via tel: 08443 35 35 35 (UK), 08 10 63 03 04 (France), or www.eurotunnel.com, or simply turn up and take the next available service. Unlike the ferries, *Le Shuttle* is never affected by bad weather, and runs 24 hours a day, all year, with from two to five departures an hour, depending on the season and time of day.

By Rail

The fast, frequent train service from London St Pancras to Paris (Gare du Nord), runs about 16

ABOVE: the Eurostar.

times a day, and takes around two hours 15 minutes. Some trains stop at Ashford and Ebbsfleet International in Kent (two hours from Paris). For reservations, contact Eurostar, tel: 08432 186 186 (UK) or 0892 35 35 39 (France) or www.eurostar.com. There are frequent fare offers, and lower fares for children aged 4–11; those under 4 travel free but are not guaranteed a seat.

Paris has six mainline railway stations, with lines radiating across France and Europe. Each connects with several Métro or RER lines, and all have left-luggage facilities *(consignes)* and coin-operated lockers *(consignes automatiques)*.The SNCF's *Train à Grande Vitesse* (TGV) high-speed trains offer fast, comfortable services from Paris to cities around France and other European countries. They are not cheap, so it pays to travel off-peak: you must reserve TGV tickets in advance, and can obtain additional discounts if you book 30 days in advance. Information and reservations are available outside France from Rail Europe, (UK) tel: 0844 848 4064, www.raileurope.co.uk, or (US) tel: 1 800 622 8600, www.raileurope.com. You can also contact French Railways (SNCF) direct, tel: 36 35 (France), www.sncf.com.

Note that before boarding an SNCF train you must have your ticket date-stamped *(composté)*

BELOW: helpful signs in Beaubourg.

for it to be valid. Simply insert your ticket in the orange *composteur* machine at the platform entrance.

By Bus

Eurolines is a consortium of around 30 European coach companies, which has daily services from London (Victoria Coach Station) to Paris that represent one of the cheaper ways to get to the French capital. The ticket includes the ferry crossing (via Dover), and there are discounts available for under-26s and senior citizens, and passes that give unlimited travel for a month or longer. For more information, contact **National Express-Eurolines**, tel: 0871 781 8178 (UK), www.eurolines.co.uk, or **Eurolines France** at Gare Routière-Coach Station Galliéni, 28 avenue du Général de Gaulle, Porte de Bagnolet (Métro Galliéni), tel: 08 92 89 90 91, www.eurolines.com.

GETTING AROUND

From the Airports

From Roissy-Charles de Gaulle

Train

Trains are the quickest and most reliable way to get to central Paris. RER line B trains go direct from Terminal 2; there is a free connecting shuttle bus *(navette) between terminals*. Trains run every 15 minutes between about 5am and 11.50pm, calling at Gare du Nord and Châtelet-Les Halles, the hub of the Métro network. The average journey time is about 30 minutes.

Bus

The Roissybus runs between the airport and Rue Scribe, near Place de l'Opéra. It runs every 15 minutes from 5.45am to 11pm and takes between 45 minutes and an hour. Alternatively, there

are Air France buses direct to northwest Paris (Porte Maillot and Charles de Gaulle-Etoile), every 12 minutes, 5.45am–11pm, and to southern Paris (Gare de Lyon, Gare Montparnasse), every 30 minutes, 7am–9.30pm. For recorded information on Air France buses in English, French, German or Italian, tel: 08 92 35 08 20. All bus services call at both airport terminals.

Taxi

Taxis are by far the most expensive, but unquestionably the easiest way, to get to Paris from the airport. This can take from 30 minutes to over an hour, depending on traffic. The cost is shown on the meter, but remember that a supplement will be charged if you put more than one item of luggage in the car's boot.

From Orly

Train

Shuttle buses run from the two Orly terminals (Orly-Sud and Orly-Ouest) to the Pont de Rungis rail station, on RER line C, which stops at Gare d'Austerlitz, St-Michel-Notre-Dame and the Musée d'Orsay. It runs every 15 minutes from 5am to 1.30pm and takes approximately 45 minutes to Gare d'Austerlitz.

The more expensive Orlyval (www.orlyval.com) automatic train runs to Antony station on RER line

BETWEEN AIRPORTS

RER line B runs from Roissy-Charles de Gaulle to Antony station, from where the fast Orlyval shuttle trains run to Orly airport. An Air France bus also links Roissy-Charles de Gaulle and Orly every 30 minutes, from 6am to 10.30pm (less frequently at weekends).

B, which has frequent trains to Châtelet-Les Halles and Roissy-Charles de Gaulle airport. It runs about every 5–8 minutes from 6am to 11pm daily, and takes 35 to 50 minutes depending on the final destination.

Bus

Air France buses run from both Orly terminals to Invalides, Etoile and Gare Montparnasse, every 20 minutes, 6am to 11pm, and take 30 minutes. Tickets are available from the Air France terminus.

The Orlybus also runs from both terminals to Place Denfert-Rochereau. There are services every 10–12 minutes, from 6am to 11.30pm every day.

Taxi

Taxis are available outside the terminal buildings at any time. The journey from Orly to the city centre takes 20–40 minutes, depending on the traffic.

BELOW: beware of imposters – hail a genuine taxi, one with a light on the roof.

Public Transport

Métro and RER

Run by the Régie Autonome des Transports Parisiens (RATP), the Paris Métro is one of the world's oldest subway systems. Used by around 9 million people every day, it is quick and efficient.

The Métro operates from 5.30am, with the last train leaving end stations at around 12.30am (2.15am on Saturdays and public holidays). You can pick up a comprehensive map free at any Métro station. The lines are identified by numbers, colours and the names of their final station, so Line 4 running north is shown as *Direction Porte de Clignancourt*, while going south is *Direction Mairie de Montrouge* (from March 2013). Follow the orange *correspondance* signs to change Métro lines.

The Métro operates in conjunction with the RER (suburban regional express train networks), which has five main lines: A, B, C, D and E, that run out into the suburbs. RER trains run daily about every 12 minutes from 5.30am to midnight (1am Friday–Saturday). They have fewer stops than the

ABOVE: down to the Métro.

Métro in central Paris, and so can be significantly faster.

Buses and Trams

Taking the bus is a pleasant way to see the city, but is much slower than the Métro because of often heavy traffic. The same tickets are used as for the Métro and RER, but you must remember to punch single tickets (though not travel cards) in the *composteur* machine by the entry doors and behind the driver every time you board a bus.

Buses don't automatically halt at every bus stop, so when you want to get off press one of the

request buttons and the *arrêt demandé* (bus stopping) sign will light up. Each bus has a map of its route posted at the front and back and at every bus stop. Most routes run from 6.30am to 8.30pm Monday to Saturday, although some routes continue until 12.30am, and some routes run all day on Sunday.

From 12.30am to 5.30am nightly over 40 *Noctilien* night bus routes operate around Paris and its region, including one that makes a circuit around the main railway stations. Tickets are the same as for daytime services. Full details of night buses can be found on www.noctilien.fr.

Another service is the *Balabus*, a special sightseeing bus that runs up and down from Gare de Lyon to La Défense, passing many of Paris's major attractions. It runs only on Sundays and on public holidays between 11 April and 26 September, from 12.30 to 8pm. The tour lasts about 50 minutes, and tickets are the same as for regular buses. Look out for bus stops marked *Balabus* or *Bb*.

Paris also has a Tramway system, which was reintroduced in 1992, the city's original tram network having closed in 1938. There are four lines in the Paris suburbs: T1 from Gare St-Denis to Noisy-le-Sec in the north, T2 from La Défense toPorte de Versailles, T3 flanking the southern *Périphérique* from Pont du

TAXIS

Taxis are readily available at airports and railway stations. In the city itself there are almost 500 taxi ranks, but be careful to hail only a genuine taxi – one with a light on the roof – as other operators may charge exorbitant fares. The white light will be on if a cab is free, while a glowing orange light means that the taxi is occupied.

Paris taxis operate on three fare rates at different times:
Tariff A 10am–5pm Monday to Saturday, in the city.
Tariff B 5pm–10am Monday to Saturday, 7am–midnight Sunday, and 7am–7pm daily in the suburbs (all areas outside the

Boulevard Périphérique).
Tariff C midnight–7am Sundays in the city, and 7pm–7am in the suburbs.
The website www.taxi-paris.net provides comprehensive information on Paris's cabs. The following companies take phone bookings 24 hours a day:
Alpha: 01 45 85 85 85
G7: 01 47 39 47 39
Taxi: 01 42 70 00 42
Taxis Bleus: 08 91 70 10 10
If you have a complaint about a taxi, send it (with the cab licence number) to: Service des Taxis, Préfecture de Police, 36 rue des Morillons, 75015, tel: 01 55 76 20 05.

TRANSPORT

ACCOMMODATION

ACTIVITIES

A – Z

LANGUAGE

ABOVE: tram line T3 – the only line so far inside the city limits.

Garigliano to Porte d'Ivry, and T4, between Bondy RER and Aulnay-sous-Bois.

Tickets and Fares

The Métro, RER, city buses and trams all use the same tickets (€1.70 for a single fare). A book or *carnet* of 10 tickets offers a considerable saving at €12.70.

Single tickets and *carnets* can be bought at Métro stations, tourist offices, tobacco shops, newsstands and some other shops. Only single tickets can be bought on board buses, so to use another ticket type you must buy it in advance at one of the other ticket outlets. With one ticket you can make a journey of any distance within fare zones 1 and 2, which includes the whole of central Paris and the Métro system, no

matter how many times you change lines or whether you use the RER. However, every time you board a bus you must use a new single ticket.

All public transport in Paris is free for children under 4, and half-price for those aged 4–11.

A range of travel passes provide good-value, time-saving alternatives to buying single tickets or *carnets*. The most popular is the *Paris Visite* card, giving unlimited travel for one, two, three or five consecutive days on the Métro, buses and railways in Paris and the Ile de France. The cards are valid for a combination of fare zones, beginning with zones 1–3 (all of central Paris), approximate prices for which are €9, €15, €21 and €31 for adults, or €4, €7, €10 and €15 for chil-

dren aged 4–11. *Paris Visite* holders also obtain discounts at several attractions, shops and restaurants. Cards can be bought from Métro, RER and SNCF stations and several other outlets; for full current details, check www.parisvisite.com.

Another option is the *Mobilis* card, which gives unlimited travel for one day on the Métro, buses, RER and other local networks, without the other benefits of the *Paris Visite*. It can be bought at all the usual ticket outlets and from all Métro stations; prices range from €6 for zones 1 and 2 to €14 for 5 zones. *Mobilis* cards are not valid for trips to either Paris airport.

Note that *Paris Visite* and *Mobilis* cards are valid for one calendar day (or series of them), not for 24 hours from the time you buy them, so to take full advantage it's best to start using them first thing in the morning.

For anyone spending longer in Paris the most useful option is the Forfait Navigo travel pass, which gives unlimited travel on all services in the zones of your choice for a month (*Mensuelle*, approximately €62, zones 1–2) or a week (*Hebdomadaire*, €19). To buy either you need to take a passport photograph to any Métro or SNCF station, and must fill in a brief form and sign your name on the card. There are also special youth and senior travel cards. For further information on all Paris transport services and fare options, check www.ratp.fr or www.parisinfo.com.

Private Transport

Driving in Paris requires confidence and concentration. In fact,

BELOW: make sure to validate tour tickets before getting on the train.

the best thing to do with a car in the city is to leave it in a car park and take public transport.

If you do intend to drive, here are a few guidelines. Seat belts are obligatory in the front and back of the car, and the speed limit in town is 50kph (30mph). Do not drive in bus lanes at any time, and at unmarked junctions give priority to vehicles approaching from the right. This applies to some roundabouts, where cars on the roundabout stop for those coming onto it. Helmets are compulsory for motorbike riders and passengers. Street parking is very difficult to find; most spaces are metered Monday–Saturday 9am–7pm (paid for not with coins but a *Paris Carte*, currently €10 or €30, purchased from a *tabac*) and the maximum stay is two hours. Most car parks are underground; see www.parkingsdeparis. com. Illegally parked cars may be towed away. Do not leave any possessions on show, as theft from cars is common.

Petrol can be hard to find in the city centre, so if your tank is almost empty head for a *porte* (exit) on the *Périphérique* (the multi-lane ringroad), where there are petrol stations open 24 hours a day all year-round.

Drivers are liable to on-the-spot fines for speeding or drunk driving. The limit in France is 50mg/litre of alcohol in the blood (equivalent to about two glasses of wine) and is strictly enforced.

Car Hire

Some fly/drive packages are good value, if you are on a short visit. The SNCF offers a good deal on its combined train/car hire bookings *(train + auto)*. Weekly rates always work out better than daily rentals, and it will often be cheaper to hire a vehicle online from the UK or the US before leaving for France. The minimum age for hiring a car varies from 21 to 23, depending on the company. The hirer must have held a full licence for at least a year, and must have a credit card.

ABOVE: traffic on Place de l'Etoile is chaotic.

Central reservation services of major car hire firms are:
Auto Europe, (UK) www.auto-europe.co.uk, (US) www.autoeurope.com. Online bookings in France and across Europe, at competitive rates.
Avis, tel: 0821 230 760, www.avis.fr.
easycar, www.easycar.com
Europcar, tel: 08 25 35 83 58, www.europcar.fr.
Hertz, tel: 0825 001 185, www.hertz.fr.

Bicycles

If you know Paris reasonably well and have nerves of steel, a bicycle is an excellent way to explore. You can hire bicycles from:
Gepetto & Velos, 59 rue du Cardinal Lemoine, 5th, tel: 01 43 54 19 95, www.gepetto-velos.com.

BELOW: vélib's waiting for customers.

Paris à Vélo c'est Sympa, 22 rue Alphonse-Baudin, 11th, tel: 01 48 87 60 01, www.parisvelo-sympa.com.

Vélib (www.velib.paris.fr) is Paris's bike transit system. You can pick up and drop off your bike at 750 locations throughout the city. Bikes are available round the clock with a credit card.

Hitchhiking

It can be difficult to get a lift out of the Channel ports, so take a bus or train for the first leg of the journey. Hitching is forbidden on autoroutes (motorways), but waiting at toll booths is allowed.

Allostop aims to connect hitch hikers with drivers. You simply pay a registration fee and a contribution towards the total petrol cost. Visit www.allostop.net.

ACCOMMODATION

SOME THINGS TO CONSIDER BEFORE YOU BOOK THE ROOM

Booking and Prices

It is always advisable to reserve accommodation in advance, either direct with the hotel, through a booking service or via the Paris Tourist Office (www.parisinfo.com). Tourist offices will also book your first night's accommodation if you arrive in person, for a small fee.

Hotel prices are not subject to controls and can change without notice, so check when booking. Most hotels also vary prices by season; low season is generally November to March, high season April to October, but this can vary, as many hotels have higher rates during certain winter trade fairs and fashion weeks. State your arrival time when booking, or your room will not be held after 7pm.

Holiday Flats

The companies below let apartments to tourists, ranging from bedsits to five-bedroom flats.
AIRBNE, www.airbnb.com/paris. International website where individuals can list a room/apartment to let, usually at much less cost than an agency.
At Home in Paris, 15 rue Friedland, 8th, tel: 01 42 12 40 40, www.at-home-in-paris.fr.
Citadines, tel:01 41 05 79 05, www.citadines.com. Aparthotels: studios and one-bed flats, with

kitchenettes and living area, but also reception and business services. Stays from one night; 17 locations around Paris.
France Ermitage, 5 rue Berryer, 8th, tel: 01 42 56 23 42, www.france-ermitage.com.

Bed & Breakfast

Alcôve & Agapes Bed & Breakfast à Paris, 8bis rue Coysevox, 18th, tel: 01 44 85 06 05, www.bed-and-breakfast-in-paris.com. Lists 125 homes; most hosts speak English. €85–195.
Good Morning Paris, 43 rue Lacépède, 5th, tel: 01 47 07 28 29, www.goodmorningparis.fr. Over 100 B&B rooms; prices from €60 for one person, and €75 for two.

Hostels

Holders of accredited Youth Hostel cards can stay in Paris hostels for about €25 per night (non-members can often use them too, for a slightly higher charge). These hostels are run by two organisations:
Fédération Unie des Auberges de Jeunesse (FUAJ), 27 rue Pajol, 18th, tel: 01 44 89 87 27, www.fuaj.fr. Affiliated to the International Youth Hostel Federation.
Ligue Française pour les Auberges de Jeunesse (LFAJ), 67 rue Vergniaud, 13th, tel: 01 44 16 78 78, www.auberges-de-jeunesse.com.

There are also non-affiliated hostels, listed under *Young Paris* on www.parisinfo.com. **MIJE,** tel: 01 42 74 23 45, www.mije.com, has three great-value "youth hotels" for groups of 10 or more, and **Ethic-Etapes,** tel: 01 40 26 57 64, www.ethic-etapes.fr, also provides youth accommodation, often combined with courses and activities.

Youth Hostels

Auberge Jules Ferry, 8 boulevard Jules-Ferry, 11th, tel: 01 43 57 55 60, www.fuaj.org. Conveniently located on the Canal St-Martin.
Auberge Internationale des Jeunes, 10 rue Trousseau, 11th, tel: 01 47 00 62 00, www.aijparis.com. Close to the Bastille.
BVJ Louvre, 20 rue Jean-Jacques Rousseau, 1st, tel: 01 53 00 90 90, www.bvjhotel.com. A large hostel near the Louvre.
BVJ Quartier Latin, 44 rue des Bernardins, 5th, tel: 01 43 29 34 80, www.bvjhotel.com. Single and double rooms as well as dormitories in the Latin Quarter.
Le Regent, 37 boulevard de Rochechouart, 9th, tel: 01 48 78 24 00, www.leregent.com. Budget accommodation in Montmartre.
St Christopher's Inn, 159 rue de Crimée, 19th, tel: 01 40 34 34 40, www.st-christophers.co.uk. Next to the Bassin de la Villette, this is Paris's coolest and most modern youth hostel.

ILE DE LA CITÉ, ILE ST-LOUIS AND THE MARAIS

Hôtel de la Bretonnerie
22 rue St-Croix-de-la-Bretonnerie, 4th
Tel: 01 48 87 77 63
❶ [p336, D2]
www.bretonnerie.com
Historic features abound in this delightful Marais hotel set in a 17th-century *hôtel particulier*. The rooms and seven suites are all furnished with lavish fabrics and rich colours; some have wooden beams and romantic four-poster beds. €€

Hôtel des Deux-Iles
59 rue St-Louis-en-l'Ile, 4th
Tel: 01 43 26 13 35
❷ [p336, C3]
www.deuxiles-paris-hotel.com
A peaceful and attractive hotel in a 17thcentury mansion house in the Ile St-Louis. Some rooms have views over a pretty courtyard. €€€€

Hôtel du Haut Marais
7 rue des Vertus, 3rd
Tel: 01 42 77 65 52
www.hotelhautmarais.com
❸ [p336, D1]
With just five rooms, two suites and an apartment, this little

hotel feels more like a B&B, especially as the friendly owners live on site. Rooms have wooden floors and beamed ceilings while the bathrooms add a contemporary twist. €€

Grand Hôtel Jeanne d'Arc
3 rue de Jarente, 4th
Tel: 01 48 87 62 11
❹ [p336, D2]
www.hoteljeannedarc.com
This affordable little place has bedrooms in bright colours which are all quite large, clean and comfortable for the price. Good location, near Place du Marché-Ste-Catherine. €

Hôtel Jules & Jim
11 rue des Gravilliers, 3rd
Tel: 01 44 54 13 13
www.hoteljulesetjim.com
❺ [p336, D1]
Opened in 2011, this super-cool, gay-friendly hotel pays homage to François Truffaut's famous film of the same name. The 23 stylish-yet-simple rooms (think wood, glass and stone) are based in three buildings around two courtyards. €€€

Hôtel du Jeu de Paume
54 rue St-Louis-en-l'Ile, 4th
Tel: 01 43 26 14 18
❻ [p336, C3]
www.jeudepaumehotel.com
There's history in spades at this charming hotel on the Ile St-Louis: the breakfast room was a real tennis court in the time of Louis XIII. Rooms, which were renovated in 2010, are simple but elegant; you get to them via a dramatic glass lift. €€€

Hôtel Lutèce
65 rue St-Louis-en-l'Ile, 4th
Tel: 01 43 26 23 52
❼ [p336, C3]
www.paris-hotel-lutece.com
The Lutèce has the same owners as the Hôtel des Deux-Iles, and is similarly charming, rich in 17th-century beams and stonework. The wood-panelled sitting room has a superb fireplace, and rooms are decorated in warm colours. €€€

Pavillon de la Reine
28 place des Vosges, 3rd
Tel: 01 40 29 19 19
❽ [p336, D2]
www.pavillon-de-la-reine.com

Arguably the smartest hotel in the Marais, in an imposing mansion in a lovely location on Place des Vosges. It has 55 rooms furnished with Louis XIII-style antiques; some overlook the beautiful Pavillon de la Reine courtyards. €€€€

Hôtel du Petit Moulin
29 rue du Poitou, 3rd
tel: 01 42 74 10 10
❾ [p336, D1]
www.hoteldupetitmoulin.com
This fashionable hotel in the Marais was designed by Christian Lacroix using sumptuous fabrics and screen-printed *trompe l'œil* to create comfort and individuality. The reception occupies an old bakery, still with its painted glass ceiling panels, while the bar marries zinc counter, murals and pop colours. €€

Hôtel de la Place des Vosges
12 rue Birague, 4th
Tel: 01 42 72 60 46
❿ [p336, D2]
www.hotelplacedesvosges.com
Carefully renovated former stables with only 16 rooms, making the hotel intimate but comfortable. It's popular, so book ahead. Note that the lift only goes as far as the fourth floor. €

BELOW: the smart Pavillon de la Reine in the Marais.

TRANSPORT

ACCOMMODATION

ACTIVITIES

A – Z

LANGUAGE

BEAUBOURG, LES HALLES, LOUVRE AND TUILERIES

ABOVE: the top-floor suite at the Hôtel Meurice is the epitomy of luxury.

Hôtel Andrea
3 rue St-Bon, 4th
Tel: 01 42 78 43 93
⑪ [p336, C2]
This modest hotel set in an early 19th-century building is handily situated just off the Rue de Rivoli. 32 rooms. €

Hôtel Brighton
218 rue de Rivoli, 1st
Tel: 01 47 03 61 61
⑫ [p336, A1]
www.esprit-de-france.com
Recently restored, this hotel has several rooms that overlook the Jardin des Tuileries, and a reception area awash with gilt, marble and glass chandeliers. Rooms are large and decorated with a mix of traditional quality fabrics, careful lighting and sober furniture and artworks. The rooms with the fine views are understandably popular, so book well ahead. €€

Hôtel Britannique
20 avenue Victoria, 1st
Tel: 01 42 33 74 59
⑬ [p336, C2]
www.hotel-britannique.fr
A comfortable hotel near the Ile de la Cité, furnished with relaxing sofas in the downstairs sitting room. Its 40 rooms are plush and decorated in red and gold. €€

Hôtel du Cygne
3-5 rue du Cygne, 1st
Tel: 01 42 60 14 16
www.cygne-hotel-paris.com
⑭ [p336, C1]
Charming, no-frills 20-room hotel in a renovated 17th-century building, a short walk from all the main sights in this area. Rooms are furnished in warm-toned, Provençal fabrics and most of the furniture has come from flea markets. €€

Le Duo
11 rue du Temple, 4th
Tel: 01 42 72 72 22
⑮ [p336, C2]
www.duoparis.com
The former Hôtel Axial Beaubourg has (under the same management) expanded into the building next door and become Le Duo, a stylish boutique hotel. Rooms are a mix of ancient and modern: eminently 21st-century colours and fabrics and state-of-the-art technology are combined with stout old wooden beams in the ceilings. Wonderfully handy for the Marais and the Centre Pompidou. €€€

Hôtel Edouard VII
39 avenue de l'Opéra, 2nd
Tel: 01 42 61 56 90
⑯ [p334, A4]
www.edouard7hotel.com
Historic hotel on one of the most beautiful avenues in Paris, Avenue de l'Opéra, close to the Opéra Garnier and the Louvre. The hotel features the Cuisine l'E7 restaurant. €€€€

Hôtel Konfidentiel
64 rue de l'Arbre Sec, 1st
Tel: 01 55 34 40 40
www.konfidentiel-paris.com
⑰ [p336, B1]
Fancy sharing a room with a French king or queen? This contemporary all-suite hotel, housed in a 15th-century building, takes its decoration inspiration from history; each room is dedicated to a different character, object or event. €€€

Hôtel Lumen
15 rue des Pyramides, 1st
Tel: 01 44 50 77 00
www.hotel-lumenparis.com
⑱ [p336, B1]
As its name suggests, "light" is the theme at this hotel and the bright, contemporary neo-Baroque style helps to achieve the desired effect. Oscar's, the Italian restaurant, is housed in a lovely conservatory overlooking St-Roch church. €€€€

Hôtel Madeleine Opéra
12 rue Greffulhe, 8th
Tel: 01 47 42 26 26
⑲ [p334, A3]
www.hotel-madeleine-opera.com
An excellent-value hotel – and if the entrance, two centuries old, looks like a shop, that's because this is what it once was. It's well located; rooms are small and their decor and fittings are fairly simple, but it's all clean, trim and pretty. There's no restaurant, but breakfast can be served in your room (for an extra charge). €€

Hôtel Meurice
228 rue de Rivoli, 1st
Tel: 01 44 58 10 10
⑳ [p336, A1]
www.meuricehotel.com
Elegant, 18th-century-style salons and a Michelin-starred restaurant are among the many assets of this historic *grand hôtel*. The 160 soundproofed, air-conditioned rooms and 28 suites are located under the Rue de Rivoli arcades, and many have great views over the beautiful Jardin des Tuileries; the top-floor suite is the ultimate in luxury, with its own terrace with panoramic views over Paris. €€€€

Hôtel Tiquetonne
6 rue Tiquetonne, 2nd
Tel: 01 42 36 94 58
㉑ [p336, C1]
Nicely situated in an old part of Paris close to Les Halles, the Tiquetonne is popular and well maintained, with 47 sizeable en suite double rooms. Closed in August. €

Hôtel Vivienne
40 rue Vivienne, 2nd
Tel: 01 42 33 13 26
㉒ [p334, B3]
www.hotel-vivienne.com
Good-value hotel close to the Bourse and well located for the Louvre, the Madeleine and the most popular shopping areas, with 45 pretty and comfortable rooms. €

GRANDS BOULEVARDS AND CHAMPS-ELYSÉES

Hôtel de Banville
166 boulevard Berthier, 17th
Tel: 01 42 67 70 16
㉓ [p332, A1]
www.hotelbanville.fr
Close to L'Etoile and
Porte Maillot, this family-
run 1920s-built hotel is
sleek and cosy. Its 38
rooms have chic marble
bathrooms, and some
have terraces looking
towards the Eiffel Tower.
Wi-Fi access in the
lobby. €€

Berne Opéra
37 rue de Berne, 8th
Tel: 01 43 87 08 92
㉔ [p332, E1]
www.paris-hotel-berne-opera.
com
Set in a quiet street near
the Opéra, this is a com-
fortable and pleasant
mid-range hotel of 36
rooms with good mod-
ern facilities, and it welcomes young families.
€€

Bradford Elysées
10 rue St-Philippe-du-Roule,
8th
Tel: 01 45 63 20 20
㉕ [p332, C2]
www.astotel.com
Large and airy rooms
close to the Champs-Ely-
sées make it a pleasure
to stay in this elegantly
furnished, intimate
1900s hotel. There are
50 rooms, and the hotel
has air conditioning, a
bar and good facilities
for children, too. €€

Le Bristol
112 rue du Faubourg St-Honoré, 8th
Tel: 01 53 43 43 00
㉖ [p332, D2]
www.lebristolparis.com
This is a discreetly
upmarket 1920s hotel
with period furniture in
all 195 rooms. Lovely
gardens complete an
extremely pleasant
experience; expensive,
but worth it. €€€€

Hôtel Chopin
46 passage Jouffroy, 9th
Tel: 01 47 70 58 10
㉗ [p334, B3]
www.hotelchopin.fr
There are few hotel
entrances as atmos-
pheric as this one, at
the end of a glass-
roofed 19th-century
shopping arcade. Staff
are helpful and friendly,
and the rooms, though
on the small side and
perhaps slightly over-
loaded with salmon-
pink decor, are clean,
comfortable and quiet.
It's great value, and

ABOVE: the Fouquet's-Barrière is close to the
Champs-Elysées.

popular, so make sure
to book well ahead. €

Hôtel de Crillon
10 place de la Concorde, 8th
Tel: 01 44 71 15 00
㉘ [p332, E3]
www.crillon.com
Perhaps the grandest of
all the grand hotels in
the capital, and probably
the best-known, the Cril-
lon enjoys a truly stun-
ning location in one of
the magnificent man-
sions that preside over
the Place de la Con-
corde, built by Jacques-
Ange Gabriel for Louis
XV in the 1750s. With
rooms in a suitably
ancien régime style,
adorned with plentiful
amounts of real marble
and gold leaf, it's fre-
quented by film stars,
heads of state and the
very, very rich; the grand
building – Marie-Antoi-
nette used to have sing-
ing lessons here – is
also home to the
Michelin-starred Ambas-
sadeurs restaurant. €€€€

Hôtel Daniel
8 rue Fréderic Bastiat, 8th
Tel: 01 42 56 17 00
㉙ [p332, C2]
www.hoteldanielparis.com
One of Paris's newest
hotels, and one of its
most luxurious: the
Daniel is only the sec-
ond Relais & Châteaux
establishment in Paris,
and it's a lovely roman-
tic marvel, five minutes
from the Champs-Ely-
sées. Top floor rooms
have balconies and
wonderful views; all are
sumptuously deco-
rated. It's expensive,
but the gourmet restau-
rant is as impressive as

BELOW: the Hôtel Bristol bar.

PRICE CATEGORIES

Price ranges, per double
room, are as follows:

€ = €55–100
€€ = €100–200
€€€ = €200–300
€€€€ = over €300

ABOVE: lavish suite at the Hôtel de Crillon.

the rest of the hotel.
€€€

Fouquet's Barrière
46 avenue George V, 8th
Tel: 01 40 69 60 00
30 [p332, C2]
www.fouquets-barriere.com
With its metal-clad
entrance, this family-
friendly luxury hotel next
door to the iconic bras-
serie Fouquet's puts its
exclusive cards on the
table from the off. Inside,
the full-on modern luxury
continues with decor by
fashionable designer
Jacques Garcia, marble
bathrooms, a spa and
more. Of the 81 rooms,
31 are suites. €€€€

Four Seasons George V
31 avenue George V, 8th
Tel: 01 49 52 70 00
31 [p332, C3]
www.fourseasons.com
The opulently furnished
rooms here have lavish
marble bathrooms, and
guests can also count
on a restaurant, a top-
class wine cellar and a
health club among its
many facilities. The
George V is supremely
elegant, stylish and
extremely exclusive. €€€€

Hôtel François 1er
7 rue Magellan, 8th
Tel: 01 47 23 44 04
32 [p332, C3]
www.the-paris-hotel.com
Nicely located for shop-
ping sprees on Avenue

Montaigne, the François
1er is a classy, calm boutique hotel with five categories of room, from
classique to suite. A lot of
care has gone into the
choice of the Belle
Epoque fabrics and furni-
ture, and there's a lot of
dark wood in the rooms.
The lounge bar with its
winter garden is a relax-
ing place for a post-shop-
ping cocktail. €€€€

Hôtel Keppler
10 rue Keppler, 16th
Tel: 01 47 20 65 05
33 [p332, B3]
www.keppler.fr
Long popular with tour-
ists and business travel-
lers, with balconies
overlooking this smart
neighbourhood near
L'Etoile, the Keppler has
recently been given a
complete overhaul to
make it a chic black-
and-white hotel, with up-
to-the-minute
electronics and enter-
tainment facilities in all
of its 39 rooms and five
suites. There's also a
hammam, a massage
service and a tearoom.
€€€€

Hôtel Mansart
5 rue des Capucines, 1st
Tel: 01 42 61 50 28
34 [p332, E3]
www.esprit-de-france.com
Named in honour of
Jules Hardouin-Mansart,

architect to Louis XIV,
and good value for this
location, just off über-
chic Place Vendôme.
The lobby has abstract
murals inspired by
designs for French for-
mal gardens, and the
spacious, high-ceilinged
rooms are furnished
with antiques and oil
paintings: the duplex
Vendôme suite looks out
over the square itself. €€

Plaza-Athénée
25 avenue Montaigne, 8th
Tel: 01 53 67 66 65
35 [p332, C3]
www.plaza-athenee-paris.com
This palatial hotel, fea-
turing lavish Versace
decor, offers 190 sound-
proofed rooms, a disco,
a restaurant and suites
furnished in Louis XVI or
Art Deco style. Super-
chef Alain Ducasse is in
charge of the fabulous
restaurant (see page
158). If you can't stretch
to the price of a room,
treat yourself to a cock-
tail in the fashionable
bar. €€€€

Hôtel Ritz
15 place Vendôme, 1st

Tel: 01 43 16 30 30
36 [p332, E3]
www.ritzparis.com
The Ritz offers pure,
unashamed luxury in
one of the finest squares
in the capital. Sadly, it is
now often remembered
as the setting for the last
supper eaten by Prin-
cess Diana and Dodi al-
Fayed (son of the
owner). Beyond most
budgets, but for a taste
of luxury, have Afternoon
Tea in Bar Vendôme.
€€€€

Hôtel de Sers
41 avenue Pierre 1er de Serbie, 8th
Tel: 01 53 23 75 75
37 [p332, C3]
www.hoteldesers.com
The Sers combines
modern style and com-
fort with the classic service of a traditional
small French hotel. It
has brushed-concrete
floors downstairs, an
interior courtyard with
perpetually changing
coloured light washes,
modern furniture and
very sleek bathrooms.
But young architect

BELOW: the five-star Plaza-Athénée.

Thomas Vidalenc has cleverly warmed up the minimalism with lots of lilac and crimson in carpets and curtains, as well as a witty nod to its Belle Epoque origins in the gallery of portraits in the hallway. €€€€

Le Sezz
6 avenue Frémiet, 16th
Tel: 01 56 75 26 26
38 [p340, A1]
www.hotelsezz-paris.com

Le Sezz opened for business in 2005: behind its antique facade it's a seriously glam boutique hotel designed by hot furniture designer Christophe Pillet, which means one-way mirrored partitions between bedrooms and bathrooms, oversized soaking tubs, large shaggy rugs in red or green, dark concrete-like walls

and a plethora of straight lines. €€€€

Hôtel de la Trémoille
14 rue de la Trémoille, 8th
Tel: 01 56 52 14 00
39 [p332, C3]
www.hotel-tremoille.com

This discreetly elegant hotel has been thoroughly modernised yet retains its sense of Parisian style – 19th-century panelling, mouldings and fireplaces meet contem-

porary lighting and fabrics, and the comforts of air conditioning, internet access and so on. There's a fitness room and spa facilities in the basement. It's a calm hideaway, and you can even have your breakfast dispatched to you in privacy through a hatch by the door. Attached is the similarly elegant Le Louis bar and restaurant. €€€€

MONTMARTRE, BASTILLE AND EAST PARIS

Hôtel Beaumarchais
3 rue Oberkampf, 11th
Tel: 01 53 36 86 86
40 [p336, E1]
www.hotelbeaumarchais.com

A fun, good-value designer hotel located in the trendy Oberkampf district, with plenty of nightlife nearby. The rooms are painted in bright, primary colours. There's a terrace for breakfast in summer, and private parking (for a separate charge); 31 rooms. €

Chat Noir Design Hotel
68 boulevard de Clichy, 18th
Tel: 01 42 64 15 26
www.hotel-chatnoir-paris.com
41 [p334, A1]

The ubiquitous black-cat image gives away that this hotel is housed in the former famous nightclub of the same name. Rooms are white, bright and contemporary with splashes of red, black and yellow. The area is a racy one. €€

Hôtel Garden St Martin
35 rue Yves-Toudic, 10th
Tel: 01 42 40 17 72
42 [p334, D3]

Situated near the Canal St-Martin, a little off the beaten track, this is a value-for-money hotel

with a small garden terrace and an even smaller lift. All the rooms are clean and compact. €€

Holiday Inn Paris – Gare de l'Est
5 rue du 8 mai 1945, 10th
Tel: 01 55 26 05 05
43 [p334, D3]
www.holidayinn.com

Reminiscent of the grand age of stream, this great railway hotel has an old-style charm and class mixed with modern luxury and sleek design. There are 200 rooms. Formerly the Mercure Terminus Est. €€

Mama Shelter
109 rue de Bagnolet, 20th
Tel: 01 43 48 48 48
www.mamashelter.com
44 [p334, E3]

Hip and stylish budget hotel designed by Philippe Starck, where the bedroom walls are black or concrete and Smart cars are available to hire. The bar-restaurant is popular with the fashionable crowd and there are DJ sets at weekends. Babysitting is on offer too. €€

Hôtel Original
8 boulevard Beaumarchais,
11th

Tel: 01 47 00 91 50
www.hoteloriginalparis.com
45 [p336, E2]

The latest offering from fashion designer Stella Cadente has five kinds of contemporary rooms, all of which are decorated differently but have bright colours in common. Great location between Place de la Bastille and Place des Vosges. €€€

Le Pavillon Bastille
65 rue de Lyon, 12th
Tel: 01 43 43 65 65
46 [p336, E3]
www.paris-hotel-pavillonbastille.com

Classy, contemporary hotel situated behind an attractive courtyard opposite the Opéra Bastille. Decor is modern and well kept, and facilities and services such as Wi-Fi are excellent. Popular with business people. €€

Regyn's Montmartre
18 place des Abbesses, 18th
Tel: 01 42 54 45 21
47 [p334, B1]
www.hotel-regyns-paris.com

Straightforward budget hotel in the heart of Montmartre, opposite Abbesses Métro station. Some of its rooms,

which are decorated in traditional Toile de Jouy fabric, have great views. Relaxed and cosy atmosphere. €€

Hôtel Royal Fromentin
11 rue Fromentin, 9th
Tel: 01 48 74 85 93
48 [p334, A1]
www.hotelroyalfromentin.com

A hotel not far from Pigalle with its own special touches typical of the neighbourhood: the lobby was formerly a cabaret dating from the 1930s, the Dom Juan, and it still has the original wood panelling and some appropriate cabaret paraphernalia. Several of its 47 rooms have views of the Sacré-Cœur; the decor is bright but fairly traditional, and rooms are spacious and clean. There's a vintage glass lift, too. €€

Hôtel Saint-Louis Bastille
114 boulevard Richard-Lenoir,

PRICE CATEGORIES

Price ranges, per double room, are as follows:

€ = €55–100
€€ = €100–200
€€€ = €200–300
€€€€ = over €300

ABOVE: the superb view from the restaurant at Terrass.

markable, but rooms do have air conditioning and Wi-Fi; breakfast is served in a vaulted basement. €€

Terrass
12–14 rue Joseph-Maistre, 18th.
Tel: 01 46 06 72 85
⑤⓪ [p334, A1]
www.terrass-hotel.com
The main attraction of this Montmartre hotel is the view from the rooftop restaurant – it is superb, taking in the whole of Paris. It's a favourite with some celebrities, who favour the hotel's plush suites. The rest of the rooms are comfortable if unre-

markable. Cosy bar area with a roaring fire in winter months. €€€

Timhôtel Montmartre
11 rue Ravignan, 18th
Tel: 01 42 55 74 79
⑤① [p334, B1]
www.timhotel.com
A reliable chain that has several hotels around the capital, including those at Place d'Italie, St-Lazare, the Louvre and on the Boulevard de Clichy. All the Timhôtels are quite modern, well equipped and individually decorated, and decent value. This one in Montmartre is located in an attractive, tree-lined square with a fountain. €

11th
Tel: 01 43 38 29 29
④⑨ [p336, E1]
www.saintlouisbastille.com
Recently renovated, this affordable hotel is a perfect base for the dedi-

cated bar-hopper, as it's on the corner of rue Oberkampf, still one of the liveliest nightlife hubs in the city. Five of the 27 rooms are singles; the decor is unre-

LATIN QUARTER AND ST-GERMAIN-DES-PRÉS

Hôtel d'Angleterre
44 rue Jacob, 6th
Tel: 01 42 60 34 72
⑤② [p336, A2]
www.hotel-dangleterre.com
This was once the home of the British Ambassador, and was the site on which the US Treaty of Independence was drawn up in 1783. Elegant yet relaxed and very comfortable, it is located in a smart corner of the Left Bank. There are 27 good-sized rooms, all en suite. €€

Aramis Saint-Germain
124 rue de Rennes, 6th
Tel: 01 45 48 03 75
⑤③ [p336, A4]
www.hotel-aramis.com
Affiliated to the Best Western group, the Aramis offers 42 attractive and comfortable rooms, with well-equipped bathrooms, TV and other facilities. Some rooms have air conditioning. It's well located, not far from

the Jardin du Luxembourg. €€

Le Clos Médicis
56 rue Monsieur-le-Prince, 6th
Tel: 01 43 29 10 80
⑤④ [p336, B4]
www.closmedicis.com
This stylish boutique hotel in an 18th-century *hôtel particulier* near the Jardin du Luxembourg offers chic bedrooms, antique tiles in the bathrooms, fabulous flower arrangements, an open fire in the lounge in winter and helpful staff. There's also a courtyard garden. €€

Hotel Cluny Sorbonne
8 rue Victor-Cousin, 5th
Tel: 01 53 54 66 66
www.hotel-cluny.fr
⑤⑤ [p336, B3]
In a quiet location opposite the Université de la Sorbonne, this small hotel with bright decor is a great base from which to explore the Latin Quarter – all the main sights are a short walk

away. Previous guests include 19th-century French poet Arthur Rimbaud who stayed in Room 62; today, he'd no doubt make good use of the free Wi-Fi. There are romantic views over the rooftops from the top floor. €

Hôtel Design de la Sorbonne
6 rue Victor-Cousin, 5th
Tel: 01 43 54 58 08
⑤⑥ [p336, B4]
www.hotels-paris-rive-gauche.com
39 recently renovated rooms decorated in bright colours, and complete with iMacs, just a pigeon's hop from the Jardin du Luxembourg. Nearby, the group's more traditional other hotels – Hôtel du Panthéon, Hôtel des Grands-Hommes and Hôtel Jardin de l'Odéon, as well as the chic new four-star La Belle Juliette – are equally good bets. €€

Hôtel Familia
11 rue des Ecoles, 5th
Tel: 01 43 54 55 27
⑤⑦ [p336, C4]
www.familiahotel.com
An excellent location within a few minutes' walk of the islands and St-Germain-des-Prés. Fifth- and sixth-floor rooms have a view of Notre-Dame. The many returning guests appreciate the hospitable Gaucheron family, who live on the premises and take great pride in every detail of the hotel. €€

Hôtel du Globe
15 rue des Quatres-Vents, 6th
Tel: 01 43 26 35 50
⑤⑧ [p336, B3]
www.hotel-du-globe.fr
Occupying a 17th-century building in St-Germain, the dinky Globe (14 rooms) was comprehensively renovated just a few years back, but retains period furniture (and a suit of armour) in its public areas and

rooms with time-worn, bare stone walls. A nice use of bright colours adds to the romance of the setting. Staff are friendly and very helpful. €€

Hôtel des Grandes Ecoles
75 rue du Cardinal-Lemoine, 5th
Tel: 01 43 26 79 23
❺❾ [p336, C4]
www.hotel-grandes-ecoles.com
At first glance, you might think you were in the French countryside; there are 51 large TV-free rooms around a cobbled courtyard, and a garden of old trees and trellised roses. It's a short uphill walk from the Métro, but you are still close enough to everything you may want to visit, including the Place de la Contrescarpe and Rue Mouffetard. A cult address, so reserve well ahead. €€

L'Hôtel
13 rue des Beaux-Arts, 6th
Tel: 01 44 41 99 00
www.l-hotel.com
❻⓪ [p336, A2]
This legendary hotel has been redecorated by Jacques Garcia, but retains something of its

old sense of decadence in the extravagant decor, dimly-lit bar and mini swimming pool. The Mistinguett suite still has the music-hall star's Art Deco mirror bed; other rooms are plushly Napoleonic, while the bedroom where Oscar Wilde died is perfect for preening, with its peacock-patterned walls. €€€€

Left Bank St Germain
9 rue de l'Ancienne-Comédie, 6th.
Tel: 01 43 54 01 70
www.parishotelleftbank.com
❻❶ [p336, B3]
Charming hotel five minutes' walk from the Seine, and only 10 minutes from the Louvre and Notre Dame. Cosy rooms with classic décor. €€€

Hôtel Lenox
9 rue de l'Université, 7th
Tel: 01 42 96 10 95
❻❷ [p336, A2]
www.lenoxsaintgermain.com
This trendy hotel is decorated in contemporary Art Deco style and is very popular among creative types such as photographers, artists and dress designers. There's a bar, and the rooms are spot-

less. It's very popular, so you should reserve well in advance if you can. €€

Hôtel La Louisiane
60 rue de Seine, 6th
Tel: 01 44 32 17 17
❻❸ [p336, B3]
www.hotel-lalouisiane.com
The Art Deco Louisiane is a relic of St-Germain's artistic, literary and jazz past. Many big American jazzmen have stayed here: Miles Davis, John Coltrane to name but two; then it was Jim Morrison's turn and, more recently, Quentin Tarantino. Facilities are basic, but people come here for the feel of the place and the lively setting overlooking Rue de Buci street market. €

Hôtel Lutetia
45 boulevard Raspail, 6th
Tel: 01 49 54 46 46
❻❹ [p336, A2]
www.lutetia-paris.com
An early Art Deco palace conveniently situated in the heart of the bustling St-Germain-des-Prés and once frequented by such literary luminaries as Dorothy Parker, Ernest Hemingway and F. Scott Fitzgerald. A monument to the Jazz

Age, it has been finely renovated and still has enough chic-appeal to attract a few famous faces: Catherine Deneuve is a regular visitor. €€€€

Hôtel des Mines
125 boulevard St-Michel, 5th
Tel: 01 43 54 32 78
❻❺ [p336, B4]
www.hotel-desmines-paris.com
In the heart of Paris and a few minutes' walk from the Jardin du Luxembourg. In a simple design with comfortable triple and quadruple rooms that make it ideal for families, and excellent value for money. Personalised and warm welcome. €€

Hôtel Montalembert
3 rue de Montalembert, 7th
Tel: 01 45 49 68 68
❻❻ [p336, A2]
www.montalembert.com
The Montalembert has an ornate Beaux Arts-style exterior and stylish rooms; some are furnished with antiques. A new suite on the sixth floor has been designed by architect Christian Liaigre. €€€€

Hôtel Notre-Dame
1 quai St-Michel, 5th
Tel: 01 43 54 20 43
www.hotelnotredameparis.com
❻❼ [p336, A3]
Overlooking the Seine and Notre-Dame, this 400-year-old building has recently been redecorated by Christian Lacroix – expect wall murals, tapestries and opulent fabrics with

BELOW: the vertigo-inducing courtyard at L'Hôtel.

PRICE CATEGORIES
Price ranges, per double room, are as follows:

€ = €55–100
€€ = €100–200
€€€ = €200–300
€€€€ = over €300

clashing patterns. There is free WiFi but no lift. €€

Hôtel de Saint-Germain
50 rue du Four, 6th
Tel: 01 45 48 91 64
68 [p336, A3]
www.hotel-de-saint-germain.fr
In an excellent location on the Left Bank, with 30 comfortable, bright rooms. There are also five family rooms. Wi-Fi access. €€

Hôtel des Saints-Pères
65 rue des Saints-Pères, 6th
Tel: 01 45 44 50 00
69 [p336, A3]
www.esprit-de-france.com
The Saints-Pères occupies a 17th-century building, with a lovely little garden and a swish little bar. If you can, book room 100, which has a fine 17th-century ceiling by painters of the Versailles school; other

rooms are a nice mix of modern and traditional touches. There's also a duplex suite with the bathroom on the upper level. €€

La Villa
29 rue Jacob, 6th.
Tel: 01 43 26 60 00
70 [p336, A2]
www.villa-saintgermain.com
A clean, sleek, modern hotel in the beating heart of St-Germain-

des-Prés. It has all the mod cons (such as Wi-Fi) you might need, and the airy public areas are equipped with Art Deco-style lamps and furniture. Rooms are decorated with faux croc-skin headboards and taffeta on the walls, and room numbers – nice touch, this – are beamed onto the floor in front of the door. €€€

MONTPARNASSE, THE EIFFEL TOWER AND INVALIDES

Hôtel Aviatic
105 rue de Vaugirard, 6th
Tel: 01 53 63 25 50
71 [p338, E3]
www.aviatic.fr
A little winter garden and a characterful lounge and reception area set the tone for this carefully put-together establishment. The breakfast room looks more like an old-fashioned bistro than part of a hotel, and rooms are decorated with objects picked up at flea markets. Book online to get the best deals. €€€

Hôtel Duc de Saint-Simon
14 rue de St-Simon, 7th
Tel: 01 44 39 20 20
72 [p338, E1]
www.hotelducdesaintsimon.com
A sense of being very pleasantly removed from the city bustle is fostered by this hotel's lovely courtyard, and maintained by the lavish Belle Epoque decor and appointments inside. There are 34 rooms in three categories, all done out with panache, creating a distinctly romantic feel; four have lovely terraces above the hotel garden. €€€

Hôtel Eiffel Rive Gauche
6 rue du Gros-Caillou, 7th
Tel: 01 45 51 51 51
73 [p338, C1]
www.hotel-eiffel.com
This is a nicely unusual hotel, in that the decor has a warm Provençal theme: lots of ochres and reds in rooms and common areas. Given its setting a short stroll from the Eiffel Tower, it's quite a bargain. €

Hôtel Istria St-Germain
29 rue Campagne-Première, 14th
Tel: 01 43 20 91 82
74 [p338, E4]
www.hotel-istria-paris.com
The "St-Germain" in the name is very cheeky – this is most definitely Montparnasse. Odd, too, that this charming hotel shouldn't play up its Montparnasse arts heritage – this is the place where Man Ray, Marcel Duchamp and poet Louis Aragon once lived, after all. Rooms (renovated since its artistic heyday) are well lit and soberly furnished, and there's a cosy cellar breakfast room. €€

Hôtel Mayet
3 rue Mayet, 6th

Tel: 01 47 83 21 35
75 [p338, D3]
www.mayet.com
This well-renovated little hotel on a quiet Montparnasse street still dotted with craftsmen's workshops proves that it is possible to find contemporary design on a budget. Bedrooms are compact but stylish in dark grey and red, and there's a comfortable salon with sofas and modern paintings. €€

Platine Hotel
20 rue Ingénieur Robert Keller, 15th
Tel: 01 45 71 15 15
76 [p338, A3]
www.platinehotel.fr
"Platine" refers to platinum blonde hair and this hotel pays homage to the world's most famous example – Marilyn Monroe. The whole place, including the 46 rooms, is decorated in 1950s retro style and there is even a small spa. €€

Hôtel Square
3 rue de Boulainvilliers, 16th
Tel: 01 44 14 91 90
www.hotelsquare.com
77 [p338, A2]
Across the river from and west of the Eiffel

Tower, this modern five-star hotel has contemporary rooms (think grey stripes and sleek lines), an in-house art gallery, a Nuxe Spa and the fashionable Zebra Square restaurant – which usually has better food than service. €€€€

Le Walt
37 avenue de La Motte Picquet, 7th
Tel: 01 45 51 55 83
[p341, C1]
www.lewaltparis.com
78 [p338, C1]
This boutique hotel certainly has the glam factor: 25 rooms decorated in classic or contemporary style – some of which have views of the Eiffel Tower, and all of which have sleek glass-and-chrome bathrooms and large oil paintings over the bed – combine with wooden floors and a stylish little courtyard restaurant. €€€€

ACTIVITIES

THE ARTS, NIGHTLIFE, FESTIVALS, PARIS FOR CHILDREN AND SPORTS

THE ARTS

Theatre, Opera, Ballet and Concerts

There is a wonderful choice of theatre, concerts, ballet and opera in Paris – though drama in any language other than French is scarce. Some of the main venues are listed below. Look out also for adventurous contemporary dance companies, concerts and performances at the Centre Pompidou, the excellent classical music seasons at the Musée d'Orsay and Musée du Louvre, and the many music recitals in churches, especially during the Festival d'Art Sacré each December.

Centre National de la Danse
1 rue Victor-Hugo, 93507 Pantin
Tel: 01 41 83 98 98
www.cnd.fr
A lavish new centre for contemporary dance, in Pantin on the northeast edge of the city.

Cité de la Musique
221 avenue Jean-Jaurès, 19th
Tel: 01 44 84 44 84
www.cite-musique.fr
Opened in 1995, this complex at La Villette includes a concert hall, information service, museum and bookshop dedicated to music.

Comédie Française
1 place Colette, 1st

Tel: 0825 10 1680
www.comedie-francaise.fr
This is France's principal national theatre, where works by such greats as Molière and Racine are performed. More recent plays, including those by Genet and Anouilh, are also shown here.

Opéra National de Paris
Palais Garnier: place de l'Opéra, 9th
Opéra Bastille: 2bis place de la Bastille, 12th
Tel: 08 92 89 90 90
www.operadeparis.fr
Opera and ballet performances are staged in the sumptuous 19th-century surroundings of the Palais Garnier and in the modern Bastille building.

Théâtre du Châtelet
2 place du Châtelet, 1st
Tel: 01 40 28 28 40
www.chatelet-theatre.com.
Opera, classical concerts and occasional ballet.

Théâtre National de la Colline
15 rue Malte-Brun, 20th
Tel: 01 44 62 52 52
www.colline.fr
Modern theatre with a focus on contemporary playwrights.

Théâtre du Vieux Colombier
21 rue du Vieux Colombier, 6th
tel: 01 44 39 87 00 www.theatre duvieuxcolombier.com.
Small-scale productions of classical and modern drama from the Comédie Française troupe.

BELOW: night out at the opulent Opéra Garnier.

Théâtre de la Ville
2 place du Châtelet, 4th
Tel: 01 42 74 22 77
www.theatredelaville-paris.com
One of Paris's liveliest venues,
hosting contemporary dance,
classical, contemporary and
world music, theatre and a wide
range of international artists.
They also have a venue in Montmartre (31 rue des Abbesses; tel:
01 48 87 54 42).

Museums

Most national museums charge
an entrance fee, but are often free
for under-18s, and municipal
museums are free for all.
Entrance at national museums is
often cheaper on Sunday, and is
free for all on the first Sunday of
each month. There are also
reductions at most museums for
senior citizens and students with
a valid student card.

If you plan to visit several
museums during your stay, buying
a *Paris Museum Pass* means you
need queue only once to visit over
60 museums or monuments –
including all the most famous
ones – in Paris and the Ile-de-
France region, and also saves a
great deal of money on entrance
prices. Tickets are available for

two, four or six days, and cost
around e39–e69 per person.
They are sold at tourist offices and
the participating museums. For
full details, see www.parismuse-
umpass.com.

As a rule, national museums
are closed on Tuesday, and
municipal museums on Monday.
Opening times at many museums
vary on Sundays and public holidays. Most museums stay open
throughout the day, but a few
small ones close for lunch from
noon–12.30pm to about
2.30pm.

WHAT'S ON AND WHERE TO GET TICKETS

The listings magazines *L'Officiel
des Spectacles* and *Pariscope*
(www.premiere.fr) both appear
every Wednesday with full
details of cultural events and
venues in and around the city.
Figaroscope, the Wednesday
supplement of *Le Figaro*
national newspaper (www.figaro-
scope.fr), is another very useful
source of entertainment information.

Music, theatre and tickets for
a big range of other events in
Paris can also be booked at dis-
counted prices through various
local websites; try www.billetre-
duc.com, www.ticketac.com or
webguichet.com. All are in
French only; normally, once you
make the booking by credit card
you will be sent an email or a
text message to a mobile phone
with a booking number, which
you must show at the venue
(about 30 minutes before the
performance) to collect your
tickets.

The Paris tourist office website provides a great deal of up-
to-date information in several
languages on what's on in the
city in theatre, music, exhibitions and other attractions,
together with news of upcoming
programmes and festivals, on
www.parisinfo.com.

Main ticket agencies
FNAC Billeterie, at FNAC stores:
1–7 Forum des Halles, rue
Pierre-Lescot, 1st; 77–81 boulevard. St-Germain, 6th; 136 rue
de Rennes, 6th; 74 avenue des
Champs-Elysées, 8th; passage
du Havre, 109 rue St-Lazare,
9th; 4 place de la Bastille, 12th;
Centre Commercial Italie, 30
avenue d'Italie, 13th; 26–30
avenue des Ternes, 17th. Bookings can also be made online at
www.fnac.com.
Virgin Megastore, 52 avenue
des Champs-Elysées, 8th. Tickets can be bought by phone,
tel: 01 49 53 50 00, online at
www.virginmega.fr or in person,
Mon–Sat 10am–midnight, Sun
noon–midnight.
Kiosque Madeleine, Place de
la Madeleine, 8th, Kiosque
Ternes, 17th, and **Kiosque
Montparnasse**, Parvis de la
Gare Montparnasse, 14th;
these kiosks sell tickets for performances the same day at half-
price. Tue–Sat 12.30–8pm,
Sun 12.30–4pm.
CROUS (Centre Régional des
Œuvres Universitaires et Sco-
laires), 39 avenue Georges-Bernanos, 5th, tel: 01 40 51 36
00, www.crous-paris.fr. Reduced-
price seats for students (with
valid student cards).

NIGHTLIFE

Paris nightlife offers something
for everyone, from elitist bars and
clubs where you can do a bit of
celebrity-spotting to underground
cafés run by squatters. You can
find jazz, salsa, tango, Congolese
storytelling, shiatsu massages
and, of course, traditional French
chansons.

Cabarets

Chez Michou
80 rue des Martyrs, 18th
Tel: 01 46 06 16 04
www.michou.fr
Drag shows every night.
Le Crazy Horse
12 avenue George V, 8th
Tel: 01 47 23 32 32
www.lecrazyhorseparis.com
Sexiest and most skimpily
dressed of the big cabarets.
Le Lido
116bis avenue des Champs-Elysées, 8th
Tel: 01 40 76 56 10
www.lido.fr
Traditional cabaret glamour, with
countless costume changes, and
three shows daily.
Moulin Rouge
82 boulevard de Clichy, 18th
Tel: 01 53 09 82 82
www.moulinrouge.fr
The original, still going strong with
two shows a night; tourist prices,
and a host of tour buses.

ABOVE: the scantily-clad dancers of the Crazy Horse.

Nightclubs

Alcazar – Mezzanine – Club Le Wagg
62 rue Mazarine, 6th
Tel: 01 53 10 19 99
www.alcazar.fr
A cool bar and even cooler DJs pull in a mixed crowd of Parisians and tourists.

Le Balajo
9 rue de Lappe, 11th
Tel: 01 47 00 07 87
www.balajo.fr
Latin dance music and rock and roll, in an old Bastille dance hall. Open Mon-Sat with a tea dance on Monday afternoons.

Barrio Latino
46–8 rue du Faubourg St-Antoine, 12th
Tel: 01 55 78 84 75
www.buddhabar.com
Lavish 3,000sq-metre (32,000sq ft) hacienda with an imposing staircase now listed as a historic monument. Gustave Eiffel designed the front of the building. The restaurant and the conservatory serve a rich variety of South American dishes. Bossa nova and salsa nights. Daily noon–2am.

Batofar
11 quai François-Mauriac, 13th
Tel: 09 71 25 50 61
www.batofar.org
Interesting live music and club events on a renovated lightship moored on the Seine.

Club 18
18 rue de Beaujolais, 1st
Tel: 01 42 97 52 13
www.club18.fr
Open on Fridays and Saturdays only, this is France's first and arguably best gay club. The music is popular: Lady Gaga, Madonna and Kylie.

Le Divan du Monde
75 rue des Martyrs, 18th
Tel: 01 40 05 06 99
www.divandumonde.com
Cheap and friendly, this former café (once frequented by Toulouse-Lautrec) is now a throbbing, eclectic club (funk, rock, indie, etc.); no elitist door policy, or a dress code.

La Java
105 rue du Faubourg-du-Temple, 10th. Tel: 01 42 02 20 52
www.la-java.fr
Swing, jazz and ska in a Belleville dance hall, with live bands at weekends. See website or listings magazines for details of specific evenings.

La Machine du Moulin Rouge
90 boulevard de Clichy, 18th
Tel: 01 53 41 88 89
www.lamachinedumoulinrouge.com
Rough and ready, mainstream and enormous, this giant venue formerly known as La Locomotive has three dance floors, and a location next door to the Moulin Rouge. Music ranges from swing to hip hop and there is occasionally live music.

Red Light
34 rue du Départ, 15th
Tel: 01 48 79 85 49
www.leredlight.com
House music and a mixed gay-straight clientele.

Rex Club
5 boulevard Poissonnière, 2nd
Tel: 01 42 36 10 96
www.rexclub.com
A techno and house stalwart with one of the best sound systems in Paris, and big-name DJs.

Silencio
142-144 rue Montmartre, 2nd
Tel: 01 53 65 65 58
www.silencio-club.com
A new club owned by American film director David Lynch, with an art library and a cinema as well as a dance floor. Open to non-members after midnight.

VIP Room
188 bis rue de Rivoli, 1st
Tel: 01 58 36 46 00
www.viproom.fr
An exclusive club with sister venues in Cannes, Saint Tropez and Monaco. Expect the clientèle to be

BELOW: Batofar, the first 'nightclub on a boat' that started the trend.

ABOVE: Fête de la Musique fun.

rich, beautiful and often famous.

Please see the bars and cafes listings at the end of each of the Places chapters.

Music Venues

L'Alimentation Générale
64 rue Jean-Pierre Timbaud, 11th
Tel: 01 43 55 42 50
www.alimentation-generale.net
A wide variety of music, from African to East European, takes place in this hip "grocery store". Open Thur-Sat 7pm-4am.

Balades Sonores
1 avenue Trudaine, 9th
Tel: 01 83 87 94 87
www.baladessonores.com
An independent record label and shop that regularly hosts concerts by its quirky artists.

Caveau de la Huchette
5 rue de la Huchette, 6th
Tel: 01 43 26 65 05
www.caveaudelahuchette.fr
Frequented by GIs in World War II, it now hosts a young clientele for cellar jazz. Sun–Wed 9.30pm–2.30am, Thur–Sat 9.30pm–6am.

La Chapelle des Lombards
19 rue de Lappe, 11th
Tel: 01 43 57 24 24
Lively world music in a popular club. Tue–Sun 11.30pm–dawn.

La Cigale
120 boulevard de Rochechouart, 18th
Tel: 01 49 25 89 99
www.lacigale.fr
A popular club hosting up-and-

A listing of all major events in Paris is available from the Tourist Office (see page 324). Here are just some of the festivals and events that occur every year:

January sales
February–March *Six Nations Rugby Tournament.* International rugby extravaganza running for three weekends.
late February–early March *Salon de l'Agriculture.* Rural France comes to Paris in a huge agricultural and food fair.
April Paris Marathon
April–early June *Foire du Trône.* France's biggest funfair; Pelouse de Reuilly, Métro: Porte Dorée.
May *Carré Rive Gauche.* Open days at the Left Bank antiques enclave.
late May–early June French Tennis Open; Stade Roland Garros, Métro: Porte d'Auteuil
early June Champs-Elysées Film Festival.
June *Fête de la Musique* (21 June). Huge street music festival; free concerts and dances all across Paris.
July Bastille Day. Celebrations begin at the Bastille on the evening of 13 July; on the 14th, a military parade starts at 10am on the Champs-Elysées. Fireworks follow at the Trocadéro.
mid-July–mid-August *Paris Quartier d'Eté.* Summer arts fes-

tival: contemporary dance, street theatre, world music and outdoor jazz provide cultural entertainment when the theatres and concert halls close down for the summer. *Paris-Plage.* The beach comes to Paris with sand, paddling pools, cafés and beach volleyball on the *quais* of the Seine. See page 113. *Cinéma en Plein Air.* Classic movies on a giant screen at the free outdoor film festival at La Villette.
September *Journée du Patrimoine* (3rd weekend). Open day at otherwise off-limits government and private buildings. *Festival d'Automne* (until Dec). Annual festival of theatre, music and dance.
October (1st Sat) *La Nuit Blanche.* Stay up all night for artistic happenings in museums and venues all over town.
November The arrival of Beaujolais Nouveau is celebrated in bars and cafés (3rd Thursday of the month).
December Notre-Dame is packed for the Christmas Eve service. On New Year's Eve, crowds fill the Champs-Elysées, and there's a giant fireworks display at Trocadéro.
mid December–late January *Patinoire de Noël.* Ice-skating in a spectacular setting: the first floor of the Eiffel Tower.

coming bands.
La Flèche d'Or
102 bis rue de Bagnolet, 20th
Tel: 01 44 64 01 02
www.flechedor.fr
A popular venue housed in a former train station, which tends to showcase up-and-coming French indie bands.

There are few better cities for movie-going than Paris, with a

choice of films each week that's unmatched anywhere in Europe. There is a high concentration of modern multi-screen cinemas showing the latest films, but if you'd rather see world cinema or a French classic than the most recent Hollywood blockbuster, there are plenty of good retro and arthouse cinemas, too. To find out what's on, check *Pariscope*.

The majority of cinemas in central Paris show films in their original language with subtitles in French (these are marked "VO" – *version originale*), but once you get out of the city centre, main-stream films are usually dubbed into French (and marked "VF" – *version française*). Ticket prices are reduced by up to 30 percent on Monday and/or Wednesday.

Cinemas on the Champs-Ely-sées (8th *arrondissement*) and around Odéon in St-Germain-des-Prés (6th *arrondissement*) show recent releases in VO, as do the Latin Quarter arts cinemas (5th *arrondissement*) for old movies. The cinemas listed here (out of 400 screens across Paris) are particularly attractive, or present interesting programmes, usually in VO:

Le Champo
51 rue des Ecoles, 5th
Tel: 01 43 54 51 60
www.lechampo.com
Ever-popular arthouse cinema in the Latin Quarter.

Le Cinéma des Cinéastes
7 avenue de Clichy, 17th
Tel: 0892 689 717
www.cinema-des-cineastes.fr
Three screens for film buffs.

Cinémathèque Française
51 rue de Bercy, 12th
Tel: 01 71 19 33 33
www.cinematheque.fr
France's official film theatre has a great new home in Bercy, to cover the whole of world cinema.

Forum des Images
Forum des Halles, 1st
Tel: 01 44 76 63 00
www.forumdesimages.net
A film archive on Paris, and always intriguing film seasons.

Gaumont Marignan
27–33 avenue des Champs-Ely-sées, 8th
Tel: 08 92 69 66 96.
One of many multi-screen com-plexes on the Champs-Elysées.

La Géode
Parc de la Villette, 19th
Tel:01 40 05 79 99
www.lageode.fr
An IMAX cinema housed inside a huge glittering dome. Mainly nature or science-themed films.

Le Grand Rex
1 boulevard Poissonnière, 2nd
Tel: 01 45 08 93 58
Art Deco cinema; one big screen.

Max Linder Panorama
24 boulevard Poissonnière, 9th
Tel: 01 48 24 00 47
www.maxlinder.com
A panoramic screen and state-of-the-art acoustics in a 1930s set-ting – the best of both worlds.

La Pagode
57bis rue de Babylone, 7th
Tel: 01 46 34 82 54
www.etoile-cinema.com
A unique cinema experience: the latest films are shown in the tran-quil setting of a mock-Japanese pagoda, complete with tearoom.

FOR CHILDREN

Most children are not really that interested in city sightseeing; Dis-neyland Paris (see pages 268) is what they are after, or failing that an afternoon in one of Paris's parks (see page 257). To find out details of other current activities and entertainments available in Paris that should appeal to chil-dren, such as plays, films, puppet shows and circuses, refer to *L'Officiel des Spectacles* and *Pari-scope*.

Taking your children out to a restaurant should not be a prob-lem (but check beforehand with more upmarket places). French children are used to eating out from an early age and so are gen-erally well behaved. Many restau-rants offer a children's menu, with smaller portions; if not, they may split a *prix fixe* menu between two. With very young children, just ask for an extra plate and give them food from your own. Alterna-tively, order a simple dish from the *à la carte* menu, such as an ome-lette or soup. With the bread that comes automatically to a French table, and ice cream or fruit to fol-low, most children will be well fed.

Animals

La Ferme de Paris
Route du Pesage, Bois de Vin-cennes, 12th
Tel: 01 71 28 50 56
Come and see farm animals in Paris's very own city farm.

Le Jardin des Papillons
Parc Floral de Paris Esplanade du château de Vincennes, Route de la Pyramide, 12th
More than 40 different types of butterfly will delight young and old.

Chocolate

Musée Gourmand du Chocolat
28 boulevard de Bonne Nouvelle, 10th
Tel: 01 42 29 68 60
Learn about chocolate through the ages and taste some before leaving.

Miniatures

Musée des Plans-reliefs
Hôtel National des Invalides

BELOW: sightseeing on two wheels.

129 rue de Grenelle, 7th
Tel: 01 45 51 95 05
A fascinating collection of scale
models of French towns and cities
dating from the reign of Louis XIV
to Napoleon III.

Puppets

Musée de la Poupée
28 rue Beaubourg Impasse Berthaud, 3rd
Tel: 01 42 72 73 11
A collection of more than 500
puppets dating from the 18th
century.
Théâtre de Marionnettes du Jardin du Luxembourg
Tel: 01 43 26 46 47 or 01 43 29
50 97 for a recorded message (in
French) about current children's
puppet shows.

SPORTS

Participant

You perhaps wouldn't go to Paris
primarily in search of sports facilities or events (except for the Tennis Open in June), but the city
does cater fairly well for the sports
enthusiast. You can find information on sporting events in *Le
Figaro* each Wednesday.

Cycling

The Bois de Boulogne and Bois de
Vincennes offer good cycling, as
do the Quais de Seine and the
Canal St-Martin. Call the **Fédération Française de Cyclotour-
isme** (www.ffct.org) for your
nearest cycling club, tel: 01 56 20
88 88.

Fitness Centres

Club Med Gym
147 rue St-Honoré
Tel: 01 40 20 03 03
www.clubmedgym.fr
One of a chain of health clubs that
offer step classes, weights, mar-
tial arts and sauna. Not all clubs
have a pool, so check first.
Club Quartier Latin
19 rue Pontoise, 5th
Tel: 01 55 42 77 88

ABOVE: roller-skating is hugely
popular in Paris.

Health club with squash courts
and pool, a fully equipped gym
and a variety of classes.

In-Line Skating

Roller-skating, in all its forms, is
hugely popular in Paris: Friday
night sees thousands gather outside Tour Montparnasse at 10pm
for the weekly three-hour skate
through town. Everybody's welcome as long as they can keep up
(www.pari-roller.com).

Paris-Plage

From mid-July to mid-August
nearly 3km (2 miles) of the Right
Bank from Pont de Sully to Pont
des Arts are converted into a
beach, with hammocks, deckchairs, showers and a small pool.
www.paris.fr. See page 113.

Swimming

Aquaboulevard
4–6 rue Louis-Armand, 15th
Tel: 01 40 60 10 00
www.aquaboulevard.com
A massive water world offering an
exciting choice of waves, flumes
and indoor and outdoor pools.
Ideal fun for the kids.
Piscine Armand-Massard
66 boulevard du Montparnasse,
15th
Tel: 01 45 38 65 19
An underground sports centre
with three pools.
Piscine Georges-Vallery
148 avenue Gambetta, 20th

Tel: 01 40 31 15 20
Built for the 1924 Olympics, when
Johnny Weissmuller (aka Tarzan
in films of old) won the gold
medal.
Piscine des Halles
Centre Suzanne-Berlioux, 10
place de la Rotonde, 1st
Tel: 01 42 36 98 44
Part of the Forum des Halles, with
a 50-metre/yd pool.
Piscine Joséphine-Baker
Quai François-Mauriac, 13th
Tel: 01 56 61 96 50
Modern floating 25-metre/yd
pool moored on the Seine next to
the Bibliothèque Nationale-Fran-
çois Mitterrand with a kid's pool, a
sundeck, a sauna and a jacuzzi.
Piscine Jean-Taris
66 rue Thouin, 5th
Tel: 01 55 42 81 90
A very pleasant 25-metre/yd pool
with a view of the Panthéon.
Piscine du Marché St-Germain
12 rue Lobineau, 6th
Tel: 01 56 31 25 40
Underground 25-metre/yd pool.

Tennis

Centre Sportif d'Orléans
7 avenue Paul-Appell, 14th
Tel: 01 45 40 55 88
A variety of sports are on offer
(athletics, football, basketball) in
addition to nine tennis courts.
Courcelles
209 rue de Courcelles, 17th
Tel: 01 48 88 00 17
Tennis lessons at all levels.
Jardin du Luxembourg
6th, tel: 01 43 25 79 18.
Anyone can play tennis here, and
it's not expensive. Summer, daily
8am–9pm; winter, 8am–sunset.

Spectator

Football fans should pay homage at the massive **Stade de
France**, designed by architects
Zubléna, Macary, Regembal and
Constantini for the 1998 World
Cup. The stadium is also used
for concerts, seating around
100,000. Located at Rue Francis-de-Pressensé, in St-Denis,
tel: 01 55 93 00 00, www.stade-
france.fr (Métro Porte de Paris;

RER B to La Plaine-Stade de France, or RER D to Stade de France-St-Denis). Guided tours are available; daily 10am–5pm (10.30am and 2.30pm in English, except during events; charge.

The huge **Palais Omnisports de Bercy** (8 boulevard de Bercy, 12th, tel: 01 40 02 60 60, www. bercy.fr) offers a vast range of events including football, ice sports, motor sports and horse riding.

Major sports events include the **Six Nations** rugby in February to March, the Marathon in April, and the **French Tennis Open** in May to June at Stade Roland-Garros. For racing fans, the **Grand Prix de l'Arc de Triomphe** is run at Hippodrome de Longchamp, Bois de Boulogne, in October. **Parc des Princes** (16th arrondissement) is home to Paris's premier football team, Paris St-Germain.

ABOVE: cooking masterclass at Ritz Escoffier.

COURSES

Paris hosts numerous schools and courses for people of all ages. **Le Centre d'Information et de Documentation Jeunesse** (CIDJ) has information sheets on education in France, available from 101 quai Branly, 15th, tel: 01 44 49 12 00, www.cidj.com. Schools may also help with travel and accommodation.

French Language

A good reference site for locating course centres is www.fle.fr.
Alliance Française
101 boulevard Raspail, 6th
Tel: 01 42 84 90 00, www.alliancefr.org
Institut de Langue et de Culture Françaises (ILCF)
12 rue Casette, 6th
Tel: 01 44 39 52 00, www.icp.fr
Ecole de Langue Française pour Etrangers (ELFE)
15 rue Montmartre, 1st
Tel: 01 48 78 73 00
www.elfe-paris.com

Eurocentres
13 passage Dauphine, 6th
Tel: 01 40 46 72 00
www.eurocentres.com

Cookery

Le Cordon Bleu
8 rue Léon-Delhomme, 15th
Tel: 01 53 68 22 50
www.lecordonbleuparis.com
Ritz Escoffier
15 place Vendôme, 1st
Tel: 01 43 16 30 50
www.ritzparis.com
Closed until 2014.

History and Culture

Collège de France
11 place Marcelin Berthelot, 5th
Tel: 01 44 27 11 47
www.college-de-france.fr
Admission to the lectures and seminars is free and open to all. About 5,000 people attend the various lectures each year.
Institut Parisien de Langue et de Civilisation Françaises
27 boulevard des Italiens, 2nd
Tel: 01 42 66 18 08
www.institut-parisien.com
Courses in language and culture.

SIGHTSEEING TOURS

By bike

Fat Tire Bike Tours
24 rue Edgar Faure, 15th
Tel: 01 56 58 10 54
www.fattirebiketoursparis.com

Veloparis
44 rue Dorsel, 18th
Tel: 01 42 64 97 39
www.veloparis.com
Explore "night-time" or "green" paris on two wheels with an English-speaking guide.

By boat

Bateaux Mouches
Pont de l'Alma (Right Bank), 8th
Tel: 01 42 25 96 10
Batobus
Port de la Bourdonnais, 7th
Tel: 0825 05 01 01
www.batobus.com

By bus

Les Car Rouges
17 quai de Grenelle, 15th
Tel: 01 53 95 39 53
www.carsrouges.com
L'Open Tour
13 rue Auber, 9th
Tel: 01 42 66 56 56
www.parislopentour.com
Hop on, hop off bus tour in an open-top bus.

By car

4 roues sous 1 parapluie
22 rue Bernard Dimey, 18th
Tel: 0800 800 361
www.4roues-sous-1parapluie.com
Tours of Paris in a 2CV in English.

On foot

Paris Walks
12 passage Meunier, Saint Denis
Tel: 01 48 09 21 40
www.paris-walks.com
Guided walking tours in English.

TRANSPORT
ACCOMMODATION
ACTIVITIES
A – Z
LANGUAGE

A – Z

AN ALPHABETICAL SUMMARY OF PRACTICAL INFORMATION

A

Addresses

Paris is divided into numbered districts – *arrondissements* – and people refer to them by number, saying, for example, that they live "in the 5th". Street names are followed by a five-digit postcode, in which the last digits are the *arrondissement* number, so an address with a 75008 code will be in the 8th *arrondissement*, and 75012 in the 12th.

Admission charges

The average entrance price to a national museum or gallery is €8-10, but a *Paris Museum Pass* or *Paris Visite* travelcard can give great savings (see page 11). Entry to the permanent collections of the city's municipal museums is free of charge. Most of the national museums offer free entry on the first Sunday of each month.

B

Budgeting for Your Trip

The price of accommodation ranges across the spectrum. You

ABOVE: most cafés and bistros offer a *formule* set menu.

can get a double room in a small pension for under €60 a night, or you can pay €300 in a luxury hotel. An average price, however, for an en suite double room in a centrally located, comfortable hotel is around €100–150.

Meals also cover a wide price range, but on average expect to pay €40-50 for a three-course meal with a half-bottle of house wine. In French restaurants the most economical (and most usual) way to order food is from a *prix fixe* set menu (also called a *menu* or a *formule*), which gives two, three or four courses, and coffee, for a set price. Drinks are not usually included. *Menus* are a real bargain, with many for €20–

30 or less. Ordering *à la carte* is always more expensive. Note too, that many restaurants only offer bargain menus for lunch, so it will be more economical to eat at mid-day than in the evening. A beer will cost around €6 but a glass of house wine can cost as little as €3 while soft drinks are about €5.

A taxi from the airport will cost around €45–70, depending on traffic, plus €1 per bag and a tip of about 5 percent. Single Métro and bus fares cost €1.70, or €12.70 for a *carnet* of 10 tickets, but, again, it's much more economical to take advantage of the various travelcards available on Paris's transport system. For details, see page 296.

Business Visitors

Business travel accounts for about a third of French tourism revenue. This important market has led to the creation of a special Conference and Incentive Department at French tourist offices in London and New York. This department deals with business travel enquiries, and helps organise hotels, conference centres and incentive deals.

Conferences and Exhibitions

Paris is a world leader for conferences, exhibitions and trade fairs, and La Défense is the largest business district in Europe. For further information, call Info-Défense, tel: 01 47 74 84 24, or visit www.ladefense.fr.

For lists of exhibitions and details on participating, contact Promo Salons agency, via www.promosalons.com, with many offices around the world.

Many châteaux and hotels offer luxurious accommodation for smaller gatherings, and it's even possible to organise a congress at Disneyland Paris.

Trade Fair Venues

Palais des Congrès, Porte Maillot, 17th, tel: 01 40 68 22 22, www.palais-congres-paris.fr.
Paris-Expo, Porte de Versailles, 15th, tel: 01 40 68 22 22, www.parisexpo.fr; Paris's biggest trade fair complex.
Parc des Expositions de Paris-Nord, Villepinte, near Roissy-Charles de Gaulle airport, tel: 01 40 68 22 22, www.expoparisnord.com.
CNIT, La Défense, tel: 01 40 68 22 22, www.cnit.fr; has links to other salons at Porte de Champerret and Carrousel du Louvre.

Chambers of Commerce

An excellent source of information on local companies, export and import technicalities, translation agencies and conference centres

CLIMATE CHART

Maximum temperature
Minimum temperature
— Rainfall

is the **Chambre de Commerce et d'Industrie de Paris**, 27 avenue de Friedland, 8th, tel: 0820 012 112, www.ccip.fr. The **Franco-British Chamber of Commerce** is at 31 rue Boissy-d'Anglas, 8th, tel: 01 53 30 81 30, www.francobrit-ishchambers.com. There are also French Chambers of Commerce in key cities around the world. In London, the Chamber is at Lincoln House, 4th floor, High Holborn, London, WC1V 7JH, tel: 020 7092 6600, www.ccfgb.co.uk.

C

Children

Paris is most definitely a child-friendly city and there are plenty of activities and sights that they will enjoy. Children under 18 usually go free in museums, even if there's a charge for adults. Many restaurants will have high chairs and children's menus while hotels will have family rooms and can often supply cots with advance notice. Larger hotels will usually have a baby-sitting service; alternatively try Mababysitter (tel: 09 66 98 08 25, www.baby-sitter-paris.fr) which provides qualified child carers for around €20 per hour.

Climate

France is the only European country that is both North European and Mediterranean. In Paris, the climate is similar to that of southern England, but less changeable, and temperatures can be higher in mid-summer. The average maximum in July and August is 25°C (76°F), the average minimum 15°C (58°F), but 27°C (80°F) is not unusual. In January, expect a maximum of 6°C (43°F), a minimum of 1°C (43°F). To check the weather for your visit, see www.weather.com.

When to Visit

Spring, when the temperature is ideal for sightseeing, is probably

ABOVE: office workers in La Défense.

the best time to visit Paris, although you should be prepared for showers. Autumn mornings can be sharp, but by midday the skies are usually clear and bright. Some believe that winter light shows Paris at its best.

What to Wear

Paris is a great city to explore on foot, so comfortable walking shoes are essential. Bring warm clothes if you're coming to Paris in winter, as the weather can be very chilly, and remember to have something waterproof (or at the least an umbrella) with you in spring or autumn, as showers are quite common.

Most Parisians are very style-conscious, and won't brave even the corner shop without displaying a fair amount of sartorial élan. Casual tourists might therefore consider taking a smart change of clothes – in case, for example, you might want to try a night out at one of the city's many upmarket restaurants, where smart dress is de rigueur.

Complaints

To complain about a purchase, return it to the shop as soon as possible. In a serious dispute, contact the local Direction Départementale de la Concurrence, de la Consommation et de la Répression des Fraudes (consult the telephone directory for details).

TRANSPORT · ACCOMMODATION · ACTIVITIES · A – Z · LANGUAGE

Crime and Safety

Police

In the event of loss or theft, a report must be made in person at the nearest police station *(commissariat)* as soon as possible after the event. This will also be required if you wish to claim from your insurance company. Visit www.prefecture-police-paris. interieur.gouv.fr for station locations, or for emergency help tel: 17.

Security

If you take sensible precautions with your possessions, you should be safe in Paris. There is a problem with pickpockets in some of the Métro stations. Obvious centres of prostitution (such as Les Halles and parts of the Bois de Boulogne) are best avoided at night. As anywhere else, use care when withdrawing money with debit or credit cards

at a bank, currency exchange office or ATM machine, and make sure others cannot see your PIN. It's always a good idea to keep a photocopy of your passport in case of theft *(see also Emergencies)*.

Customs Regulations

There are no official restrictions on the movement of goods within the European Union, provided that the goods were purchased within the EU. However, people of all nationalities must declare, upon arrival or departure, sums of cash exceeding €10,000.

Duty-paid goods

If you are an EU resident and buy goods in France on which you pay tax, there are no longer any restrictions on the amounts you may take home with you. However, EU law has set "guidance levels" on the amounts that are acceptable of the following:

Tobacco 800 cigarettes, or 400 cigarillos, or 200 cigars, or 1kg of tobacco
Spirits 10 litres
Fortified wine/wine 90 litres (not more than 60 litres may be sparkling wine)
Beer 110 litres
   If you exceed these amounts you must be able to show that the goods are for personal use, for example a family wedding.

Duty-free goods

If you are from outside the EU and buy goods duty-free in France, the following limits still apply (these quantities may be doubled if you live outside Europe):
Tobacco 200 cigarettes, or 100 cigarillos, or 50 cigars, or 250g of tobacco
Alcohol 1 litre of spirits or liqueurs over 22 percent volume, or 2 litres of fortified, sparkling wine or other liqueurs, 4 litres of still wine and 16 litres of beer.

USEFUL INFORMATION

The following guides are useful for people with disabilities:
Access in Paris A guidebook that provides essential information for anyone with a mobility problem, including the elderly or parents travelling with young children. It can be obtained from Access Project, 39 Bradley Gardens, West Ealing, London W13 8HE, www. accessinparis.org.
Door to Door The UK government's online guide to travel for disabled people, with a section on travelling abroad. http://dptac.independent.gov. uk/door-to-door/
Michelin Red Guides Both the *France* and *Camping-Caravanning* guides indicate hotels that have facilities for guests with disabilities.
See www.ricksteves.com/plan/ tips/easyaccess.htm and www. ricksteves.com/plan/destinations/europe/easyaccess.htm for tips on travelling

BELOW: Parisians love their pooches.

Perfume 50g of perfume, plus 250ml of eau de toilette.

There are no restrictions on the amount of currency you can take into France.

For more information contact Centre de Renseignements des Douanes, tel: 08 11 20 44 44, or check www.douane.gouv.fr.

Disabled Travellers

Travellers with mobility problems are advised to book accommodation in advance. Official hotel lists use a symbol to denote wheelchair access, but it's a good idea to check with the hotel regarding the exact facilities available. Information on hotels with good access facilities can be found on the Paris Tourist Office website, www.parisinfo.com.

Hotels in the Accor group (www.accorhotels.com) and Louvre Hotels group (www.louvrehotels.com) have at least one room for disabled guests in a variety of chains to suit all budgets.

Fédération Française des Clubs UNESCO, 173 rue de Charenton, 12th, tel: 01 42 58 68 06, has accommodation for disabled young people.

Wheelchairs to rent

CRF Matériel Médical, 153 boulevard Voltaire, 11th, tel: 01 43 73 98 98, www.go2sante.fr.

French Organisations

Association des Paralysés de France, 17 boulevard Auguste-Blanqui, 13th, tel: 01 40 78 69 00, www.apf.asso.fr.
The association may be able to answer specific enquiries and can provide branch addresses.
CIDJ (see page 322, Study in France) youth information service has extensive information on services for less-able young travellers. It publishes *Vacances pour Personnes Handicapées* and leaflets on activity and sports holi-

EMBASSIES AND CONSULATES

Australia
4 rue Jean-Rey, 15th
Tel: 01 40 59 33 00
www.france.embassy.gov.au
Canada
35 avenue Montaigne, 8th
Tel: 01 44 43 29 00
www.canadainternational.gc.ca/france
New Zealand
7ter rue Léonard-de-Vinci, 16th
Tel: 01 45 01 43 43
www.nzembassy.com/france
Republic of Ireland
12 avenue Foch, 16th
Tel: 01 44 17 67 00
www.embassyofireland.fr
South Africa
59 quai d'Orsay, 7th
Tel: 01 53 59 23 23
www.afriquesud.net
UK
35 rue du Faubourg-St-Honoré, 8th, tel: 01 44 51 31 00
Consular services: 18bis rue d'Anjou, 8th, tel: 01 44 51 31 00
http://ukinfrance.fco.gov.uk
US
2 avenue Gabriel, 8th
Tel: 01 43 12 22 22
http://france.usembassy.gov
Office of American Citizen Services (consular services for US travellers or residents): 4 avenue Gabriel, 8th

days for young disabled people.
Union Nationale des Associations de Parents d'Enfants Inadaptés (UNAPEI), 15 rue Coysevox, 18th, tel: 01 44 85 50 50, www.unapei.org. Parents may wish to contact this organisation for information about facilities for children with disabilities.
Comité de Liaison pour le Transport des Personnes Handicapées, Conseil National des Transports, 34 avenue Marceau, 8th, tel: 01 53 23 85 85. Gives brief information on accessibility and arrangements for less-able passengers on public transport, and contacts for special transport schemes in France.

French Embassies

Australia
6 Perth Avenue, Yarralumla ACT 2600, Canberra
Tel: (02) 6216 0100
www.ambafrance-au.org
Canada
42 promenade Sussex, Ottawa, Ontario K1M 2C9
Tel: (613) 789 1795
www.ambafrance-ca.org
New Zealand
34-42 Manners Street, Wellington, 6142
Tel: (04) 384 25 25
www.ambafrance-nz.org
Republic of Ireland
36 Ailesbury Road, Ballsbridge, Dublin 4
Tel: 1 277 5000
www.ambafrance-ie.org
South Africa
250 Melk Street, New Meuckleneuk, 0181 Pretoria
Tel: (0) 12 425 1600
www.ambafrance-rsa.org
UK
58 Knightsbridge, London, SW1X 7JT
Tel: 0207 073 1250
www.ambafrance-uk.org
US
4101 Reservoir Road NW, Washington DC20007
Tel: 202 944 6000
www.info-france-usa.org

Ptitcar, 27-29 rue Raffet, 16th, 09 77 07 14 32, www.ptitcar.com, is an excellent transport company that operates a fleet of wheelchair-accessible vehicles for transport and tours. They also prepare vacation itineraries for wheelchair users, and offer other helpful services.

UK Organisations

RADAR, The Royal Association for Disability and Rehabilitation, 12 City Forum, 250 City Road, London EC1V 8AF, tel: 020 7250 3222, www.radar.org.uk. Provides helpful and friendly advice.
Mobilise (Disabled Drivers' Association and Disabled Driv-

TRANSPORT
ACCOMMODATION
ACTIVITIES
A – Z
LANGUAGE

ABOVE: the Marais is the most gay-friendly neighbourhood in Paris.

ers' Motor Club), tel: 01508 489449, www.mobilise.info.

US Organisations

Society for Accessible Travel and Hospitality (SATH), 347 Fifth Avenue, Suite 605, New York, tel: 212-447 7284, www.sath.org. A non-profit organisation that represents travellers with disabilities, and can also provide information.
MossRehab Resource Net www. mossresourcenet.org. A website with a very wide range of information on travelling and other disability-related issues.

Electricity

The standard voltage is 220 volts. Round-pin plugs are used, so pack an adaptor (available at airports as well as any store selling travel-related items). Visitors from North America with 110v equipment will also need a transformer for the higher voltage.

Etiquette

If you walk into a small shop or restaurant with people in it, it is

usually polite to say "bonjour". And if someone says "bonjour" to you it is polite to reciprocate; it is nice to add "monsieur" or "madame" or "mademoiselle" (for young women) after it eg. "bonjour, madame". If you enter a church or other place of worship, be sure to cover up with no bare shoulders, cleavage or legs on show for women.

Gay Travellers

The Marais (the 4th *arrondissement*) is the most gay-friendly district in Paris, with gay-oriented restaurants, wine bars, boutiques, bookstores, beauty salons, hotels, bars and discos. For more information check out the websites www.legayparis.fr, www.paris-gay.com and www.gay-paris.net (all in French and English). There are various free magazines you can pick up in most gay bars in the 3rd and 4th *arrondissements*. The gay magazine *Têtu* is a useful source of information, and can be bought at most news kiosks in the city.

EMERGENCIES

Ambulance: 15
Police: 17
Fire service: 18
Emergency calls from a mobile phone: 112
SOS Help English-language-helpline (daily 3–11pm): 01 46 21 46 46

Health & Medical Care

If you are an EU national and you fall ill in France, you can receive emergency medical treatment from doctors, dentists and hospitals. You will have to pay the cost of this treatment, but are entitled to claim from the French *Sécurité Sociale*, which refunds up to 70 percent of your medical expenses. To receive a refund you must have a **European Health Insurance Card** (**EHIC**). These are available online at www.ehic.org.uk or can be ordered through post offices and health centres. While travelling, keep the card safe.

If you need to see a doctor, expect to pay at least €23 per consultation, with prescription charges on top. The doctor will provide a statement of treatment *(feuille de soins)*. With this, EU citizens can reclaim around 70 percent of the cost of treatment. If you buy any medicines on prescription, check that the price stamp *(vignette)* is attached to the *feuille de soins* by the chemist, so that you can reclaim this cost too. When complete, the *feuille de soins* and prescription should be sent as soon as possible to the local *Caisse Primaire d'Assurance Maladie* (the doctor or chemist will have the address, or see the phone book under *Sécurité Sociale*) for your refund. It can also be a good idea to include a photocopy of your EHIC, and keep copies yourself of the other documents. The refund will be sent to your home, which will take about a month. If you have any difficulties, contact the **Caisse Primaire d'Assurance Maladie de Paris**, 27 rue Georges Auric, 75019 Paris, www.ameli.fr or in the UK call tel: 0191 218 1999.

For more information, consult the leaflet **Health Advice for Travellers** (available from post offices, online at www.dh.gov.uk or by tel: 020 7210 4850). Reciprocal EU health agreements do not cover all medical expenses, such as the cost of bringing a sick person back to the UK, so the Department of Health advises travellers also to take out private insurance. If you plan to drive in France, you should check that your motor insurance covers you for accidents abroad.

For travellers from North America, a comprehensive travel insurance policy with full medical cover is essential. You can also contact the **International Association for Medical Assistance to Travellers (IAMAT),** based in Guelph, Ontario, tel: 519 836 0102, www.iamat.org. This non-profit-making group offers members fixed rates for treatment from participating physicians. Members receive a passport-sized medical record and a directory of English-speaking IAMAT doctors in France. Membership is free, but a donation is requested.

In Paris, you can find English-speaking health services at the private **American Hospital** (Hôpital Américain de Paris, tel: 01 46 41 25 25, www.americanhospital. org), which is highly regarded and very expensive, or the **British Hospital** (Hôpital Franco-Britannique, tel: 01 46 39 22 22, www.british-hospital.org), which is covered by the French social security system. However, not all the staff are bilingual, and the hospital is mainly known for its maternity unit.

Pharmacies

Most pharmacies display flashing green neon crosses, and are open from 9 or 10am to 7 or 8pm. At night, they all post the addresses of the nearest late-opening pharmacies in their windows. Staff can provide basic medical advice and services. The following pharmacies also open late every night:
Dhéry, 84 avenue des Champs-Elysées, 8th (Métro George V), tel: 01 45 62 02 41. Open 24 hours.
Pharmacie Européenne de la Place de Clichy, 6 place de Clichy, 9th (Métro Place de Clichy), tel: 01 48 74 65 18. Open 24 hours.
Pharmacie des Halles, 10 boulevard de Sébastopol, 4th (Métro Châtelet), tel: 01 42 72 03 23, fax: 01 42 72 52 10. Mon–Sat 9am–midnight and Sun 9am–10pm.

ABOVE: pharmacy sign.

Publicis Drugstore, 133 avenue des Champs-Elysées, 8th (Métro Etoile), tel: 01 47 20 39 25.Open 24 hours.

Internet

WiFi (pronounced "wee-fee" in France) is now widely available in French hotels, although there is often a charge. For a list of free Wi-Fi spots around the city, including public buildings, parks and squares see www.paris.fr. A list of cafés with free Wi-Fi can be found here www.cafes-wifi.com. There are cyber cafés all over the city – ask at the tourist office for current ones or see www.parisinfo.com.

There is an enormous wealth of information available over the web, from pages telling you how to get to your destination, to how to speak the language when you get there. The following entries are only the tip of the iceberg:
www.parisinfo.com official site of the Paris Tourist Office, with information on hotels, sites, events, exhibitions, transport, weather and more
www.franceguide.com official site of the French Tourist Office,

---

HOSPITALS

All state hospitals have casualty departments (urgences). A complete list is available on www.aphp.fr. The following are some of the larger ones:
Hôpital Bichat
46 rue Henri-Huchard, 18th
Tel: 01 40 25 80 80
Hôpital Fernaud-Widal
(poisons control centre)
200 rue du Faubourg St-Denis, 10th
Tel: 01 40 05 45 45
Hôpital Hôtel-Dieu
1 place du Parvis-Notre-Dame,

4th
Tel: 01 42 34 82 34
Hôpital Necker
(children's hospital)
149 rue de Sèvres, 15th
Tel: 01 44 49 40 00
Hôpital de la Pitié-Salpêtrière
47 boulevard de l'Hôpital, 13th
Tel: 01 42 16 00 00
Hôpital St-Louis
1 avenue Claude-Vellefaux, 10th
Tel: 01 42 49 49 49

Maison de la France, for general information on France
www.magicparis.com travel, shops, hotels, events and more
www.paris.fr site of the Mairie de Paris, the Town Hall
www.ratp.fr the Paris transport system site
www.culture.fr official site of the Ministry of Culture
www.monuments-nationaux.fr official site of France's Department of National Monuments
www.rmn.fr guide to national museum exhibitions
www.meteo.fr weather online
www.pagesjaunes.fr the French Yellow Pages
www.lemonde.fr France's most respected newspaper
www.mondediplo.com *Le Monde*'s supplement *Le Monde Diplomatique* in English
www.figaroscope.fr online edition of *Le Figaro*'s weekly Paris arts and restaurant supplement
www.timeout.com/paris *Time Out* city guide for Paris
www.gogoparis.com a guide to what's hip and happening in the city
www.girlsguidetoparis.com a guide to Paris for women with a focus on shopping

Maps

Essential Paris (Editions de l'Indispensable) is the most useful map for visitors. It can be bought for about €5 at any of the ubiquitous news-stands and kiosks around the city. You may also be able to get by on the tourist office maps. Free maps of the public transport network can be picked up in the metro stations.

Media

Newspapers

The two main national dailies are *Le Monde*, the most influential paper in the country, which has a

ABOVE: *Le Parisien*, the most popular daily newspaper in France.

rather dry and leftish slant on politics and economic news, and sells about 300,000 copies daily. The more conservative *Le Figaro* sells about 525,000 copies.

The paper representing the Communist Party is *L'Humanité*, and not veering so heavily left is Jean-Paul Sartre's brainchild, *Libération*. The major weekly news magazines are *Le Point* (right), *L'Express* (centre) and *Le Nouvel Observateur* (left), which each sell around 350,000–500,000 copies. British, American and other European dailies are available on the same day at

city-centre kiosks and shops showing *journaux* or *presse* signs.

The *International Herald Tribune*, published in Paris, has listings for the city. To find out what is going on in Paris, try *L'Officiel des Spectacles or Pariscope* (both out on Wednesday), which give listings of movies, clubs, exhibitions, concerts, theatres and more.

Radio

France Inter (87.8 MHz) is the biggest station, offering something to suit all tastes. Radio Classique (101.1 MHz) plays non-stop lightweight classical music.

LOST PROPERTY

If your documents, cash, credit cards or other belongings are lost or stolen, go to the *commissariat de police* closest to the scene of the incident as soon as possible – even before contacting your credit card company or your consulate.

If you lose your passport, report it to your consulate immediately after notifying the police. There is a complete list of consulates in the local Yellow Pages (*Pages Jaunes*).

If credit cards are lost or stolen, local numbers are:

American Express, tel: 01 47 77 72 00
Diners Club, tel: 0820 82 01 43
MasterCard, tel: 01 45 67 84 84
Visa, tel: 0892 705 705
To reclaim anything else lost in Paris, go (with ID) to the **Bureau des Objets Trouvés**, 36 rue des Morillons, 15th, tel: 08 21 00 25 25 (Métro Convention); Mon–Thur 8.30am–5pm, Fri 8.30am–4.30pm. You must go in person: don't expect to sort out any enquiry by phone.

For something a bit less mainstream, try France Musiques (91.7 and 92.1 MHz). RTL (104.3 MHz), a popular station throughout France, plays music from the charts interspersed with chat.

Europe 1 (104.7 FM) is the best for morning news coverage, while France Info (105.5 FM) is a non-stop French news channel.

Television

TF1, France 2, France 3, France 5/Arte and M6 are the five main television stations. There is also a huge choice of cable channels, which are often available in larger hotels.

Canal+ is a subscription channel, which shows big-name films. CNN and BBC World are also available in many hotels.

Money

Currency

The euro (€) is the official French currency and is available in 500, 200, 100, 50, 20, 10 and 5 euro notes, and 2 euro, 1 euro, 50 cent, 20 cent, 10 cent, 5 cent, 2 cent and 1 cent coins. There are 100 cents to 1 euro.

Credit Cards

Most large shops and restaurants and almost all hotels accept credit cards. The most common in France are Visa, MasterCard and Carte Bleue (often called "CB"). American Express (Amex) and Diner's Club (DC) are

PUBLIC HOLIDAYS

New Year's Day, Easter Monday, 1 May (Labour Day), 8 May (end of World War II in Europe), Ascension Day – mid/late May, Whit Monday – late May, 14 July (Bastille Day), 15 August (Feast of the Assumption), 1 November (All Saints' Day), 11 November (Armistice Day, 1918), 25 December (Christmas).

ABOVE: postboxes are yellow.

widely recognised, and many places also accept Maestro and Cirrus, but if you don't see a card's sticker in a hotel or restaurant window, it's advisable to double-check.

Exchange

Bureaux de change at train stations vary their hours in high or low seasons, but most are open Monday to Friday 7am–7pm. In banks, separate exchange counters are increasingly rare.

Exchange offices at **Roissy-Charles de Gaulle** (terminals 2A, 2B and 2D) and **Orly Sud** airports are open daily until 11pm.

Travelex at 194 rue de Rivoli, 1st, tel: 01 47 03 49 52, or for other locations visit: www.travelex.fr. Mon-Sat 9.15am-7.30pm, Sun 10.45am-5.45pm.

Multi Change at 180 boulevard St-Germain, 6th, tel: 01 42 22 41 00, www.multi-change.com. Mon-Sat 9.30am-6.30pm. Take your passport if you want to cash travellers' cheques.

Cash Machines

You can draw cash from bank dispensing machines (ATMs) using a credit card or European bank cashpoint card, using your PIN if your card is one of the following: Visa, MasterCard, Maes-

tro or Cirrus. Be sure to confirm with your home bank that both your card and PIN can be used abroad.

Tipping

Restaurants By law, restaurant bills must include a service charge, which is usually 12 or 15 percent. Nevertheless, it is common to leave a small additional tip (not more than 5 percent) for the waiter if the service has been especially good. Address waiters as *Monsieur* (never *garçon*) and waitresses as *Mademoiselle*, if they are young, or *Madame*, if they are older.

Taxis Rounding up to the nearest euro is the norm.

O

Opening Hours

Office workers normally start early (8.30am is not uncommon) and often stay at their desks until 6pm or later. This is partly to make up for the long lunch hours (two hours, from around noon) traditional in public offices. Many companies are changing to shorter lunch breaks, as employees appreciate the advantages

TRANSPORT

ACCOMMODATION

ACTIVITIES

A – Z

LANGUAGE

of getting home earlier in the evening.

Traditionally **banks** open from Monday to Friday 9am to 5.30pm and are closed on Saturday and Sunday. However, many banks now close on Monday instead, and open on Saturday morning.

Food shops, especially bakers, tend to open early. Most boutiques and department stores open about 9am, but some do not open until 10am. Traditionally most French shops close from around noon to 2.30pm, but in Paris many remain open until 7 or 7.30pm. Big department stores do not close at lunchtime, and open until 9 or 10pm on Thursday. Most shops close on Sunday, but bakers and patisseries are usually open in the morning.

Suburban hypermarkets are usually open all day until 8 or 9pm. Most shops are closed on Monday morning, some all day Monday. If you want to buy a picnic lunch, remember to get everything you need before midday.

P

Postal Services

The French post office is run by the PTT (*Poste et Télécommunications*). The main branches are open on average Mon–Fri 8am–8pm and Sat 9am–1pm. The central post office at 52 rue du Louvre, 1st, tel: 36 31, www.laposte.fr, operates a daily 24-hour service. Another large post office is at Place de la Bourse, 2nd, tel: 36 31, Mon–Fri 8.15am–8pm, Sat 9.30am–1pm. Fax and photocopying facilities and limited Internet access are available in all larger post offices.

Stamps (*timbres*) are available at most *tabacs* (tobacconists) and other shops selling postcards or greetings cards. For postcards and letters weighing up to 20 grams, postage costs €0.57 within France and €0.77 to the rest of the EU. Sending a letter airmail to Australia, the US and Canada costs €0.89.

R

Religious Services

Most religious believers in France are Catholic, and Paris's many churches, including Notre-Dame, are open to the public. For a list of all denominational churches, mosques, temples and synagogues, look out for the guide Essential Paris from a kiosk or bookshop. For information on catholic services contact the **Service d'Information Réligieuse**,www.paris.catholique.fr.

There are services in English around Paris, notably in the **American Church**, 65 quai d'Orsay, 7th, tel: 01 40 62 05 00, or visit www.acparis.org.

S

Student Travellers

Students and young people under the age of 26 can get cut-price travel to Paris. For a prolonged stay, it may be worth finding out about an exchange visit or study holiday. The following organisations provide information or arrange visits.

UK Services

The **British Council** provides opportunities for international youth experience, exchange and other projects. Contact the **Youth in Action**, British Council, 10 Spring Gardens, London SW1A 2BN, tel: 0116 242 7400, www.britishcouncil.org/youth inaction.htm.

Those who can speak French could approach UK-based camping holiday operators, such as **Holidaybreak** (Hartford Manor, Greenbank Lane, Northwich, Cheshire CW8 1HW, tel: 01606 787 522, www.holidaybreakjobs. com, which often employ students as site attendants in France and other European countries in summer.

US Services

American Council for International Studies (ACIS), Boston Regional Office, 343 Congress Street, Suite 3100, Boston, MA, 02210, tel: 1 800 888 ACIS, www.acis.com.

Council on International Educational Exchange (CIEE), 300 Fore Street, Portland, ME 04101, tel: 1 800 407 8839, www.ciee.org. Work and study programmes overseas.

Youth for Understanding, 6400 Goldsboro Road, Suite 100, Bethesda, MD 20817, tel: 240 235 2100, www.yfu.org. One of the world's oldest and largest international exchange organisations.

Study in France

Several French tour operators can organise study tours and language courses.
Office National de Garantie des Séjours Linguistiques, 8 rue César-Franck, 15th, tel: 01 42 73 36 70, www.loffice.org, is a national association that quality-check all its members that offer language courses. Write for a list of schools, or try the following organisations:

Centre d'Information et de Documentation Jeunesse (CIDJ), 101 quai Branly, 15th, tel: 01 44 49 12 00 (from Monday to Friday 1–6pm, Sat 1-5pm), www.cidj. com. A national organisation that disseminates information on youth and student activities. CROUS, 39 avenue Georges-Bernanos, 5th, tel: 01 40 51 36 00, www.crous-paris.fr. Provides information on student accommodation, Resto-U canteens and courses and enrolment for British students studying in France.

For further suggestions about courses in Paris, see page 313.

OPERATOR SERVICES

Directory Enquiries
118 218
International Directory Enquiries
32 12
International Operator
32 12 + country code
Reverse charges/collect calls: You cannot normally make reverse-charge calls within France, but you can to other countries where such calls are accepted. Go through the international operator and ask to make a PCV (pay-say-vay) call.

ABOVE: most French people use the 24-hour clock.

T

Telephones

All telephone numbers in France have 10 digits. Paris and Ile de France numbers begin with 01, while the rest of France is divided into four zones: Northwest 02; Northeast 03; Southeast and Corsica 04; and Southwest 05. Toll-free phone numbers begin with 0800; all other numbers beginning with 08 are charged at variable rates; and 06 numbers are mobile phones. You get 50 percent more call-time for your money if you ring between 10.30pm and 8am on weekdays, and from 2pm at weekends.

The main mobile networks in France are Orange, SFR and Bouygues Télécom and they are compatible with GSM 900 and GSM 1800 phones. It is a good idea to check with your network provider that your phone is set up for roaming before you head to France and also to find out the cheapest way to make and receive calls while abroad. If you plan to make a lot of calls, especially within France, it will be cheaper to buy a French pay-as-you-go (prépayé) SIM card with a French number (from a network provider compatible with your

phone) to use in your phone during your stay. It is also possible to hire SIM cards and phones from a wide variety of specialist companies in the UK and US for a trip.

Most public phone boxes in Paris are now operated with a card (télécarte). A télécarte can be bought from kiosks, tabacs and post offices for 50 or 120 units (currently €8 or €15). Insert the card and follow the instructions on the screen. You can only receive calls at phone boxes displaying a blue bell sign.

You can also phone from post offices. To call long-distance, ask at the counter and you will be assigned a booth – you pay when the call is over. Cafés and tabacs often also have public phones, which usually take coins or jetons, coin-like discs bought at the bar.

To dial Paris from the UK: 00 (international code) + 33 (France) + 1 (Paris) + an eight-figure number. To call other countries from France, first dial the international code (00), then the country code: Australia 61, UK 44, US and Canada 1. If using a US credit phone-card, call the company's access number: Sprint, tel: 08 00 99 00 87; AT&T, tel: 08 00 99 00 11; MCI, tel: 08 00 99 00 19.

Time Zone

France is one hour ahead of Greenwich Mean Time (GMT) and six ahead of Eastern Standard Time. Most French people use the

24-hour clock, so 1pm appears as 13h00 on timetables and is referred to as treize heures.

Tour Operators

In the UK

British Airways Holidays, tel: 0844 493 0787, www.britishairways.com. Short breaks by plane.
Cresta, tel: 0844 879 8036, www.crestaholidays.co.uk. Breaks to Paris by plane or Eurostar.
Eurostar, tel: 08432 186 186, www.eurostar.com. Booking a train and hotel together usually saves money.
Railbookers, 14 Bonhill Street, London, EC2A 4BX, tel: 0203 327 0800. Short breaks to Paris by train.
Riviera Travel, New Manor, 328 Wetmore Road, Burton-on-Trent, Staffs, DE14 1SP, tel: 0844 826 2122, www.rivieratravel.co.uk. Escorted four-day trips to Paris by Eurostar.
Travel Editions, 69-85 Tabernacle Street, London, EC2A 4BD, tel: 0207 251 0045, www.traveleditions.co.uk. Escorted short theme breaks by Eurostar: Gastronomic Paris and Secret Paris on Foot.
Travelsphere, tel: 0844 567 9961, www.travelsphere.co.uk. Escorted short breaks to Paris by coach.
VFB, tel: 0800 171 2160, www.vfbholidays.co.uk. Short cultural breaks to Paris by plane or Eurostar.

In the US

Academic Travel, 1920 N Street NW, Suite 200, Washington, DC 20036-1601, tel: 800 566 7896, www.academic-travel. com. Educational tours for adults.

Adventures and Voyages, PO Box 352, Lincoln, California 95648, tel: 888 868 5688, www. adventuresandvoyages.com. Personalised itineraries to Paris.

France Journeys, 12381 Fenton Road, Fenton, MI 48430, tel: 888 357 6978 or 810 714 3803, www.francejourneys.com. Organises individual breaks to Paris and elsewhere in France.

Tour Vacations to Go, tel: 800 680 2858, www.tourvacationst-ogo.com. Individual and escorted tours to Paris for all budgets.

In Paris

Cityrama, 2 rue des Pyramides, 1st, tel: 01 44 55 60 60, www. parisvision.com. Excursions to Versailles, Giverny, Normandy, the Loire and elsewhere in France.

FcomFrance, 11 avenue de l'Opéra, 1st, tel: 01 42 61 24 64, www.fcomfrance.com. Coach excursions to Versailles, Giverny and the châteaux of the Loire.

France Tourisme, 33 quai des Grands Augustins, 6th, tel: 01 53 10 35 35, www.francetourisme.fr. Excursions include Champagne, Normandy beaches and Fontainebleau.

Tourist Offices

The French Tourist Board Lincoln House, 300 High Holborn, London WC1V 7JH, tel: 0906 824 4123 (calls 60p per minute), http://uk.franceguide.com. Mon–Fri 10am–4pm. Useful source of information before you travel.

Tourist Offices in Paris

All provide ample information and can book hotels. Most are closed 1 May and 25 Dec.

25 rue des Pyramides, 1st, Métro: Pyramides. May–Oct daily 9am–7pm, Nov–Apr Mon–Sat 10am–7pm.

Champs-Elysées, corner of avenue Marigny, 8th, Métro: Champs Elysées-Clémenceau. May–Oct daily 10am–7pm.

Gare de Lyon, 20 boulevard Diderot, 12th, Métro: Gare de Lyon. Mon–Sat 8am–6pm.

Gare du Nord, 18 rue de Dunkerque, 10th, Métro: Gare du Nord. Daily 8am–6pm.

Anvers, outside 72 boulevard Rochechouart, 18th, Métro: Anvers. Daily 10am–6pm.

Montmartre, 21 place du Tertre, 18th. Métro: Abbesses. Daily 10am–6pm.

Hôtel de Ville, 11 place de l'Hôtel de Ville, 4th. Métro: Hôtel de Ville. July–Aug 10am–6pm.

Notre Dame, Parvis de Notre Dame, 4th. Métro: Cité. May–Oct daily 10am–7pm.

Bastille, 4 place Bastille, 12th.

TOURIST INFORMATION

www.parisinfo.com has details of all services.
To call the Paris Tourist Office, tel: 08 29 68 30 00; calls cost €0.34 per minute.

Métro: Bastille. July–Aug daily 11am–7pm.

U

Useful Addresses

RATP Information, in English, tel: 32 46, www.ratp.fr.
SNCF, tel: 36 35, www.sncf.fr, for train information.

V

Visas and Passports

All visitors to France require a valid passport. No visa is required by visitors from European Union (EU) member states, the US, Australia, Canada or Japan. Nationals of other countries may need a visa; if in doubt, check with the French Consulate in your home country. For anyone (including EU nationals) who wants to stay longer than 90 days, it is no longer obligatory to obtain a *carte de séjour*, but it is still advisable to get one, from French Consulates or the Préfecture de Police, 9 boulevard du Palais, 4th, tel: 01 58 80 80 80.

W

Weights & Measures

Metric measurements are always used in France. For a quick conversion: 1 metre is about a yard, 100 grams is just under 4oz, 1kg is 2lbs 2oz. Distance is in kilometres: 1km equals five-eighths of a mile, so 80km is 50 miles.

BELOW: sightseeing on the Seine.

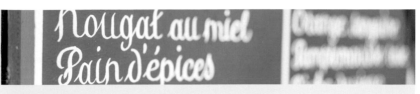

LANGUAGE

UNDERSTANDING THE LANGUAGE

GENERAL

French is the native language of more than 90 million people and the acquired language of 180 million. It is a Romance language descended from the Vulgar Latin spoken by the Roman conquerors of Gaul. It still carries the reputation of being the most cultured language in the world and the most beautiful. People often tell stories about the impatience of the French towards foreigners who do not attempt to speak their language. In general, however, if you attempt to communicate with them in French, they will appreciate it and may even overcome their reluctance to respond in English.

Since much of the English vocabulary is related to French, thanks to the Norman Conquest in 1066, travellers will often recognise many helpful cognates: words such as *hôtel*, *café* and *bagages* hardly need to be translated. You should be aware, however, of some misleading "false friends" *(faux amis)*, words that look like English words but mean something different.
le car coach, also railway carriage
le conducteur bus driver
personne can mean either person or nobody, depending on the context.

The Alphabet

Learning the pronunciation of the French alphabet is a good idea. In particular, learn how to spell out your name.
a = ah, **b** = bay, **c** = say, **d** = day, **e** = uh, **f** = ef, **g** = zhay, **h** = ash, **i** = ee, **j** = zhee, **k** = ka, **l** = el, **m** = em, **n** = en, **o** = oh, **p** = pay, **q** = kew, **r** = ehr, **s** = ess, **t** = tay, **u** = ew, **v** = vay, **w** = dooblah vay, **x** = eex, **y** = ee grek, **z** = zed.

Basic Rules

If you speak no French at all, it is worth trying to master a few simple phrases. The fact that you have made an effort is likely to break the ice. More and more French people like practising their English on visitors, especially waiters and the younger generation. Pronunciation is the key; they really will not understand if you get it very wrong. Remember to **emphasise each syllable**, but not to pronounce the last consonant of a word as a rule, unless it is followed by a vowel. Also bear in mind "er", "et" and "ez" endings are pronounced "ay" (this includes the plural "s") and "h"s are silent.

Whether to use "**vous**" or "**tu**" is a vexed question; increasingly the familiar form of "tu" is used, but it is safer to be formal, and use "vous". It is very important to be courteous; always address people as **Mademoiselle**, **Madame** or **Monsieur**, and address them by their surnames until you are confident first names are acceptable. When entering a shop always say, *"Bonjour Monsieur/Madame/Mademoiselle,"* and *"Merci, au revoir,"* when leaving.

Garçon is the word for waiter but is never used directly; say *Monsieur, Madame* or *Mademoiselle*, to attract a waiter's attention.

USEFUL WORDS & PHRASES

How much is it? *C'est combien?*
What is your name? *Comment vous appelez-vous?*
My name is... *Je m'appelle...*
Do you speak English? *Parlez-vous anglais?*
I am English/American *Je suis anglais(e)/américain(e)*
I don't understand *Je ne comprends pas*
Please speak more slowly *Parlez plus lentement, s'il vous plaît*
Can you help me? *Pouvez-vous m'aider?*
I'm looking for... *Je cherche...*
Where is...? *Où est...?*

I'm sorry *Excusez-moi/Pardon*
I don't know *Je ne sais pas*
No problem *Pas de problème*
Have a good day! *Bonne journée!*
That's it *C'est ça*
Here it is *Voici*
There it is *Voilà*
Let's go *On y va/Allons-y*
See you tomorrow *A demain*
See you soon *A bientôt*
Show me the word in the book *Montrez-moi le mot dans le livre*
At what time? *A quelle heure?*
When? *Quand?*
What time is it? *Quelle heure est-il?*
yes *oui*
no *non*
please *s'il vous plaît*
thank you *merci*
(very much) *(beaucoup)*
you're welcome *de rien*
excuse me *excusez-moi*
hello *bonjour*
hi/bye *salut*
OK *d'accord*
goodbye *au revoir*
good evening *bonsoir*
here *ici*
there *là*
left *gauche*
right *droite*
straight on *tout droit*
far *loin*
near *près d'ici*
opposite *en face*
beside *à côté de*
over there *là-bas*

BELOW: like anywhere else in the world: the green man means go.

today *aujourd'hui*
yesterday *hier*
tomorrow *demain*
now *maintenant*
later *plus tard*
right away *tout de suite*
this morning *ce matin*
this afternoon *cet après-midi*
this evening *ce soir*

On Arrival

I want to get off at... *Je voudrais descendre à...*
Is there a bus to the Louvre? *Est-ce qu'il y a un bus pour le Louvre?*
What street is this? *Sur quelle rue sommes-nous?*
Which line do I take for...? *Quelle ligne dois-je prendre pour...?*
How far is...? *A quelle distance se trouve...?*
Validate your ticket *Compostez votre billet*
airport *l'aéroport*
railway station *la gare*
bus station *la gare routière*
Métro stop *la station de Métro*
bus *l'autobus, le car*
bus stop *l'arrêt*
platform *le quai*
ticket *le billet*
return ticket *aller-retour*
hitch hiking *l'autostop*
toilets *les toilettes*
This is the hotel address *C'est l'adresse de l'hôtel*
I'd like a (single/double) room... *Je voudrais une chambre (pour une/deux personnes)...*
...with shower *avec douche*
...with bath *avec salle de bain*
Is breakfast included? *Le prix comprend-il le petit-déjeuner?*
May I see the room? *Puis-je voir la chambre?*
washbasin *le lavabo*
bed *le lit*
key *la clé*
elevator *l'ascenseur*
air-conditioned *climatisé*

Emergencies

Help! *Au secours!*
Stop! *Arrêtez!*
Call a doctor *Appelez un médecin*
Call an ambulance *Appelez une ambulance*
Call the police *Appelez la police*
Call the fire brigade *Appelez les pompiers*
Where is the nearest telephone? *Où est le téléphone le plus proche?*
Where is the nearest hospital? *Où est l'hôpital le plus proche?*
I am sick *Je suis malade*
I have lost my passport/purse *J'ai perdu mon passeport/porte-monnaie*

Shopping

Where is the nearest bank (post office)? *Où se trouve la banque (Poste) la plus proche?*
I'd like to buy *Je voudrais acheter*
How much is it? *C'est combien?*
Do you take credit cards? *Est-ce que vous acceptez les cartes de crédit?*
I'm just looking *Je regarde seulement*
Have you got? *Avez-vous...?*
I'll take it *Je le prends*
I'll take this one/that one *Je prends celui-ci/celui-là*
What size is it? *C'est quelle taille?*
Anything else? *Avec ceci?*
size (clothes) *la taille*
size (shoes) *la pointure*
cheap *bon marché*
expensive *cher*
enough *assez*
too much *trop*
a piece of *un morceau de*
each *la pièce (eg ananas, €2 la pièce)*
receipt *le reçu*
chemist *la pharmacie*
bakery *la boulangerie*
bookshop *la librairie*
library *la bibliothèque*
department store *le grand-magasin*
delicatessen *la charcuterie/ le traiteur*
fishmonger *la poissonnerie*
grocery *l'alimentation/l'épicerie*
tobacconist *le tabac* (also sells stamps and newspapers)
market *le marché*

supermarket *le supermarché*
junk shop *la brocante*

Sightseeing

town *la ville*
old town *la vieille ville*
street *la rue*
square *la place*
abbey *l'abbaye*
cathedral *la cathédrale*
church *l'église*
keep *le donjon*
mansion *l'hôtel*
hospital *l'hôpital*
town hall *l'hôtel de ville/la mairie*
nave *la nef*
stained glass *le vitrail*
staircase *l'escalier*
tower *la tour (La Tour Eiffel)*
walk *le tour*
country house/castle *le château*
Gothic *gothique*
Roman *romain*
Romanesque *roman*
museum *le musée*
art gallery *la galerie*
exhibition *l'exposition*
tourist information office
l'office du tourisme/le syndicat d'initiative
free *gratuit*
open *ouvert*
closed *fermé*
every day *tous les jours*
all year *toute l'année*
all day *toute la journée*
swimming pool *la piscine*
to book *réserver*
town map *le plan*
road map *la carte*

Dining Out

Table d'hôte (the "host's table") is one set menu served at a set price. *Prix fixe* is a fixed-price menu. *A la carte* means differently priced dishes chosen from the menu.
breakfast *le petit-déjeuner*
lunch *le déjeuner*
dinner *le dîner*
meal *le repas*
first course *l'entrée/les hors d'œuvre*
main course *le plat principal*
made to order *sur commande*
drink included *boisson comprise*

wine list *la carte des vins*
the bill *l'addition*
fork *la fourchette*
knife *le couteau*
spoon *la cuillère*
plate *l'assiette*
glass *le verre*
napkin *la serviette*
ashtray *le cendrier*
I am a vegetarian *Je suis végétarien(ne)*
I am on a diet *Je suis au régime*
What do you recommend?
Qu'est-ce que vous recommandez?
Do you have local specialities?
Avez-vous des spécialités locales?
I'd like to order *Je voudrais commander*
That is not what I ordered *Ce n'est pas ce que j'ai commandé*
Is service included? *Est-ce que le service est compris?*
May I have more wine? *Encore du vin, s'il vous plaît*
Enjoy your meal *Bon appétit!*

Breakfast and Snacks

baguette **long thin loaf**
pain **bread**
petits pains **rolls**
beurre **butter**
poivre **pepper**
sel **salt**
sucre **sugar**
confiture **jam**
miel **honey**
œufs **eggs**
...à la coque **boiled eggs**
...au bacon **bacon and eggs**
...au jambon **ham and eggs**
...sur le plat **fried eggs**
...brouillés **scrambled eggs**
tartine **bread with butter**
yaourt **yoghurt**
crêpe **pancake**
croque-monsieur **ham and cheese toasted sandwich**
croque-madame **...with a fried egg on top**
galette **type of cake**
pan bagna **bread roll stuffed with salade niçoise**
quiche **tart of eggs and cream with various fillings**
quiche lorraine **quiche with bacon**

First Course

An *amuse-bouche, amuse-gueule* or appetiser is something to "amuse the mouth", before the first course
anchoïade **sauce of olive oil, anchovies and garlic, served with raw vegetables**
assiette anglaise **cold meats**
potage **soup**
rillettes **rich fatty paste of shredded duck, rabbit or pork**
tapenade **spread of olives and anchovies**
pissaladière **Provençal pizza with onions, olives and anchovies**

Main Courses

Viande **Meat**
bleu saignant **rare**
à point **medium**
bien cuit **well done**
grillé **grilled**
agneau **lamb**
andouille/andouillette **tripe sausage**
bifteck **steak**
boudin **sausage**
boudin noir **black pudding**
boudin blanc **white pudding (chicken or veal)**
blanquette **stew of veal, lamb or chicken with creamy egg sauce**
bœuf à la mode **beef in red wine with carrots, onions, mushroom and onions**
à la bordelaise **beef with red wine and shallots**
bourguignon **cooked in red wine, onions and mushrooms**
brochette **kebab**
caille **quail**
canard **duck**
carbonnade **casserole of beef, beer and onions**
carré d'agneau **rack of lamb**
cassoulet **stew of beans, sausages, pork and duck from southwest France**
cervelle **brains (food)**
châteaubriand **thick steak**
choucroute **Alsace dish of sauerkraut, bacon and sausages**
confit **duck or goose preserved in its own fat**
contre-filet **cut of sirloin steak**

TRANSPORT

ACCOMMODATION

ACTIVITIES

A–Z

LANGUAGE

coq au vin **chicken in red wine**
côte d'agneau **lamb chop**
daube **beef stew with red wine, onions and tomatoes**
dinde **turkey**
entrecôte **beef rib steak**
escargot **snail**
faisan **pheasant**
farci **stuffed**
faux-filet **sirloin**
feuilleté **puff pastry**
foie **liver**
foie de veau **calf's liver**
foie gras **goose or duck liver pâté**
gardian **rich beef stew with olives and garlic from the Camargue**
cuisses de grenouille **frogs' legs**
grillade **grilled meat**
hachis **minced meat**
jambon **ham**
langue **tongue**
lapin **rabbit**
lardons **small pieces of bacon, often added to salads**
magret de canard **breast of duck**
médaillon **round piece of meat**
moelle **beef bone marrow**
mouton navarin **stew of lamb with onions, carrots and turnips**
oie **goose**
perdrix **partridge**
petit-gris **small snail**
pieds de cochon **pig's trotters**
pintade **guinea fowl**
Pipérade **Basque dish of eggs, ham, peppers and onion**
porc **pork**
pot-au-feu **casserole of beef and vegetables**
poulet **chicken**
poussin **young chicken**
rognons **kidneys**
rôti **roast**
sanglier **wild boar**
saucisse **fresh sausage**
saucisson **salami**
veau **veal**

Poissons **Fish**

à l'américaine **made with white wine, tomatoes, butter and cognac**
anchois **anchovies**
anguille **eel**
bar/loup **sea bass**

barbue **brill**
belon **Brittany oyster**
bigorneau **sea snail**
Bercy **sauce of fish stock, butter, white wine and shallots**
bouillabaisse **fish soup, served with grated cheese, garlic croutons and spicy rouille sauce**
brandade **salt cod purée**
cabillaud **cod**
calamars **squid**
colin **hake**
coquillage **shellfish**
coquilles Saint-Jacques **scallops**
crevette **shrimp**
daurade **sea bream**
flétan **halibut**
fruits de mer **seafood**
hareng **herring**
homard **lobster**
huître **oyster**
langoustine **large prawn**
limande **lemon sole**
lotte **monkfish**
morue **salt cod**
moule **mussel**
moules marinières **mussels in white wine and onions**
oursin **sea urchin**
raie **skate**
saumon **salmon**
thon **tuna**
truite **trout**

Légumes **Vegetables**

ail **garlic**
artichaut **artichoke**
asperge **asparagus**
aubergine **eggplant, aubergine**
avocat **avocado**
bolets **boletus mushrooms**
céleri rémoulade **grated celery with mayonnaise**
cèpes **boletus mushrooms**
champignon **mushroom**
chanterelle **wild mushroom**
chips **potato crisps**
chou **cabbage**
chou-fleur **cauliflower**
concombre **cucumber**
cornichon **gherkin**
courgette **zucchini, courgette**
cru **raw**
crudités **raw vegetables**
épinards **spinach**
frites **chips, French fries**
gratin dauphinois **sliced potatoes baked with cream**
haricot **dried bean**

haricots verts **green beans**
lentilles **lentils**
maïs **corn**
mange-tout **snow pea**
mesclun **mixed-leaf salad**
navet **turnip**
noisette **hazelnut**
noix **nut, walnut**
oignon **onion**
panais **parsnip**
persil **parsley**
pignon **pine nut**
poireau **leek**
pois **pea**
poivron **bell pepper**
pomme de terre **potato**
pommes frites **chips, French fries**
primeurs **early fruit and vegetables**
radis **radis**
roquette **arugula, rocket**
ratatouille **Provençal vegetable stew of aubergines, courgettes, tomatoes, peppers and olive oil**
riz **rice**
salade niçoise **egg, tuna, olives, onions and tomato salad**
salade verte **green salad**
truffe **truffle**

Fruit **Fruit**

ananas **pineapple**
cerise **cherry**
citron **lemon**
citron vert **lime**
figue **fig**
fraise **strawberry**
framboise **raspberry**
groseille **redcurrant**
mangue **mango**
mirabelle **yellow plum**
pamplemousse **grapefruit**
pêche **peach**
poire **pear**
pomme **apple**
raisin **grape**
prune **plum**
pruneau **prune**
reine claude **greengage**

Sauces **Sauces**

aïoli **garlic mayonnaise**
béarnaise **sauce of egg, butter, wine and herbs**
forestière **with mushrooms and bacon**
hollandaise **egg and butter**

lyonnaise **with onions**
meunière **fried fish with butter, lemon and parsley sauce**
meurette **red wine sauce**
Mornay **sauce of cream, egg and cheese**
Parmentier **served with potatoes**
paysan **rustic-style, ingredients depend on the region**
pistou **Provençal sauce of basil, garlic and olive oil; vegetable soup with the sauce**
provençale **sauce of tomatoes, garlic and olive oil**
papillotte **cooked in paper**

Dessert **Pudding, dessert**

chèvre **goat's cheese**
clafoutis **baked pudding of batter and cherries**
coulis **purée of fruit or vegetables**
crème anglaise **custard**
crème caramel **caramelised egg custard**
crème Chantilly **whipped cream**
fromage **cheese**
gâteau **cake**
île flottante **whisked egg whites floating in custard sauce**
pêche melba **peaches with ice cream and raspberry sauce**
poire Belle-Hélène **pear with ice cream and chocolate sauce**
tarte tatin **upside-down tart of caramelised apples**

In the Café

les boissons **drinks**
café **coffee**
...au lait or crème **...with milk or cream**
...déca/décaféiné **...decaffeinated**
...espresso/noir **...black espresso**
...filtre **...filtered coffee**
thé **tea**
tisane **herb infusion**
verveine **verbena tea**
chocolat chaud **hot chocolate**
lait **milk**
eau minérale **mineral water**
gazeux **fizzy**
non-gazeux **non-fizzy**
limonade **fizzy lemonade**

citron pressé **fresh lemon juice served with sugar**
orange pressée **fresh squeezed orange juice**
entier **full (eg full cream milk)**
frais, fraîche **fresh or cold**
bière **beer**
...en bouteille **...bottled**
...à la pression **...on tap**
apéritif **pre-dinner drink**
kir **white wine with cassis, blackcurrant liqueur**
kir royale **kir with champagne**
avec des glaçons **with ice**
sec **neat**
rouge **red**
blanc **white**
rosé **rosé**
brut **dry**
doux **sweet**
crémant **sparkling wine**
vin de maison **house wine**
vin de pays **local wine**
carafe/pichet **pitcher**
...d'eau/de vin **...of water/wine**
demi-carafe **half-litre**
quart **quarter-litre**
panaché **shandy**
digestif **after-dinner drink**
armagnac **brandy from the Armagnac region of France**
calvados **Normandy apple brandy**

Where is this wine from? *De quelle région vient ce vin?*
cheers! *santé!*
hangover *gueule de bois*

Days of the Week

Days of the week, seasons and months are not capitalised in French.
Monday *lundi*
Tuesday *mardi*
Wednesday *mercredi*
Thursday *jeudi*
Friday *vendredi*
Saturday *samedi*
Sunday *dimanche*

Seasons

spring *le printemps*
summer *l'été*
autumn *l'automne*
winter *l'hiver*

Months

January *janvier*
February *février*
March *mars*
April *avril*
May *mai*
June *juin*
July *juillet*
August *août*
September *septembre*
October *octobre*
November *novembre*
December *décembre*

Saying the date

20 October 2013 *le vingt octobre, deux mille treize*

Numbers

0 *zéro*
1 *un, une*
2 *deux*
3 *trois*
4 *quatre*
5 *cinq*
6 *six*
7 *sept*
8 *huit*
9 *neuf*
10 *dix*
11 *onze*
12 *douze*
13 *treize*
14 *quatorze*
15 *quinze*
16 *seize*
17 *dix-sept*
18 *dix-huit*
19 *dix-neuf*
20 *vingt*
21 *vingt-et-un*
30 *trente*
40 *quarante*
50 *cinquante*
60 *soixante*
70 *soixante-dix*
80 *quatre-vingts*
90 *quatre-vingt-dix*
100 *cent*
200 *deux cents*
500 *cinq cents*
1000 *mille*
1,000,000 *un million*
Note that the number 1 is often written like an upside down V, and the number 7 is always crossed.

FURTHER READING

History

A Concise History of France, by Roger Price. Excellent historical overview.
The Eiffel Tower: And Other Mythologies, by Roland Barthes. A collection of essays by this influential French critic.
Marie Antoinette, by Antonia Fraser. An interesting biography of France's most famous queen.
Parisians: An Adventure History of Paris, by Graham Robb. A fascinating look at the individuals who shaped the city.
Sylvia Beach and the Lost Generation: A History of Literary Paris in the Twenties and Thirties, by Noel Riley Fitch. The origins of Shakespeare & Company bookshop and the writers who went there.

Art and Architecture

A Propos de Paris, by Henri Cartier-Bresson. Some 130 stunning black-and-white photographs of the capital, spanning 50 years.
Brassaï: Paris. A great collection of the photographer's images spanning 50 years.
The Cathedral Builders, by Jean Gimpel. The story of the hands and minds behind the cathedrals of France.
Paris: An Architectural History, by Anthony Sutcliffe. A great book on the architecture of the capital across the ages.
Paris: Art and Architecture by Martina Padberg. A comprehensive guide to the city's art and

architecture from its origins to the 21st century.
Robert Doisneau: Paris. A compact book featuring more than 600 of the photographer's images of Paris.

Expat Memoirs

A Moveable Feast, by Ernest Hemingway. Life with the literati in 1920s Paris.
A Year in the Merde, by Stephen Clarke. The best-selling humorous tale of an expat in Paris.
Almost French: A New Life in Paris, by Sarah Turnbull. An engaging story of a woman who moves to Paris for a man but falls in love with the city.

Fiction

Murder in the Palais Royal, by Cara Black. One of a series of entertaining crime novels set in and around Paris.
The Elegance of the Hedgehog, by Muriel Barbery. A moving tale of a friendship between a young girl and the concierge of her apartment building.
The Sun King Rises, by Yves Jégo and Denis Lépée. Intrigue and mystery in the court of Louis XIV.

Food

Paris Bistro Cooking, by Linda Dannenberg. Tasty dishes from a wealth of Paris brasseries.
The Little Paris Kitchen, by Rachel Khoo. Easy-to-make versions of French classics.
The Paris Café Cookbook, by

Daniel Young. Recipes and excerpts on recommended cafés in the capital.
The Sweet Life in Paris, by David Lebovitz. The Paris-based American chef's observations on Paris and cooking, including 50 recipes.

Other Insight Guides

Insight Guide: France is the major book in the French series covering the whole country, with features on food and drink, culture and the arts. Other titles include *Southwest France*, *Northern France*, *Provence* and *The French Riviera*.

Insight Fleximaps

Insight Fleximaps have a tough, laminated rainproof finish and feature a list of the top 10 sites in a city or area, and an in-depth index. Fleximaps in the French series include *Paris* and *Nice, Cannes & Monaco*.

Insight Step by Step

Insight's Step by Step guides provide a series of timed itineraries, with recommended stops for lunch. The itineraries are plotted on an accompanying pull-out map. Titles incude *Paris* and *Nice & the French Riviera*.

Insight Select Guides

Insight Select Guide: Paris offers a collection of over 100 inspiring ideas for your stay in the city, with plenty of secret gems and offbeat haunts in the mix – all carefully selected by a local writer who knows Paris inside out.

PARIS STREET ATLAS

The key map shows the area of Paris covered by the atlas
section. An index of street names and places of interest
shown on the maps can be found on the following pages. For
each entry there is a page number and grid reference

Map Legend

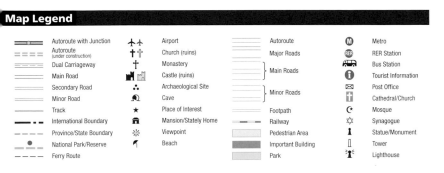

Autoroute with Junction		Airport		Autoroute	M	Metro
Autoroute (under construction)		Church (ruins)		Major Roads	RER	RER Station
Dual Carriageway		Monastery		Main Roads		Bus Station
Main Road		Castle (ruins)			i	Tourist Information
Secondary Road		Archaeological Site		Minor Roads		Post Office
Minor Road		Cave				Cathedral/Church
Track	★	Place of Interest		Footpath		Mosque
International Boundary		Mansion/Stately Home		Railway		Synagogue
Province/State Boundary		Viewpoint		Pedestrian Area		Statue/Monument
National Park/Reserve		Beach		Important Building		Tower
Ferry Route				Park		Lighthouse

A

B

Restaurants ❶

Louvre & Tuileries
32 L'Ardoise E3
36 Kinugawa E3

Grands Boulevards & Champs-Elysées
38 CPH B2
39 Alain Ducasse at the Plaza Athénée C3
40 L'Atelier de Joel Robuchon B2
41 Brasserie Printemps E2
43 Guy Savoy B2
44 Ladurée C2
45 Lavinia E3
47 Market D3
48 Savy C3
49 Al Ajami C3

Eiffel Tower, Trocadéro & Les Invalides
94 L'Affriolé C4
95 L'Ami Jean C4
97 Au Bon Accueil C4
98 L'Esplanade D4
99 La Fontaine de Mars C4
100 Jules Verne B4
101 Tokyo Eat D3/4
102 Le Vin de Bellechasse E4
103 Petrossian D4

Bars & Cafés ❶

Louvre & Tuileries
13 Jean-Paul Hévin E3

Grands Boulevards & Champs-Elysées
15 Café Jacquemart André D2
16 Café Le Nôtre D3
18 Kitty O'Shea's E3

Eiffel Tower, Trocadéro & Les Invalides
39 Bellota Bellota C4

Hotels ❶

Grands Boulevards & Champs-Elysées
12 Hotel Brighton E3
19 Hotel Madeleine Opéra E2
20 Hotel Meurice E3
23 Hotel de Banville A1
25 Bradford Elysée C2
26 Le Bristol D2
28 Hotel de Crillon E3
29 Hotel Daniel C2
30 Fouquet's Barrière C2
31 Four Seasons George V C3
32 Hotel François Ier C2
33 Hotel Keppler B3
34 Hotel Mansart E3
35 Plaza Athénée C3
36 Hotel Ritz E3
37 Hotel de Sers C3
39 Hotel de la Trémoille C3

Montmartre, Bastille & East Paris
24 Berne Opéra E1

CIMETIÈRE DE MONTMARTRE

La Fourche

MONTMARTRE

Moulin de la Galette
Moulin du Radet
Musée de Montmartre
PARC DE LA TURLURE

Château Rouge

Moulin Rouge

Espace Montmartre S.Dali
St-Pierre
Basilique du Sacré-Cœur

Abbesses
Halle St-Pierre

St-Jean Montmartre
Rochechouart
Barbès Rochechouart

Pl. Clichy
Pigalle
Anvers

St-André de l'Europe

Musée de la Vie Romantique

Th. de l'Œuvre

Dt. Evang. Christuskirche

Th. de Paris

Casino de Paris

Musée Gustave-Moreau

St-Georges

St-Constantin/ Ste-Hélène

Gare St-Lazare

Ste-Trinité

N.-D. de Lorette

N.-D. de Lorette

St-Lazare

L. Condorcet

Folies Bergère

St-Louis d'Antin

Au Printemps

Galeries Lafayette

Chaussée d'Antin

Comédie Caumartin

Havre Caumartin

Palais Garnier

Haussmann

Richelieu Drouot

Grévin

Musée du Parfum

Olympia

Opéra

Pl. de l'Opéra

Grands Boulevards

Bd Montmartre

Bonne Nouvelle

Bd de la Madeleine

4 Septembre

Quatre - Septembre

Bourse

Palais Brongniart

Crédit Foncier de France

Ministère de la Justice

N.-D. de L'Assomption
Cour des Comptes

Place Vendôme

Bibliothèque Nationale-Richelieu

Basilique N.-D. des Victoires

Sentier

Pyramides

St-Roch

Banque de France

JARDIN DU PALAIS ROYAL

Hôtel des Postes

Rue de Rivoli

Tuileries

Restaurants ❶

Marais
10 Au Bascou D4

Beaubourg & Les Halles
21 L'Escargot Montorgueil C4

Louvre & Tuileries
28 A Casaluna B4
29 La Ferme Opera A4
31 L'Absinthe A4
32 L'Ardoise A4
34 Le Grand Véfour B4
35 Restaurant du Palais Royal B4
36 Kinugawa A4
37 Takara B4

Grands Boulevards & Champs-Elysées
41 Brasserie Printemps A3
42 Drouant A4
45 Lavinia A4
46 Aux Lyonnais B3

Montmartre
50 L'Auberge du Clou B2
51 Le Bouclard A1
52 Chez Jean B2
53 Chez Michel C2
54 Chez Toinette B1
55 La Famille B1
56 Pétrelle C2
57 Le Relais Gascon B1
58 Wally le Saharien B2
59 Just Be A1

Bastille & East Paris
60 Astier E4
61 Auberge Pyrénées-Cévennes E4
62 La Bellevilloise E3
64 Chez Prune D3

Bars & Cafés ❶

Marais
2 Andy Wahloo C4

Beaubourg & Les Halles
11 Le Tambour B4

Louvre & Tuileries
13 Jean-Paul Hévin A4
14 Juvéniles B4

Grands Boulevards & Champs-Elysées
17 Café de la Ville C3
18 Kitty O'Shea's A4

Montmartre
19 Le Café qui Parle A1
20 L'Etoile de Montmartre B1
21 La Fourmi B1
22 Le Sancerre B1

Bastille & East Paris
24 Café Cannibale E3
25 Café Charbon E4
26 Le Café Noir E3
27 Au Chat Noir E3
28 Le Jemmapes D3
29 Plein Soleil E4
30 Au P'tit Garage E4

Hotels ❶

Ile de la Cité & Ile St-Louis, Marais
3 Hotel du Haut Marais D4

Beaubourg, Les Halles, Louvre & Tuileries
21 Hotel Tiquetonne C4

Grands Boulevards & Champs-Elysées
12 Hotel Brighton A4
16 Hotel Edouard VII D4
18 Hotel Luman A4
19 Hotel Madeleine Opéra A3
20 Hotel Meurice A4
22 Hotel Vivienne B3
27 Hotel Chopin B3
34 Hotel Mansart A4
36 Hotel Ritz A4

Montmartre, Bastille & East Paris
41 Chat Noir Design Hotel A1
42 Hotel Garden St Martin D3
43 Holiday Inn Gare de l'Est D3
44 Mama Shelter E4
47 Regyn's Montmartre B1
48 Hotel Royal Fromentin A1
49 Hotel Saint Louis Bastille E4
50 Terrass A4
51 Timhotel Montmartre B1

Bars & Cafés ❶

Ile de la Cité & Ile St-Louis
1 Le Flore en l'Ile C3

Marais
2 Andy Wahloo C4
3 L'Apparement Café D2
4 La Perle D2
5 Au Petit Fer à Cheval D2
6 Stolly's D2

Beaubourg & Les Halles
7 Bistrot Beaubourg C2
8 Le Café des Initiés B1
9 Le Père Fouettard C1
10 Le Petit Marcel C1

Louvre & Tuileries
12 Café Marly A/B1

Bastille & East Paris
23 Bistrot à Vins Mélac

Latin Quarter & St Germain
31 Le Bar Dix B3
32 Café de Flore A2/3
33 Café de la Mairie A3
34 La Pousse au Crime A3
35 Le Procope B3
36 La Rhumerie B3

Montparnasse
37 Café de l'Atelier A4
38 Les Tontons

Hotels ❶

Ile de la Cité & Ile St-Louis, Marais
1 Hotel de la Bretonnerie D2
2 Hotel des Deux Iles C3
3 Hotel du Haut Marais D1
4 Grand Hotel Jeanne d'Arc D4
5 Hotel Jules et Jim D1
6 Hotel du Jeu de Paume C3
7 Hotel Lutèce C3
8 Pavillon de la Reine D2
9 Hotel du Petit Moulin D1
10 Hotel de la Place des Vosges D2

Beaubourg, Les Halles, Louvre & Tuileries
11 Hotel Andrea C2
13 Hotel Britannique C2
14 Hotel du Cygne C2
15 Le Duo C2
17 Hotel Konfidentiel D1
18 Hotel Lumen A1
21 Hotel Tiquetonne C1

Montmartre, Bastille & East Paris
40 Hotel de Beaumarchais E1
45 Hotel Original E2
46 Le Pavillon Bastille E3
49 Hotel Saint Louis Bastille E1

Latin Quarter & St-Germain-des-Prés
52 Hotel d'Angleterre C3
53 Aramis St Germain A4
54 Le Clos Medicis B4
55 Hotel Cluny Sorbonne B3/4
56 Hotel Design de la Sorbonne B3
57 Hotel Familia C4
58 Hotel du Globe B3
59 Hotel des Grandes Ecoles C3
60 L'Hotel A2
61 Left Bank St Germain B3
62 Hotel Lenox A2
63 Hotel La Louisiane B3
64 Hotel Lutetia A2
65 Hotel des Mines A4
67 Hotel Notre Dame C3
68 Hotel de Saint Germain A3
69 Hotel des Saints Pères A3
70 La Villa A2

Restaurants ❶

Ile de la Cité & Ile St-Louis
1 Brasserie de l'Ile C3
2 Café Med C3
3 L'Escale C3
4 L'Ilot Vache C3
5 Taverne Henri IV B2
6 Ismai C3

Marais
7 Le Petit Marché C3
8 L'Ambassade C1
9 L'Ambroisie D2
10 Au Bascou D1
11 Breizh Café D1
12 Le Dôme du Marais D2
13 Aux Vins des Pyrénées D3
14 L'Osteria D2
15 Candelaria D1
16 Chez Omar D1
17 Thai Spices D3

Beaubourg & Les Halles
18 Joe Allen C1
19 Benoit C2
20 Au Chien qui Fume D1
21 L'Escargot Montorgueil C1

22 La Fresque C1
23 Georges C2
24 Le Hangar C1
25 Au Pied de Cochon B1
26 La Tour de Montlhéry B1
27 Saveurs Végét'halles B1

Louvre & Tuileries
30 Oh mon Cake! B1
33 Le Fumoir B2
35 Restaurant du Palais Royal B1
37 Takara B1

Bastille & East Paris
63 Bofinger E3
65 Comme Cochons E4
66 Crêperie Bretonne E3
67 L'Encrier E3
68 Paris Main d'Or E3
69 Le Train Bleu E4
70 Le Janissaire E4

Latin Quarter & St Germain
71 Bayon C4
72 L'Alcazar B2
73 Les Bouquinistes B2
74 Chez René C3

75 Le Comptoir du Relais B3
76 Lapérouse B2
77 Moissonnier C3
78 L'Ourcine B4
79 Pierre Gagnaire à Gaya A2
80 Le Voltaire A2
81 Ze Kitchen Galerie B2
82 Le Grenier de Notre Dame C2

Montparnasse
83 L'Assiette B4
84 L'Avant-Gout C4
86 La Closerie des Lilas B4
88 L'Entrepot A4
89 Le Parc aux Cerfs A4
90 Le Select A4
91 Wadja A4
92 Paradis Thai C4
93 Bambou C3

0 100 200 300 400 500 m
0 100 200 300 400 500 yds

332

Notable Graves
1 - Abélard et Héloïse
2 - Édith Piaf
3 - Georges Bizet
4 - Gertrude Stein
5 - Guillaume Apollinaire
6 - Honoré de Balzac
7 - Jim Morrison
8 - Marcel Proust
9 - Maria Callas
10 - Molière
11 - Oscar Wilde
12 - Sarah Bernhardt
13 - Yves Montand